I0482865

LEONARDO DA VINCI'S
MONA LISA

NEW PERSPECTIVES

Fielding University Press
Santa Barbara, CA

Fielding University Press is an imprint of Fielding Graduate University.
Its objective is to advance the research and scholarship of Fielding faculty,
students and alumni around the world, using a variety of publishing platforms.

For more information, please contact the Editor at Fielding University Press via email to jisbouts@fielding.edu,
or via postal mail to Fielding Graduate University, 2020 De la Vina Street, Santa Barbara, CA 93105. On the web at www.fielding.edu/
universitypress.

© 2019 Fielding Graduate University
Published in the United States of America

All Rights reserved. No part of this publication may be reproduced or transmitted, in any form or by any means,
without the prior permission of Fielding University Press.

Library of Congress Cataloging-in-Publication data
Leonardo da Vinci's Mona Lisa
1. Humanities – Art history – the Renaissance
2. Leonardo da Vinci - oeuvre

LEONARDO DA VINCI'S
MONA LISA

NEW PERSPECTIVES

Edited by Jean-Pierre Isbouts

Fielding University Press
Editorial Review Board

Katrina Rogers, Ph.D.

Monique Snowden, Ph.D.

Patrice Rosenthal, Ph.D.

Jean-Pierre Isbouts, D.Litt.

Ad Hoc Reviewers

David Blake Willis, Ph.D.

Fredrick Steier, Ph.D.

Rich Appelbaum, Ph.D.

Connie Corley, Ph.D.

TABLE OF CONTENTS

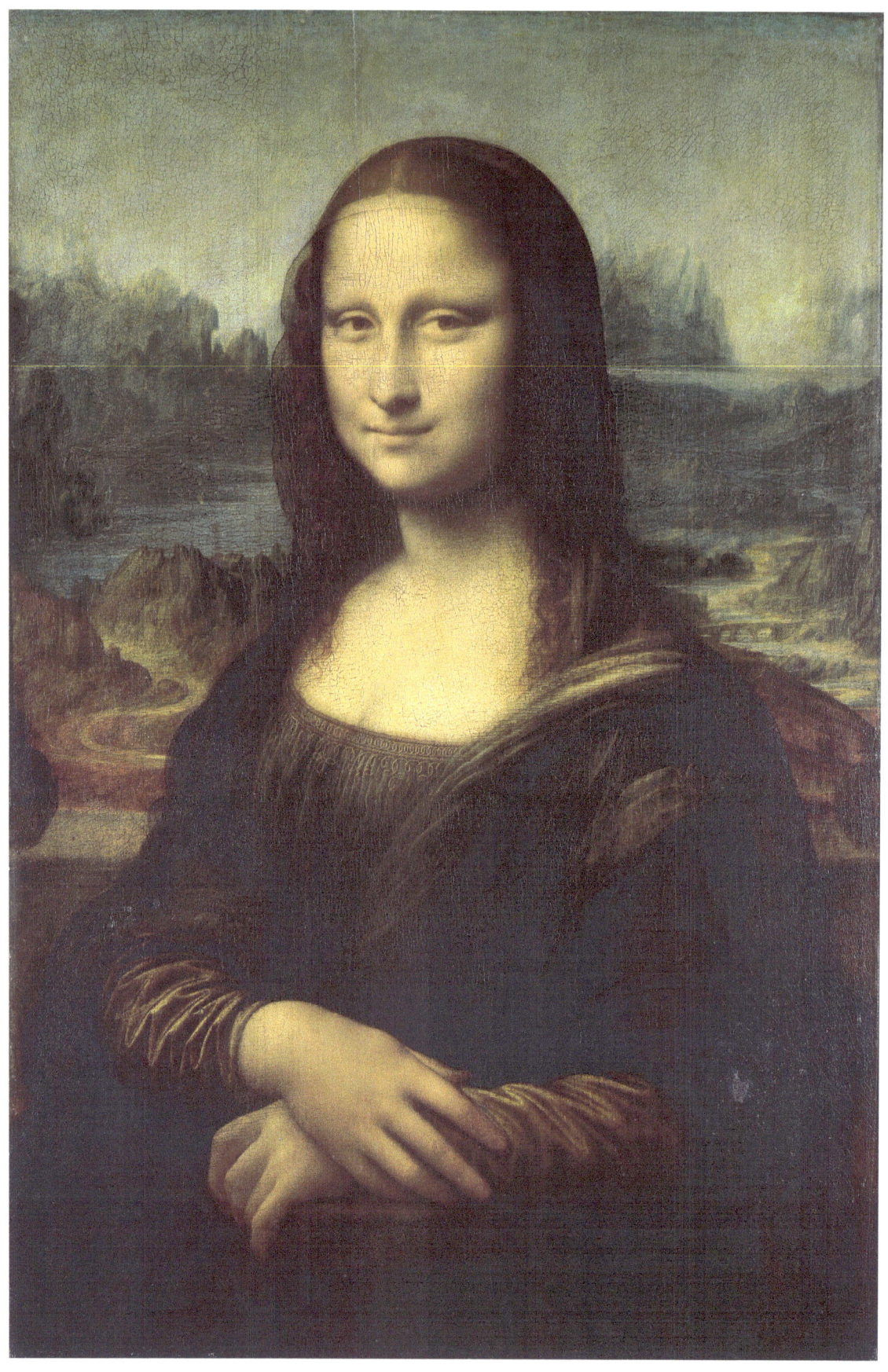

Fig. 1. Leonardo da Vinci, *Mona Lisa*, Louvre version, ca. 1508-1516. Oil on wood, c. 53.3 cm x 79.2 cm.

INTRODUCTION

Prof. Jean-Pierre Isbouts
Fielding Graduate University
Santa Barbara, CA

One of the great riddles of our time is how a portrait of a woman of no known rank, title or fame continues to hold the world in thrall, some 500 years after it was painted. What is it about the *Mona Lisa* that makes it such a fascinating work of art? Why do six million visitors rush the stairs of the Louvre's Denon Pavilion each year, just to catch a glimpse of this small painting, hidden behind a double layer of bullet-proof glass? And more to the point, why does it continue to cast a spell on modern critics and historians, as evidenced by the continuing wave of publications on the subject?

One reason, perhaps, is that even today, the events surrounding the origins of the *Mona Lisa* are shrouded in mystery. The reason is simple: most of the evidence about the painting is confusing and contradictory.

Take, for example, the first and most obvious problem: the identity of the lady. Giorgio Vasari, one of Leonardo's first biographers and the author of the 1550 book *The Lives of the Painters,* wrote that the portrait represents Lisa del Giocondo (*née* Gherardini), the wife of a Florentine silk merchant named Francesco del Giocondo. This would suggest that the portrait originated sometime between 1503 and 1506, during Leonardo's extended sojourn in Florence before his return to Milan. But Leonardo himself, when questioned about the portrait in 1517, declared that the work represents "a certain Florentine woman, done from life, at the behest of the late Magnificent Giuliano Medici." That would place the origin of the portrait at least ten years later, between 1513 to 1516, when Leonardo lived at the Medici court in Rome under Giuliano's patronage. And since, as Leonardo said, it was *facta di naturale*, "done from life," that

would suggest that the sitter lived in Rome, possibly at the court of Pope Leo X, Giuliano's brother, who were both Florentines themselves.[2] According to that argument, a possible candidate would be Pacifica Brandano, Giuliano's mistress, who gave birth to his son Ippolito in 1511. Tragically, Pacifica is believed to have died shortly after the birth, which may have been a motive for Giuliano to order a posthumous portrait of her. The identification of the *Mona Lisa* as Pacifica Brandano, which until recently had little support in the scholarly community, was boosted by a series of multispectral images taken by the French scientist Pascal Cotte, published in 2015. Cotte claimed that these scans reveal the image of a lady underneath the *Mona Lisa*, which looks strikingly different than the final portrait and may have been a lady at the court in Rome, such as Pacifica Brandano—an assumption that inspired a BBC documentary.[3]

But there are obvious problems with this hypothesis. First off, Pacifica was not a "Florentine lady" as Leonardo's statement suggests, but a daughter of Urbino. Second, Giuliano's brother Giovanni, the future Pope Leo X, was not elected to the papacy until March 9, 1513, some two years after Pacifica's death. Though Giovanni briefly moved from Florence to Rome on March 23, 1492 after being admitted (at age 17) to the College of Cardinals, he soon returned to his native city upon the untimely death of his father, Lorenzo de' Medici. He then lived with his brother Piero in Florence until he was elected to the papacy. In other words, Pacifica never attended the Medici court of Leo X in Rome, since it did not come into being until 1513. One could, of course, argue that Giuliano commissioned a posthumous portrait of Pacifica while he was still living in Florence, but the evidence suggests that he was not very interested in his son by his deceased mistress, and consequently, not in the memory of Pacifica herself. Indeed, it fell on Giovanni to take little Ippolito under his wing, and ultimately made sure he enjoyed a prominent ecclesial career. And most importantly, Leonardo was not living in Florence at the time, save for some brief visits.

The most important argument against the Pacifica hypothesis is, as always, the simplest one: why would Leonardo paint a portrait of the mistress of his patron, Giuliano de' Medici, only to cover it up with a portrait of an entirely different lady with no known connection to the Medicis, or the papal court in Rome? Indeed, mere months after Giuliano's death in 1516 (which could have marked an end to the commission), Leonardo was on his way to France, carrying a *Mona Lisa* portrait in his baggage that by then was virtually complete.

To further confuse the issue, various modern authors have offered other theories with regards to the identity of the lady. For example, some claim that she is either Isabella Gualanda, daughter of a courtier to Alfonso of Aragon; or Costanza d'Avalos, the Duchess of Francavilla.[4] The fact that today, she is known under different names doesn't help either: in Italy she is known as *La Gioconda* (after the family name of her husband), in Spain as *La Joconda*, and in France by a derivative of that name, *La Joconde*. For the rest of the world, she is known as *The Mona Lisa*.

Apart from the sitter's identity, we also have the problem of when the portrait was actually painted. Though darkened by various layers of varnish, the *Mona Lisa* is very clearly the product of Leonardo's late period, as evidenced by the rich *sfumato* of the skin that is carried through in the opaque, atmospheric treatment of the background. These features are also present in two other late works, *The Virgin and Child with St Anne* and *St John the Baptist*. Significantly, these are the three paintings that Leonardo decided to

bring with him when in 1516 he moved to Amboise, France, to spend the last years of his life. Indeed, until recently most Leonardo scholars dated the *Mona Lisa* between 1513 and 1516.

This assumption, which was considered an infallible axiom in Leonardo scholarship, was thrown in doubt by an astonishing discovery in 2005. In that year, a professor at Heidelberg University, Armin Schlechter, was working on an inventory of volumes at the university library when he chanced upon a publication of letters by the Roman orator and statesman Marcus Tullius Cicero (106-43 B.C.E.). This particular book had been published under the title *Epistulae ad Familiares* ("Letters to his Friends") in Bologna in 1477, and had been in the possession of either Niccolò Machiavelli, a secretary to the Chancery of Florence, or his assistant, Agostino Vespucci.

At one point in the book, Cicero refers to the Greek artist Apelles, who among others created the famous painting of Alexander the Great defeating King Darius III at the Battle of Issus.[5] Cicero then notes how Apelles had been commissioned to paint the portrait of the goddess Venus, but left it unfinished. In his *Natural History,* Pliny the Elder explains *why* Apelles never completed the painting: as it happened, the artist died before he could do so. Cicero, on the other hand, implies that Apelles' choice to leave the portrait unfinished was deliberate.[6] This must have struck a chord with Vespucci, who was reminded of Leonardo's reputation for not always completing his works. He grabbed a pen and scribbled a note in the margin, next to the Cicero passage. Written in Latin, it said,

> "Apelles the painter. That's the way Leonardo da Vinci works in all of his paintings, like, for example, the portrait of Lisa del Giocondo and Anne, the mother of the Virgin. We will see what he's going to do with the chamber of the great council, the thing for which

he's just come to terms with the gonfaloniere."[7]

And then, most importantly, Vespucci added a date: "1503 8.^bris," or *October, 1503.*

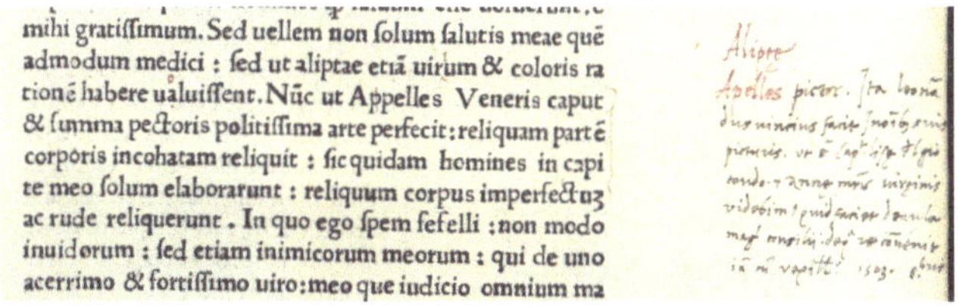

Fig 2. The Heidelberg marginalia in *Epistulae ad Familiares,* 1503.

It is safe to say that this scribble in the margin of an obscure book has transformed *Mona Lisa* scholarship. And yet, it has also made the attempt to establish a firm date for the painting's genesis more difficult. How to reconcile a work that is clearly the product of Leonardo's late period with a putative date some 10 years earlier?

In response, a number of art historians have advanced the theory that while Leonardo began working on the portrait in 1503, he never actually delivered it to Francesco del Giocondo—who, according to Vasari, commissioned the work—but kept it with him so as to continue to work on it. At first glance, this appears to be a plausible argument. As we know, Leonardo often spent an extraordinary length of time on his paintings, in the pursuit of the most perfect expression of his ideas. His fresco of *The Last Supper* at the Santa Maria delle Grazie in Milan took nearly four years to complete—in part because, as one eyewitness wrote, he spent days "without his touching the work, yet each day he would spend several hours examining it and criticizing the figures to himself."[8] Similarly, *The Virgin and Child with St Anne* had an exceptionally long genesis, not reaching its final form as a painted work until 1513 or 1515. Yet the idea for such a "St. Anne Trinity" may have originated with a 1501 commission by the Servite friars (or "Servants

of Mary" as they were officially known) for a new altarpiece for their church, the *Santissima Annunziata* in Florence. The evidence is provided in a letter by a prominent Carmelite cleric from Mantua, the vicar-general Pietro da Novellara, who visited Leonardo's studio on April 8, 1501.[9] Some authors believe that the *St Anne* goes back even further, to a commission by the French King Louis XII while Leonardo was still living in Milan.[10]

In other words, the idea that Leonardo could hang on to a work like the *Mona Lisa* and continue to explore new ideas and solutions is not far-fetched, and indeed, this is still a hypothesis in the *Mona Lisa* literature today.

Three formidable pieces of evidence argue against this hypothesis, however. The first one is that Giorgio Vasari, in his detailed description of the *Mona Lisa,* wrote that:

> Leonardo undertook to execute, for Francesco del Giocondo, the portrait of *Monna Lisa,* his wife; and after toiling over it for four years, he left it unfinished; and the work is now in the collection of King Francis of France, at Fontainebleau.[11]

The reference to "four years," an unusually specific number, suggests that this must be a historical fact. That means that, if Leonardo was well advanced on the portrait in 1503, as the Vespucci marginalia indicate, he must have stopped work on it in 1506—and for a very good reason, as we will explore in Chapter 3. This would eliminate the possibility that Leonardo kept working on the portrait of Lisa del Giocondo for the remainder of his career.

The second problem is that Vasari insists that the work was left unfinished. But anyone who is familiar with Leonardo's oeuvre would readily admit that of all his works, the *Mona Lisa* in the Louvre is undoubtedly

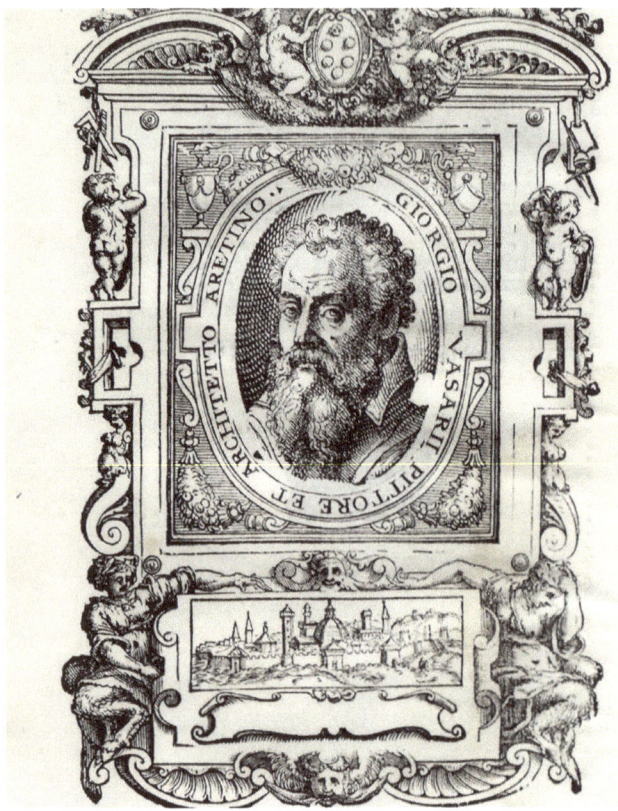

Fig 3. Giorgio Vasari, *Le vite de' piu eccellenti pittori scultori e architettori*. Florence, 1568.

his most finished work. That is not the case for many of Leonardo's other paintings that were indeed left unfinished, such as *The Adoration of the Magi* (1479-1481), *St. Jerome in the Wilderness* (1480-1490), *Portrait of a Musician* (1485-1487), as well as passages in the *Madonna Litta* (1491-1495) and the *St Anne* (1501-1515). By comparison, the Louvre *Mona Lisa* is as polished and complete as a Leonardo work would ever get. So why does Vasari claim that Leonardo left the portrait unfinished?

The third piece of evidence is contained in the end of Vasari's paragraph: "the work is now in the collection of King Francis of France, at Fontainebleau." This we know is true, because when Leonardo died in 1519, the *Mona Lisa*, the *St Anne*, and the *St John* passed into the estate of the French king as part of Leonardo's bequest. What's more, Vasari then proceeds to describe the *Mona Lisa* in great detail:

"The eyes had their natural luster and moistness, and around them were the lashes and all those rosy and pearly tints that demand the greatest delicacy of execution. The eyebrows were completely natural, growing thickly in one place and lightly in another and following the pores of the skin. The nose was finely painted, with rosy and delicate nostrils as in life. The mouth, joined to the flesh-tints of the face by the red of the lips, appeared to be living flesh, rather than paint. On looking closely at the pit of her throat, one could swear that the pulses were beating."[12]

It will be obvious to the reader that no one could have produced such a vivid analysis of the painting unless he had actually seen it with his own eyes. There was no digital photography or any other form of mechanical color reproduction in the 1500's; the only way one could see a painting in all its glory was to travel to the place where it was on display.

But here is the fundamental problem: how could Vasari have seen the *Mona Lisa* if the portrait had already left Italy for France in 1516? Vasari—who was born in 1511, just five years earlier—never traveled to France, let alone visit the French royal court. Indeed, he did not start to work on his book until the late 1530's, when he began to take trips to the principal cities in Tuscany to see the work of Italian artists up close. This very likely put him in contact with the del Giocondo family, who as he wrote, were responsible for the *Mona Lisa* commission. In fact, Francesco del Giocondo, Lisa's husband, died in June of 1538 and was given a lavish funeral in Florence. It is conceivable that Vasari attended the funeral and was thus brought into contact with the surviving spouse,

Lisa herself. At this time, Lisa was still living in the Giocondo house on the Via della Stufa. If the portrait of the *Mona Lisa* was still in the family collection at the time, Vasari would have had an opportunity to see it.

There is another important reason why Vasari would have made every effort to see works by Leonardo that were still in Florence. Though this is often forgotten in art scholarship, Vasari's *Lives* is not a work of art history in the modern sense. To produce and publish a book of such size and ambition was an expensive exercise in the Cinquecento, the 16th century, and few authors were in a position to embark on it unless there was a patron who could foot the bill. In Vasari's case, that patron was none other than Duke Cosimo I de' Medici, who ruled the state of Florence as an autocrat after the overthrow of the legitimate Florentine republic in 1530. Indeed, Vasari's book is dedicated to the duke.

Cosimo realized that the ducal Medici rule was under a cloud of illegitimacy, and used every means at his disposal to cement his status as the recognized ruler of the state. Art played a key role in this form of propaganda and the personality cult of Cosimo himself. That is why Vasari's book is almost exclusively preoccupied with artists who lived in the territory ruled by the Medici—the Florentine Duchy, formerly a republic, and the Medici papal court in Rome. Vasari has often been criticized by modern critics for this highly selective focus, but that is because they never grasped the true purpose of *Lives of the Painters*: to serve as an act of official propaganda, espousing the blessings of Medici patronage. And in the first half of the Cinquecento, one of Florence's most prominent artists was undoubtedly Leonardo da Vinci. Unlike Michelangelo, who had fallen out with the Medicis for supporting the republican cause, Leonardo had retained his mystique—despite the fact that few, if any, works by him were still in the city.

In response, Cosimo was eager to tie Leonardo's fame to the Medici family, even though historically this was utter nonsense: as a young artist in Florence, Leonardo had been largely eschewed by Lorenzo the Magnificent and his social circle. That is why a detailed description of one of Leonardo's few surviving paintings in Florence, the *Mona Lisa*, was of considerable political significance, and why Vasari would lavish such attention on this portrait.

But this still doesn't resolve the essential problem: how could Vasari have seen a portrait in Florence in the late 1530's or early 1540's, when that portrait was actually in France, and had been in the possession of the French king for well over two decades?

There is an obvious solution to this quandary. It is this: our sources about the *Mona Lisa* contradict each other for the simple reason that *they are not referring to the same painting*. If we consider this possibility, that Leonardo painted more than one version of the *Mona Lisa*, then all of these problems begin to resolve themselves. Indeed, in his 1584 biography of Leonardo, the artist Paolo Giovanni Lomazzo refers to two versions of the portrait: *il ritratto della Gioconda, e di Mona Lisa* ("A portrait of the *Gioconda*, and of *Mona Lisa*").[13] It is this hypothesis that the present monograph aims to examine in depth, by juxtaposing various arguments by our distinguished contributors.

The idea that Leonardo would paint not one, but two versions of the portrait is entirely in character. Throughout his life, Leonardo would often return to a motif or composition for a variety of reasons. One, as we saw, is that he always strove for perfection. Another reason is that his slow pace of working also meant that his output was limited—certainly compared to other Florentine workshops like those run by Verrocchio, Ghirlandaio or Botticelli. That was a problem, because Leonardo had many pupils and associates who depended on him for their livelihood. Even Verrocchio, who enjoyed a steady stream of commissions from the Medici circle, wrote on his 1457 tax statement that he was "losing his shirt" trying

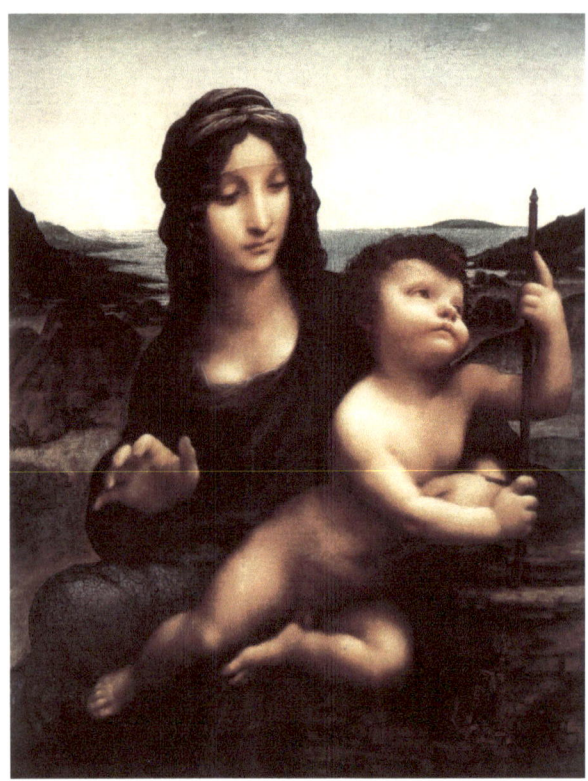

Fig. 4. Leonardo da Vinci and assistant, *Madonna of the Yarnwinder*, Buccleuch version, 1501-1507.

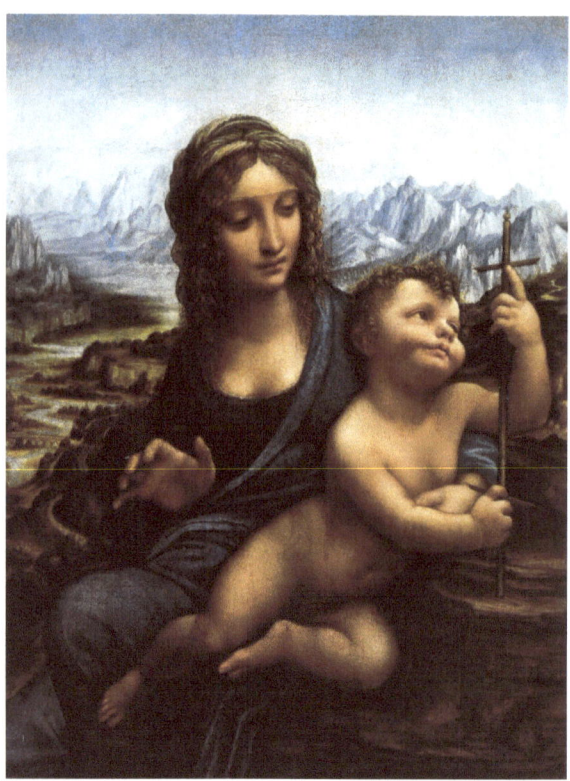

Fig. 5. Leonardo da Vinci and assistant, *Madonna of the Yarnwinder*, Lansdowne version, 1501-1507.

to keep the shop operating (the Italian expression is *non guadagniamo le chalze*, "can't keep our hoses on").[14]

The answer, then, was to create multiple versions of the paintings that Leonardo was working on, so as to maximize the studio's output. Thus we have at least two versions of *The Virgin of the Rocks*, both painted by Leonardo with the De Predis brothers. The first version, now in the Louvre, was painted between 1483 and 1486, and a second version, now in the National Gallery in London, was produced well over a decade later, possibly between 1495 and 1508.[15] Similarly, Leonardo painted two versions of the *Madonna of the Yarnwinder* (or *Madonna dei Fusi* in Italian), the first of which was probably commissioned in 1499 by Florimond Robertet at the French court in Milan, who served as counselor to King Louis XII. This work, commonly referred to as the Buccleuch version (as it was acquired by the Duke of Buccleuch in 1767),

appears to be the first as evidenced by the tender *sfumato* on the faces of the Madonna and child, which indelibly mark the work as a Leonardo autograph. Other passages, however, were clearly executed by a pupil or associate of considerably less talent, particularly with regards to the rather disappointing background.

A second version of this work, known as the Lansdowne version (after the Marquess of Lansdowne, who bought the work in 1809) or the Reford version (after Robert Reford, who acquired it in 1928), rectified this problem by adding a landscape that is strongly reminiscent of the background panorama of both the Louvre *Mona Lisa* and the *St Anne*. This would put the work in a much later time frame, possibly between 1508 and 1513. Other parts of the painting, however, betray the hand of pupils, though numerous alterations or *pentimenti* underneath the work suggest that it originated under Leonardo's close supervision. Critical passages, such as the faces and hands, are most likely by his own hand.

Consequently, the proposition that Leonardo may have painted not one, but two versions of the *Mona Lisa* is by no means far-fetched, as some critics have claimed.

Nonetheless, this hypothesis raises another question. If Leonardo did paint more than one *Mona Lisa*, where is this earlier version today? And if we can locate it, how can we determine that this painting is indeed an autograph, rather than one of the many *Mona Lisa* versions and copies that are still extant today?

Versions and Copies

To answer this question, we must first recognize the innate difference between a "version" of a Leonardo painting, painted by himself and his assistants at his studio; and a copy of such a work executed by his pupils or later followers—the so-called *Leonardeschi*—without the guidance of the master himself. And in judging this difference, we must remember that our understanding of what constitutes an "original" versus a "copy" is different from the norms that prevailed in the Renaissance, and certainly in the workshop of Leonardo da Vinci. In our age, digital technology has made it possible to mechanically reproduce a work of art with such fidelity that it is sometimes difficult to distinguish it from the original. That has made any suggestion that a work could be a "copy" inherently suspect, at least in our eyes; for us, only the original matters.

But that distinction did not exist in the Renaissance, nor did the largely pejorative meaning that we attach to the idea of a "copy" today. Any form of mechanical reproduction did not exist in the 15th and 16th century, other than the nascent technology of the

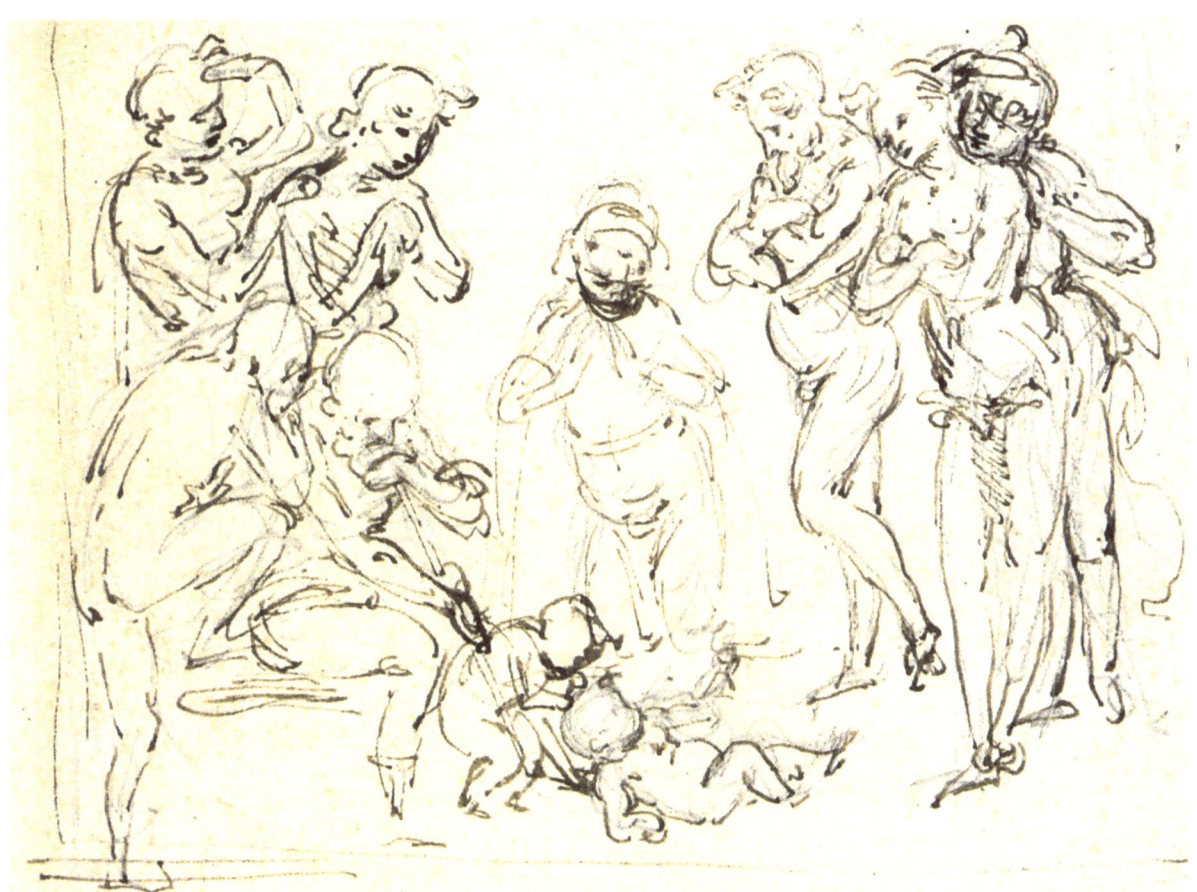

Fig. 6. Leonardo da Vinci, *Study for a Nativity*, c. 1480.

woodcut or copper engraving, in black and white ink. The only way a painting could be reproduced in all of its nuance and color was to copy it, painstakingly, by hand.

This was particularly true for Leonardo, who maintained a strict pedagogical system for the pupils under his sway. First, aspiring students had to hone their incipient talent by learning how to draw. In this, Leonardo probably followed the curriculum of Verrocchio's studio, who also emphasized the art of drawing as the principal educational agency of his workshop. Whereas a painting involves a long and laborious effort with an uneven outcome, a drawing could be sketched quickly, and then modified or improved upon with just a few strokes. Virtually everything Leonardo did was informed by studies in the form of drawings: his observations of nature, his engineering designs, his anatomical studies, his ideas about composition, and lastly, his preparatory drawings and studies for paintings, including "cartoons" for murals *al fresco*.

In short, drawings were the principal medium by which Leonardo communicated his artistic ideas to his followers. According to Paolo Giovio, one of Leonardo's earliest biographers, Leonardo went as far as to forbid his pupils, until twenty years of age, to "use a paintbrush or paints." Instead, he made them "work with lead point to choose and reproduce diligently the excellent models of earlier works, to imitate with simple line drawings the force of nature, and outlines of bodies that present themselves to our eyes with a great variety of movement." Thus, Giovio believed, Leonardo prevented his students from being "seduced by the brush and colors" before they learned to represent "the exact proportions of things."[16]

In his *Trattato della Pittura* or "Treatise on Painting," which probably reflects the lessons taught in his workshop, Leonardo explained why drawing was so important.[17] "First," he instructs the reader, "copy the drawings of accomplished masters made

directly from nature, and not practice drawings; follow this through with drawings of relief works alongside drawings taken from the same relief; then move on to drawing from life."[18]

It was only when a pupil had demonstrated his facility with drawing that he moved on to the next stage: to paint a faithful copy of one of Leonardo's paintings, under the master's direct supervision. By copying a work like *Leda and the Swan*, for example, of which a number by Leonardo's pupils are still in existence today, the student could study a composition in-depth and recognize the unique solutions that Leonardo had brought to its realization. "For Leonardo, that was something that's absolutely integral to an artist's training," says Maya Corry, an art historian at Oxford's Oriel College. "You have to learn first through copying and also not just copying in terms of pouncing and tracing and those sorts of technical aspects of copying, but even through the memorization of design."[19]

Once a pupil had reached a certain level of mastery, he could then be charged with painting a complete panel in oils, based on a Leonardo drawing or cartoon. This appears to be the case with Giampietrino's *Leda and the Swan* of 1506-1510, now in Karlsruhe. The work most likely drew its inspiration from one of several Leonardo drawings on the subject, such as the version in the Devonshire Collection in Chatsworth, dated between 1503 and 1504.

In sum, then, this copying activity served two outcomes. One, it gave talented young artists the opportunity to learn their craft by working from a detailed model; and two, it provided the workshop with additional product to sell to the marketplace, particularly given the low output of Leonardo "originals."

But even then, the border between master and pupil was not as sharply drawn as our modern use of terms like "original" and "copy" would suggest. Infrared reflectographic studies of some of these

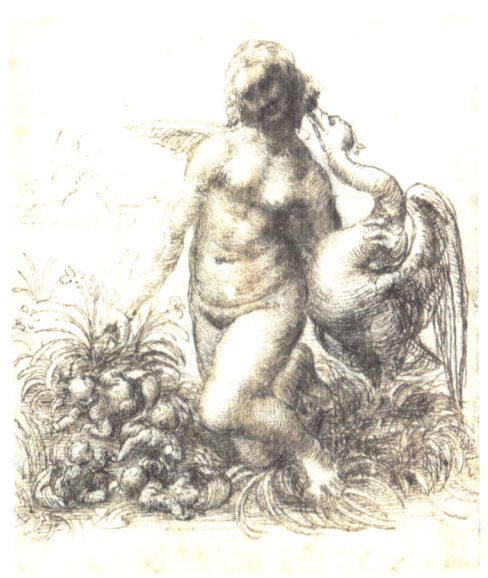

Fig. 7. Leonardo da Vinci, *Study for Leda and the Swan*, ca. 1503-1504.

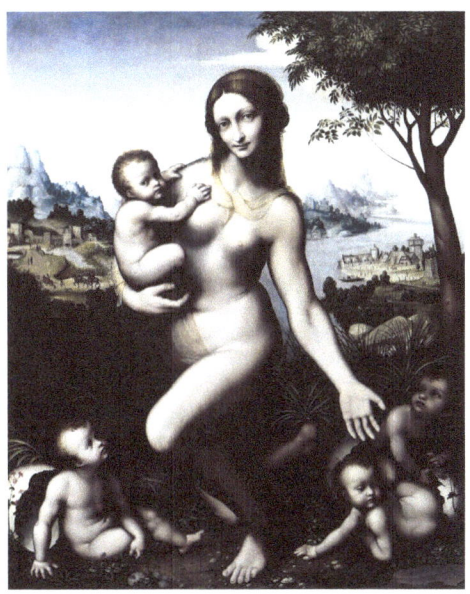

Fig. 8. Giampietrino, *Leda and the Swan*, 1510-1515.

copies have revealed numerous *pentimenti* that show that Leonardo could intervene and correct the student, or point him into a different direction entirely. In the case of Giampietrino's *Leda and the Swan,* for example, modern tests have revealed an underdrawing of the *St Anne*, which suggests a correlation with one of Leonardo's other studies for of this time.

Another factor that complicates our search for a possible second autograph of the *Mona Lisa* is that Leonardo's pupils and followers would continue to work from the master's models after they left the studio and set themselves up as independent artists. This indicates that Leonardo gave them access to his cache of drawings and cartoons when they chose to leave the workshop, or after the second Milan studio disbanded in 1513. In the decades to follow, these sketches and drawings would become treasured possessions that enjoyed broad circulation among the *Leonardeschi*, as evidenced by countless later copies of works such as *Leda and the Swan,* the *St Anne Trinity*, *The Virgin of the Rocks* and a great number of variations on Leonardo's Madonna motifs. In addition, former pupils such as Solario, Giampietrino, d'Oggiono, Boltraffio, Il Sodoma, da Sesto, Luini and

Salaì would time and again fall back on Leonardo drawings and sketches in the development of their own original works. Bernardino Luini's *The Holy Family with Saint Anne and the infant John the Baptist* (c. 1515-1520), for example, appears to be inspired by the Burlington Cartoon.

But no composition proved to be as popular a source for copies as the *Mona Lisa*. In 1952, to mark the 500th anniversary of Leonardo's birth, a group of French art historians undertook the task of creating an inventory of all versions and copies of the *Mona Lisa* from the 16th to the 19th century. They came up with an astounding 61 works that are "worthy of scholarly attention."[20] Some of these works, dated to the first part of the 16th century, continue to be the source of speculation about their authorship.

This is the subject of Chapter 2, *A Comparative Evaluation of the Different Versions and Copies,* by Profs. Salvatore Lorusso and Andrea Natali of the Università di Bologna. Their conclusion is that of three particularly promising versions—the Prado *Mona Lisa*, the Reynolds *Mona Lisa*, and the Isleworth *Mona Lisa*—it is the latter that has the strongest claim as a possible Leonardo autograph.

This idea—that the Isleworth *Mona Lisa* could be the earliest, or perhaps *earlier*, version of the motif, painted *before* the portrait now in the Louvre, is then discussed in contributions by a number of scholars. They include Prof. John Asmus, University of California at San Diego; Prof. Vadim Parfenov at the State Electrotechnical University in St. Petersburg, Russia; Prof. Salvatore Lorusso and Prof. Andrea Natali at the Università di Bologna; Prof. Átila Soares da Costa Filho of the Universidade Cândido Mendes in Rio de Janeiro, Brazil; Prof. Jason Halter of the University of Michigan; and some of my own articles. In addition, this monograph includes contributions by noted art critic Gérard Boudin de l'Arche and two artists, Albert Sauteur and Joe Mullins. Moreover, Prof. Robert Myrick of the School of Art at Aberystwyth University has contributed an in-depth analysis of the events surrounding the "discovery" of the Isleworth *Mona Lisa* in 1913 by the British art collector Hugh Blaker. While these authors do not always agree on key points of argument and evidence, as one would expect in an academic publication, they do agree on one point: that the Isleworth *Mona Lisa* is arguably the first version of the *Mona Lisa*, painted by Leonardo between 1503 and 1506, thus preceding the Louvre *Mona Lisa* by a decade.

Before we can examine this evidence in detail, however, Chapter 3 will address a question that few publications on the *Mona Lisa* have ever addressed in detail: *why* did Leonardo da Vinci paint a portrait of Lisa del Giocondo? Why did he accept this commission when, as the vicar from Mantua asserted, by 1501 he was "tired of the brush," and longed for more challenging assignments than creating *another* portrait of a young woman? After all, that is exactly what he had been doing while serving Ludovico Sforza, the duke of Milan, for the preceding two decades. Leonardo was an artist who was always looking for new ideas that could challenge his intellect. In that context, his decision to paint an unknown Florentine housewife, after refusing to finish the portrait of the most influential woman in Renaissance Italy, Isabella d'Este, doesn't seem to make sense.

Therefore, we can only begin to understand the genesis of the *Mona Lisa,* and the feasibility of the two-version hypothesis, by delving into his mindset as he returned to Florence from his long sojourn in Milan.

[1] Giorgio Vasari, "Lionardo da Vinci," in: *Le Vite de' più eccellenti pittori, scultori e architetti;* first published by Torrentino in 1550; second edition by Giunti in 1568.

[2] Antonio de Beatis, "Account of the Visit of Cardinal Louis d'Aragon paid to Leonardo, at the Château de Cloux, October 10, 1517," in Delieuvin, Vincent, *Saint Anne: Leonardo da Vinci's ultimate Masterpiece;* p. 199.

[3] See *Secrets of the Mona Lisa*, BBC documentary, hosted by Andrew Graham-Dixon; December 9, 2015. Full disclosure: the editor of this monograph, Jean-Pierre Isbouts, appeared in this documentary as well.

[4] Isabella Gualanda's mother, Bianca, was a cousin of Cecilia Gallerani, subject of the '*Lady with an Ermine*', painted by Leonardo c.1489-1490. Isabella was orphaned as a baby, and from 1492 she was raised under the protection of the Aragonese court in Naples. By 1514, then widowed and a mother, she possibly lived in Rome, and moved in the circle of Vittoria Colonna, which also included Costanza d'Avalos, the Duchess of Francavilla, and other intellectual '*emigres*' from Naples. The suggestion that she may be the sitter of the Mona Lisa portrait rests on the fact that the day after Cardinal Louis d'Aragon visited Leonardo in Amboise, his secretary recorded the prelate's visit to Blois, where they saw "an oil painting of a certain Lady of Lombardy, done from life, a beautiful woman indeed: but in my opinion *less so than Signora Gualanda*" (our italics). This, in the opinion of some, would suggest that the Lombardy portrait compared unfavorably with the *Mona Lisa* portrait seen the previous day. This raises the question, however, why de Beatis would not have identified the sitter of the *Mona Lisa* as such while describing the portrait in his diary entry on October 10. Certainly, the roundabout reference to "a Florentine lady" would have provided the perfect opportunity to do so, if indeed Isabella Gualanda was the sitter. Furthermore, Isabella was not a Florentine but born and raised in Naples.

The identification with Costanza d'Avalos was advanced by Adolfo Venturi in a series of articles beginning in 1929.

Costanza d'Avalos Piccolomini was a noblewoman of Spanish origin and daughter of Innico I d'Avalos, who joined the Naples court of Alfonson V of Aragon in 1442. She married Federico del Balzo, brother of the Queen of Naples, Isabella, but he died in the 1480's, leaving Costanza childless. The evidence for the claim that she is the *Mona Lisa* is the presence of a veil around the lady's head, which would suggest widowhood. Venturi cited the poet Enea Irpino, who claimed that "Vinci" painted Costanza d'Avalos as a widow, *sotto il bel negro velo* ("under a beautiful black veil"). However, it is highly unlikely that in 1513, when Leonardo came to Rome, Costanza would still be wear mourning dress, more than 25 years after her consort's death. Indeed, at that time she was the center of a renowned salon of artists and poets, living in Ischia. So renowned was her influence in artistic circles that Emperor Charles V gave her the territory of Pescara and raised her to the title of princess. If she had truly been the subject of Leonardo's portrait, her name would undoubtedly been attached to the painting, given her status and prominence at the time.

[5] This work by Apelles, which was famous throughout the ancient world, has been preserved in a mosaic in the House of the Faun in Pompei. A copy is still visible *in situ*; the original is in the Archeological Museum in Naples.

[6] Pliny the Elder, *Natural History,* Book 35.

[7] The original text of Vespucci's handwritten note reads: "Apelles pictor. Ita Leonardus Vincius facit in omnibus suis picturis, ut enim caput Lise del Giocondo et Anne matris virginis. Videbimus, quid faciet de aula magni consilii, de qua re convenit iam cum vexillifero. 1503 8.bris." From: Probst, Veit, "Rätselhafte Mona Lisa: Wer ist die geheimnisvoll lächelnde Dame auf Leonardo da Vincis Bild?" in *UniSpiegel*, University of Heidelberg, 2008.

[8] Matteo Bandello, *Novelle* (1554), in Claire Farago (Ed.), *Biography and Early Art Criticism of Leonardo da Vinci;* p. 198.

[9] As he dutifully reported to his patron, the Marchioness Isabella d'Este, Leonardo had produced only one drawing since his return to Florence, "a cartoon of a child Christ, about a year old, almost jumping out of his mother's arms to seize hold of a lamb." Mary herself, he continued, "is in the act of rising from St. Anne's lap, and holds back the child from the lamb. See Copsey, Richard O. Carm., "A Carmelite Link to Leonardo da Vinci", from *The British Province of Carmelite Friars,* December 26, 2011.

[10] When he succeeded Charles VIII as king of France, Louis had decided to marry Charles' widow, Anne of Bretagne. Naturally, St. Anne was the queen's patron saint, which could have inspired the king to ask Leonardo—who was already working on a Madonna for the king—to paint a portrait of this saint.

[11] Giorgio Vasari, "Leonardo da Vinci," in *Lives of the Artists,* 1568 edition, in Claire Farago (Ed.), *Biography and Early Art Criticism of Leonardo da Vinci;* p. 88.

[12] Claire Farago (Ed.), *Biography and Early Art Criticism of Leonardo da Vinci;* page 88.

[13] Lomazzo, Gian Paolo: *Trattato dell'arte della pittura, scoltura et architettura* [Milano 1584] in *Scritti sulle arti* Vol. II, Roberto Paolo Ciardi, Florence 1974.

[14] Burke, Peter, *Culture and Society in Renaissance Italy;* p. 69.

[15] The second version of *The Virgin of the Rocks*, now in London, may have come about as a result of a dispute with the commissioning agency, the Confraternity of the Immaculate Conception in Milan. Leonardo's panel was supposed to function as the "cover piece" of an elaborate wooden reliquary of sorts, which housed a venerable Madonna sculpture known as the *Immacolata*, symbol of Mary's Immaculate Conception. This sacred event had only become an official feast day on the Catholic liturgical calendar in 1477, as part of a decree by Pope Sixtus IV, which could have motivated the development of this altarpiece. One theory suggests that the Confraternity refused to pay the agreed price for the work because in Leonardo's composition, the emphasis is clearly on the Virgin and the infant John. Jesus, strangely,

is relegated to a lesser role at the very base of the triangular composition. Leonardo may therefore have sold the painting to the French king, as attested by an inventory of the French royal collection from 1625. In due course, the Confraternity changed their mind and requested a second version, possibly because of the growing fame of Leonardo at that time. This second version may initially have been executed by Leonardo's associates, most likely Ambrogio de Predis, possibly using the same cartoons used for the first. But once again, the Confraternity balked at paying for this work, because in their view the painting was still "unfinished." Translated properly, this meant that the Confraternity believed the painting was more Ambrogio than Leonardo; the magic touch of the *real* master, or so it was felt, was clearly missing. As a result, Leonardo had to return to Milan and undertake major revisions of the work, as evidenced by a detailed 2010 study by National Gallery conservators. For more information see Jean-Pierre Isbouts and Christopher H. Brown, *Young Leonardo*; pp. 160-166.

[16]Paolo Giovio, "The Life of Leonardo," in P. Barocchi, *Scritti d'arte del Cinquecento.* Milan and Naples: 1961; pp. 20-21.

[17]After Leonardo's death, Melzi tried to organize the master's various sheets and notebooks in some order, while transcribing many of Leonardo's scribbles in something approximating standard Italian grammar. He was particularly focused on Leonardo's texts for a treatise of painting, as a guide for artists. These and other texts were combined in a compendium known as the Codex Urbinas, which wound up in the Vatican Library. Through copies, this manuscript circulated for more than a century in private collections until it was edited as the *Trattato della Pittura* by Raffaelo du Fresne in 1651, both as an Italian edition published in Rome, and a French translation published in Paris. This first print included several illustrations drawn by the renowned Nicolas Poussin, the most important artist of French 17th century classicism.

[18]*Libro di Pittura*, in manuscript A, folio 113, Institut de France.

[19]As quoted in the film *The Search for the Last Supper*, produced by Pantheon Studios; broadcast on PBS stations during Easter, 2018.

[20]McMullen, Roy, *Mona Lisa: The Picture and the Myth.* Boston: Houghton Mifflin Co., 1976; p. 139.

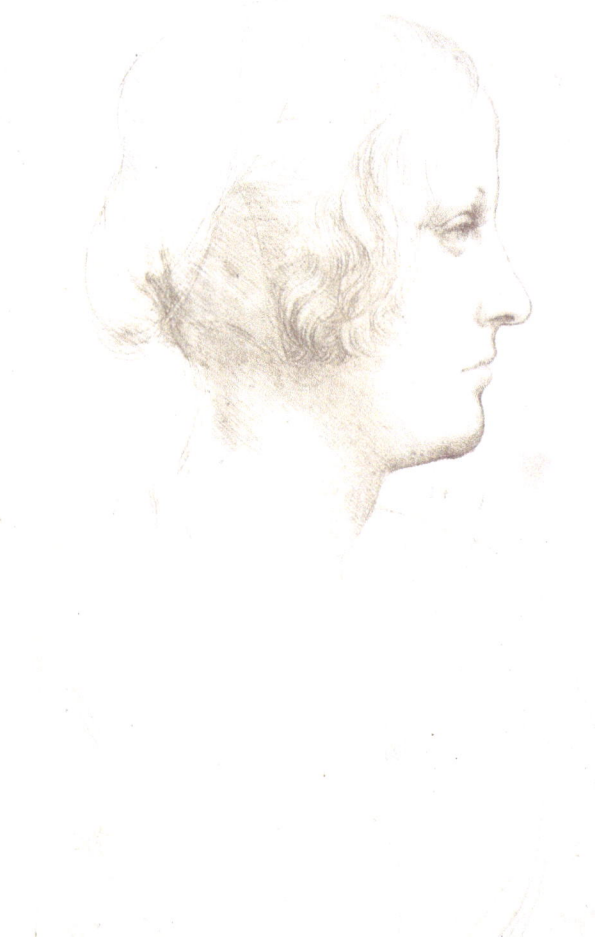

Fig. 9. Leonardo da Vinci, *Head of a Young Woman*, ca. 1485-1490.

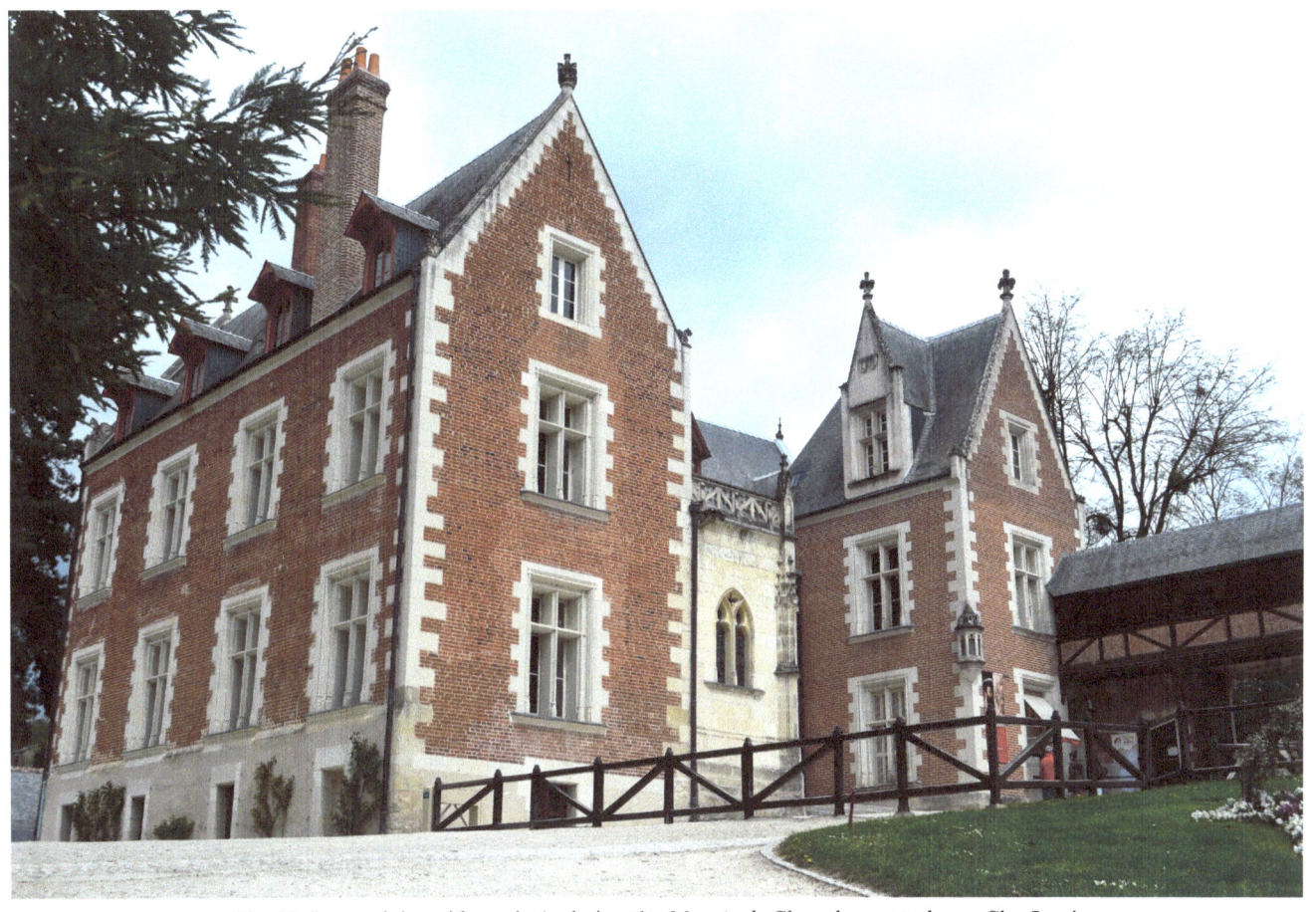

Fig. 10. Leonardo's residence in Amboise, the *Manoir de Cloux*, known today as Clos Lucé.

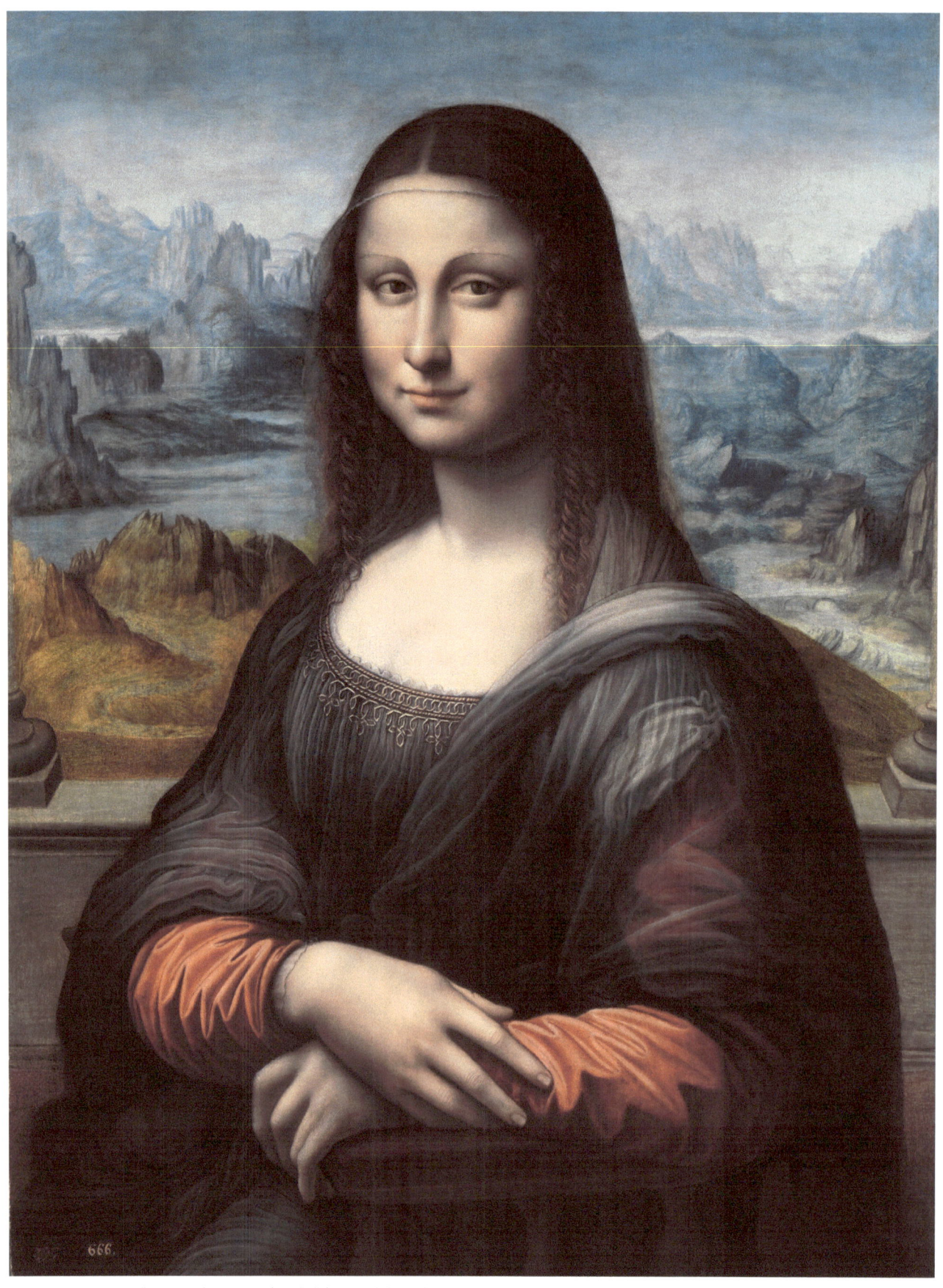

Fig. 1. Unknown artist (Salai or Melzi?), The Prado *Mona Lisa*, ca. 1516, after the 2012 restoration.

THE MONA LISA: A COMPARATIVE EVALUATION OF DIFFERENT VERSIONS AND COPIES

Prof. Emeritus Salvatore Lorusso
Dipartimento di Beni Culturali
Alma Mater Studiorum Università di Bologna, Ravenna, Italy

Prof. Andrea Natali
Dipartimento di Beni Culturali
Alma Mater Studiorum Università di Bologna, Ravenna, Italy

This chapter will examine a group of *Mona Lisa* paintings that at various times have either been identified as Leonardo autographs; as works originating from Leonardo's workshop; or as copies by *Leonardeschi* and their followers. The article includes an in-depth analysis of the *Isleworth Mona Lisa* as conceivably an autograph predating the Louvre *Mona Lisa*.

A previous study of stylistic and diagnostic analyses found that the oil painting on canvas known as the *Mona Lisa with Columns*, part of a private collection and now in a museum in St. Petersburg (Figure 2), is a copy of the *Mona Lisa* by Leonardo (Figure 3), though dating to a period between 1590 and 1660.[1] Noteworthy features include the good quality, readability and expressiveness emanating from the work, which presumably is of Nordic influence, specifically German-Flemish.

This study reached its conclusions based on detailed investigations carried out by J. P. Mohen in 2004 on the Louvre *Mona Lisa* on behalf of the Center for Research and Restoration of the Museums of France, and published in the book *Au coeur de La Joconde – Léonard de Vinci Décodé*.[2] These investigations – which were not aimed at authentication – were examined together with the conclusions of the National Gallery in London with regards to its painting of *The Virgin of the Rocks*, thus enabling a comparison between the two works by Leonardo.[3]

The present paper examines and compares a number of works depicting the same subject: Leonardo's *Mona Lisa*. The paintings were chosen on the basis of their acknowledged artistic quality and a series of technical data obtained by consulting diagnostic-analytical tests by several laboratories. A key factor in this comparison is the particular role played by the presence of the columns in the paintings. Another focus of this article is to examine how over the years, different authors have tried to interpret Leonardo's highly original treatment of his subject, and to see what prompted the obvious differences in their iconography and technique.

The *Mona Lisa* Versions

Of course, there are many copies of the *Mona Lisa*; some are of good quality, while others are not. In 1952, on the occasion of the 500th anniversary of the birth of Leonardo, an official count identified no less than 61 works, though many other copies have been identified in the years since.[4] Among those worthy of note are those in the Hermitage in St. Petersburg, the Walker Art Gallery in Liverpool, the private copy known as the Vernon *Mona Lisa* in the United States,

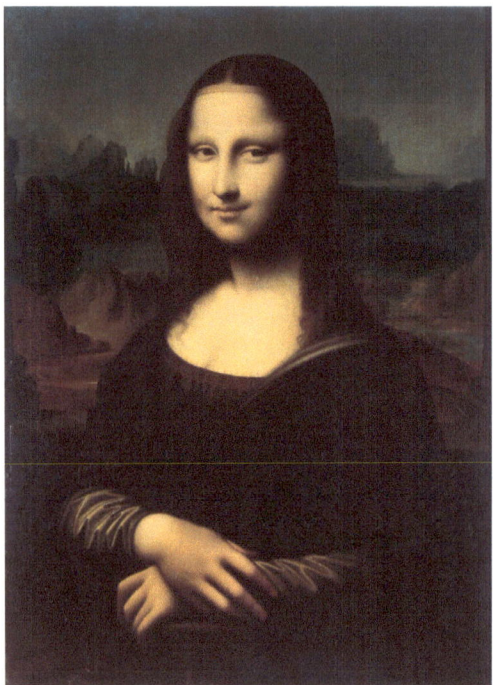

Fig. 2. Unknown Artist, *Mona Lisa with Columns*
("The St. Petersburg *Mona Lisa*"), 16th century.
Oil on canvas 63.2 x 85.2

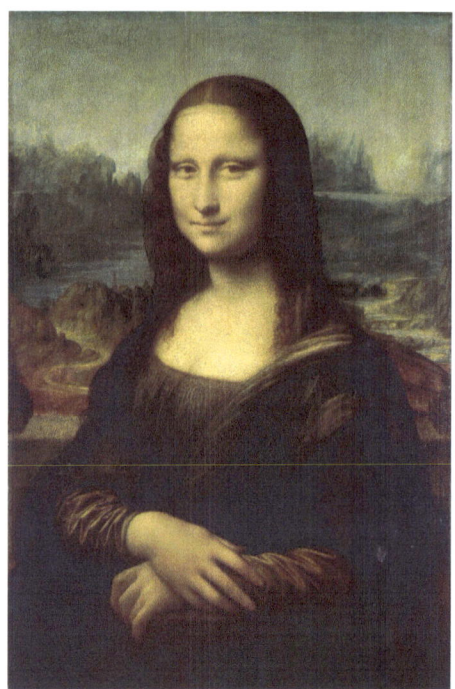

Fig. 3. Leonardo da Vinci, The Louvre
Mona Lisa, ca. 1508-1516

one in the collection of the Earl of Wemyss in the UK, and another in Salzburg. Of particular interest in this study the Isleworth *Mona Lisa*. As discussed later, it depicts a much younger figure than the Louvre version, poised between the columns, but in a pose that is similar. This painting is currently the subject of extensive study by the scientific community, as it is believed that it could be another autograph version by the Master, from which other copies have drawn inspiration. There are in fact, copies with a landscape similar to the *Isleworth* version, including that in Oslo, which have been attributed to Joos van Cleve, Gabriel Ferrier and other authors. Other interesting copies can be found in the Alte Pinakothek in Munich, Germany; the Luchner Collection in Innsbruck; and the Musée des Beaux-Arts in Tours.

Leonardo's work has been studied in great detail: the particular characteristics of the master, his brushwork, composition, and structure. The degree of innovation that characterizes his work is the result of an extraordinary talent, praised by poets and writers of the time, and from which stems the uniqueness

of his production. Nevertheless, careful archival and bibliographic research has only yielded reliable data for 13 copies. For some, only a small amount of technical and historical data was available, while for others, more in-depth study was possible.[5]

In order to highlight the differences and similarities in the production of the various copies of the *Mona Lisa*, three detailed case studies will be discussed here: the Prado *Mona Lisa,* the Reynolds *Mona Lisa*, and the Isleworth *Mona Lisa*. Owing to their differences, these three cases provide us with a significant, but not exhaustive, informative picture.

The Prado *Mona Lisa*

The Prado *Mona Lisa* (Figure 1), is an oil painting on wood, probably produced at the beginning of the sixteenth century. The first reference to this portrait appears for the first time in the 1666 inventory of the Gallery of the Mediodia del Alcazar as "*mujer de mano de Leonardo Abince*." The painting differs from other copies in several ways. In January, 2012 the work underwent major restoration. The results

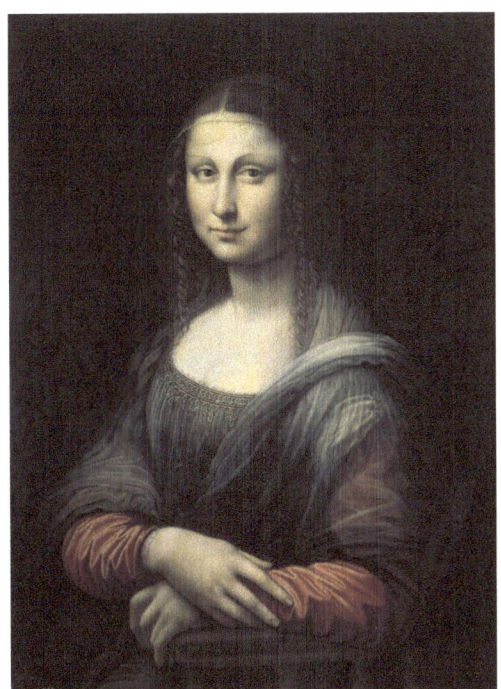

Fig. 4. Unknown artist (Salaì or Melzi?), The Prado *Mona Lisa*, ca. 1516, before the 2012 restoration.

led to a surprising discovery: the black background hid a landscape and a parapet flanked by column bases similar to those of the *Mona Lisa* in the Louvre. Furthermore, infrared reflectography highlighted the similarity of the preparatory drawing of the copy with the portrait in the Louvre. These results, together with the excellent state of conservation, have revealed the original colors of the Prado painting. However, there is no substantial evidence that Leonardo himself used a palette similar to the version now in the Louvre. The two portraits, therefore, are different works and were executed on panels of wood from different trees.

The 2012 investigation by the Prado team supports the argument that the portrait was probably executed before Leonardo left Italy for France, which would mean that it was probably painted in Rome around 1516. In fact, there has never been any hypothesis that the copy in the Prado was painted by Leonardo. Bruno Mottin, head curator at the Center for Research and Restoration of the Museums of France, has suggested that the painting could be attributed to one of Leonardo's favorite apprentices, perhaps Salaì or

Melzi. But it is also true that Salaì did not possess the talent to paint such a lifelike picture, and Melzi could not have produced such a painting, since he was only 15 when he met Leonardo in 1506, and was therefore too inexperienced to paint this copy. On the other hand, if we assume that the painting is by Melzi after completion of his apprenticeship and as an artist in his own right, it could have been painted a few years after Leonardo's death. A further theory is that the painting was done by one of Leonardo's Spanish pupils: in this case the painting may have been completed in Spain. Another theory explaining the present location of the work is that the painting was taken by the Spaniards when they sacked Rome in 1527.

However, a press release issued by the Prado in February 2012, states that:

> "Following its rediscovery, this copy of the "Mona Lisa" in the Prado Museum, which has now been confirmed as a work by one of Leonardo's pupils or followers working in his studio while the original was being painted, has not only been confirmed as the oldest known copy of this enigmatic image, but also acquires considerable importance for its potential to cast more light on the Louvre painting."[6]

At about the same time, conservators at the Louvre announced the re-dating of their "Mona Lisa" to a period from 1503-1519. The reason for this decision is unclear. Of course, if, as the Prado scientists have theorized, the copy in Spain was painted by someone who "... sitting next to Leonardo da Vinci, was trying to duplicate his every brush stroke", it would have meant that this artist stayed with Leonardo for 16 years, a period when in fact, the Master alternated his work and travels between Florence and Milan, and Rome and France—hardly a plausible situation.

Moreover, we know that Leonardo very likely

suffered a stroke in 1514, while in Rome. When Cardinal Luigi d'Aragona visited him in 1517, the cardinal's secretary and diarist, Canon Antonio de Beatis, reported that "... nothing good can be expected from his paintbrush as he suffers from a paralysis in his right hand."[7] Leonardo was known to be left-handed, but at the time was over 65 years of age and most likely incapacitated. In addition, de Beatis reported that the portrait of the "Florentine woman," now considered to be the painting the *Mona Lisa* in the Louvre, was "quite perfect"—in other words, completed. All these documented reports exclude the possibility that the Louvre version was completed in the year of Leonardo's death, in 1519.

Perhaps the main argument that highlights the non-contemporaneity of the Prado copy with the *Mona Lisa* in the Louvre is that the two women are physically different: the woman in the Prado is significantly younger than the Parisian *Mona Lisa* and has a more robust appearance. The hairstyle is curlier and more intricate, and the fingers of her right hand, which are slimmer and longer, have been beautifully rendered. Although the qualitative representation of the embroidery pattern is simplified, it is evident that to paint the face, hands and clothing with such finesse must have required a talent far greater than the average pupil.

On the other hand, the landscape is in some ways incomplete and appears to reproduce some of the intermediate layers of Leonardo's original landscape, as revealed by the infrared photography of the original. This suggests that the copyist stopped working before the original was finished.[8]

Analytical-diagnostic investigation

In February of 2012, a joint investigation of the Prado *Mona Lisa* by the Prado and the Louvre sought to ascertain the constituent materials used by the artist, and to highlight the original compositional and conservative procedures. The inquiry revealed that the work suffered repeated invasive restoration over the centuries, including the transfer of the painting from a wooden support to a textile one.[9] The analysis was particularly important for understanding the methods used in Leonardo's workshop for depicting light. As a result, the Prado *Mona Lisa* is perhaps the most important copy of the *Mona Lisa* known today.

This comparison of the Prado painting with that of the Louvre has further contributed to a better understanding of the *Mona Lisa* in the Louvre and the sequence of its execution phases. The higher resolution images produced during investigation of the Prado copy revealed features of the original which had previously remained undetected. In addition, data resulting from the comparative investigation of the two works has confirmed what was already known about the way in which Leonardo's workshop operated.

The existence of a landscape beneath the black background was revealed by infrared reflectography and the examination of the surface in raking light before the restoration. This was subsequently confirmed by X-ray scans. Even with these tests however, it was important to determine whether the black substance had been added after completion of the painting, and if so, if it had caused any damage. The study found that the dark background was the result of a re-varnishing done after 1750, using linseed oil as a binder. The landscape beneath the coating of dark color was well preserved but not completely finished, which may have been one of the reasons why it was covered. An organic layer, probably a lacquer, found between the background and the overpainting, allowed the two layers to remain separate. This information, along with solubility tests, supported the decision to remove the layer of black overpainting, since it bears no relation to the original conception of the painting. The recovered landscape conforms to the chromatic range and shapes of Leonardo's ethereal landscapes, apart from the obvious differences in the pictorial quality: for example, the rock in the area of

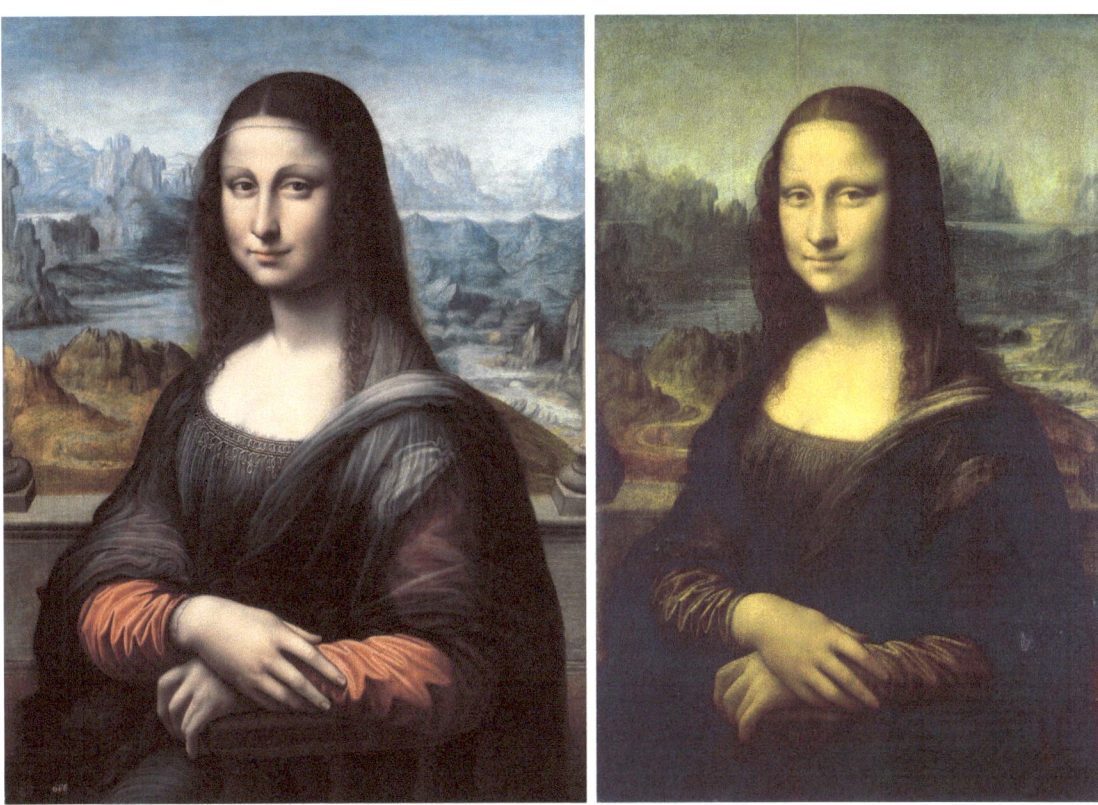

Fig. 5. Comparison between the Prado *Mona Lisa* and the Louvre *Mona Lisa*

the mountains, located to the right of the figure, is similar to that in the autograph drawing by Leonardo in the Royal Collection at Windsor (c. 1510-15).

As for the support, the work was originally painted on a walnut panel, a support customarily used by Leonardo and his circle in Milan, as in the case of the *Lady with an Ermine*, *La Belle Ferronnière* and *St. John the Baptist*.[10] The preparation of the panel, however, does not have the traditional plaster substrate. Instead, it has a double preparation (a more orange-like inner layer and a whiter outer layer) consisting mainly of lead white. Test results, published in Volume 32 of the National Gallery Technical Bulletin, conducted on other works by Leonardo, such as *Lady with an Ermine* and *La Belle Ferronière*, show that although unusual, this type of preparation was used in Leonardo's workshop when a walnut panel was used as support.[11] Finally, the blue pigment made from costly lapis lazuli, imported from the country now called Afghanistan, seems to suggest that the copy was

intended for a precise destination and owner; it can therefore be assumed that it was not just a "workshop experiment". All in all, the materials used in the Prado panel are of high quality and the work has been expertly executed.

Comparative analysis

The Prado copy is of particular interest because the process used to create this *Mona Lisa* can be retraced from the preparatory drawings to the final layer, without any evident sign to indicate it was a copy. Furthermore, the comparative analysis between the Prado and Louvre versions revealed identical details underneath the paint layers. The figures are of the same size and shape, and were probably transferred onto their respective supports using the same cartoon. The preparatory drawing of the original is not so accurate as that of the copy (Figure 5) however, which has lines that indicate how the position of the figure was moved; in addition, the intermediate phases of execution, also found on the copy, are evident.

The brushstrokes that define the forms in the original painting also appear beneath the pictorial surface of the Prado figure, though slightly displaced. They are found beneath the figure, on the waist, on the shoulders and hands, on the line of the breast, on the folds of the sleeves and on the knees. Some of the contour lines of the initial figure in the Prado version were corrected by hand, and some fine lines drawn in black pencil and brush bearing no relationship with the painted forms, are visible. As such, they reflect the artist's experiments and hesitations, thus suggesting a much more complex creative process than that of a normal copy.

The most important point, however, is that each of the corrections to the underdrawing in the original can also be found in the Prado version: the change in the contour of the waistline which, as in the original, is covered by drapery on the surface, the position of the fingers, the outline of the veil and head, including minor changes to the contours of the cheeks and neck. A "traditional" copyist reproduces what can be seen on the surface, but not what is hidden beneath. The existence of these changes beneath the surface, common to both versions, reveals that the artist who painted the Prado copy saw the entire procedure used for the *Mona Lisa* from conception to completion. In addition, he included elements that Leonardo drew on the underlayers, but did not repeat on the surface, including the right armrest of the chair and some internal parts of the robe.

Considerations

The Prado and Louvre investigation led to the thesis that a 'habitué' of Leonardo's workshop, either a pupil or associate, must have produced the Prado painting, and that the copy and the original were executed in parallel during the same time period. As for who the actual artist was, the pictorial treatment cannot be readily associated with the style of students or assistants such as Boltraffio, Marco d'Oggiono and Ambrogio Predis, who all had well-defined artistic personalities. Stylistically, however, the work can be placed in a Milanese context, approaching that of Salaì or Francesco Melzi, who were perhaps Leonardo's most trusted students and heirs of his work with direct access to his landscape drawings.

In sum, the high quality of the materials used in the Prado painting suggests it involved an important commission. The work must have been executed at the same time as the original, which supports the hypothesis of a "duplicate", produced at the same time by someone who had direct access to the gradual procedure of creating Leonardo's original work.[12]

The Reynolds *Mona Lisa*

In 1790, Sir Joshua Reynolds presented the 5th Duke of Leeds (a friend and member of the Society of Dilettanti) with a self-portrait, now in the Royal Collection. The self-portrait was a gift from Reynolds to the Duke, as a token of his gratitude for the copy of the *Mona Lisa*, an oil work painted on wood he had earlier received from the Duke (Figure 6).

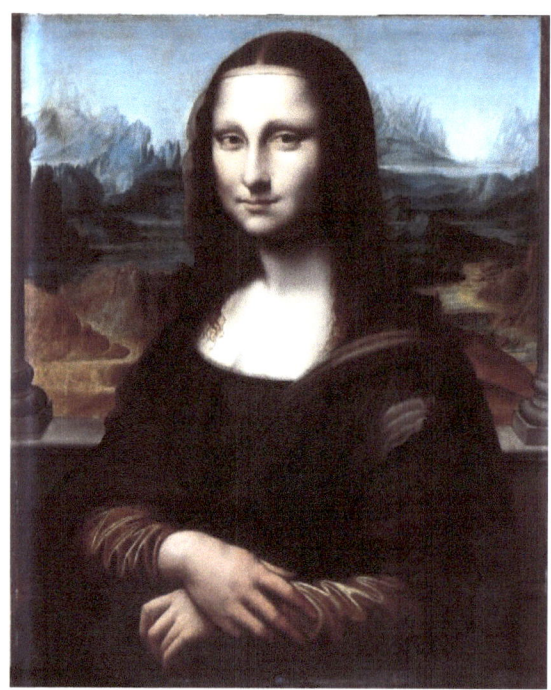

Fig. 6. The Reynolds *Mona Lisa*. Oil on oak panel, ca. 1624-1640

Although certainly not by Leonardo, this painting is of considerable interest. It is a well-made copy that in some ways has elements, such as the color, that are not easily visible in the actual painting in the Louvre. Furthermore, the fact of having been in the Reynolds collection gives it considerable historical relevance. The painting was probably copied by a French artist in the early seventeenth century from the original *Mona Lisa* then in the palace of Fontainebleau, or from a very accurate copy. In terms of its quality, this seems to be a copy that most closely matches the original. Reynolds, a leading artist of the English Baroque, was keenly interested in Leonardo, having studied him from an early age. While in Italy during his Grand Tour from 1750-1752, he spent most of the time in Rome. Here, he studied the old masters, both ancient and modern, assiduously. In the notebooks he kept during this period, Reynolds refers only three times to Leonardo, while Michelangelo and Raphael are cited numerous times. However, only a few works attributed to Leonardo were available for viewing and none were in Rome.

In one of his notebooks, Reynolds made an accurate drawing of a Madonna breastfeeding the infant Jesus, writing "Leonardo da Vinci / Barberini".[13] This painting, housed in Palazzo Barberini, is actually a copy or version of the *Virgin of the Green Cushion* by Andrea Solario, a masterpiece influenced by Leonardo's work, painted between 1507-1510, and now in the Louvre. Leonardo's technique of overlapping colors to intensify areas of light with thin layers of light colored pigment, or vice versa, to darken areas of shadow with layers of light brown, is repeatedly emphasized by Reynolds, and certainly had an influence on the art and techniques used by Reynolds himself.

As for the origin of the Reynolds copy, a late owner of the painting, Sir Abraham Hume, states in the catalog of his collection (1829) that the painting had "very probably" been owned by Jonathan Richardson (1665-1745), the English portrait painter and collector of drawings by old Masters.[14] Richardson's essay on the theory of painting (1715) must have influenced the young Reynolds in his successive speeches, so much so that Reynolds bought many of his drawings. As mentioned earlier, the painting was given to Reynolds by Francis Osborne, the 5th Duke of Leeds (1751-1799), who served as Foreign Secretary under William Pitt. Reynolds writes in his catalog that he asked the French secretary of the Académie Royale, through a certain 'Monsieur Barbier', if the original *Mona Lisa* was still present in the King's study. The answer was that the work was still there, but not considered to be an original and so of little prestige. The response must have encouraged Reynolds in his opinion that the painting in his possession was actually the original.

Sir Abraham Hume (1749-1838), a famous collector of old masters, bought the painting when Reynolds' estate went up for sale in 1795.[15] In his catalog, Hume refers to Reynolds' opinion that the painting was an original despite of the presence of the *Mona Lisa* in Paris, which curiously he considered to be a fake. Nevertheless, when Waagen saw the Reynolds *Mona Lisa* in Hume's collection, he accurately identified it as "a new, very delicate and beautiful copy."[16] Hume then bequeathed most of his collection, including the Reynolds *Mona Lisa,* to his nephew, John Hume Cust, Viscount Alford (1812-51), son of the first Earl of Brownlow. After Hume's death, in 1838, his grandson moved the collection to Ashridge Park, Hertfordshire. The painting was exhibited at the British Institution in 1823 and at the Royal Academy Winter Exhibition in 1902.[17]

Analytical and diagnostic studies have shed new light on the history of the copy and how it was produced. A 2005 Courtauld study found that the artist must have been a highly qualified painter, as demonstrated by the refined preparatory drawing, his use of pigments, including the sophisticated use of azurite for the sky and mountains, and also by the excellent condition of the paint film. The materials and techniques are consistent with traditions in northern Europe from the end of the sixteenth century until the early seventeenth century. It should also be noted that the right edge of the three horizontal panels, on which the work was painted, was cut after the imprimatura was applied. This could mean that the panel was probably originally designed for a larger painting, possibly a landscape. Ian Tyers used a dendrochronological dating method for the support and concluded that the three panels came from two oak trees of eastern Baltic origin, felled around 1602 and probably originally used before 1634.[18]

Comparative analysis

A comparative analysis carried out by Matthew Landrus involved overlapping the outlines of the copy with those of the Louvre painting.[19] The comparison shows that the majority of the contours and proportions in this work coincide with that in Paris. This suggests that the painting may have been copied from the original, or from an exact copy, through a mechanical process: it was probably traced with great accuracy on the original painting. This thesis is supported by the fact that there is no trace of a quadratura on the drawing beneath the painting. There are proportional coincidences in the composition of the sections, both in the upper (head and landscape) and the lower sections (hands and sleeves), suggesting that the copying process was done section by section. Some outlines are not precisely accurate and do not perfectly match the original forms; but they are, by and large, almost identical. The differences can probably be attributed to unintentional slips during the tracing operation.

Among the copies of a high standard listed by Frank Zöllner and André Chastel, the Reynolds seems to be the best, even if the face of the painted figure lacks the softness and radiance of the original. The cheeks appear a little too wide and the chin too short, but the face is delicately painted with a composed expression. The hands too, are well painted. The technique of using opaque layers of paint, however, is very different from the original. The dress is of a color closer to black than dark green and the garment's folds must have been painted when the original was already difficult to read. The sleeves seem to have a reddish-brown enamel glaze tending to yellow, while the original, from descriptions, must have been yellow, but now appears as a dull gold.[20] The landscape and the mountains, even if summarily painted, are more accurate than those of other copies and have more details. The modelling of the parapet and its linear decoration appear accurate. The chair armrest is difficult to see, but in the underdrawing appears to be accurate as well. The base of the column to the right of the female figure likewise appears to be very precise.

An interesting detail copied from the original that does not appear in other copies is the shadow projected forward from the base (which is unclear in the original). The Reynolds copy, like many others, enlarges every detail. Martin Kemp suggests that copyists were unnerved by the 'daring' way Leonardo had just hinted at the columns, and so increased their size to create a more conventional setting. However, this cannot explain why Raphael drew full columns in his sketch of the *Mona Lisa* he saw in Leonardo's studio in 1504. The column slivers on the Louvre version were most likely only added later after the painting was completed. But this is possibly one reason why Reynolds and Hume made the claim that their copy is better than the original, precisely because it has colors and details that are not easily visible in the Louvre version, even if such details may have been obscured by discolored paint.

Around the cleavage of the figure is a decoration that appears to form part of the smock worn under the *gamurra* (a typical female dress of that period). Similar frills appear in four copies: in one of

Leonardo's treatises on painting in 1651; in a print by Jean Masard of 1806, which came out after the drawing of Bouillon; in the first French edition of the complete paintings of Leonardo; and in the engraving by Calamatta. By contrast, there is no lace trimming on the original. There are darker areas above the breast line, that could be the remains of some lace trimming rather than a shadow from the top of the dress. Kemp has stated that this kind of detail is the last to be painted and the first to be lost in any restoration.

The Reynolds *Mona Lisa* is currently on exhibition in the Dulwich Picture Gallery. The Gallery director has said that the original in the Louvre has lost much of its original color, the tones having become very dark. This worsening condition may be due to the technique used by the Master, which was to create overlapping layers
of infinitely thin color, a process that may have gone on for years. The change in the original tone of color, also because of the age of the painting, has made it hard to read.

By contrast, more traditional techniques have been used on the Reynolds *Mona Lisa*, and the painted surface has suffered much less. It still has a surprisingly bright background, and in this case too, as in the original, a pigment obtained with extremely expensive lapis lazuli has been used to create the intense blue of the sky.[21]

The Isleworth *Mona Lisa*

In 1550 and also in 1568, Vasari declared in one of his writings that Leonardo had left the painting of the "lady on the balcony" unfinished. The version in the Louvre, however, had already been completed by 1517, when it was shown by Leonardo himself to the Cardinal of Aragon in Cloux. In this regard, the critical confrontation between the oil painting on canvas, the Isleworth *Mona Lisa* (Figure 7), and the Louvre *Mona Lisa* proves to be of great importance in determining, as some scholars sustain, that the Isleworth *Mona Lisa*

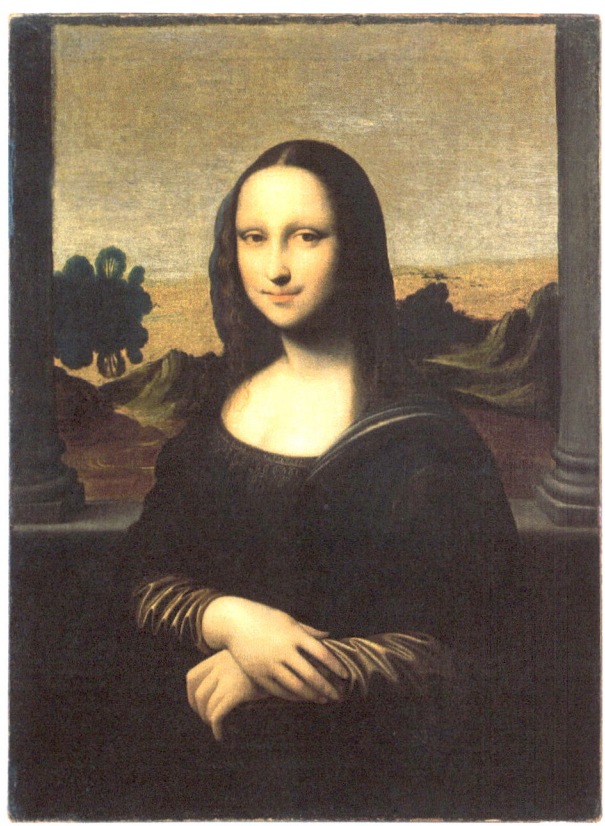

Fig. 7. The Isleworth *Mona Lisa*, c. 1502-1506. Oil on canvas, c. 64.5 cm x 86 cm

may be an original by Leonardo.

Further proof of the possible existence of an earlier version of the portrait is represented by a pen and ink drawing, depicting a young woman on a balcony with columns by Raphael. Dated around 1504, the work was probably executed when Raphael was in Florence to observe Leonardo's work at his studio (Figure 8).[22] According to some historians, it was actually the Isleworth *Mona Lisa* and its composition that would influence Raphael's style in subsequent years. Since the compositional elements in it are unique and do not appear in any other painting, this *Mona Lisa* must have been nearing completion when Raphael saw it in 1504. Several scholars have therefore hypothesized that both versions of the *Mona Lisa* have generated copies. As we saw, the Louvre *Mona Lisa* has been the basis for numerous copies throughout the centuries. By contrast, each copy in which the columns appear in full may have been inspired by the Isleworth version: for

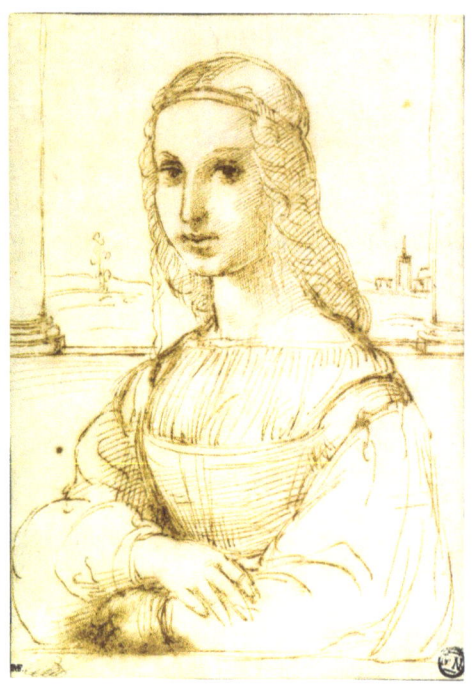

Fig. 8. Raphael, *Head and shoulders of a woman*, ca. 1504.

binder since his apprenticeship under Verrocchio. Until then, wood had been the most important support for painting and before 1470 important works were almost never painted on canvas in Western art. Both *Lady with an Ermine* and *La Belle Ferronnière* were painted on walnut panels from the same block of wood. By contrast, the *Mona Lisa* in the Louvre is painted on poplar wood, a wood most often used in Lombardy and Tuscany.

It should be remembered that Leonardo was not only a great inventor and innovator, but also someone who assiduously experimented with new ideas and technologies. Canvas was already being used in 1500 by many Italian artists, particularly in the Veneto. It is worth noting that a small work of art, executed on parchment in 1490, has recently been authenticated as the work of Leonardo. This is particularly noteworthy, given that until now no known finished works of Leonardo are on this material. In his book *The Beautiful Princess*, Martin Kemp writes: "He uses a medium that has not been previously observed in his work, but that is closely connected with his interest

example, the Oslo *Mona Lisa* (Figure 9) seems to be a direct copy of the Isleworth, as is also the *Mona Lisa with Columns* in a private collection in St. Petersburg, Russia (Figure 2).

When comparing the Isleworth *Mona Lisa* with all other paintings of the same subject, additional impressive features are found that can only be attributed to the hand of a great master. Among them are the details in the rendering and design of the embroidery on the dress, which suggest a brilliant mind. Furthermore, results from computerized regression analysis, which uses forensic techniques, have confirmed that the portraits are of the same woman at different ages, the difference between the one and the other being approximately 11 years.[23]

Analytical-diagnostic investigation

The beginning of the sixteenth century marked a period of transition that was extremely significant for the development of new artists' materials. Venetian and Flemish masters' knowledge of new media became widespread. Artificial oil paints and pigments began to be popular. In fact Leonardo had used oil as a

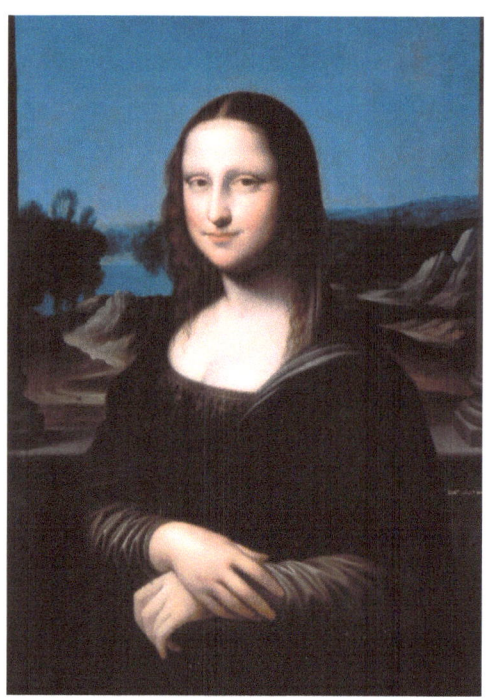

Fig. 9. The Oslo *Mona Lisa*, 17th century.
Oil on canvas, 57.6 cm x 80.5 cm

in the French artist Jean Perreal. It bears witness to his spectacular exploration and development of new media, tackling each commission as a new technical and aesthetic challenge."

In his *Treatise on Painting*, Leonardo describes in detail not only how to prepare a canvas for painting, but also how to paint on it ("The mode of painting on canvas...").[24] Leonardo probably developed the technique of working on canvas during his apprenticeship in the workshop of Verrocchio. One of the first references to the work of Leonardo on canvas is by Giorgio Vasari, according to whom the master often used linen or Rensa canvas, which was suitably prepared, to use in his studies. The Isleworth *Mona Lisa* consists of a hand-made linen cloth, a material with which Leonardo had had significant experience before 1500, and is actually similar to the material used for his studies on drapery. The main features of this linen cloth are simple "tabby" weaves with an average count of 18 threads per cm^2 in the warp and 16 threads per cm^2 in the weft, that cross one another regularly, with some variation in thickness. The result is a deformation in which the warp is slightly tighter than the weft.

It is no coincidence that Leonardo's studies on drapery (now in the Louvre), dating back to 30 years before had almost identical features. Just like the cloth of the *Mona Lisa*, the cloth in his studies was hand woven.

In 2005, the painting of a *Young Christ*, oil on thin cloth, probably linen, was presented by Alessandro Vezzosi as an unpublished work by Salaì. In 1504, Salaì was introduced to Isabella d'Este as a talented and worthy pupil of Leonardo. It was also at this time that canvas was used in Leonardo's studio, and during this period that the Isleworth *Mona Lisa* was painted. In 2011, Vezzosi presented other paintings with a canvas support from the same period by Salaì. This lends further credence to the idea that this material was used in Leonardo's studio in the late fifteenth century.

It is evident that from the time of Leonardo's work on, the use of canvas as a support became more common not only among Flemish and Venetian masters, but also among German, Dutch, Florentine and other Italian masters. A more particular detail is the presence of the lining. This was commonly used on very old canvases to reinforce the original support by connecting it to a second new canvas. The lining not only strengthened the original support, but helped in the overall preservation of the picture. In the case of the Isleworth *Mona Lisa*, the lining was attached by means of a mixture of glues: a combination of Venetian turpentine, flour paste and gum as a plasticizer. The original canvas was cut slightly when the lining was applied, but the rough edges with the original paint have not been touched. The lining consists of a uniform fabric, obtained industrially, using a flat tabby weave, with an average number of 14 threads per cm^2 in the warp and 14 threads per cm^2 in the weft. The canvas is attached to a wooden frame, known as the stretcher, with nails. Since there are no holes from nails in the previous lining, it can be assumed that the current stretcher was inserted when the painting was lined.[25]

The base ground layer is of a red-brown color, a combination of red-brown ochre calcite and some grains of quartz. Using this as a base color, the artist was able to create a sense of warmth throughout the whole of the painting. The pigments are mainly earths. The obvious lack of strong colors contributes to the intrinsic beauty of the picture: all the chromatic elements are in organic harmony and contribute to accentuating the beautiful skin tones. Part of this effect is in fact due to the undercoat of reddish-brown. It is not the only painting where Leonardo used this technique. For example, it can be seen in *Lady with an Ermine*, which underwent diagnostic tests at the National Museum in Warsaw between 1952 and 1954. These revealed that the background of the painting is a combination of bone black, earth of burnt umber and natural sienna. Since *Lady with an Ermine* was executed in Milan in 1490, it is likely that pigments similar to those used in Florence were available.[26]

La Belle Ferronnière was examined in the laboratories of the Louvre in the early fifties. In his book, *Leonardo da Vinci – The Complete Paintings*, published in 2003, Pietro Marani reports on an investigation carried out by Sylvie Beguin, the renowned French curator, which revealed a thin paint surface and an imprimatura of red earth already found in Leonardo's work. Marani later declared that a microscopic examination of the Louvre *Mona Lisa* had revealed there were at least two colors in the preparatory layer: blue beneath the upper section, in the landscape; and red beneath the lower section. Leonardo used the same type of two-tone earth for *La Belle Ferronière*, *The Musician* and *Trinity of Saint Anne*.[27]

In 1974, the American conservator and scientist, H. Travers Newton, was in Florence to try to find out if there were any remains of the "Battle of Anghiari" by Leonardo that might still be present under Vasari's frescoes in Palazzo Vecchio. According to Charles Nicholl, all the core samples showed a layer of red pigment under Vasari's plaster, as well as other pigments with the same red preparation. Two of them are typical of Leonardo's painting technique: a copper carbonate green, similar to that used for *The Last Supper*, for which Leonardo provides a recipe in his *Treatise On Painting*; and smalt blue, found in the *Virgin of the Rocks* in the Louvre. Furthermore, traces of azurite were found, a rather unsuitable pigment for frescoes, which makes this particular fresco an unconventional work.[28]

Based on these studies, it could be argued that in *The Battle of Anghiari* (c.1503), the use of a red ground is predominant, which is also true for the Isleworth *Mona Lisa* of the same period, as it has the same red base. The dates of the two commissions are also the same, so it is quite conceivable that the palette was the same as well. The background landscape in the Isleworth *Mona Lisa* also has traces of enamels and azurite, as mentioned above in the results by H. Travers Newton.

A recent analysis of the pigments in Leonardo's *Last Supper* has drawn significant attention. During restoration of the painting, Antoinette Galone from the Politecnico di Milano revealed the presence of traces of calcite (calcium carbonate) in the preparatory layers. It also identified a number of pigments that demonstrate the work can be attributed to the Renaissance period. During the Congress of the International Institute for Conservation of Historic and Artistic Works in Dublin in 1998, Jill Dunkerton and Marika Spring of the National Gallery in London presented additional information. They found that "With reference to the tinted and colored preparations, the thin pigmented layers found immediately above the plaster may be part of some monochromatic underdrawings."[29] The first layer of gray, found in many Italian paintings of this period, corresponds to materials found in samples from the Isleworth *Mona Lisa*.

It can therefore be argued that the reddish-brown ground in the Isleworth *Mona Lisa* is compatible with other known paintings by Leonardo of this period, which testifies to his creative ability and detailed knowledge of pigments. This talent enabled him to overcome the challenge of reproducing natural colors—or the way colors should be perceived by the human eye in real life. The reddish-brown ground can also be seen in many of his drawings and studies, some of which are in the Royal Library in Windsor and the Uffizi Gallery Museum in Florence. The successive layer, which is grey with a slight purplish hue, is made from calcite, lead white and bone black. The same colors and techniques are again mentioned by Leonardo in his Treatise.

In 1996, Larry Keith and Ashok Roy published an article in the *National Gallery Technical Bulletin* entitled "Giampietrino, Boltraffio, and the influence of Leonardo." They found that "In Leonardo's paintings, the overall pictorial unity, produced using a tightly controlled, restricted range of tones, was a central feature. The sculptural plasticity of the London National Gallery's cartoon of the *Virgin and Child with Saint Anne* and *St. John the Baptist*, together with the use of a restricted palette, illustrate Leonardo's primary concern with the creation of depth through the manipulation of the sfumato and not of colour. In his painting, while developing techniques to exploit colour by decreasing its intensity so as to create aerial perspective, the intrinsic beauty of certain naturally high-key pigments was, as a rule, deliberately and consistently subordinated to the constraints dictated by his great discipline in the use of sfumato."[30]

In order to identify the complete range of pigments and other media used, as well as determining some of the techniques used in preparing the support, two campaigns of analytical investigations were performed on the Isleworth *Mona Lisa*: the first in 1977, by Hermann Kuhn, under the supervision of the Swiss Institute for Art Research; and the second, in 2005 by Maurizio Seracini. The results are not only consistent with each other, but are entirely compatible with the palette used in the version of the Louvre. Reflectographic investigations performed in January 2011 by Pascal Cotte, show that the painting has some clear preparatory drawings below the painting surface. This therefore means that it is not a direct copy.

What's more, Leonardo's interest in geometry is well-known and well-documented. In this regard, the Isleworth *Mona Lisa* is perfectly in line with the "golden ratio". The painting has also been subjectedto two different sets of dating analyses: radiometric (210Pb) and radiocarbon. 210Pb dating was carried out on a sample of white lead in order to determine whether the work was executed pre- or post- 1750: the chemical composition after this date changes. The materials present in the examined sample indicate a date prior to 1750, a date that includes the early sixteenth century. Radiocarbon dating conducted on the canvas yielded a dating of the canvas between 1492 and 1652, with a higher probability in the earlier part of that period. This date range is a standard and is one that is typically expected for dating results of paintings executed in the early 1500s. This is in line with the hypothesis of the painting being executed at the beginning of the sixteenth century.

Comparative analysis

When comparing the two versions of the *Mona Lisa* by Leonardo, some significant differences immediately come to notice, which suggest that Leonardo's intention from the very beginning was to paint two separate portraits.

• Firstly, the different dimensions: the Isleworth version is 64.5 cm wide and 86 cm high; the Louvre version has a slightly irregular width of 53.3 cm at the top, and 53.4 cm at the bottom, with a height of 79.2 cm on the right, 79.1 cm on the left and 79.4 cm in the middle.

• As for the support, the Isleworth painting is on canvas, the Louvre version is on poplar wood.

• Though the work appears to represent the same sitter, their ages are markedly different: in the Isleworth version the woman is 22 or 23; in the Louvre version the subject is 11 or 12 years older.

• As for the composition, the young Mona Lisa in the Isleworth version is sitting in an open loggia framed by two columns, one on either side. The woman appears to face the viewer more directly. Her head and right shoulder are tilted slightly forward. Her neck muscles are tense, allowing the artist to emphasize this angle with superb effects of light on the neck.

• Despite the smaller size, in the Louvre version the mass of the figure leans further forward. The female figure occupies more space, the geometry being further accentuated by the effect of the glaze, a technique perfected by Leonardo after 1508.

• There are slight traces of the pillars at the edge of the picture, but it is possible they were not part of the original composition. They may have been added by a restorer who had taken into consideration the Isleworth version. The woman is sitting more upright, making the neck appear more relaxed.

• One of the predominant features of Leonardo's portraits is the contrast between the warmer tones of the hands and pale complexion of the face and chest. In the Isleworth version the hands are thinner, the fingers more slender and the index finger of the right hand is more relaxed than in the Louvre version.

• The background in the Isleworth *Mona Lisa* is markedly different. It has remained largely unfinished (as is the area of the sky). This topic is discussed in several original texts and is also mentioned by Vasari in his *Lives of the Artists*. Reference is made to an unfinished *Mona Lisa* and no mention is made of any type of landscape. Originally, the group of trees on the left side was reflected in a small blue lake. A trace of blue is visible beneath the paint, indicating that the area was completely repainted during a restoration carried out by someone whose talent by no means matched that of the original master.

• Leonardo's imaginary landscapes in the Louvre *Mona Lisa* remain a mysterious enigma. The landscape below is certainly more comprehensible and, in this regard, some scholars have come to identify the place through recognition of the famous bridge behind the figure. The landscape higher up is pure fantasy. Carlo Pedretti wrote that: "The landscape in the painting in

the Louvre, is more in line with Leonardo's scientific views in 1508 or later versions." This comment further explains the dating of the painting, which can be considered as one of Leonardo's last works. Having said that, it is certainly true that Leonardo used the device of a background with rocky formations on many occasions, such as the *Annunciation* of 1472-1475 and the *Madonna of the Carnation* of 1478-1480.

Considerations

The results from the previous analyses indicate that all the pigments found on the painting were already available and in use at the beginning of the sixteenth century. A comparison between the pigments used in the two paintings of the *Mona Lisa* has led to interesting results. The white lead, for example, is an important component in both works. Both Kuhn and Seracini detected the presence of lead white in each single analysis, including the grey ground.[31] The Louvre report on the state of the *Mona Lisa* confirms that lead is present in the form of white lead throughout the painting.[32] Other pigments common to both works are azurite, copper blue, vermilion and umber. In fact, both paintings have a substantial amount of earth pigments, such as the different range of siennas, ochres and umbers, which was quite common for this period, when artificial pigments were not yet available. There are, in addition, many variations of black.

Burnt umber is an earth tone used in both paintings, with wonderful mineral properties. This suggests that the burnt umber, or at least a pigment rich in manganese oxide, plays an important role in achieving the famous *sfumato* effect typical of Leonardo. The relative absence of craquelure in the shadows of the face may be related to the drying properties of this pigment, which originally comes from Umbria, a region famous for the quality of its pottery. Traces of smalt were found exclusively in the landscape background of the younger version of the

Mona Lisa. The popularity of the pigments used by the artist became widespread only in the second half of the sixteenth century. However, according to scientists from the Centre for Research and Restoration of the Museums of France, the use of smalt in easel painting was already well known, albeit to a lesser extent, in the second half of the fifteenth century.[33]

One problem that many artists of that time faced was the lack of availability of the pigments they needed. Creating the right colors and tones from minerals and earths, using suitable binders to obtain the appropriate texture, was a laborious process and therefore costly. Many of these pigments were imported from the major art centers of Italy, the Netherlands, France and England, but they were expensive and not always readily available. One can therefore imagine how eager artists were to learn the process of creating artificial pigments that could serve as alternatives to the traditional palette.

In Leonardo's *Treatise*, there is a reference to "... a veil of color diluted with dry cinnabar". This is present in the Isleworth *Mona Lisa,* in a sample of the flesh tones, but not in the Louvre *Mona Lisa.* In the latter painting, there is a small amount of vermilion in some of the flesh tones, as in the younger version. Leonardo mentions the red lake pigment as being the correct one for shadows and areas of light. Again, both paintings show traces on the young woman's face, and in the Louvre version, on the hands.

As a result, many experts, are inclined toward authenticating the Isleworth painting as genuine and executed in a period that is earlier than the version in the Louvre.

This paper will next investigate certain key aspects of the *Mona Lisa* in more detail by comparing four versions: the Isleworth, the Oslo, the Louvre and the Prado. These features involve (1) the presence of the columns, and (2) the decoration embroidered on the dress.

The Role of the Columns

When looking at the Louvre version, the female figure naturally stands out from the background. This has led to the supposition that the wood panel, at one time, must have been wider, thus allowing for the insertion of the columns or other device, so as to frame the figure in a more particular composition, as the base of the columns and barely visible vertical lines would seem to indicate. In 1959, the distinguished German art historian Richard Friedenthal stated that "... [the *Mona Lisa* in the Louvre] was cut by about 10 cm on each side." This would confirm that the panel was larger by about 20 centimeters.[34] Pedretti also declared that the architecture of the Louvre version of the *Mona Lisa* would have been better with columns framing the composition. As he wrote, "The lady sits by the parapet of a loggia, which was originally extended at each side to include two columns framing the landscape, as in a window. These are now reduced to little more than vertical strips, but their bases are easily visible and their foreshortening offers the only element of linear perspective in the picture. Originally therefore, the overwhelming presence of the lady was kept in check by the architectural structure of her setting."[35] Serge Bramly agreed, and wrote that "the panel has lost a strip of about seven centimeters from each side: we can no longer see the two columns that originally framed the landscape, which appear in old copies and in Raphael's drawing.[36] In a later book Bramly added: "Like so many of Leonardo's works, the *Mona Lisa* has suffered both from the ravages of time and from rough treatment by restorers: it has been narrowed by six or seven centimeters on both the right and left."[37] On the other hand, in his letter to Murray Urquhart of 25 February 1943, the scholar Kenneth Clark opined that the columns were evidently intended to be part of the original design, but were added later.

However, all this speculation ended, when, in October 2004, the Louvre version was subjected to a series of diagnostic tests carried out by a group of 39 international experts. The results showed that over the centuries, the sides of the panel had indeed been trimmed a little, but only on the unpainted part: "Careful examination of the side edges in section reveals open burrow holes caused by parasites, which indicate that the plank's width was trimmed a second time. This trimming clearly only involved the bare wood and not the painted layer." Additional Louvre documents posit that "The absence of any preparation on the covered edges thus provides us with irrefutable testimony of the original dimensions of the painting itself". The report therefore arrived at the following conclusions:

• It is clear that the *Mona Lisa* in the Louvre originally had no columns;

• It follows, therefore, that any version or copy of the *Mona Lisa* in which the columns are represented, must have originated from another painting, probably the younger version of the *Mona Lisa* (the Isleworth version).

• Many scholars currently believe that copies with columns were influenced by the Isleworth *Mona Lisa*, which provides for a clear development of the columns in their entirety.

This does not however exclude a further hypothesis: there are barely visible vertical lines, as well as bases, in the Louvre *Mona Lisa*. In general, Leonardo's compositions followed strict mathematical principles. Certainly, the Master's ability in capturing reality was already mature by the beginning of the sixteenth century. Therefore, if he had intended to frame the Louvre *Mona Lisa* between two columns, he would certainly have painted them in the correct manner, by giving them a special space in the geometry of the structure. Leonardo himself points out that: "No human investigation can be a real science unless it can be demonstrated mathematically."

Hence, there is a strong feeling that, at some point in the painting's history, a restorer considered that the portrait would look better with columns, despite the fact they were not really evident. This assumption, however, has not yet been scientifically proven.

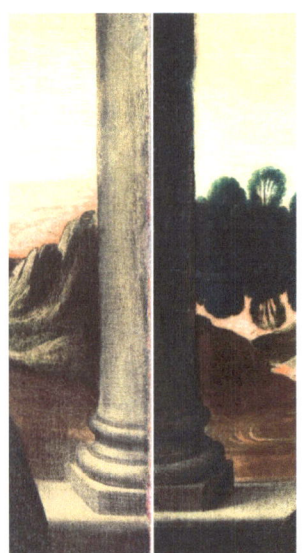 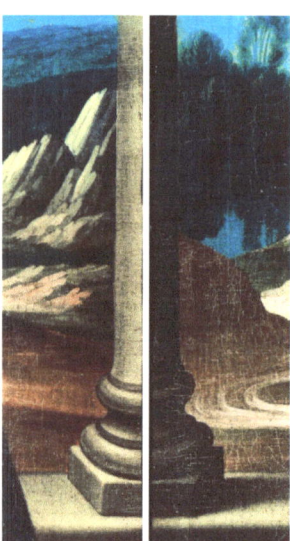 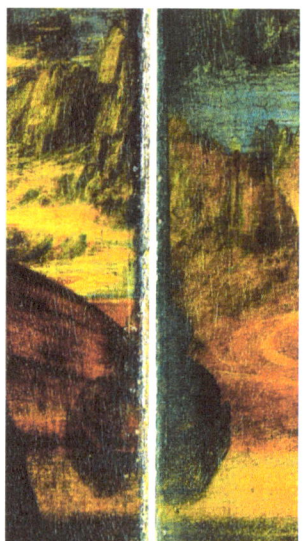 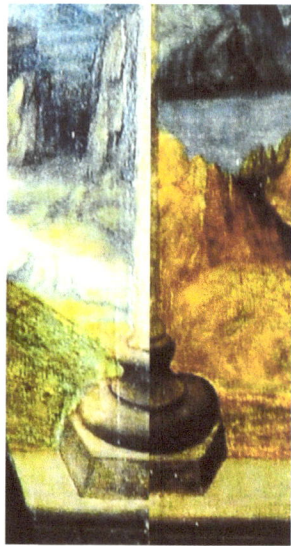

'*Earlier Mona Lisa*'   Oslo '*Mona Lisa*'   Louvre '*Mona Lisa*'   Prado '*Mona Lisa*'

Fig. 10. Comparison of the columns

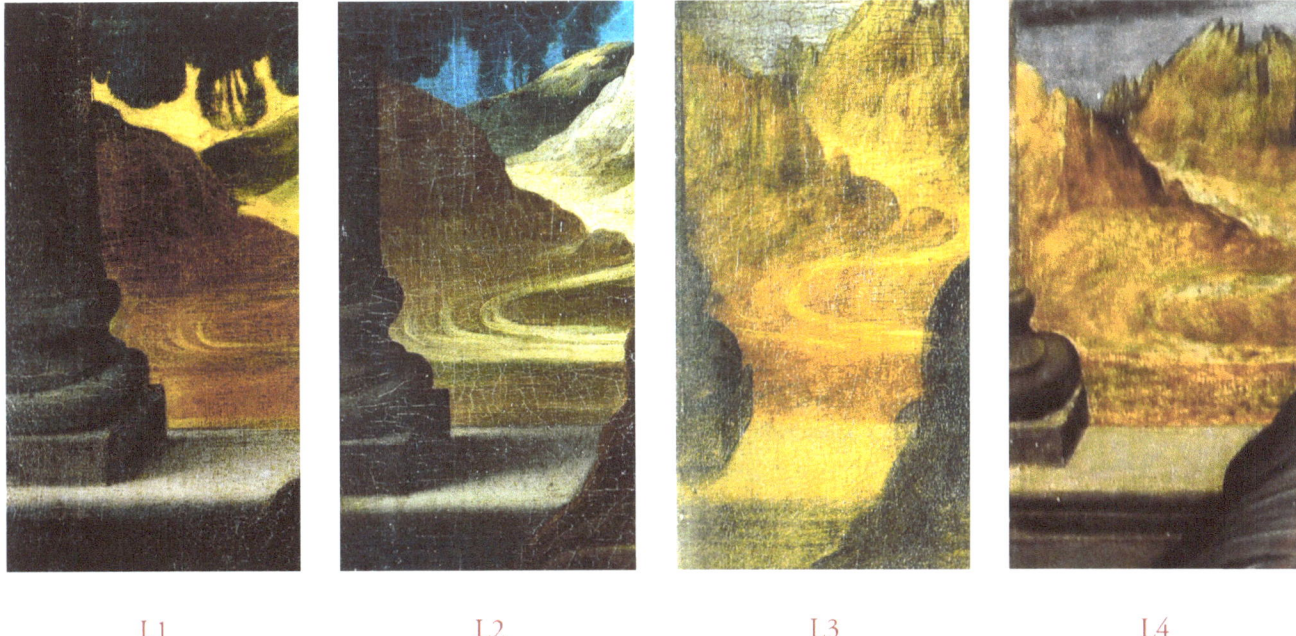

L1   L2   L3   L4

Fig. 11. Comparison of the left column in the Isleworth, Oslo Louvre, and Prado *Mona Lisa*

As regards the left-hand column, in more detail (Figure 11):

L1. Isleworth version: in this work, the column and its base are clearly part of the original composition and not an afterthought. In addition, in accordance with Leonardo's studies on light, the shadow of the columns falls softly on the balcony ledge.

L2. Oslo copy: in this work, the details and composition of the Isleworth version have been copied: in particular, the column, the base, the shadow on the ledge and most of the landscape through the trees.

L3. Louvre version: the column, barely visible, and its base, seem to have been added later, by another artist. The base has been painted inaccurately and there is no shadow on the balcony ledge.

L4. Prado copy: the base of the column is more shapely than the one in the version of the Louvre, which they have tried to reproduce, and once more, the shadow on the balcony ledge is missing [5.7].

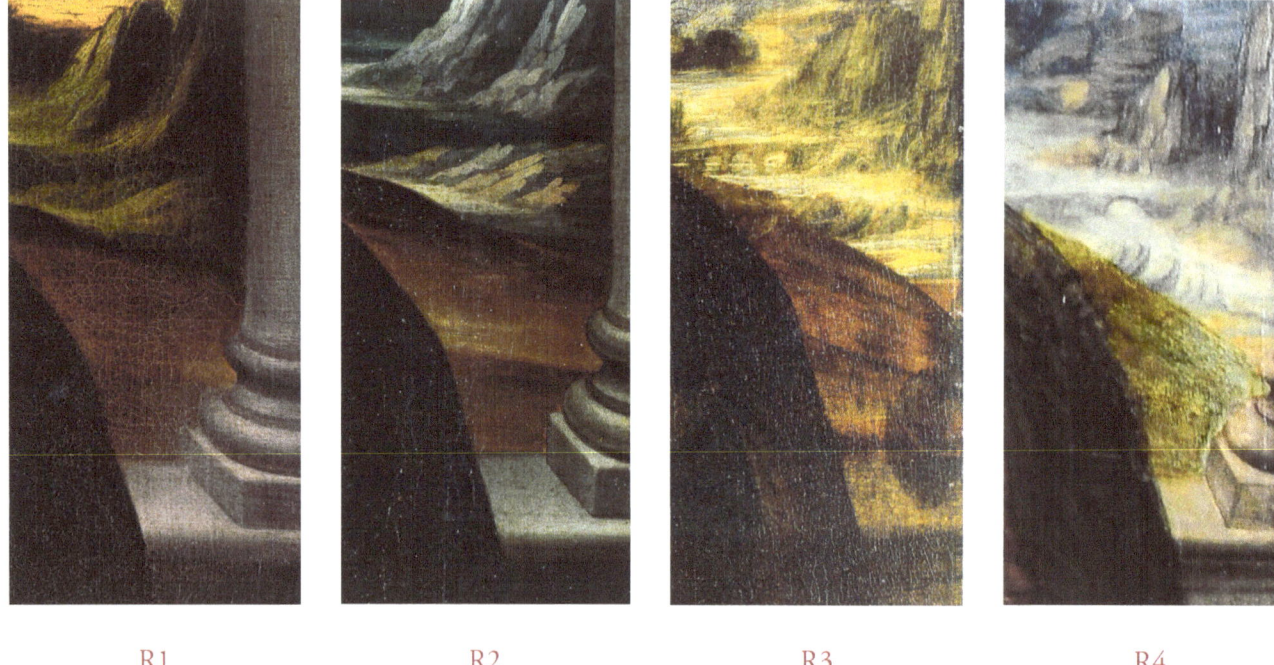

R1   R2   R3   R4

Fig. 12. Comparison of the right column in the Isleworth, Oslo, Louvre, and Prado *Mona Lisa*

As regards the right-hand column (Figure 12):

R1. Isleworth version: among the different versions and copies of the *Mona Lisa* the right-hand column and base demonstrate confidence in the design and knowledge of classical architecture. This painting is believed to be the true genesis in relation to the composition of the flanking columns and may also have been a model for some of Raphael's early works from the sixteenth century.

R2. Oslo copy: as with the left side of the painting, the copyist accurately reproduces the composition with the columns on each side, as well as Leonardo's Florentine landscape from the Isleworth version.

R3. Louvre version: on the right side too, the column is barely visible, and the base is evidence that it was painted on the landscape and was therefore probably not part of the original composition.

R4. Prado copy: in this case too, there is a great deal of evidence (including the bridge) that proves it is based on the Louvre version. However, the details on the base have a different shape to those on the left and the perspective is imprecise.

The Role of the Embroidery

Likewise, there are several significant differences in the embroidery on the dress, in the various copies and the original. Once again, a comparison will be made of the Isleworth *Mona Lisa* (the earlier *Mona Lisa*), the Oslo copy, the Louvre *Mona Lisa* and the Prado copy, with regard to the embroidered dress (Figure 13). This comparison reveals that:

• in the Isleworth version, the embroidery is done in a loose horizontal style (Figure 14);

• in the Louvre version, the design of the embroidery has a closer oval vertical pattern, further evidence of the diversity of the two paintings (Figure 15);

• in the Oslo copy, the embroidery follows the samehorizontal pattern of the Isleworth version (Figure 16);

• in the Prado copy, unlike in the others, the pattern in the embroidery is more rounded (Figure 13) [5-19].

Some further considerations can be made regarding certain details of the embroidery relating to the repetition of the "cloverleaf" pattern, the regularity in the design, the irregularities in the interwoven

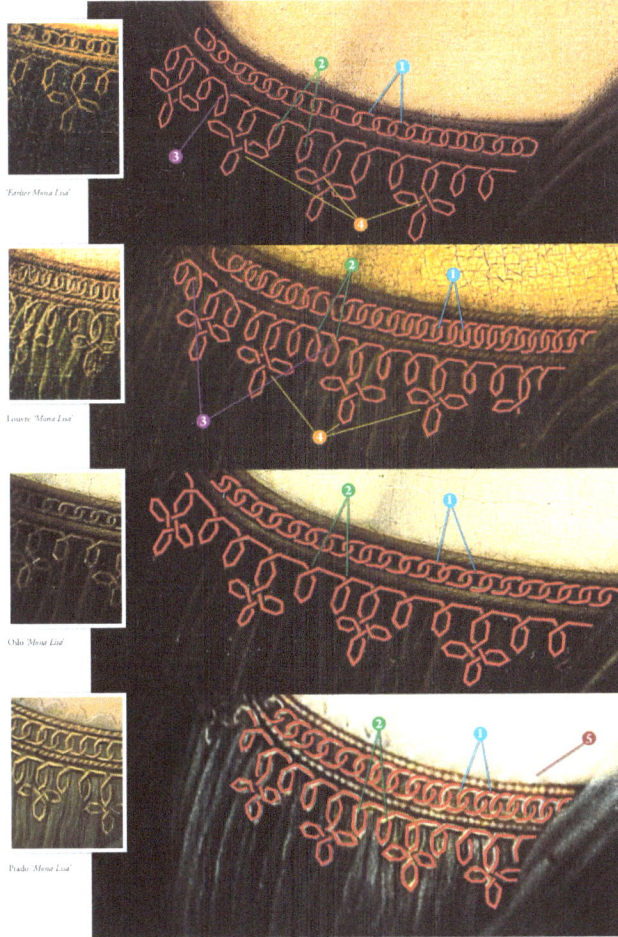

Fig. 13. Comparison of the embroidery on the Isleworth,
Louvre, Oslo and Prado *Mona Lisa*

"cloverleaf" and the gala (trimming). As regards the recurrence of the 'cloverleaf', the following differences have been noted.

• The Isleworth version shows continuity in the repetition of the "cloverleaf" twice on the bodice.
• In the Louvre version, Leonardo went 'out of sequence' in the center by using three rings among the cloverleaves. From this, it can be assumed that this painting is not only different from the Isleworth *Mona Lisa* but that – the bodice at least – was probably painted at a later date. The three rings in the center are another indication of Leonardo's intent to differentiate the paintings. The *Mona Lisa* in the Louvre is the only painting of this subject in which the detail of the three rings is found.

• In the Oslo and Prado copies a repetitive pattern of two cycles can be seen between each cloverleaf.

With regards to the irregularities in the interweaving of the 'cloverleaf', in the Isleworth version each individual group of cloverleaves has a unique pattern, identified by a slight difference in the threading of the pattern; no two are the same. This feature itself identifies the Isleworth version in a significant way, as being a unique original version. In the Louvre version and the Oslo and Prado copies, the cloverleaves have a repetitive pattern.

The gala, a delicate ruffle at the top of the bodice, is clearly visible only in the Prado copy. In the other works examined, however, this detail is no longer visible.

Final considerations

The workmanship of the *Mona Lisa* copies is heterogeneous: there are over sixty recorded copies and probably others that have yet to be discovered. The works are often of good quality and painted by talented artists, while others are of inferior quality. This is probably also due to the fact that after the death of its author, the *Mona Lisa* became a true "icon". This also meant that it was studied and used as a means of testing the skills of those who wanted to pursue a career in the arts and inevitably had to look to the greatest master of the Italian Renaissance – an artist who had invented a new way of doing and feeling art.

Carlo Pedretti claims that none of the known copies reproduces the transparent veil which follow the woman's contours in the original (such as in the left arm up to and past the elbow).[38] Just as there is difficulty in reading the color of the dress and the folds of the clothes on the figure, it is equally difficult to reproduce the infinitely subtle gradations of the bright tones transposed in the modeling of the face and hands, tones that Leonardo produced layer by layer, over many years, with small transparent brushstrokes.[39]

Indeed, part of the *Mona Lisa's* charm is in the difficulty of reproducing it.

As the literature has shown, virtually all copies and prints of the *Mona Lisa* have given rise to discussions regarding their date of execution and sources used. The way in which the figure is given substance and depth through the transparent veils, the scarf and the folds of the clothes, often escapes the copyists, just as the complexity of the landscape does, with its aerial perspective, gradually receding into the distant mountains that gently merge into the sky. The brushstrokes in the copies are generally not full-bodied, unlike the original, in which the landscape is characterized by the typical thickness of the colors, often obtained by spreading them with the fingertips. As a result, it is almost impossible to find the same depth, the luministic vibrations, and the same play of chiaroscuro, the suffused glow, so typical of Leonardo's masterpiece.

Nowadays, works that have been generally attributed to Leonardo, and exhibited in major museums and galleries, are not always universally recognized as originals. Experts' opinions are likely to change, often on the basis of new evidence, further reflection, studies, or simply a change of mind. But it is the thorough technical examination of a painting that can often reveal important features that are not readily evident to connoisseurship or provenance documentation. Art historical judgements are not a "definitive" science, but the art world still relies heavily on the opinions of experts.

The fame of the *Mona Lisa* also derives from the cult of its author, Leonardo, and the acclaim the painting has received from the time it was painted to the present day. All the above highlight the distinctive artistic features of this universal art work.
As regards the copies described in this article, we can conclude that:
• the Prado copy was painted in Leonardo's workshop in parallel with the original

• the Reynolds *Mona Lisa* is one of the copies that provides the most clues about what the original has lost over time, but also succeeds in demonstrating the "magic" of Leonardo's work. However, the Reynolds *Mona Lisa*, though well executed, is unable to recreate the infinitely subtle shades of light and shadow, especially in the modelling of the face and hands;
• the Isleworth Mona Lisa is a Leonardo original most likely executed before the version in the Louvre [5].

The following statement by Kemp, a leading Leonardo scholar and curator of the exhibition of Leonardo's drawings at the Victoria and Albert Museum in London, sums up the exclusive and shared characteristics of Leonardo's genius: "There is something intangible and unique when you are in front of a work by Leonardo, it cannot therefore be compared, much less, replicated".
This study of the paintings has highlighted not only the presence of two versions of the *Mona Lisa,* but also the necessary distinction between *copies* and autograph *versions*, to wit, the Isleworth *Mona Lisa* and the Louvre *Mona Lisa.* These are to be considered, therefore, as two original works, since they were both painted by Leonardo in two different periods. The subject is the same, but the paintings vary considerably, making them two works in their own right and not a copy of each other. Consequently, it can be argued that all subsequent copies of the *Mona Lisa* are in fact copies of one of these versions or the other, or a combination of both.

About the Authors
Salvatore Lorusso, former full Professor in "Chemistry of the Environment and Cultural Heritage" in the Department of Cultural Heritage at the University of Bologna (Ravenna Campus), continues his academic activities in various fields. His scientific activity continues as a member of the Scientific Committee of the project "Joint Research Laboratory

for Cultural Heritage Diagnosis and Conservation", as part of the Agreement of Cooperation between the University of Bologna, Italy, and Zhejiang University, China. He is the founder and Director of two book series: *I beni culturali e l'ambiente*, consisting of 11 volumes (Pitagora Editrice, Bologna), and *La formazione e la ricerca nel settore dei beni culturali eambientali*, in 2 volumes (Mimesis Edizioni, Milano-Udine). He is also Editor-in-Chief of the historical-technical journal *Conservation Science in Cultural Heritage* (Mimesis Edizioni, Milano-Udine). Prof. Lorusso is the author of more than 400 publications in national and international scientific journals and congress proceedings, and of 22 volumes covering subjects such as commodity science and the system: artifact-environment-biota. He is a Foreign Member of the Russian Academy of Natural Sciences; a former vice-president and now a Councilor of the Presidency of the Società Italiana per il Progresso delle Scienze (SIPS – founded in 1839); Director General of the Academy of Food and Wine Culture; member of the Scientific Committee of the network "Gardens of Babylon – Green Hub"; Emeritus Professor and Visiting Professor of the Cultural Heritage Institute of Zhejiang University (China); and President of the Academic Committee of National Cultural Heritage Preservation (Cultural Relics Bureau of Zhejiang Province). His biography appears in the 2016 Marquis Edition of "Who's Who in the World".

Andrea Natali is Adjunct Professor and Research Fellow at the Department of Cultural Heritage of the Alma Mater University of Bologna. He graduated in "Conservation of Cultural Heritage" at the University of Tuscia, Viterbo. He carries out scientific and didactic activities in the field of conservation environment, employing diagnostic techniques for evaluating the conservation state of cultural heritage, art diagnostics and authentication of art works, including the management and valorization of cultural heritage and landscape, and planning and promotion of artistic and cultural events. He is a mediator/conciliator (as per Ministerial Decree n.180, 18th October 2010). He is professor on the Master (1st level) "Planning and Promotion of artistic and Cultural Events" at the Alma Mater Studiorum University of Bologna. He is author and co-author of over 40 publications covering the preservation and valorization of cultural heritage, andmonographs and scientific treatises used as university text books. Prof. Natali is also a member of the Scientific Committee and Coordination of the Journal *Scienze e Ricerche*, and the Editorial Coordinator of the Journal *Conservation Science in Cultural Heritage*. He is an honorary member of the Academy of Food and Wine Culture.

References

[1]Lorusso S, Matteucci C, Natali A, Apicella S., Fiorillo F. (2013) "Diagnostic-analytical study of the painting "Gioconda with columns"." *Conservation Science in Cultural Heritage*, vol. 13, pp. 75-127 ISSN: 1974-4951

[2]Mohen J.P. (2005). *Au coeur de La Joconde. Léonard de Vinci décodé.* (ed.) Center for Research and Restoration of the Museums of France, Musée du Louvre éditions.

[3]Keith, L., Roy A., Morrison R., Schade P. (2011). "Leonardo da Vinci's Virgin of the Rocks: Treatment and Display." *National Gallery Technical Bulletin*, n. 32.

[4]*Hommage à Léonard de Vinci: exposition en l'honneur du cinquieme centenaire de sa naissance.* (1952). Musée du Louvre.

[5]See *The International Art Magazine*, www.apollo-magazine.com

[6]Museo del Prado, "Advance information on the study of the Mona Lisa in the Prado." February 3, 2012. Retrieved from https://www.museodelprado.es/en/whats-on/new/advance-information-on-the-study-of-the-mona-lisa/4befae32-d1ba-4002-86ee-acd372ddd77e?searchMeta=mona%20lisa.

[7]Antonio de Beatis, "Account of the Visit of Cardinal Louis d'Aragon paid to Leonardo, at the Château de Cloux, October 10, 1517," in Delieuvin, Vincent, *Saint Anne: Leonardo da Vinci's ultimate Masterpiece;* p. 199.

[8] Ed. Piva G. (2007). *L'arte del restauro: il restauro dei dipinti nel sistema antico e moderno, secondo le opere di Secco-Suardo e del Prof. R. Mancia.* Milano, Editore Ulrico Hoepli.

[9]Zöllner, F. (2007). *Leonardo da Vinci, tutti i dipinti e disegni.* Modena, Taschen.

[10]The Metropolitan Museum Of Art. (2003). *Leonardo da Vinci, Master Draftsman* (exhibition catalog). New York, Metropolitan Museum of Art.

[11]Keith, L., Roy A., Morrison R., Schade P. (2011). "Leonardo da Vinci's Virgin of the Rocks: Treatment and Display." *National Gallery Technical Bulletin*, n. 32.

[12]*Leonardo da Vinci, Volume 1* (Ed). (1956). Istituto Geografico de Agostani, Novara.

[13]Giovanna Perini Folesani, "Sir Joshua Reynolds in Rome, 1750-1752: The Debut of an Artist, an Art Collector or an Art dealer?" in: Paolo Coen (Ed.), *The Art Market in Rome in the 18th century.* Brill: 2018.

[14]*A descriptive catalogue of a collection of pictures comprehending specimens of all the various schools of painting belonging to Sir Abraham Hume.* London: W. Nicol, 1824.

[15]The sale in 1794 of 2,253 drawings from Reynolds's collection, all stamped with his collector's mark, included 12 attributed to Leonardo.

[16]Gustav Friedrich Waagen, *Works of Art and Artists in England*, Vol. 2. John Murray, 1838; p. 203.

[17]*The International Art Magazine*, www.apollo-magazine.com

[18]The Mona Lisa Foundation, www.monalisa.org

[19]Laurie Hurwitz, "Is She Smiling for Two?" in *ArtNews*, January 1, 2007.

[20]See, for example, Rinaldi S., Quartullo G., et al. (1995). *La fabbrica dei colori. Pigmenti e col-oranti nella pittura e nella tentoria.* Roma, Bagatto libri.

[21]Ibid.

[22]Pedretti, C. (1973). *Leonardo – A study in chronology and style.* London, Thames and Hudson

[23] Joe Mullins. (2015). "The Regression Project." *Leonardo da Vinci's Earlier Mona Lisa.* The Mona Lisa Foundation, second edition; pp. 132-133.

[24] Ed. Piva G. (2007). *L'arte del restauro: il restauro dei dipinti nel sistema antico e moderno, secondo le opere di Secco-Suardo e del Prof. R. Mancia.* Milano, Editore Ulrico Hoepli.

[25]Bramly S. (1994). *Leonardo: The Artist and the Man.* Penguin, New York.

[26]Pedretti, C. (2005). "Leonardo, La pittura," in *Art Dossier*, no. 215, Milano, Giunti

[27]Fiori C., Lorusso S., Pentrella L. (2003). *Restauro, manutenzione, conservazione dei Beni Culturali: materiali, prodotti e tecniche.* Bologna, Pitagora Editrice.

[28]Ed. Piva G. (2007). *L'arte del restauro: il restauro dei dipinti nel sistema antico e moderno, secondo le opere di Secco-Suardo e del Prof. R. Mancia.* Milano, Editore Ulrico Hoepli.

[29]"Painting Techniques: History, Materials and Studio Practice," in *Proceedings of the Congress of the International Institute for Conservation of Historic and Artistic Works*, Dublin: 1998.

[30]Larry Keith and Ashok Roy (1996). "Giampietrino, Boltraffio, and the influence of Leonardo." *National Gallery Technical Bulletin*, Vol. 17.

[31] "Scientific Analysis of the Paint Pigments" (2015). *Leonardo da Vinci's Earlier Mona Lisa.* The Mona Lisa Foundation, second edition; pp. 85-87.

[32]*Hommage à Léonard de Vinci: exposition en l'honneur du cinquieme centenaire de sa naissance.* (1952). Musée du Louvre.

[33]Rinaldi S., Quartullo G., et al. (1995). *La fabbrica dei colori. Pigmenti e coloranti nella pittura e nella tentoria.* Roma, Bagatto libri.

[34]Friedenthal, R. (1959). *Leonardo da Vinci; a pictorial biography.* New York, Viking Press.

[35]Pedretti, C. (1973). *Leonardo – A study in chronology and style.* London, Thames and Hudson

[36]Bramly S. (1994). *Leonardo: The Artist and the Man.* Penguin, New York.

[37]Bramly S. (1998). *Léonard de Vinci.* Éditions Lattès.

[38]Pedretti, C. (2005). "Leonardo, La pittura," in *Art Dossier*, no. 215, Milano, Giunti.

[39]See, for example, Martin G. (1970). *The Flemish school, 1600-1900.* London, National Gallery Catalogues, and Villers, C., (1981). "Artists' canvases." *Proceedings of the ICOM committee for conservation*, vol. 2, pp. 1-12. Ottawa.

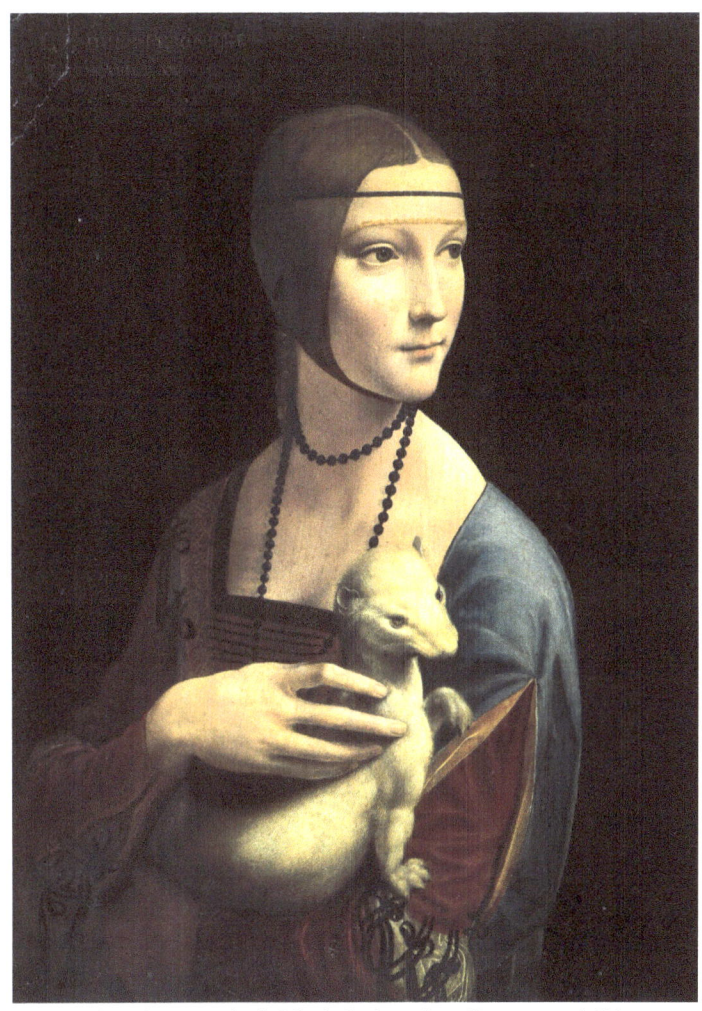

Fig. 14. Leonardo da Vinci, *Lady with an Ermine,* ca. 1490.

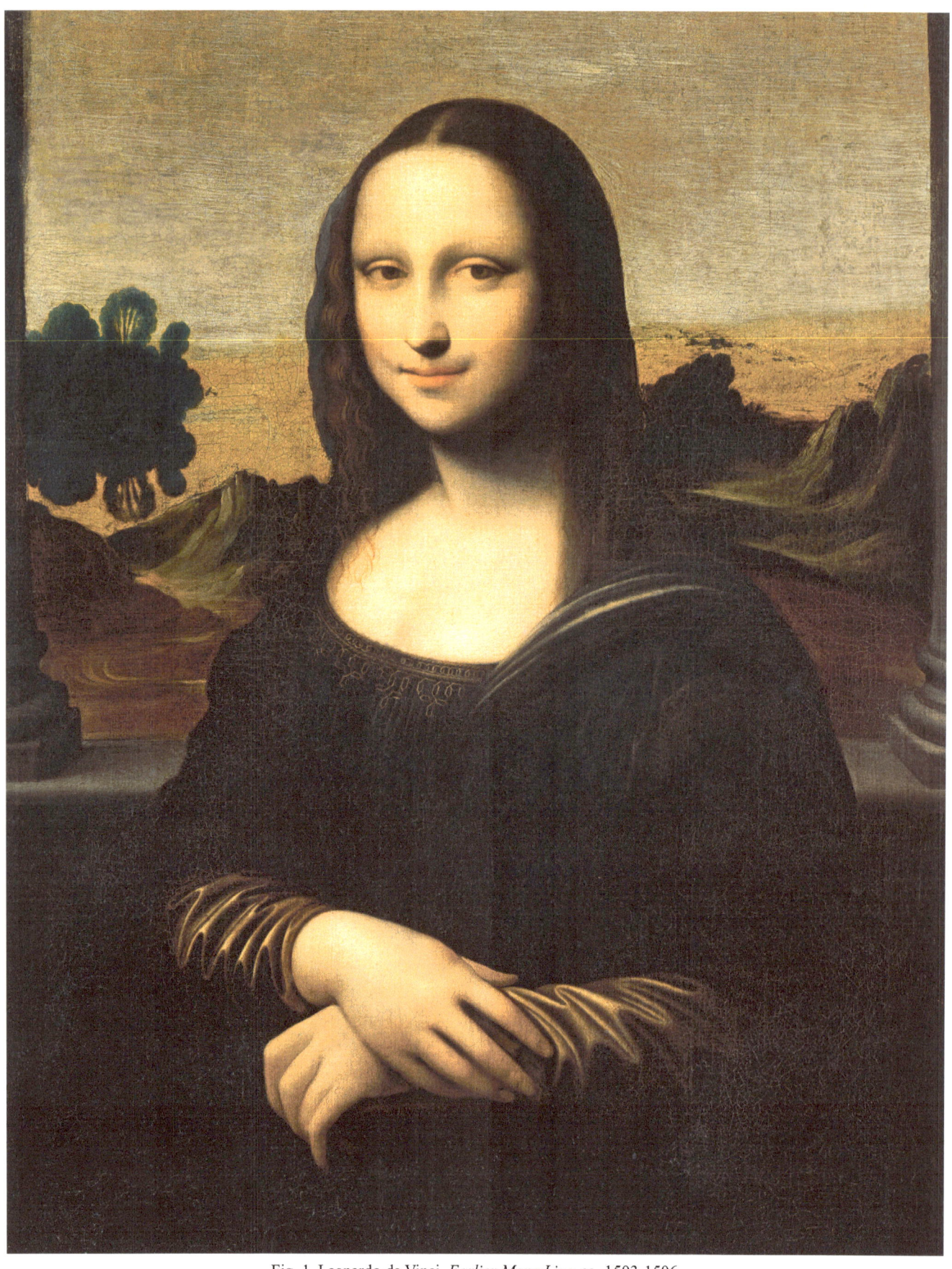

Fig. 1. Leonardo da Vinci, *Earlier Mona Lisa*, ca. 1503-1506

WHY DID LEONARDO PAINT THE MONA LISA?

Prof. Jean-Pierre Isbouts
Fielding Graduate University
Santa Barbara, CA

It seems a relatively straightforward question: why did Leonardo agree to paint the portrait of a Florentine housewife, the spouse of Francesco del Giocondo? That he was working on such a painting by 1503 has been shown by the Heidelberg marginalia, which in turn confirmed Vasari's account in his book *Lives of the Artists*. But the real question is: what motivated him to do so?

With regards to modern art, this question is rarely pertinent. Most art from the 20th century onwards is the product of the artist's inspiration—his desire to create a composition informed by his creativity and imagination. To do so, all he has to do is to go to the nearest art supply store and purchase a suitable canvas, brushes, and an array of paint tubes. But in the Middle Ages and the early Renaissance, those off-the-shelf implements were not available. To begin a painting project, the painter (or his pupils) had to acquire the appropriate pigments, and grind them with a binding agent, whether egg yolk (for tempera) or linseed oil (for an oil painting). Pigments could be expensive; ultramarine blue, often specified for the blue mantel of the Virgin Mary, was derived from lapis lazuli from Afghanistan, and cost more than its weight in gold.

For support, the Renaissance artist would select a suitable slab of wood, whether poplar, walnut or willow, usually cut across the tree as a radial piece for greater stability against warping and splitting. This wooden panel would then be carefully planed and sanded to produce a smooth surface. It was sometimes enlarged with other panels if a sizeable work (such as an altarpiece) was required. And once the panel was dry, it was primed with at least ten layers of gesso (a mixture of animal glue, gypsum, pigment and chalk), each of which was carefully sanded until the panel shone like an enamel-like surface.

In other words, the Renaissance artist did not undertake the development of a painting on a whim. Nor did he have the freedom to explore a subject as his inspiration might suggest. Creating a painting of a sacred subject, such as a *Baptism of Christ* or *The Adoration of the Magi* was ruled by strict iconographic conventions to ensure that the mostly illiterate masses would recognize the meaning of the scene. As a result, religious institutions were always vigilant to ensure that the painting matched what the believers would expect.[1] Secular subjects were still rare in the *Quattrocento*, the 15th century, and invariably involved a portrait or a mythological subject, commissioned by an affluent family. Renaissance paintings, in sum, were almost always "bespoke" works for a particular patron, who had a great deal of say in what the subject should be and how it should be executed.

For that reason, it would be fascinating if we could have a glimpse of the original contract for the *Mona Lisa*, but unfortunately that has not survived. This is not unusual when we remember that this was a *private* commission. Unlike commissions tendered by churches or the state, private contracts did not involve the civic or ecclesiastical authorities and were thus rarely recorded in an official archive, such as the Archivio dello Stato di Firenze, the official state archives of Florence.

Fortunately, we do have other contracts from Quattrocento Florence that can give us an idea of what such an agreement would have entailed. It typically stipulated the key elements of the work to be produced, including (1) the subject matter; (2) the size and format of the painting; (3) the estimated cost of the materials; (4) the fee for the artist, and (5) the date by which the artwork was expected to be finished. The painter sometimes enclosed a sketch or preparatory drawing that the patron signed off on. For example, in a letter from Filippo Lippi to his patron, Giovanni di Cosimo de' Medici dated 20 July 1457, the artist wrote that:

> "If you agree .. to give me sixty florins to include materials, gold, gilding and painting, I will… have the painting completely finished by 20 August… And to keep you informed, I send a drawing of how the triptych is made of wood, and with its height and breadth. Out of friendship for you I do not want to take more than the labor costs of 100 florins for this; I ask no more."[2]

This contract reveals the comparably high cost of materials (sixty florins, or roughly $12,000 today) versus the cost of labor ($20,000). Admittedly, this contract involved a large work—a triptych—but a similar cost was quoted by Domenico Ghirlandaio for a painting for the *Spedale degli Innocenti,* the Foundling Hospital and children orphanage in Florence, some thirty years later. This contract specified that the price of the painting was 115 florins, *including* all expenses to be borne by the painter, on condition that the painting, when completed, "was

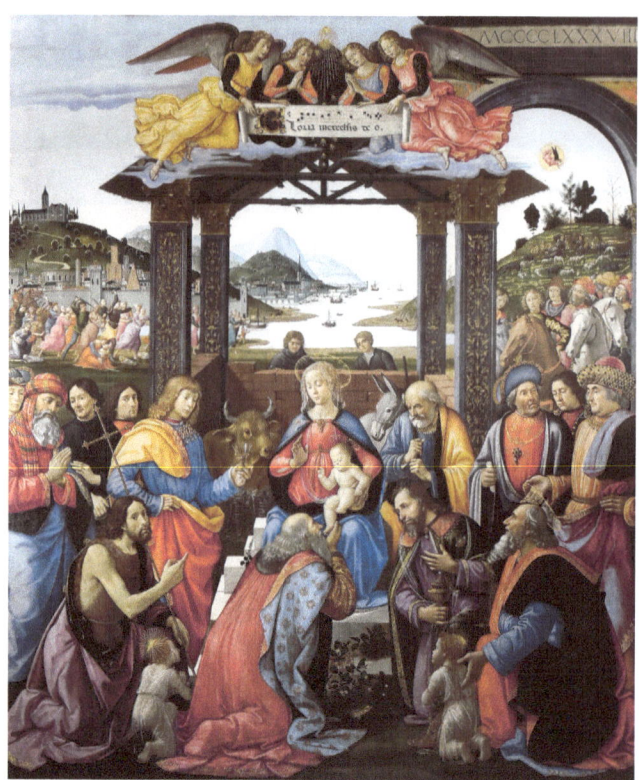

Fig 2. Domenico Ghirlandaio, *Adoration of the Magi*, 1485-1488. Ospedale degli Innocenti, Florence

worth it."[3]

These and other contracts show a growing concern with the length of time in which the work was to be completed. This was probably a reflection of the rising workload in artist workshops during the Quattrocento, when the amount of commissions grew and projects often had to be prioritized based on the seniority and prominence of the client.

The tremendous power that a patron could wield in specifying the terms of a contract could often put an artist at a disadvantage. When Leonardo embarked on his first major bespoke work as an independent artist, the *Adoration of the Magi*, his client—the Augustinian monks of San Donato a Scopeto—insisted that he complete this vast work (more than eight feet wide and seven feet tall) in less than 30 months. What's more, Leonardo was to finance all the costs himself, including the fees of his assistants over a period of two and a half years, and would not be paid until the painting was completed to the monk's satisfaction.

Even then, he would not be paid in cash, but be given a portion of a small estate in the Val d'Elsa, left to the monks by a merchant donor.

Most of these contracts involved sacred art. For much of the Middle Ages, it was the Church—and its aggregate of parishes, convents and monasteries—that served as the principal funding agency of art in Italy and beyond. Before 1400, portraits of living human beings were rare, except in the case of prominent kings, clergy or noblemen. The reason is that such paintings were considered an unseemly expression of personal vanity. To the medieval mind, the body was a mere mortal shell; what mattered was the soul, which would find eternal peace in heaven if the person had lived a pious and moral life. In this context, one's physical likeness was of little account, just as the importance of the individual was subsumed by the overarching role of the Christian community, governed by the Church. When portraits of lay citizenry did appear, it was usually in their role as "donors," the patrons who paid for the work, painted on the margins of a sacred scene.

After 1400, however, the growing power of the merchant class in Florence led to a fundamental change in attitude towards secular portraits, for the simple reason that wealth always seeks an outlet. During the preceding century, authors such as Dante, Petrarch and Boccaccio had laid the groundwork for a new appreciation of the individual by creating a literary tradition on the classical humanist model. Their works advanced the idea that the human experience was a subject worthy of study and discussion, just as Greek and Roman authors had done in Antiquity. During the Quattrocento, this encouraged sculptors and architects like Donatello, Ghiberti and Brunelleschi to turn to classical models for inspiration—despite the fact that in a previous era, such models would had been denounced as pagan art, exposing the artist to charges of heresy. This is captured in the word "Renaissance" (or *Rinascità* in Italian) that Vasari uses to describe the 'revival' of ancient models during the 15th century.

There was only one problem: whereas Renaissance sculptors and architects could draw their inspiration from Roman statuary and architectural ruins scattered across the Tuscan countryside, such models were not available to the painter. Painters were well aware that the Greeks and Romans had some outstanding artists—such as the Greek Apelles, as we saw in a previous chapter—but actual Roman paintings and frescoes had not survived, or still slumbered in their graves in Pompeii and Herculaneum.

There was one exception, and fortuitously, it pertained to portraiture. Ancient coins, which were avidly collected in Renaissance Italy, gave painters an idea of what portraiture in Antiquity may have looked like. These coins typically depicted rulers such as Roman emperors in profile view, since this was the most efficient way of reducing the human physiognomy to a two-dimensional surface. The sudden rage for ancient coins coincided with a new interest in secular portraiture—particularly among

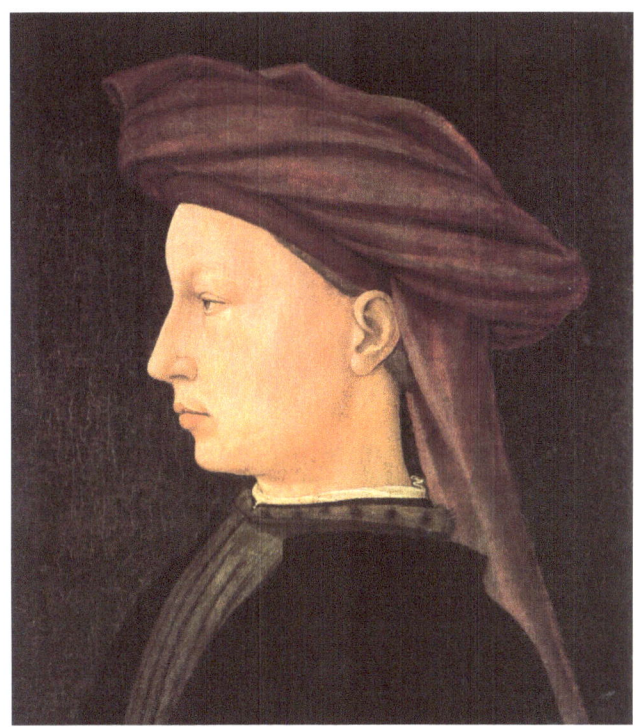

Fig. 3. Masaccio, *Portrait of a Young Man*, ca. 1425.

those patrons whose wealth and privilege enabled them to collect such coins and discuss them with their humanist friends. It is therefore not surprising that the first exclusively secular portraits of the Florentine Renaissance—meaning, art for the specific purpose to document the features of the sitter—use a coin-like profile view.

Even as the century progressed, the profile portrait remained the preferred format among the upper classes because of its obvious classicizing tenor; it signaled to the beholder that the person was fully *au courant* with ancient art. Even in the group paintings of Masaccio and Mantegna (such as the latter's *Ludovico II Gonzaga with Cardinal Francesco Gonzaga and his Sons* of 1474), most of the men, women and children are depicted *en profil*. What's more, the head, torso and limbs of these figures are all facing the same direction.

Significantly, Leonardo was one of the first painters who broke with that trend. Not only did he paint his sitters in a *trois-quarts* or "three-quarter" position; he also deliberately turned the head in a different direction than the torso. As a result, the figure seems to be in the process of *turning towards us*, imbuing the portrait with a sense of movement. This heightens the impression that we are dealing with a real, living person, with a distinct personality of her own.

We can see the beginning of this process in Leonardo's portrait of Ginevra de' Benci, possibly begun at the occasion of her wedding (at age 16) in 1474. The *contrapposto* motif, the classical ideal of moving the head, torso and limbs in different directions from its center axis, was then fully developed in Leonardo's masterful portrait of *The Lady with an Ermine* of 1490. Its familiarity has made it difficult for us to grasp its truly revolutionary quality: the soft tonal play of light and shadow on the skin; the daring turn of the head, as if something beyond our view has caught attention of the lady; and the dark background, a black limbo, that enhances the almost photographic realism of the painting.

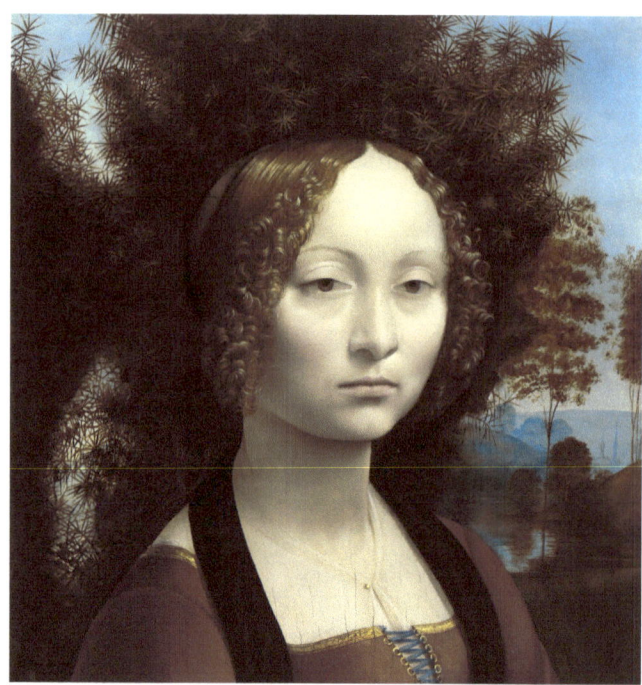

Fig 4. Leonardo da Vinci, *Portrait of Ginevra de' Benci*, ca. 1474-1478.

To truly recognize the transformative quality of this work, we must compare it to the entirely conventional portrait of Bianca Maria Sforza, painted three years later by Leonardo's partner, Giovanni Ambrogio de Predis.[5] While the artist adapted the dark background from *Lady with an Ermine*, in all other aspects he remained true to Lombard form, including the profile position of the lady and the detail of her garments.

Another important feature of *Lady with an Ermine* that would return in the *Mona Lisa* is Leonardo use of the lady's hands to enhance the portrait's psychological depth. With her slender, slightly elongated fingers, the young woman is absentmindedly caressing the neck of an *ermine*, thus enhancing the pensive, almost intellectual air of the portrait. The ermine, a weasel-like animal, also provides the key to identify the lady. The ermine was a favorite pet of the aristocracy, and one of the emblems of Duke Ludovico Sforza of Milan. But as many of the educated elite at the Duke's court would know, the Greek name for an ermine is *gale* or *galay*. These clues point towards Cecilia Gallerani, a young woman whom the Duke took as his lover when she was sixteen.

Portraiture would remain the focus of Leonardo's remaining nine years at the ducal court of Milan, culminating in his great masterpiece, *The Last Supper*, at the convent of Santa Maria delle Grazie in Milan. Here, with infinite care, Leonardo tried to portray the full range of human emotions, cued to the unique personality and physiognomy of each Apostle. In this painting, Christ has just revealed that one among the twelve will betray him, and this announcement is met with shock, disbelief, indignation, fear, and sadness— all the drama and intensity of a live play. Leonardo was well familiar with stage performance, having directed many of Ludovico's masques, including *Festa del Paradiso* and the theatrical comedy *Danae* by Baldassare Taccone. Leonardo's notebooks and drawings show how much work he invested in capturing lifelike expressions of his *Last Supper* "cast" in a realistic and convincing manner. Many of these studies appear to have been drawn from life, using characters that Leonardo would have met in the streets and alleys of Milan.

Leonardo Returns to Florence

Leonardo spent 18 years in Milan, after which his appointment as court painter and impresario came to an end. In 1499 the new French king, Louis XII, suddenly turned on Duke Ludovico, France's erstwhile ally, and marched south to enforce his claim on the Duchy of Milan. Ludovico had no choice but to flee. Leonardo, too, was compelled to disband his Milanese studio and leave the city. Together with the noted friar and mathematician Luca di Pacioli he traveled to Venice, arriving in the lagoon city in March of 1500. But first, he was invited to the court of the Marchioness of Mantua, Isabella d'Este. It is possible that he had already been introduced to Isabella during the wedding celebrations of her sister Beatrice to Duke Ludovico in 1491. A rich and highly educated woman, Isabella was renowned as a leading arts patrons in Northern Italy. This pursuit that was, to some degree, facilitated by the frequent absences of her husband, Marquess Francesco Gonzaga, who served as the commander of Venice's armed forces. It also enabled Francesco to indulge in a passionate love affair with

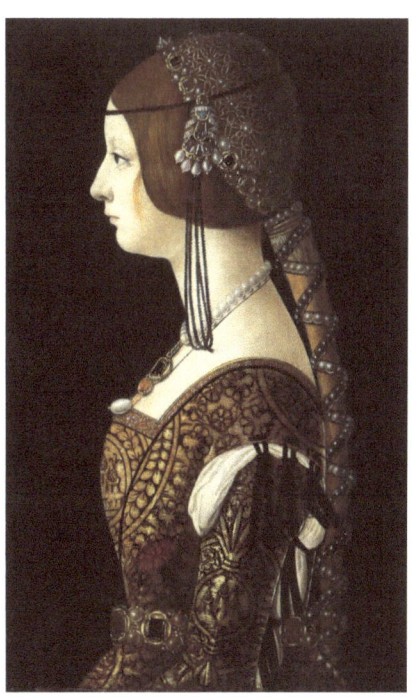

Fig. 5. Leonardo da Vinci, *The Lady with an Ermine*, ca. 1489-1490.

Fig. 6. Ambrogio de Predis, *Portrait of Bianca Maria Sforza*, c. 1493

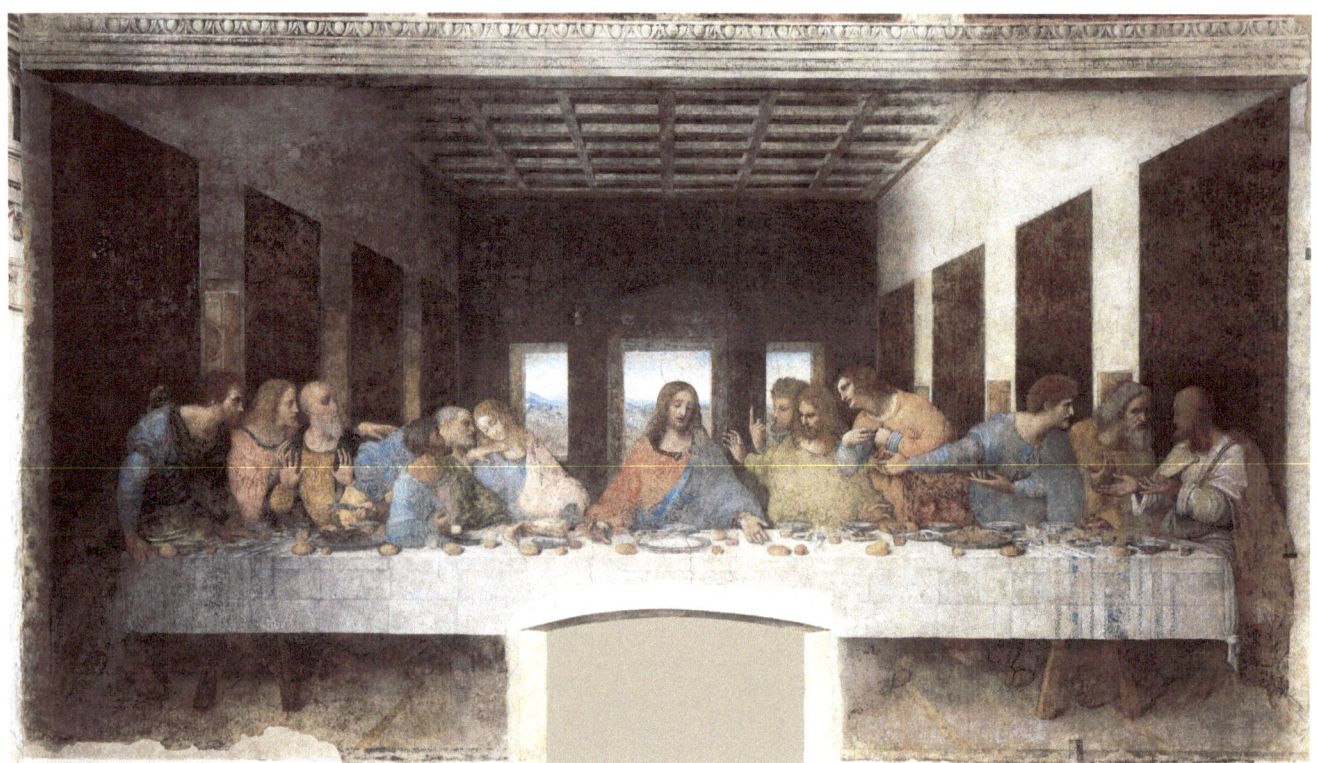

Fig. 7. Leonardo da Vinci, *Last Supper*, c. 1495-1498

Lucrezia Borgia.

It was Isabella who had conceived the idea of creating a *studiolo*, a private gallery of all the paintings in her collection—something that would soon become the rage in 16th century Italy and much of Europe. It therefore did not come as a surprise that, while Leonardo was enjoying her hospitality at the Mantuan court, she asked him to paint her portrait. Leonardo obliged her by creating a beautiful drawing in black and red chalk, now in the Louvre. Surprisingly, the young Isabella is shown resolutely in profile, while her torso in turned towards the viewer in Leonardo's now familiar *trois-quarts* composition. Then again, Isabella had a large collection of Roman coins, and may have insisted that Leonardo paint her in this position. Indeed, the artist Gian Cristoforo Romano created several medals with her likeness in profile.

In every other aspect, however, this drawing is a signature Leonardo portrait, with a composition that clearly anticipates the *Mona Lisa*. Though the drawing has been cut on the bottom, a 16th century copy reveals that the hands were originally in full view, resting on a parapet, one hand on top of the other.[8] Despite its obvious beauty, however, the drawing was not likely to satisfy the marchioness's wishes. She wanted a painted portrait. Indeed, when the prominent Carmelite vicar of Mantua, Pietro da Novellara, was invited by the church of Santa Croce to come to Florence to give the Lenten sermon of March, 1501, Isabella instructed him to visit Leonardo's workshop and find out what was happening with her portrait, and why on earth it was taking him so long.

Alas, Leonardo had not even begun the work. Having spent most of his time in Milan working on portraits, the idea of painting *another* likeness was probably furthest from his mind. Instead, he was fully occupied with matters of science, geometry and engineering. That is probably the reason why he and Pacioli had traveled to Venice in the first place, because the city served as Europe's leading gateway to the ideas, products and science of the East. What's more, Venice was a city built on a lagoon,

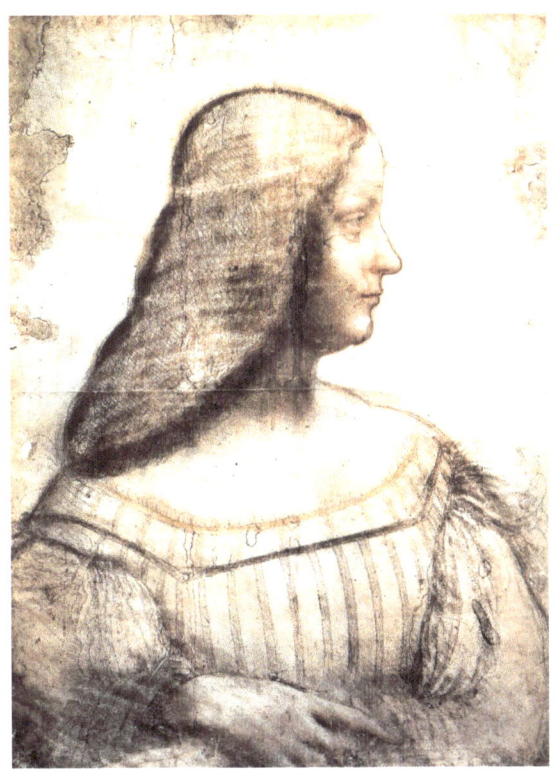

Fig. 8. Leonardo da Vinci, *Portrait of Isabella d'Este*, c. 1499-1500

he was undoubtedly impressed by the use of canvas by artists like Mantegna, whom he may have met in either Mantua or Venice. Canvas did not warp or split like wooden panels, but it required additional layers of animal glue, gesso and white paint to achieve the smooth surface that Renaissance artists had come to expect. Unlike modern artists, the Renaissance painter did not want the fabric of canvas to be visible, and went to great lengths to cover it in order to simulate the polish of wood. This is attested by a detailed chapter on the use of canvas in Leonardo's *Treatise on Painting,* which reads:

> "Stretch the canvas onto a chassis, then apply a light coat of fluid glue and let it dry. Then draw your painting with tone using silk brushes adding, in your style the "sfumato" technique to place the shadows while the paint is still fresh."[9]

The detailed nature of this narrative suggests that Leonardo had actual, hands-on experience with painting on canvas, as we will see shortly. Then again, he was always fascinated by any new techniques or inventions that could improve the quality of his work. In that sense, canvas had the potential of revolutionizing the art of painting because of its low cost, light weight, ease of transportation, and ability to sustain multiple layers of oils—as North European artists such as Jan van Eyck and Robert de Campin had already discovered.

While Leonardo was in Venice, exciting news arrived. Duke Ludovico Sforza had launched a daring bid to restore his rule in Milan. Troops loyal to the former duke, including a contingent of Swiss mercenaries, had forced themselves into the city and defeated the French troops stationed within its walls. For Leonardo, this could have been very good news. It may have filled him with hope that once the Duke was restored in his domain, he could return to Milan, reassemble his studio and resume his work at

and Leonardo had always been intrigued by the flow of water. Having witnessed first-hand the disastrous flooding of the Arno River in 1466 and 1478, he was fascinated by the technology of channeling the awesome power of water through locks and sluices. As a result, he soon found himself drafting a report for the Venetian Senate for ways in which the Isonzo River could be fortified in the event of a Turkish invasion. This was no idle threat, for in 1480 Ottoman forces had captured Otranto in Apulia, and were planning to march up north.

There were scores of other innovations to be found in Venice. One was a new form of etching whereby engravers used acid to create painterly effects on a copper plate that could not be made with the lines of a burin. Another novelty was a revolutionary type of support—one that was lighter, cheaper, and more durable than wood. This was the use of canvas, derived from the stitching of sails for the Venetian shipbuilding industry. Leonardo had come in contact with canvas before, notably in the workshop of Verrocchio. But court. Unfortunately, that is not what came to pass. When he heard the news, French King Louis XII immediately dispatched an expeditionary force that caught up with Ludovico in the city of Novara, west of Milan. Fatefully, his troops included a large company of Swiss mercenaries as well. When the Swiss on Ludovico's side found out, they promptly surrendered their arms and left the city, for no Swiss would ever fight another. Bereft of his troops, Ludovico tried to escape by disguising himself as a servant, but was promptly recognized and captured. The former duke was then taken to France where he died, unmourned, in a dungeon at the Château de Loches in 1508. In one of his notebooks, Leonardo wrote of his former patron, "The Duke lost his state, and his goods, and his freedom, and none of his works was completed."[10]

Now that the road back to Milan was cut off—at least for the time being—there was only one thing for Leonardo to do. He would return to his native town of Florence.

Leonardo in Florence

What went through Leonardo's mind as he slowly made his way back to Tuscany? It was almost two decades since he had turned his back on the city of his youth, in the hope of finding a more amenable patron in the North. Many decades later, the Medici propaganda machine would manufacture the myth that Leonardo had been "sent" by Lorenzo de Medici to the court of Milan on a diplomatic mission, but this is pure fiction.[11] As we will see, Leonardo had never enjoyed the patronage of Lorenzo the Magnificent, for the simple reason that unlike his rivals in Florence, Leonardo was uneducated and unlettered, unable even to write or read Latin. For Lorenzo, who considered himself the leading intellectual of his day, such an artist was not worthy of his attention, certainly when he had yet to produce anything of merit. Indeed, when in 1481 Pope Sixtus IV asked Lorenzo to send him six of the city's finest painters to decorate the new

Sistine Chapel in the Vatican, Leonardo was studiously omitted from the list of recommended artists. In sum, what prompted Leonardo to leave Florence for Milan was his inability to penetrate the clannish circles of Medici patronage, exacerbated by the order from the Augustinian monks to stop working on the *Adoration of the Magi*.[13]

But now he was back, having arrived in early 1501, still wearing the fine livery from the ducal court that may have been the extent of Leonardo's possessions at that time. "He owned next to nothing," Vasari wrote, "and worked little, yet he always kept servants and horses." More than likely, he headed to the home of his father, the notary Ser Piero, who lived on the Via Ghibellina. In one letter that has survived, Leonardo expresses his "pleasure" upon hearing that his father was "in good health," and adds that he is "unhappy to learn of your trouble."[14] Perhaps he was referring to the fact that Ser Piero's first two wives, Albiera and Francesca, had tragically died childless. His third wife, Margherita, had presented him with his first legitimate child, a son, in 1476. Other offspring followed in rapid succession, but Margherita eventually died, and was replaced by Ser Piero's fourth wife, Lucrezia di Guglielmo, who continued to bear him children as well. As a result, Leonardo would have been in for a shock. The house on the Via Ghibellina must have reverberated with the cries and laughter of eleven children, ranging from a 24-year old to a toddler who was still in diapers.

The idea that Leonardo would visit his father is not idle speculation, because most authors agree that it was Ser Piero who then introduced Leonardo to the Servite friars, or "Servants of Mary" as they were officially known, who were looking for an artist to paint an altarpiece for their church, the *Santissima Annunziata*. This must have been welcome news, because Leonardo was nearly broke, and had been forced to withdraw 50 florins from his account at the Santa Maria Nuova. The friars liked what Leonardo had to say, and accepted his services as the painter of the altarpiece. Together with Salaì and possibly Fanfoia, he moved into quarters provided by the friars at the *Annunziata*, and set to work – or so it was assumed. But actually, while Leonardo did produce some sketches, he could never bring himself to picking up a brush. Various other job offers began to pour in, including several restoration projects in and around Florence and the design of a new villa for Francesco da Gonzaga. This must have further increased the anxiety of the Servite monks, since, as Vasari tells us, they were "picking up the expenses for Leonardo and of all his household."[16]

This, then, is the moment when Isabella d'Este beseeched the vicar general of Mantua, Pietro da Novellara, to visit Leonardo's studio and see what was going on. The prelate soon discovered that Leonardo "was difficult to pin down," since he seemed to "live from day to day;" but eventually he made his way into Leonardo's chambers, where he recorded everything he saw in a letter dated April 3, 1501.

"Since he has been in Florence, he has only made one sketch," Father Pietro observed, "a cartoon of a child Christ, about a year old, almost jumping out of his mother's arms to seize hold of a lamb." Mary herself, he continued, "is in the act of rising from St. Anne's lap, and holds back the child from the lamb."[17] Clearly, Father Pietro is referring to a drawing or cartoon for *The Virgin and Child with St. Anne,* which was probably developed based on an earlier version of this theme, known as the Burlington Cartoon, now in the National Gallery in London. The painted version, executed sometime after 1508, now hangs in the Louvre.

In 2008, a curator discovered several drawings on the back of the Louvre painting, including a sketch showing the infant Jesus playing with a lamb. Quite possibly, these sketches convey something of the drawing that Father Pietro saw. The Carmelite vicar added a few lines that reveal Leonardo's state of mind.

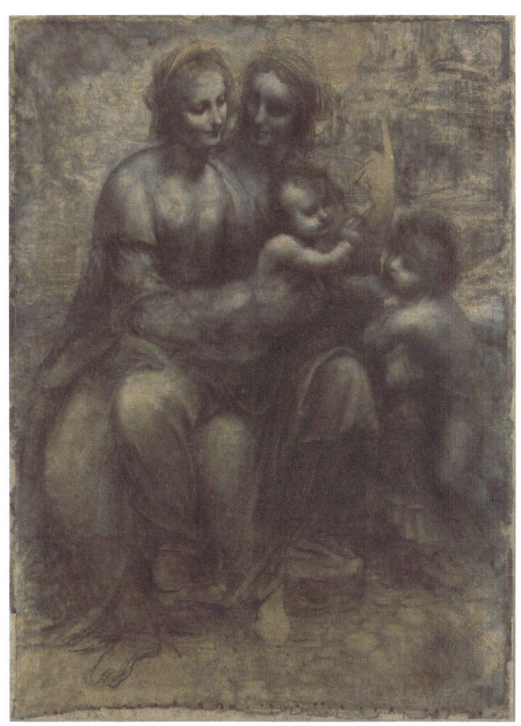

Fig. 9. Leonardo da Vinci, *Saint Anne, Mary, Jesus and John* (the Burlington Cartoon), ca. 1499-1500.

"He has done nothing else," he wrote, "excepting that two of his apprentices are painting portraits to which he sometimes adds a few touches. He is working hard at geometry, and is quite tired of painting" (*Altro non ha facto senon che dui suoi garzoni fano retrati et lui ale volte in alcuno mette mano. Da opra forte a la geometria impacientissimo al pennello*).[19]

Knowing that the marchioness was waiting impatiently for the portrait that Leonardo had promised he would paint based on the drawing made in Mantua, the vicar added a bit of wishful thinking. He wrote, "as soon as he has finished a little picture which he is painting for a certain Robertet, a favorite of the King of France, he will do your portrait immediately and send it to you." That "little picture" was most likely the first version of the *Madonna of the Yarnwinder* as discussed in the Introduction to this book.

Whether Leonardo was truly contemplating a portrait of Isabella d'Este is extremely doubtful, because in the meantime, another patron had appeared: the son of Pope Alexander, Cesare Borgia. And this patron was not interested in Leonardo's brush; he wanted the master's skill as a military engineer. Today, we tend to associate Cesare Borgia with all sorts of nefarious doings—including murder, extortion, even incest with his sister.[20] But Borgia was also a cunning strategist and a talented military commander, who had every intention of finishing what Pope Sixtus IV had begun in the 1470's: to extend the papal territories into a vast central state, including the province of Romagna. This expansion would allow the papal state to hold the balance of power between Milan, Venice and Naples. To do so, Borgia needed a military engineer: one who could ford rivers with bridges; build siege engines to subdue recalcitrant towns; and fortify those towns once they'd been captured. Borgia had probably met Leonardo in Milan, and may have seen some of the engineering drawings he'd created for Ludovico Sforza. Of course, Leonardo leapt at the opportunity. Here, at last, was the opportunity to deploy his talents as a scientist and engineer.

And so, by the summer of 1502 Leonardo was busy inspecting the fortifications of Piombino; drawing maps for Borgia's captain Vitellozzo Vitelli; and assisting in the siege of Arezzo, which had revolted against the Borgias. Many of these observations are recorded in a small book known as "Manuscript L." It's possible that during this siege, Leonardo studied the city's famous Ponte Buriano across the Arno; some historians believe its slender design would return in the bridge in the background of the *Mona Lisa*. Along the way, he produced a bird's eye view map of Imola so as to better study ways to fortify the town, thus inventing the concept of modern urban cartography.[21]

But Leonardo's engagement with the Borgia forces was not destined to last, for reasons that are still disputed today. On the one hand, it is certainly true that when the winter of 1502 set in, troops were sent into their winter quarters and there was little for Leonardo to do. On the other, life in the Borgia circle was becoming precarious. Cesare had discovered that

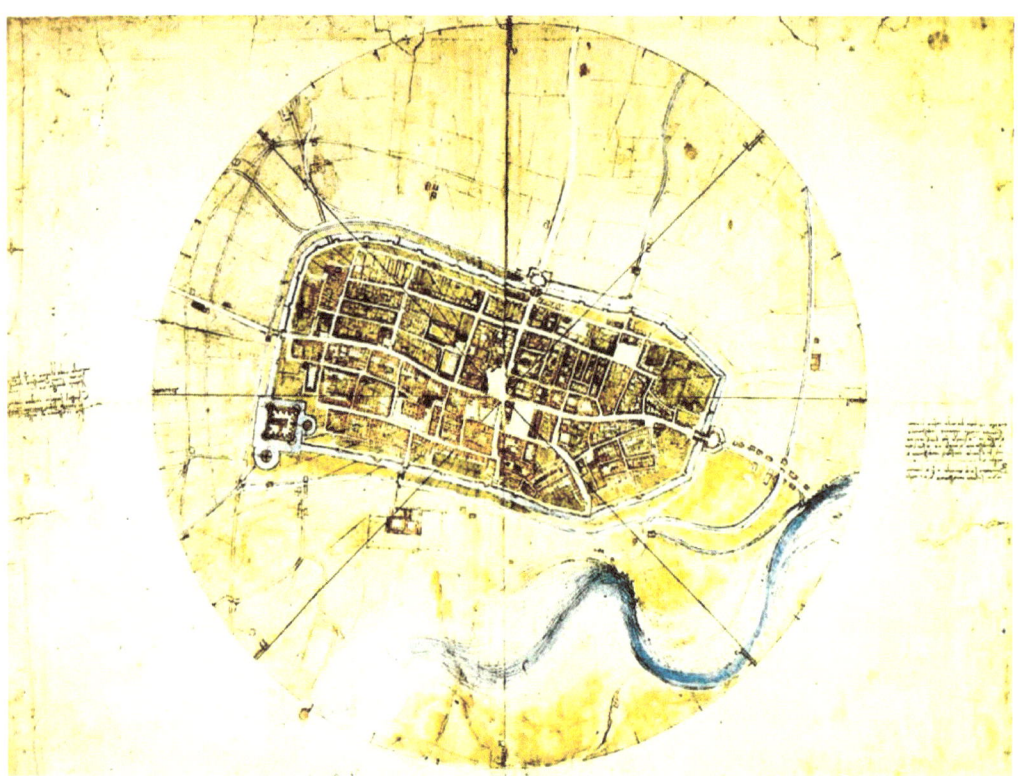

Fig. 10. Leonardo da Vinci, *Map of the Town of Imola*, ca. 1502.

several officers were plotting against him. In response, he invited them to his headquarters in Senigallia with offers of gold and promotions—and then had them murdered as soon as they entered his chambers. Yet another hypothesis suggests that Leonardo found out that Borgia had begun to plot the conquest of Tuscany—Leonardo's native region. Others believe that Borgia's power had begun to wane; indeed, in the summer of 1503, he was forced to flee to Spain. Unfortunately, Leonardo's notes are silent on the matter. The only entries of this period contain the usual expenses for Salaì—a pink hose, among others—and a reminder to write to a monk at Santa Croce.[22]

What we do know is that in March of 1503, Leonardo was back in Florence, without a job, without commissions, and apparently, without money. He once again began to draw from his savings account at the Ospedale di Santa Maria Nuova, and would continue to do so, every three months, until the summer.[23] This suggests that the Borgia engagement had not ended in amicable fashion; a satisfied patron may have sent Leonardo on his way with a purse of gold.

To make matters worse, the city of Florence was experiencing a severe economic recession. Between 1494 and 1498, the Dominican monk Savonarola had established a virtual theocracy, urging citizens to burn any pagan effigies on a "bonfire of the vanities" on the Piazza della Signoria. Though the monk himself was hanged and burned on May 23, 1498, his fiery rule had led many of the city's patrons to sour on their enthusiasm for secular art. Meanwhile, the endless war with Pisa—exacerbated by the revolt of another dependency, the town of Arezzo, in 1502—had emptied the city's coffers, forcing the Signoria to raise taxes. In sum, these were anxious, volatile times; in some trades, business was so bad that several guilds were on the verge of bankruptcy.[24] The city was hardly in a mood to receive its prodigal son with open arms, and to offer him new commissions.

But there was a silver lining: during Leonardo's sojourn in the Borgia camp, he had been introduced to the thirty-year old envoy from Florence, named Niccolò Machiavelli. The Signoria had dispatched Machiavelli, a Secretary of the Second Chancery, to see what Borgia was up to and determine if he posed a threat to Florence, which was definitely a possibility. Machiavelli was very reluctant to embark on this mission since he had just been married, and desperately missed his young bride. But he was delighted to find a fellow compatriot in Leonardo, and the two formed a strong bond. Machiavelli must have been pleasantly surprised to discover that Leonardo had made extensive studies of the movement of water. It is even possible that Leonardo showed him the designs he had made for the fortification of the Isonzo River in Venice.

As it happened, the new *gonfaloniere* or "president" of the Florentine republic, Piero Soderini, had come up with a drastic scheme to bring an end to the war with Pisa: by depriving it of its lifeline, the Arno River. If that river could be diverted, Pisa would lose its link to the sea, and thus its trade, food and military supply. Plans such as these had been percolating for many years, for if the Florentines were successful in that endeavor, they would also be able to canalize the river and make it navigable for Florentine ships, thus creating a waterway directly to the sea. Indeed, Machiavelli himself had visited the "front" near Pisa in June and July of 1500, to see what could be done. But until now, such plans had rarely moved beyond the realm of fantasy.

Of course, when Machiavelli told Leonardo of this scheme, presumably during their stay in the Borgia camp, Leonardo must have been intrigued. To divert the Arno was exactly the type of project that would summon all of his scientific experience: his study of soil, of geological formations, of the movement of water, of weirs and sluices, of floodgates and bulwarks. Unfortunately, it would also be extremely

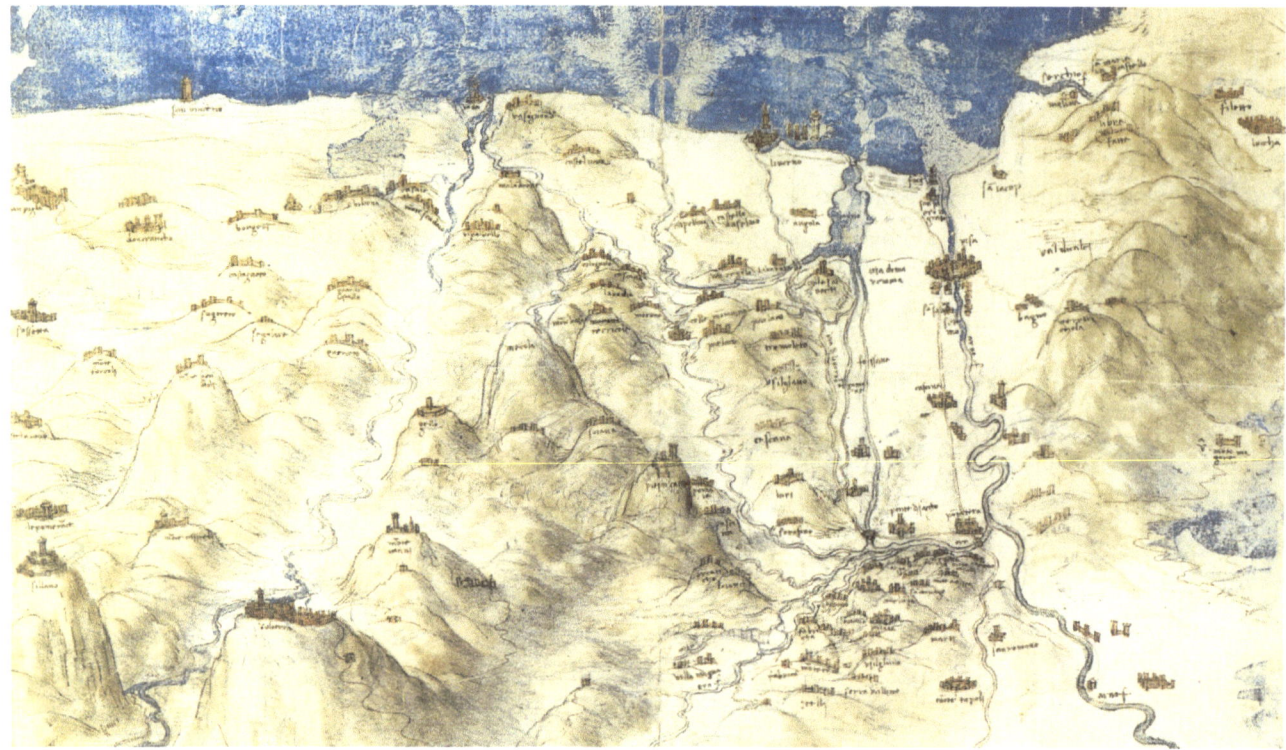

Fig. 11. Leonardo da Vinci, *Study of Tuscany with the Arno River*, 1502-1503.

expensive; in one of his preparatory studies, Leonardo calculated that it would require some 54,000 man days just to create a 12-mile diversion of the Arno. Such projects were not entered into lightly.

This may explain why, by the time Leonardo returned to Florence in March of 1503, the Arno project had not yet been approved, and wouldn't be approved for quite some time. In the meantime, Leonardo and his companions needed to eat and have a place to sleep. Naturally, a return to the Servite monks of the *Annunziata*, who were still waiting for their altarpiece, was out of the question. Leonardo had no choice but to fall back on his savings; a withdrawal of fifty gold ducats on March 4 was followed by another drawdown of fifty ducats on June 14. In one of Leonardo's notebook pages, now a part of the Codex Atlanticus, someone wrote, '*Tra noi non ha a correre denari*'—"there's not a lot of money around here."[25]

But then, Machiavelli may have come to his aid. The young secretary probably knew that the Signoria, though impressed with Leonardo's design

for the diversion of the Arno, was not about to place such a vast undertaking in the hands of a man with a reputation for not finishing what he started—as the monks of the *Annunziata* could affirm. They continued to rely on his plans and drawings—even inviting Leonardo to review his design with the senior military commander on the scene, Francesco Guiducci—but did not go as far as to actually charge him to supervise the work.[26] Indeed, when in August 1504, the Signoria finally approved the project, Leonardo found himself excluded from the engineering team.

But Machiavelli also knew that Soderini was contemplating another project that might be in Leonardo's reach. The *gonfaloniere* had decided to create a large propaganda work to buck up the spirits of his citizens who were weary of the war, the taxes, and the loss of so much of their former prosperity. He wanted to commission a vast mural in the newly built hall of the Palazzo della Signoria, the government building that today is known as the Palazzo Vecchio. This hall was the meeting place of the *Consiglio*

Maggiore, the Grand Council of 500 members who served as the bedrock of Florence's new republican foundation.

The subject that Soderini had in mind was the famed Battle of Anghiari, one of the few victories in Florence's rather checkered military history. In 1440, the allied armies of Florence, Venice and the Papal States—a rather motley assortment of no more than around 8,000 troops—was attacked by the vastly superior forces of Milan near the town of Anghiari, close to Arezzo. In a furious clash that lasted over four hours, the Florentine general, Micheletto Attendolo, had held the bridge that led directly to the allied camp, thus denying the Milanese the ability to make their numbers count and ultimately driving them from the field. Though the battle actually ended in a draw, it was touted by the Florentines as a major victory.

The sheer size of the mural, however—55 feet wide and 22 feet high, or 17 by 7 meters —posed a challenge. It would require a veritable army of assistants and scaffold-builders to paint such a vast surface. Then again, this was an area in which Leonardo had made his mark—by painting the large fresco of the *Last Supper*. Machiavelli may have been aware of that feat, but he doubted that the gentlemen of the council knew it as well. Many, including Soderini himself, were inclined to give the project to Michelangelo instead.

That it was Machiavelli who first alerted Leonardo to the project seems plausible; among Leonardo's notebooks is a detailed description of the battle, translated from the original Latin by Agostino Vespucci, Machiavelli's secretary. But whether Machiavelli was also in a position to persuade the Signoria to choose Leonardo, instead of Michelangelo, is questionable. Machiavelli was secretary to the Chancery, with the ability to whisper into Soderini's ear, but he did not have any voting powers himself. And Leonardo's *non finito* reputation—his rumored inability to finish what he started—was quite

pervasive, for Florentines have a long memory. No doubt, there were many among the Signoria who bridled at the idea of conferring this important commission on a wayward artist who had yet to accomplish anything of note in his native town.

Francesco del Giocondo

This, then, is the moment when I believe Francesco del Giocondo entered the scene. Giocondo had built his wealth on the trade of silk. Silk was far more difficult to produce than wool—the mainstay of Florence's cloth industry—but Giocondo realized that Florence's wool trade was bound to be eclipsed by the growing competition from England and Spain. What's more, the silk industry was not governed by the same onerous restrictions that had been imposed by the Lana Guild on wool manufacturers.[27] A keen observer of city politics, Giocondo had steadily parlayed his growing wealth into a network of contacts among the *prominenti* of the city, even serving as a member of the advisory council of the *Dodici Buonuomini,* the "Twelve Good Men." In fact, between 1480 and 1520, the members of the Giocondo family would hold no less than forty positions at various levels of the Florentine government.[28] Here, then, was a man who could bring his influence to bear to swing the vote Leonardo's way—if, that is, he could be incentivized to do so.

We don't know whether it was Machiavelli or Leonardo's father, Ser Piero, who introduced Leonardo to the Giocondo family, but as the Heidelberg marginalia indicate, at some point in late 1502 or early 1503 they must have met. During that meeting, Giocondo may have stressed the great odds that he would face in persuading the Signoria to give Leonardo the fresco contract; it was less than two years since Leonardo had walked away from a painting for one of the city's most prominent churches, the *Santissima Annunziata.*

Research by Giuseppe Pallanti has revealed that

Giocondo was a tough, even ruthless negotiator. To cite just one example: while negotiating the terms of his marriage to Lisa with her father, Antonmaria Gherardini, Giocondo had balked at Gherardini's claim that the family was too poor to come up with a dowry. In the end, Gherardini was able to scrape together 170 florins, but in some ways that paltry sum was worse than nothing at all. Another man might have let the matter rest and get on with enjoying the pleasures of matrimonial love, but Francesco was not like other men. He ordered what today we would call a financial "discovery," and found out that aside from the farms that the Gherardini's rented in Chianti, they also owned some properties. There was a mill on the Pesa river and a house in San Donato, but the best place of all was a farm known as San Silvestro. Acquired by Antonmaria's father Noldo in the early 1450s, it lay nestled in the soft hills of Poggio, just 10 miles north of Siena, and produced grapes and olives that were second to none.

Giocondo was determined to get his hands on that farm, and in the end, he did. On the very day of his wedding to Lisa, he dragged Gherardini to the Palazzo del Podestà, the Court of Justice, today known as the Bargello. There, they signed the deed of transfer, which has survived to this day. It identifies Giocondo's new wife as *uxor dicti Francisci*. And indeed, as of that day, 15-year old Lisa was "the wife of said Francesco."

It was this seasoned merchant whom Leonardo now faced in his affluent home on the Via della Stufa, just off the Church of San Lorenzo. Would Giocondo be willing to lobby the Signoria in his favor? Well, perhaps, but what could Leonardo offer in return? Perhaps Giocondo had already introduced the artist to his wife, the lovely Lisa, and the young children that populated the Giocondo household. As it happened, Lisa was in the flush of motherhood once more. She had presented Giocondo with her first child, a boy named Piero, in 1496, just one year after her wedding

day. This was followed by the birth of a daughter, Piera, but unfortunately the little girl only lived to age 2. Shortly after her death, in 1499, Lisa gave birth to another daughter, whom they named Camilla, possibly in memory of Giocondo's first wife. Another daughter, Marietta, was then born in 1500, followed by a boy named Andrea in 1502.[31]

If anything, the string of births would have reminded Giocondo that the life of a young mother was perilous. His first wife, Camilla, had died shortly after giving birth to his first son, Bartolomeo, so the boy would never know what his mother had looked like. Furthermore, there is every indication that Giocondo was deeply in love with Lisa—not an inevitable outcome in an age when most marriages were arranged. When in 1537 Giocondo's testament was drawn up, this somber document in Latin, not usually given to effusive declarations of love, was found to extol the "mutual love between said testator and his beloved wife Lisa" and the "exceptional quality" of her character."[32]

All this could explain why, shortly after the birth of Andrea, Giocondo may have decided to have a portrait made of his wife while she was still a quintessential Florentine beauty—with her luscious dark hair, her large brown eyes, fine cheekbones and full lips. And now, Giocondo was in a position to obtain such a portrait from one of the most renowned artists in Italy. That man was sitting right across from him, full of hope that Giocondo could intervene on his behalf for the *Anghiari* project. It was a moment Giocondo must have savored. In business, as in everything else in life, it is leverage that matters.

Of course, we have no hard documentation that this is how the *Mona Lisa* project came into being. But the circumstantial evidence is compelling. Not only do the Heidelberg marginalia clearly imply a link between the portrait of Lisa del Giocondo and the *Anghiari* fresco in the Great Council Hall; Vespucci even specified that "We will see what he's going to

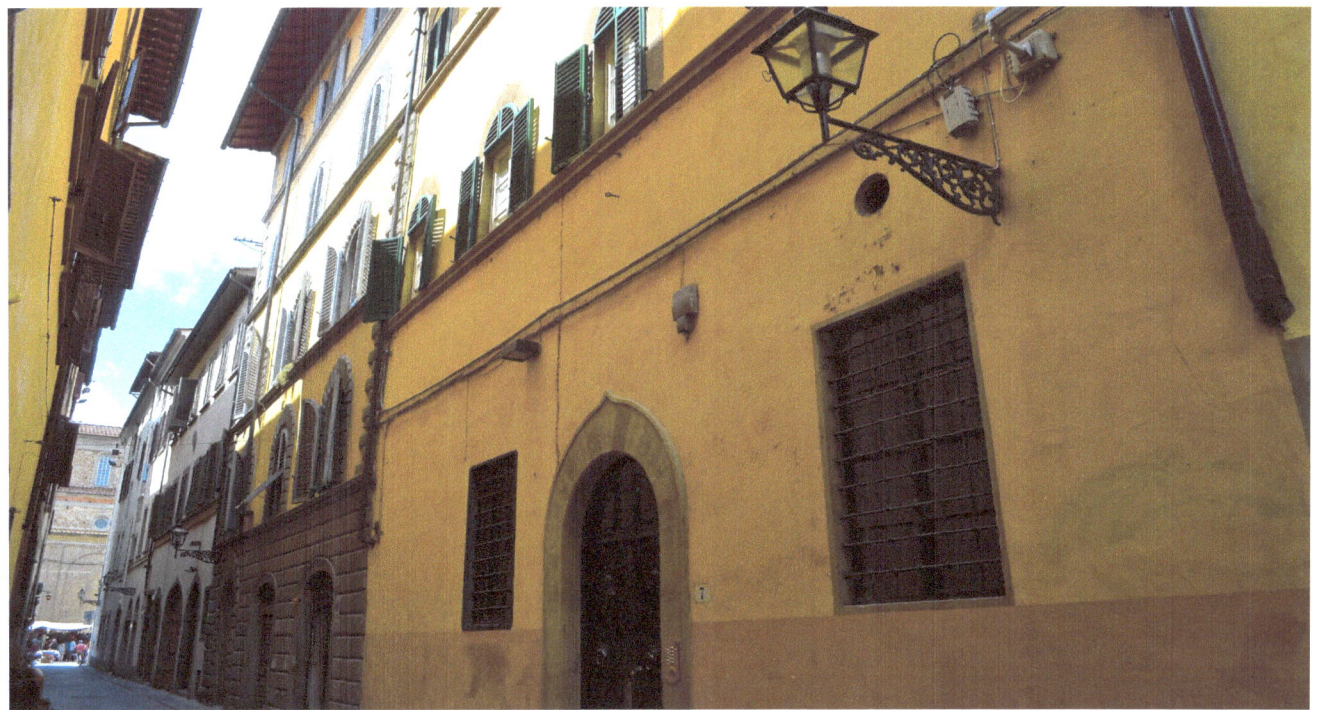

Fig. 12. The Via della Stufa in Florence.

do with the chamber of the great council, the thing for which *he has just come to terms with the gonfaloniere* (my italics; the original Latin text reads *Videbimus, quid faciet de aula magni consilii, de qua re convenit iam cum vexillifero.*)[34] The phrasing "for which he has *just* come to terms" suggests that Machiavelli and his secretary, Vespucci, were not only informed about the progress of these negotiations, but may also have played a role in securing a successful outcome. It is Machiavelli who served as the critical link: a close friend of Leonardo's (or at least as close as any of Leonardo's friends would get), he also served as secretary to the Chancery, charged to conduct much of the state business in that office. He was therefore in a position to know that of all the leading citizens of Florence, Francesco del Giocondo was the one who could lobby the Chancery on Leonardo's behalf.

If this assumption is correct, then it would explain a key mystery that we first identified in the Introduction: why would Leonardo agree to paint the portrait of a nobody, a Florentine housewife, when he previously had resisted the pressure to paint a portrait of Isabella d'Este, one of the most powerful women of his time? Why did he agree to do so when he was "tired of the brush," tired of painting the type of portraits he had made in Milan, and longed for new challenges, such as the creation of a massive fresco depicting a major battle? That prospect, of capturing the *terribilità* of human conflict—something he had just witnessed among Borgia's forces—must have fascinated him for the same reason that he had been attracted to the *Last Supper* theme. In the Milan fresco, he had purposefully discarded the centuries-old iconography of the Last Supper as the institution of the Eucharist, and instead picked an entirely different moment in the Gospels: when Christ declares that one of the men gathered at the table will betray him. That announcement literally sends shockwaves through the group of the twelve, producing shock, dismay, violent denial, and stunned silence.

That is what Leonardo was after: to depict the full scale of human emotions—the same idea that had animated his unfinished *Adoration of the Magi.* And now, here in his home town, was an opportunity to do what he had done in Milan: to create a monumental painting of the same visceral intensity, of a group of men caught in the throes of death. If he succeeded, as he knew he could, it would silence his critics and seal his reputation for all time. And if the price for securing such a work was the production of a small painting of a merchant's wife, then so be it; the tedium would be worth it.

Leonardo Paints Lisa del Giocondo

Characteristically, as soon as he accepted the work to paint the portrait of *la Gioconda* he sought for ways to make it more interesting, more challenging, just as he had experimented with his gesso and pigments for the *Last Supper*. He decided to use the form of support that he had just seen in Venice: a frame of stretched canvas, rather than wood panel. Most of Leonardo's patrons at the time, including the French King, would have rejected such a suggestion, simply because painting on wood panel was a time-honored and therefore trusted tradition. A Florentine cloth merchant like Francesco del Giocondo, who (as far as we know) had never commissioned a painting before, probably did not have such scruples. What's more, the subject—a portrait of his pretty wife—was an acceptable risk, in case the experiment went awry.

And so it came to pass. As Vespucci wrote, Leonardo was well underway on the *caput*, the "head" or face of Lisa in 1503, when the contract for *Anghiari* was signed. This makes sense if the fulfillment of the portrait contract was the condition for Giocondo to get moving and bring his influence to bear for the *Battle of Anghiari*. But then something extraordinary happened, and this is where, in my opinion, the *Mona Lisa* story takes a radical turn.

When in early 1503, Lisa sat for Leonardo in her home on the Via della Stufa, she was around 24 years old. It was nine years since she had been wed to her husband Francesco as a blushing 15-year old —not an unusual age for nuptials in the Middle Ages. As soon

as a young girl started her menses, she was considered fit for marriage. Significantly, Leonardo's mother, a young orphan named Caterina di Meo Lippi, was also 15 years old when she gave birth to him. More importantly, Lisa was only a few years older than Caterina when Leonardo was forcibly taken away from her, to be raised by his grandfather.[35] Why was Leonardo taken out of his mother's house? The answer is that Leonardo was the unintended outcome of a fling between a promising notary-apprentice called Ser Piero, then just 26, and Caterina, a comely farm maid, who lived with her brother Papo at their grandmother's decrepit farm in Vinci. Of course, marriage was out of the question; the social gulf between Ser Piero and Caterina was simply too wide. What's more, Ser Piero was probably betrothed at that time; just eight months after the birth of Leonardo, he married a young woman of his class, a daughter of a Florentine notary named Albiera di Giovanni Amadori.

Shortly after giving birth to Leonardo, Caterina married as well, possibly through the intervention of Ser Piero's family, who gave her a modest dowry. Caterina's new husband, Antonio, worked in a local kiln and went by the nickname *Accattabriga,* or 'troublemaker.' Thus, for the first five years of his life, Leonardo was raised by his natural mother, who lived with an irascible character who wasn't his father, while his true father lived with his young bride in Florence. We don't need Freud's lengthy exposé to understand that for most children this would lead to unhealthy consequences: an innate sense of insecurity, as well as a deep-seated attachment to the mother, untempered by the intervention of a strong and benign father figure.

Thus, as tax records from 1457 attest, when Leonardo was five years old he was taken away from his mother to be raised in his grandfather's house. Caterina had just given birth to a daughter named Maria, after another daughter named Piera had been born in 1454. We can imagine Accattabriga's reasoning: there were too many mouths to feed, room had to be made, and at the end of the day Leonardo was not his son. It probably broke Caterina's heart—and perhaps young Leonardo's as well. At a vulnerable age in his development as a child, he was separated from the only true source of love he had known all his life.

Did Leonardo's traumatic childhood instill a lifelong yearning for motherly love? And is this the reason why here, in the Via della Stufa, he was so struck by this woman, this young Florentine lady in the full bloom of motherhood? If so, then it would explain the unusual care and tenderness with which he captured her likeness, as evidenced by Vasari's rapt description of the portrait's beauty.

But this leads us to an important question: which *Mona Lisa* portrait did Vasari see? As we saw in the Introduction, by the time Vasari began his research for his book, the Louvre *Mona Lisa* had been in France for many years. So how could he have seen it? Or did he perhaps see another version?

The Earlier *Mona Lisa*

In the previous chapter, Salvatore Larusso and Andrea Natali argued that of all the high-quality versions of the *Mona Lisa* that could conceivably qualify as autographs, the Isleworth *Mona Lisa* stands out for the reasons cited. In subsequent chapters of this book, a number of other scholars and critics will add their voice to this attribution, each citing specific reasons why the Isleworth painting, rather than the Louvre version, is the original portrait that Leonardo began in early 1503. This is particularly evident when we compare the Isleworth painting to Vasari's detailed description of the portrait he saw in the late 1530s or early 1540s:

> "The eyes had their natural luster and moistness, and around them were the lashes and all those rosy and pearly tints that demand the greatest delicacy of execution. The eyebrows were

completely natural, growing thickly in one place and lightly in another and following the pores of the skin. The nose was finely painted, with rosy and delicate nostrils as in life. The mouth, joined to the flesh-tints of the face by the red of the lips, appeared to be living flesh, rather than paint. On looking closely at the pit of her throat, one could swear that the pulses were beating." [36]

It is difficult to imagine any version of the *Mona Lisa* that better matches this description than the Isleworth, particularly with regards to the delicate tints and treatment of the eyes, nose and lips that so impressed Giorgio Vasari. Even allowing for the many layers of varnish that have darkened the *Mona Lisa* in the Louvre, it is difficult to reconcile Vasari's description of a young woman with the Louvre's mature and matronly figure.

There are many other factors that support the authentication of the Isleworth portrait as the earlier version, each of which will be addressed in subsequent chapters. In the meantime, however, we must address two pivotal problems prompted by Vasari's other comment:

> "Leonardo undertook to execute, for Francesco del Giocondo, the portrait of *Monna Lisa*, his wife; and after toiling over it for four years, he left it unfinished; and the work is now in the collection of King Francis of France, at Fontainebleau." [37]

The first question is: if the Isleworth is indeed the earlier version, then what happened to it? How could Vasari describe the painting in such loving detail, while at the same time claiming that the portrait was in France? As far as we know, Vasari never traveled to France or any other country across the Alps. What's

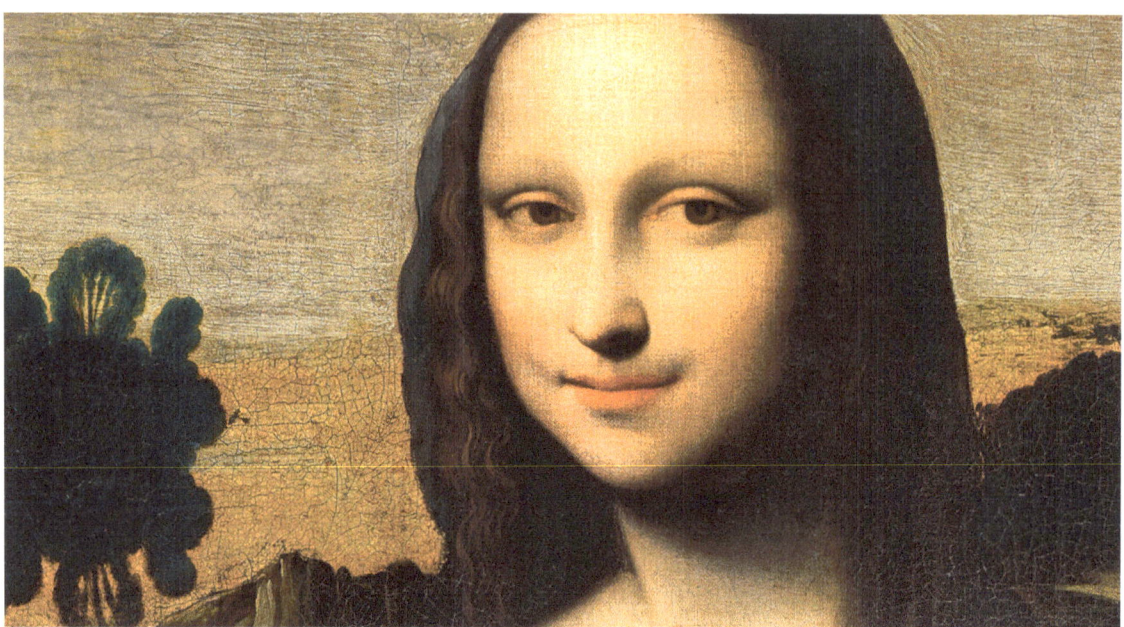

Fig. 13. Leonardo da Vinci, The Earlier *Mona Lisa*, ca. 1503-1506; detail of the face.

more, Vasari was five years old when Leonardo left for France, taking the *Mona Lisa* with him. So how could he have seen it?

And the second question is, why would he claim the painting was unfinished? Antonio de Beatis, who together with Luigi Cardinal of Aragon visited Leonardo in Amboise in 1517, saw the *Mona Lisa* and pronounced it "most perfect." As the eminent scholar Edward McCurdy wrote, "of all his pictures, (the Louvre *Mona Lisa*) is carried farthest in degree and finish." It is, quite simply, as polished as any da Vinci painting would ever get. So why would Vasari claim otherwise?

To answer to these questions, we once again have to base our assumptions on two sources: the Heidelberg document, which shows that by 1503 the portrait of Lisa del Giocondo was well underway; and Vasari's quote shown above, which emphatically states that Leonardo worked on the portrait "for four years" before leaving it unfinished. This would clearly indicate that after 1506 or 1507, Leonardo no longer worked on this portrait, and left it in the unfinished state we presumably see today.

When we consider these facts in the context of what we know of Leonardo's subsequent movements, this chronology suddenly begins to make sense. To understand that, we must return to the project that brought Leonardo in contact with the Giocondo family to begin with: the fresco of the *Battle of Anghiari* in the hall of the Great Council.

On October 24, 1503, Leonardo was officially presented with the keys to a large refectory in the monastery of Santa Maria Novella, which would serve as his studio for the *Anghiari* project. Attached to the monastery was a Dominican church, which in 1470 had been graced with a beautiful Renaissance façade designed by Alberti, and paid for by Giovanni Rucellai; it still faces the Piazza de Santa Maria Novella to this day. The refectory, known as the *Sala del Papa* (or "hall of the Pope"), was no longer in use, which suited Leonardo's needs; he wanted a very large space to accommodate the full-size cartoon, which if all the pieces were joined together, probably measured around 55 feet wide and 22 feet high –the dimensions of the future fresco itself.

Several months later, a young artist named Raffaello Sanzio decided to leave his native Urbino to absorb the latest artistic developments in Florence.

Up to this point, Raphael had been apprenticed in the workshop of Pietro Perugino, who like Leonardo had begun his career under the tutelage of Verrocchio. Vasari claims that when Raphael arrived in the city, he first learned of Leonardo's fame from a group of workmen talking about the large cartoon for the *Battle of Anghiari*. This piqued Raphael's interest, and a few months later he was admitted to Leonardo's *bottega* as one of his apprentices. Significantly, perhaps, Raphael took rooms in the Taddei palazzo, which faced the Giocondo residences on the Via della Stufa.[40]

It was in Leonardo's studio that he saw the *Mona Lisa* as a work in progress. It made an immediate impact. Captivated by the originality of the composition, he grabbed a pencil and drew a sketch of the portrait, which closely matches the Earlier version, as we will see described in greater detail later in this book. It is, however, important to make a few observations at this point.

Looking at this drawing, we instantly see things that are familiar—and things that are not. The *trois-quart* position of the sitter is certainly familiar, based on the portraits of Gallerani and Crivelli (also known as *La belle ferronnière*). So is the simple treatment of the gown she is wearing, or the absence of any ornament save for a headband around her forehead, which stands in sharp contrast to the court portraits painted in Milan by Lombard artists. The hands are folded below the lady's chest—a posture that first appeared in Leonardo's metal point study of hands at Windsor. The lady's gaze, moreover, is pointed directly at us; not unlike Crivelli's intent gaze, that is, although Crivelli's look seems to graze just off our eye-line to focus onto an object above our right. In all these aspects, therefore, the *Mona Lisa* that Raphael saw in early 1504 is a logical development of Leonardo's portraits that preceded her in Milan.

In other respects, however, the painting explores new ground. The most obvious feature is the fact that the lady is not depicted against a dark background,

but is placed on a balcony of some sort, flanked by pillars that separate her from the deep vista of a Tuscan landscape beyond. This is a North European motif, and noticeably different from Leonardo's use of landscape in his early Madonna paintings, as well as the *Virgin of the Rocks* and the *Last Supper*. Here, the primary setting is that of an interior, whether natural or man-made, in which windows give out to a glimpse of the landscape beyond. In the *Mona Lisa* observed by Raphael, by contrast, it is the sitter herself who determines the primary space; the balcony, framed by columns, merely serves as a screen, a device to negotiate the transition between her space and the vista beyond. The immediate precedent for such a dramatic, monumental use of the sitter is the *Madonna of the Yarnwinder*, which was probably observed by our vicar, Pietro da Novellara, in Leonardo's studio in 1501. In fact, there is some similarity between the landscape in the Buccleuch version of the *Yarnwinder*

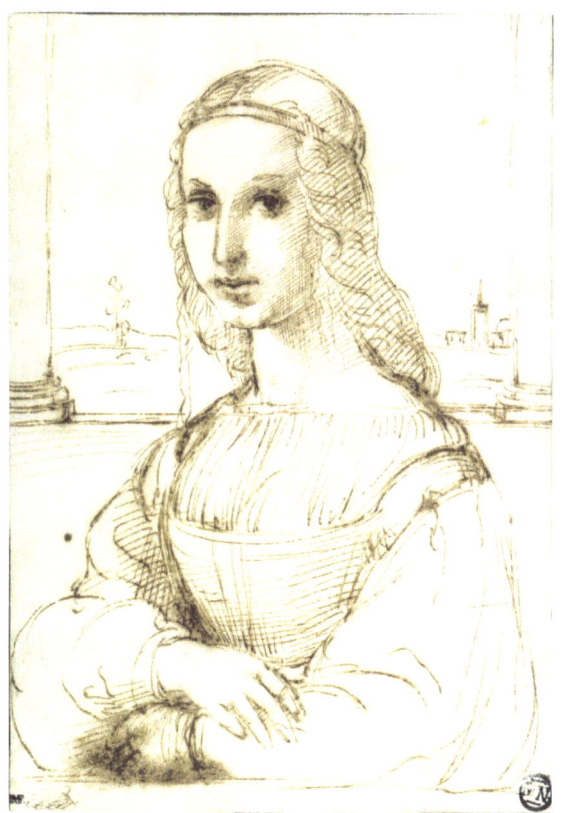

Fig. 14. Raphael, *Portrait of a Young Woman*, 1504.

and the Raphael drawing. Both are relatively flat and compressed, with little suggestion of depth, and with the horizon positioned well below the gaze of the sitter. In these compositions, the purpose of the landscape is to merely suggest a sense of scale, so as to emphasize the monumentality of the principal figure. That would change, of course—both in the second version of *Madonna of the Yarnwinder* and the second version of the *Mona Lisa*. But it supports the idea that this *Mona Lisa* drawing is a key link, heretofore missing, between Leonardo's art of the early 1500s and that of his works later in the decade.

The other insight is that what Raphael saw and sketched in 1504 *cannot*, by any measure, be the same *Mona Lisa* portrait that hangs in the Louvre today. The woman who looks so intently at us in the drawing is obviously much younger, with the slightly hesitant look of that age; we would be hard-pressed to see any resemblance between her and the matronly, self-confident figure in the Louvre.

What's more, the two prominent pillars in the drawing are missing in the Louvre panel, save for a small fragment of their bases. It was long assumed that the Louvre portrait once featured two fully developed pillars as well, before being trimmed at some point, but this theory, as explained in detail in the previous chapter, was roundly rejected by a detailed spectro-analysis of the panel.

Most importantly, the dramatic mountainous background of the Louvre *Mona Lisa* is nowhere in sight. That this is not the result of impatience or indifference on Raphael's part—as has sometimes been suggested—is clearly shown by Raphael's *Lady with a Unicorn,* painted a year later, and the *Portrait of Maddalena Doni,* completed between 1506 and 1507. In almost every respect, these portraits are a tribute to the *Mona Lisa* that Raphael observed in Leonardo's studio in 1504. The tepid, foreshortened landscape behind Maddalena is almost a replica of Raphael's sketch, down to the inclusion of a solitary tree to the

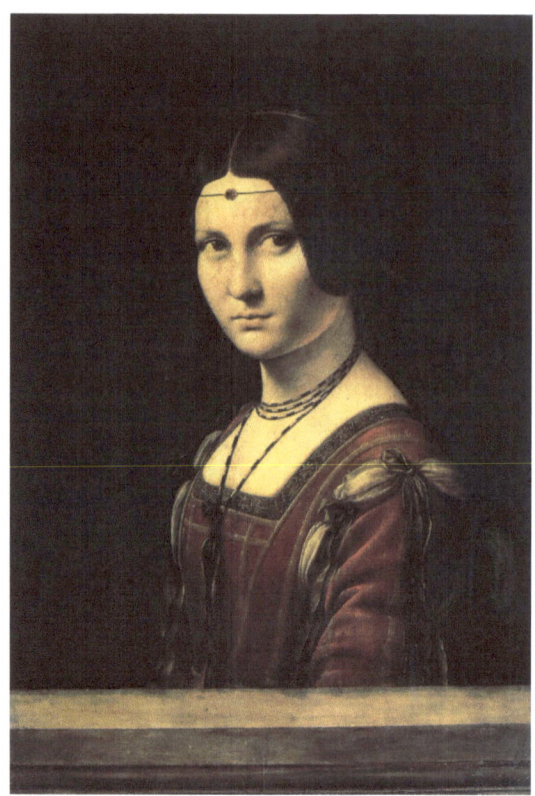

Fig. 15. Leonardo da Vinci, *La belle ferronnière*, ca. 1490.

left.

While this drawing does not match the Louvre *Mona Lisa*, it does resemble the Isleworth *Mona Lisa*—or the Earlier *Mona Lisa*—to an astonishing degree. Both versions depict a young woman in the prime of her beauty. Both feature a highly compressed landscape with few details. And most importantly, in both works the young lady is flanked by columns that screen her from the vista beyond.

Of course, there are also discrepancies: in Raphael's drawing the left hand is left indistinct, so that the right hand does not as yet rest on the left, as in the Earlier version. The prominent structure in the distance at left does not appear in the Earlier version either. Perhaps these details were still being developed when Raphael sketched the portrait, and modified at a later stage—which is entirely plausible, given Leonardo's deliberate style of working.

Taken together, this evidence would clearly indicate that what Raphael saw in Leonardo's studio in 1504 was the gestation of the Earlier *Mona Lisa*, rather

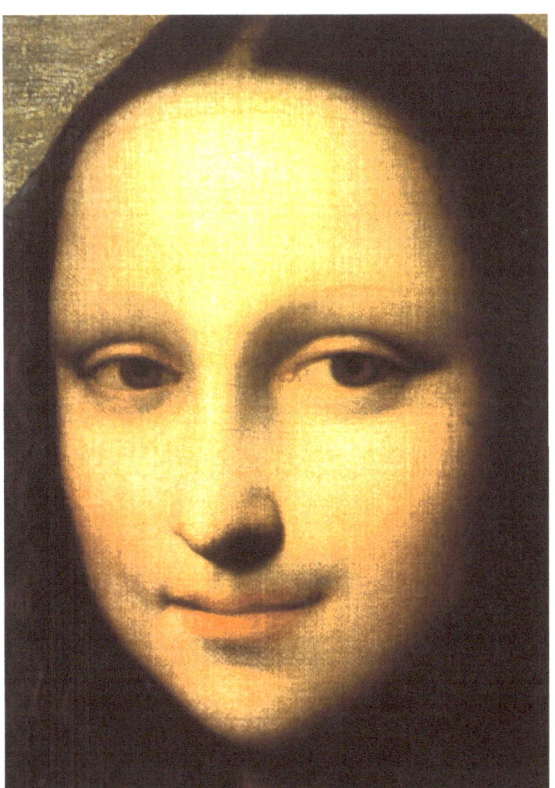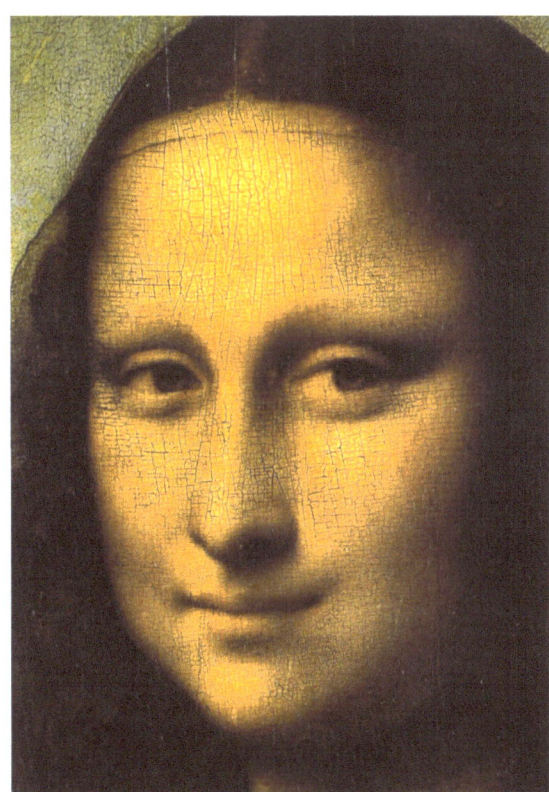

Fig. 16. Young vs. Old: detail of the Earlier *Mona Lisa* (left) and the Louvre *Mona Lisa* (right).

than the portrait in the Louvre.

But what happened with this Earlier version after 1504? To answer that question, we have to return to the project that precipitated the *Mona Lisa* portrait to begin with: the fresco of the *Battle of Anghiari*.

The Failure of the *Battle of Anghiari*

From 1504 onwards, Leonardo was wholly consumed by work on the *Anghiari* fresco, his largest and most prestigious civic commission to date. He carefully studied a detailed description of the battle, composed by the Dominican humanist Leonardo di Piero Dati in the early 1400s. Written as a Latin poem entitled *Trophaeum Anglaricum* ("Victory at Anghiari"), the story had, as we saw, been translated into Italian by Agostino Vespucci, since Leonardo's grasp of Latin was rudimentary. [41]

Soon thereafter, the first sketches began to appear. As revealed in the drawings now in the Accademia in Venice, Leonardo very early gravitated to the idea of a violent clash of cavalry at the peak of the fighting. "If

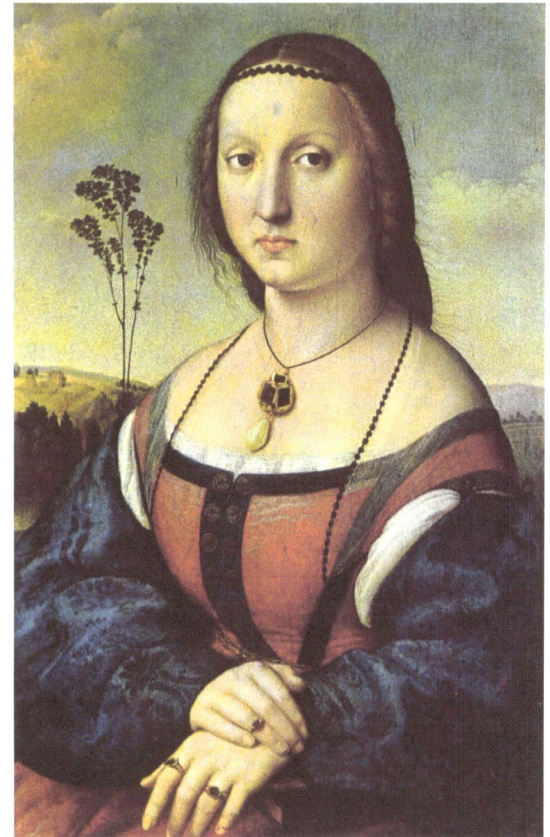

Fig. 17. Raphael, *Portrait of Maddalena Doni*, 1506-1507.

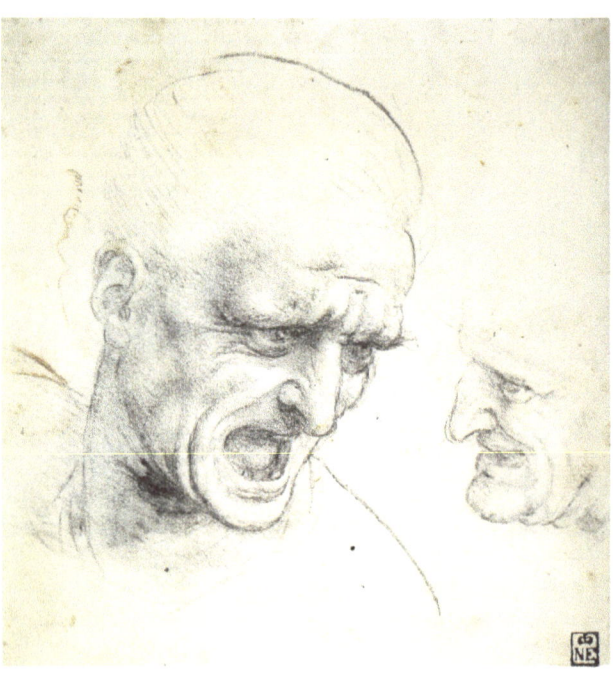

Fig. 18. Leonardo da Vinci, *Study for the Battle of Anghiari*,
ca. 1504-1505.

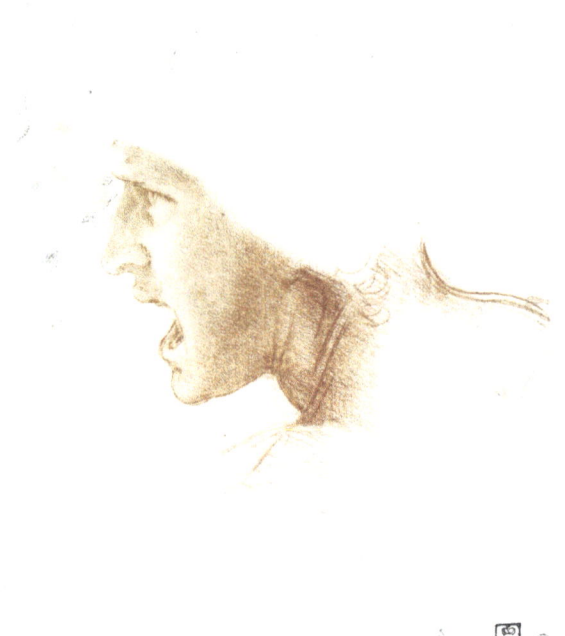

Fig. 19. Leonardo da Vinci, *Study for the Battle of Anghiari*,
ca. 1504-1505.

you, poet, were to portray a bloody battle, you would
write about the dark and murky air amid the smoke
of fearful and deadly engines of war," he wrote in his
Treatise, perhaps with Dati's poem in mind; "it would
be a long and tedious thing in poetry to portray all the
movements of the participants in such a war… but the
painter can display this in an instant."[42] That moment
slowly crystallized into the ultimate moment of
victory: the battle for the standard. In the final sketch,
we see a dense tangle of four mounted officers slashing
at each other, while infantry casualties cower below
the horses' hooves. With this composition established,
he then moved to close-ups of individual combatants,
as shown in the studies now in the Szépművészeti
Múzeum in Budapest.

Alas, the distractions that vied for his attention
continued to pile up. The indefatigable Isabella d'Este
sent a letter, reminding him that she hoped "we can
get from you what we have so much desired, which
is something from your hand." She noted his promise
to turn the charcoal drawing he had made of her "into
color," but since this would now be unlikely, she

offered him to "keep your good faith by a portrait
of Jesus as a young man, of about twelve years old,
at the age when he disputed in the Temple." What
the marchioness was particularly looking for, she
confessed, was "that sweetness and soft ethereal
charm, which is the peculiar excellence of your art."[44]
The letter was delivered by her agent, the merchant
Angelo del Tovaglia. The answer, dutifully relayed
back to Isabella, was a "perhaps." As Tovaglia wrote
in his response, he "may do it when he can spare the
time from the project he has begun for the Signoria."
Translated into Leonardonese, that meant 'no'.

Then came a request from the Signoria to serve on
an *ad hoc* committee that would decide where to place
the towering sculpture of *David,* just completed by
Michelangelo Buonarotti. Michelangelo was then just
28 years, a quarter-century younger than Leonardo,
and already considered the *Wunderkind* of the new
century. Nowhere is the contrast between the old
and the new made more vivid than in a comparison
between the strong, purposeful pose of Michelangelo's
sculpture and the *David* by Verrocchio, for which

Leonardo may have posed as a model. A strong sense of rivalry between Michelangelo and Leonardo was therefore inevitable; there are anecdotes, never truly verified, of the two exchanging sharp words in public. The committee, which included Sandro Botticelli, Filippino Lippi, Pietro Perugino, and Andrea della Robbia, voted to put Michelangelo's *David* in a place of honor, right next to the entrance of the Palazzo della Signoria (where a copy of the statue still stands today). Leonardo dissented; he suggested that it should be placed deep in the Loggia dei Lanzi, "lest it interfere with state ceremonies"—that is, well away from the public view. His opinion was ignored.

But the Signoria had a surprise in store. According to Vasari, *gonfaloniere* Soderini, who considered Michelangelo something of a protégé, had come up with the brilliant idea to commission the artist to create a battle fresco in the *same* Grand Council Hall where Leonardo was working on his *Battle of Anghiari*. By the summer of 1504 they had struck a deal with Michelangelo for the fresco, which was supposed to depict another great victory from Florence's past, the *Battle of Cascina*. As some have suggested,

Michelangelo was to create this painting right opposite the wall designated for the *Battle of Anghiari*. Leonardo was not amused—certainly not when it transpired that Michelangelo's fee was higher than his own, which was a mere 150 florins, doled out at a rate of 15 florins a month.

Then, on July 9, Leonardo's father, Ser Pietro, passed away. The event merits a brief mention on a page in the Codex Atlanticus, which otherwise lists various expenses for his household: "On Wednesday at the 7th hour Ser Piero da Vinci died, on the 9th day of July 1504." Ser Piero was 78. Elsewhere, Leonardo wrote that he left "ten sons and two daughters," including himself in that tally, even though he was his father's illegitimate son. That illegitimacy now came back to haunt him. Either Ser Piero had deliberately omitted Leonardo from his will, or his sons colluded to ensure that Leonardo would not receive his share; the record is not clear. But Leonardo was not to receive a single cent from his father's inheritance.

In response, Leonardo's uncle Francesco, with whom he always felt close, vowed to make amends. Childless himself, Francesco changed his will to

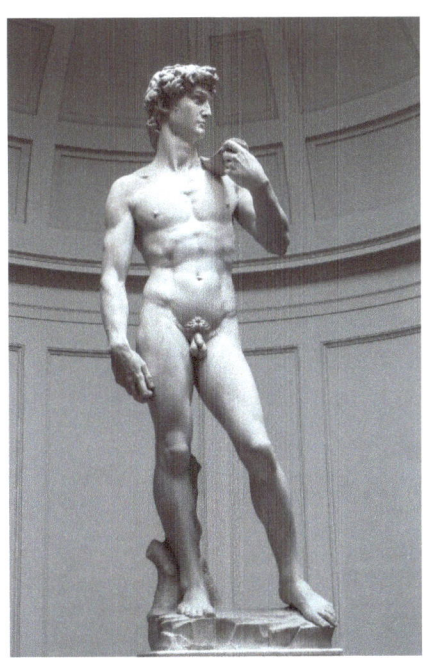

Fig. 20. Michelangelo Buonarotti, *David*, ca. 1501-1504.

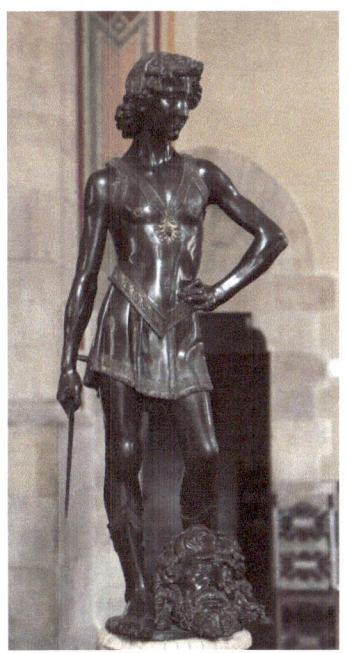

Fig. 21. Verrocchio, *David,* ca. 1473-1475.

ensure that all of his properties around Vinci would be bequeathed to his nephew Leonardo, exclusively. Charles Nicholl cites a Tuscan historian named Renzo Cianchi, who suggests that this property would have been located in Forra di Serravalle, some 4 miles east of Vinci.

As it happened, Leonardo was in Vinci—perhaps to meet with his uncle—when a devastating rainstorm swept over Tuscany. Among others, the storm destroyed the trenches that had been dug at the start of the Arno diversion project, which was now proceeding under the supervision of a professional engineer named maestro Colombino. Gusts of rain flooded the plain and quickly filled the ditches that had been so painstakingly dug over the preceding two months. Worse, eighty workers drowned. As soon as word of the disaster reached Florence, work was suspended. Thus ended another unfulfilled dream from the mind of Leonardo da Vinci, this time at the cost of some "seven thousand ducats."[45]

Two months later, in February 1505, Leonardo completed the massive *Anghiari* cartoon and was ready to transfer it to the wall of the Grand Council Hall. An ingenious scaffold enabled him to move up and down across the vast expanse of the wall. But on June 6, 1505, when the wall had been prepped and part of the cartoon had already been transferred, disaster struck once more. Another fierce spring storm hit Florence. As Leonardo wrote, "the cartoon came loose," "water spilled from its jug," and "rain poured until nightfall." But worse was to come.

Leonardo couldn't help but indulge in his fascination with experimental pigments. As in the case of the *Last Supper*, the quick-drying tempera technique didn't suit him; he wanted to move slowly, deliberately, applying layer upon layer, so as to achieve the rich spatial and atmospheric effects of his oil paintings. To do so, he needed an undercoat that could absorb multiple layers of oil paint, rather than tempera. According to the anonymous author known

as Anonimo Gaddiano, Leonardo created a concoction based on Pliny the Elder's book *Natural History,* which recommended the use of Greek pitch to seal the plaster wall. But the experiment didn't work; the wall refused to absorb the pigments and caused the paint to drip and run. Paolo Giovo believed that the undercoat was "resistant to paints mixed with walnut oil." As with the *Last Supper*, the fresco began to deteriorate almost as soon as Leonardo's brush left it.[46]

Desperate to stem the running paint, Leonardo called for braziers to be hung in front of the painting, hoping that this would make the fresh paint dry more quickly. Alas, all that the heat accomplished was to make the paint run even more. No matter how hard he struggled to save his grand vision, the painting continued to decay. By early 1506, Leonardo recognized that the fresco that was to be the crowning achievement of his career was ruined.

And yet, what remained of this work would still attract a steady stream of artists and visitors for a half-century to come. As Paolo Giovio wrote, "our sorrow for the unforeseen damage seems only to have wondrously increased the fascination of the unfinished work." Vasari was even more effusive, praising "the inventiveness of Leonardo's design of the soldiers' uniforms, which he sketched in all their variety, or the crests of the helmets and other ornaments, not to mention the incredible skill he demonstrated in the shape and features of the horses."

Several copies were made, including an oil painting known as the *Tavola Doria*, which reveals that the core of the painting, the battle for the standard, was already far advanced, even though the standard itself—the banner of the Milanese army—is missing; only the pole is visible.[47] We will never really know what the painting looked like, because between 1555 and 1572, the hall was substantially enlarged, and the unfinished paintings of both Leonardo and Michelangelo were lost. It was Vasari himself who in 1563 overpainted Leonardo's fresco with a mural

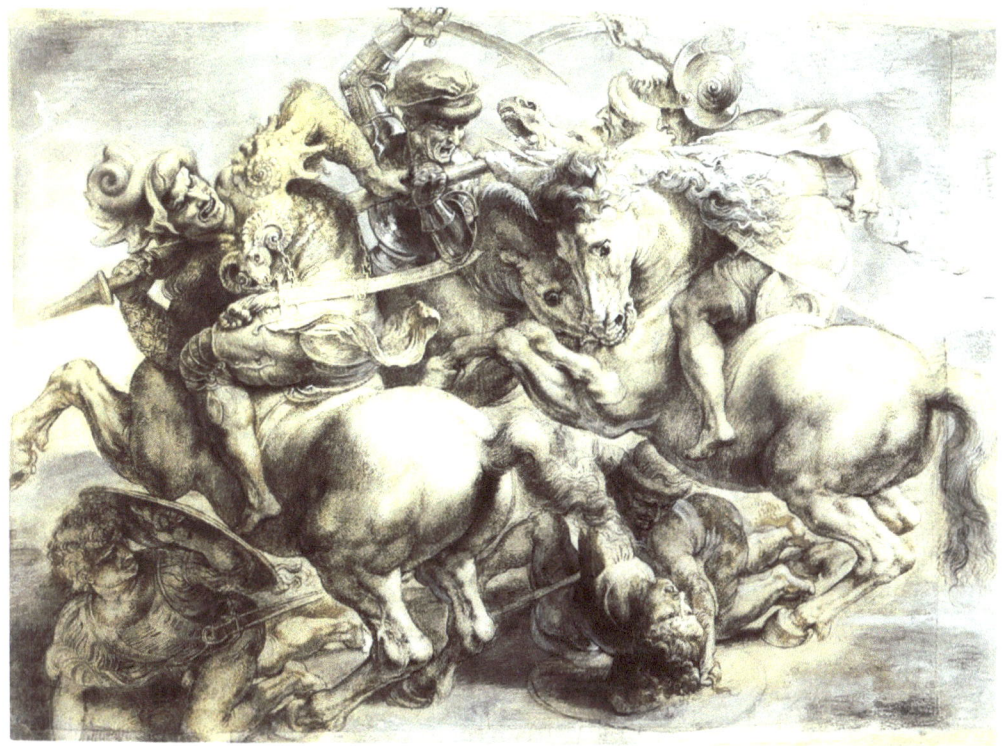

Fig. 22. Leonardo da Vinci, *Battle of Anghiari*, ca. 1505. Copy by Peter Paul Rubens, ca. 1603.

of his own, entitled *The Battle of Marciano in Val di Chiana.* A persistent modern theory claims that Vasari might have found a way of "preserving" Leonardo's masterpiece underneath his own, admittedly mediocre, work of art. Precisely how Vasari could have accomplished that is not known. Using NASA-developed surface-penetrating radar, followed by an examination of samples taken from underneath the Vasari fresco, the Italian scholar Maurizio Seracini announced in March of 2012 the discovery of a so-called "curtain wall," which would have left a gap of 1 to 3 centimeters. Behind this wall, Seracini claimed to have found pigment fragments that are consistent with certain ochre-brown and black base paints in the *Mona Lisa* and the *John the Baptist*.[48] This is where the investigation ended; after Seracini's methods came under attack, the Italian government forbade any further invasive techniques that could destroy Vasari's fresco. Perhaps some non-invasive techniques will be developed in the future to determine whether remnants of Leonardo's masterpiece still exist.

In the meantime, Leonardo had little to look forward to but the wrath of the Signoria, the *gonfaloniere* Soderini, and by extension Giocondo himself, whose recommendation the city fathers had presumably accepted against their better judgment. Fortunately, this is when the place of his erstwhile glory, Milan, came to his rescue. As it happened, Leonardo and his Milanese collaborator, Ambrogio de Predis, were still owed payments for their work on the second version of the *Virgin of the Rocks*, which de Predis had delivered to the Confraternity of the Immaculate Conception in 1502. Frustrated in his attempt to recover the final payment, De Predis lodged a complaint with the King of France (and nominal ruler of Milan), Louis XII. The king ordered a hearing, but the judge found against the artists; the painting, or so the Confraternity claimed, was still "unfinished." Translated properly, this meant that the Confraternity believed the painting was more Ambrogio than Leonardo; the magic touch of the master, or so it was felt, was clearly missing. Ergo, Leonardo had to return

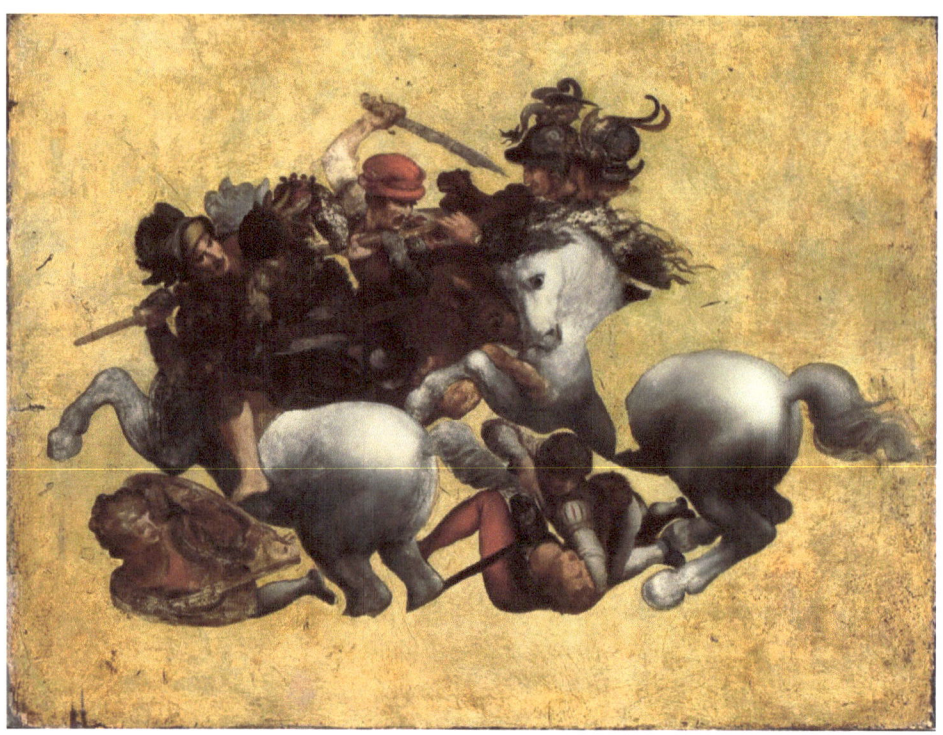

Fig. 23. Leonardo da Vinci, *Battle of Anghiari*, ca. 1505. Anonymous copy known as the *Tavola Doria*, 16th century.

to Milan and do whatever it took to see the client satisfied, and himself and his partner paid.

Of course, it wasn't quite as easy as that. Leonardo was still under contract to the Signoria, and they were not about to let him leave the city before he finished the *Anghiari* fresco. Eventually, Leonardo had to prevail on the French governor of Milan, Charles d'Amboise, to intervene on his behalf. Pressed by the French, Florence grudgingly issued Leonardo a travel permit on May 30, 1506, with the understanding that the furlough would not exceed three months, and that Leonardo would have to leave a deposit of 150 florins to guarantee his return. If he failed to do so, he would forfeit the escrow and—it was left unsaid—incur the enmity of the Republic of Florence.

In my opinion, this is the moment when Leonardo recognized the urgency of delivering the still unfinished *Mona Lisa* to Francesco del Giocondo. As we saw, Giocondo was an exceedingly shrewd businessman, who probably was well aware of what was transpiring between the Signoria and the French court. If that assumption is correct, he must have

suspected, given Leonardo's penchant for leaving things unfinished, that once the artist was allowed to leave for Milan he was not likely to return. Whether it was Giocondo who called in the debt, or whether Leonardo saw the need to fulfill his pledge before his departure, is not known. What we do know is that, four years after Leonardo received the commission, he stopped work on the portrait and left it unfinished. That is Vasari's claim, and the chronology now makes perfect sense. After he begun the work in late 1502 or early 1503, Leonardo delivered the work to Giocondo in the late Spring of 1506, just before his departure for Milan.

That also explains why the portrait was unfinished, as the Earlier *Mona Lisa* most certainly is, because in the intervening years Leonardo had become too absorbed in the *Anghiari* project. The landscape behind the lady, with its rather unconvincing depiction of rock formations, were probably painted by one of his assistants, Ferrando Spagnolo, 'Ferrando the Spaniard', who previously worked on the first version of the *Madonna of the Yarnwinder*.[49] This sequence of events is supported by ultraviolet scans of the Earlier *Mona Lisa*, which show that the background areas to the left and the right of the face fluoresce less than the adjacent paint values, thus indicating a clear discrepancy in the execution of the figure and the background. Other than these modest additions, the space beyond shows little more than an ochre underpainting, without any additional features. Similarly, the sky above never moved beyond its preparatory layer of calcite, lead white, and a pale powdered cobalt known as *smalt*. Simply put, Leonardo was in a rush to satisfy his client, and to remove the possibility of any legal action that could prevent him from leaving Florence.

The Earlier Mona Lisa after 1506

After Leonardo left for Milan—prompting an extended tug-of-war between the Signoria and the French governor in Milan, who wanted him to stay in the duchy permanently —the Earlier *Mona Lisa* was most likely hung in the Giocondo home on the Via della Stufa, and there it would have remained for the next 30-odd years. Leonardo, meanwhile, divided his time between Milan, Florence and Vinci until he moved to Rome in 1513, and on to Amboise, France in 1516.

In the meantime, he had begun a second version of the *Mona Lisa*, for reasons we shall examine in a subsequent chapter. Two of Leonardo's assistants accompanied him to Amboise: Francesco Melzi, a young nobleman, and Leonardo longtime companion Salaì. But at some time in 1517, Salaì moved back to Milan. The most likely reason is that Leonardo had left many of his unsold paintings—copies of his original works, mostly—in a house on his vineyard property in Milan, since he could only take a few works with him across the Alps to France. Perhaps he was hoping to sell these works in the near future, on the Italian market, where his name was much better known than among buyers in France. Salaì was obviously the best man to facilitate such sales, since many of these copies

were by his hand. What's more, it must have grated on Salaì that once at the French court, Melzi—who after all was a young aristocrat—was welcomed as "an Italian gentleman living with master Leonardo" and given a grant of 400 écus, whereas Salaì, now 40 years old, was identified as Leonardo's "servant" who merited a salary of only 100 écus. A new book, *The Da Vinci Legacy,* argues that there was a subsequent falling out between Leonardo and Salaì, which explains why Leonardo wrote Salaì out of his will, even though Salaì had served Leonardo faithfully for nearly three decades.[50]

Then, on May 2, 1519 Leonardo died in Amboise. Melzi was designated as Leonardo's executor, and received all of Leonardo's intellectual property, with the exception of the three paintings that Leonardo had brought to France: the *St Anne*, the *John the Baptist*, and the second version of the *Mona Lisa*. These were bequeathed to the royal collection of his host, King François, which is how the paintings eventually wound up in the collection of the Louvre Museum. Pleased with this gift, the king invited Melzi to remain at the manor house, supported by a generous pension, so that he could continue his work of organizing Leonardo's notebooks. Not until 1520 or 1521 did Melzi finally decide to return to Italy.

Three years later, on January 15, 1524, Salaì married a Milanese lady, Bianca Coldiroli d'Annono. The marriage was not destined to last: seven months later Salaì became involved in a duel and was killed with a crossbow. An inventory of his estate, discovered in 1990 in the State Archives of Milan, lists numerous paintings—proof positive of the valuable cache of art that Leonardo left in his care in 1517.[51] Among these is an intriguing reference to a painting called *La Honda*. Some scholars have argued that this is evidence that the Louvre *Mona Lisa*—*La Gioconda* in Italian—was actually in Salaì's possession at that time. They cite the high valuation of the work—505 lire—as evidence that the portrait must have been an autograph by Leonardo. In 2003, the chief curator of the Louvre paintings department, Cécile Scailliérez, dismissed that theory, arguing that there is no way that the Louvre *Mona Lisa* could have somehow made its way back from Amboise to Salai's art collection in Milan.[52] It is more likely that this entry is referring to the Prado *Mona Lisa*, which may have been executed by Salaì in Rome while Leonardo was painting the Louvre portrait, as we will see in a later chapter. This is further corroborated by the presence of a *Saint Anne* in the inventory, also valued at 505 lire, which is most likely Salaì's or Melzi's copy of Leonardo's *Saint Anne*, now in the collection of the Hammer Museum, but on loan to the Getty Museum in Los Angeles.

Fourteen years later, in June of 1538, Francesco del Giocondo died in Florence, just a year after writing his will. It is likely that the young Giorgio Vasari, then just 27 years old, attended the funeral— a lavish event attended by all the notables in the city. Vasari had been apprenticed at the studio of Andrea del Sarto, a Florentine artist who himself had eagerly absorbed the lessons of Leonardo's *Battle of Anghiari*. "When Andrea had any time to himself, particularly on feast-days," Vasari would later write, "he would spend the whole day in company with other young men, drawing" from the fresco in the Hall of the Five Hundred. The young Vasari had already spent time in Rome and soon after his return became a protégé of the new authoritarian Medici regime led by Duke Cosimo I.

It is generally believed that Vasari began his research for his book *Lives of the Artists* in the late 1530s, when many artists and eyewitnesses of the works he planned to write about were still alive. This makes it very plausible that he sat down with Lisa del Giocondo, the widow of Francesco del Giocondo and the model for the *Mona Lisa*, who was still living in the family house on the Via della Stufa. This, I believe, is the moment when Vasari saw the Earlier version, and documented it for his future book. We should

remember that at the time, the second version—the Louvre portrait—had already been in France for two decades, in King François's new royal palace at Fontainebleau. There is therefore no way that Vasari could have arrived at his famous description of the *Mona Lisa*, other than by seeing the Earlier version at the Giocondo home.

Soon thereafter, Lisa moved to the convent of Sant'Orsola in Florence, where her youngest daughter, Suor Ludovica, lived as a nun.[53] It is here, in this monastery, that the lady known as *Monna Lisa* died on July 15, 1542.

Meanwhile, Vasari continued to travel widely, not only for commissions but also to research his book, visiting all the locations where prominent works—such as frescoes—were still on display. In his book, hardly a reference is made to a painting or a sculpture without a detailed description of its location; indeed, this is what makes the book so valuable for art historians. Among others, Vasari visited Milan, where he saw certain drawings by Bramantino, as well as the tomb of Gaston de Foix in the Santa Marta, designed by Agosto Milanese.[54] While in Milan, he could have been in touch with representatives and royal purveyors of the French king, since the city was still under French rule at the time. It is therefore plausible that during these conversations, Vasari learned that three of Leonardo's principal works—the *St Anne,* the *St John the Baptist* and the *Mona Lisa*—were now in the royal collection in France. Another possible source for this information is Vasari's friend, the sculptor Giovanni Francesco Rustici. Though mostly forgotten today, Rustici was considered one of the leading sculptors of his time. Like Leonardo, he had been apprenticed to the workshop of Verrocchio, and later shared lodgings with Leonardo while working on bronze figures for Florence's Baptistery. Not surprisingly, several of Rustici's terracotta sculptures of warriors betray a strong influence of Leonardo's *Battle of Anghiari*.[55] In 1528, when the city was briefly controlled by anti-

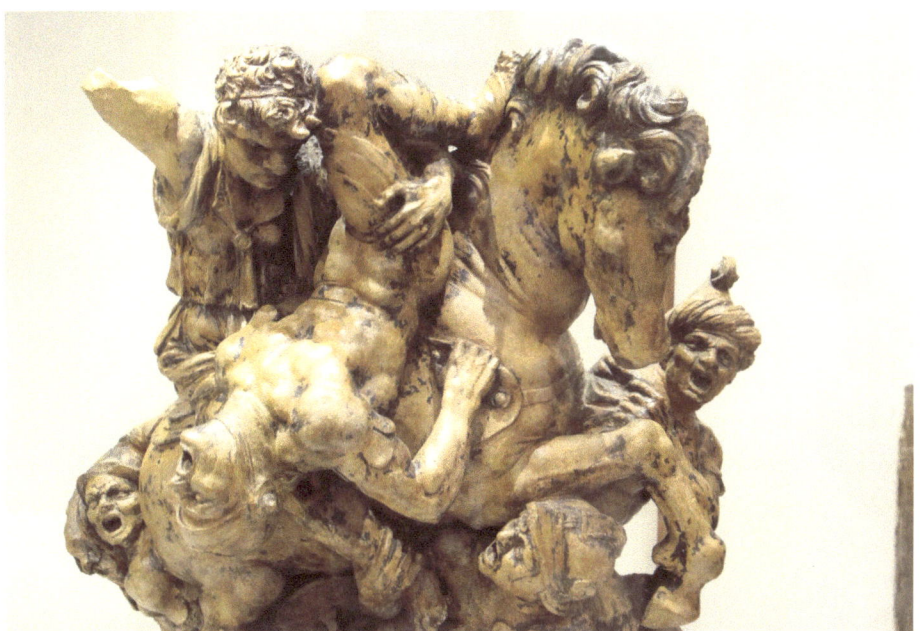

Fig. 24. Giovanni Francesco Rustici, *Battle Scene*, early 16th century.

Medici forces, Rustici accepted an offer from the French King Francois I to move to France on a royal pension, just as Leonardo had done a decade earlier. As a result, Rustici (who also merits a chapter in *Lives of the Artists*) must have been a valuable source of information for Vasari, particularly during his subsequent stay in France.

The news that the portrait of the *Mona Lisa* was now in France would not have come as a surprise to Vasari. After the death of a prominent personage, it was common for his spouse or heirs to sell any valuable items in his possession, since their principal source of income had now come to an end. What's more, the keen interest of the royal French court in all things Leonardo was well known. For Vasari, then, it was not unreasonable to think that Lisa must have sold the painting to representatives or intermediaries of the French governor in Milan, and that the painting thus found its way to France—as many other Italian works did. But as we know, that is not what happened.

Vasari's book, properly known as *Lives of the Most Excellent Italian Painters, Sculptors, and Architects, from Cimabue to Our Times*, was first published in

1550 by the Florentine publisher Lorenzo Torrentino. It has served ever since as the primary source about Leonardo's life and work that continues to be cited and parsed in modern scholarship today, even though many historians take issue with Vasari's occasional penchant for gossip and trivial anecdotes.

In the meantime, the silk business founded by Francesco del Giocondo was continued by his sons and grandsons. But in 1564, the firm suffered a devastating collapse. This was largely due to the dealings of Guasparri del Giocondo, Francesco's grandson, who was known around town as a heavy gambler. The repercussions of this bankruptcy reverberated throughout the silk and wool trade in the city, affecting scores of vendors, agents and employees. Major holdings of the family, including valuable artifacts and paintings, were put up for auction. If the Earlier version was still in the collection of the family at the time, it is very likely that portrait was sold to an unknown Italian bidder in order to satisfy Giocondo's creditors.

From that point on, the canvas began its long journey that would ultimately take it to an English

nobleman's manor in Somerset in the 18th century, and
its discovery by Hugh Blaker in 1913. Long before,
however, it must have become common knowledge
that Leonardo had produced two versions of the *Mona
Lisa*, just as he had made multiple versions of other
paintings. Some twenty years after the Giocondo
bankruptcy, the Italian artist and author Gian Paolo
Lomazzo wrote a treatise that explicitly refers to *two*
paintings by Leonardo: one entitled *La Gioconda*, and
one known as the *Mona Lisa*, as we will see in a later
chapter. As far as we know, this is the first 16th century
reference to Leonardo's two autograph versions of the
Mona Lisa portrait.[56]

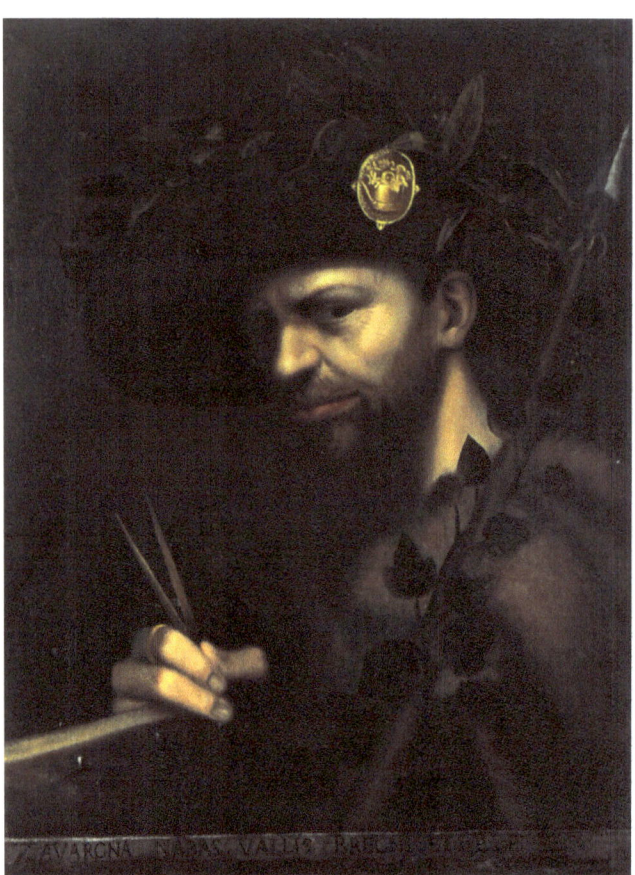

Fig. 25. Paolo Giovanni Lomazzo, *Self-Portrait*, ca. 1565.

References

[1] That such was common in Italy is attested by the agreement that the Fraternity of Santa Maria della Misericordia contracted with Piero della Francesca on July 11, 1445, for a panel for their church. The contract specified that the painting should be executed "with those images, figures and ornaments as stated and agreed with the above-said Prior and advisor or successors in office." See Michael Baxandall, *Painting and Experience in Fifteenth-Century Italy,* p. 20. This is also the likely reason why the Augustinian friars rejected Leonardo's *Adoration of the Magi,* since it utterly ignored the iconographic canon of this scene.

[2] C. Gaye, *Carteggio inedito d'artisti dei secoli XVI, XV, XVI,* Vol. I; Florence, 1840; pp. 175-176.

[3] Baxandall, Michael, *Painting and Experience in Fifteenth Century Italy*; p. 6.

[4] On the plus side, the property had been valued at three hundred florins (roughly forty thousand dollars in modern currency). On the downside, half of it was supposed to serve as the dowry for the patron's daughter—which, incidentally, the artist was expected to advance as well. And if at any time the painter decided to walk away from the commission, he would, as the friars told him, "forfeit that part of it which he has done." See Jean-Pierre Isbouts and Christopher Brown, *Young Leonardo: The Evolution of a Revolutionary Artist*; p. 7-8.

[5] Bianca Maria Sforza was the daughter of the legitimate Sforza duke, Galeazzo Maria Sforza, who was assassinated in 1476. Her uncle, Ludovico Sforza who subsequently seized power in Milan, tried to marry her off to various prominent rulers in Europe in an effort to cement his legitimacy as duke. While still a toddler, she was betrothed to Philibert I, Duke of Savoy, but her groom died when Bianca was only ten. Three years later she became engaged to Janus Corvinus, son of the Hungarian King Matthias, but the actual marriage never took place. Finally, in 1494 (a year after de Predis painted her portrait), she was married to the King of the Holy Roman Empire, Maximilian I, in exchange for Maximilian bestowing upon Ludovico the longed-for title of Duke of Milan. The deal did not come cheap: Ludovico agreed to pay Maximilian a dowry of 400,000 ducats (around thirty-two million dollars in today's currency). This gigantic sum was raised by the expedient of sharply increased taxes on the hapless populace of the Duchy of Milan.

[6] Jean-Pierre Isbouts and Christopher Brown, *Young Leonardo,* p. 182.

[7] Pietro C. Marani, "Leonardo in Venice and the Veneto, Documents and Evidence," in Claire Farago (Ed.), *Leonardo da Vinci: Selected Scholarship.* New York: Garland Publishing, 1999; pp. 1-14.

[8] Charles Nicholl, *Leonardo da Vinci: Flights of the Mind.* New York: Penguin, 2004; p. 316.

[9] Leonardo da Vinci, "*Modo Di Colorir In Tela*" (CCCLIII), in *Trattato della Pittura,* published by Raffaelo du Fresne in 1651.

[10] Paris MS L, as reproduced in Charles Nicholl, *Leonardo da Vinci: Flights of the Mind*, p. 330.

[11] Regrettably, this myth is once again perpetuated in Walter Isaacson's 2017 biography, *Leonardo da Vinci.*

[12] There may be another reason why Lorenzo chose to ignore the young Da Vinci. In 1476, Leonardo had been arraigned in court with three other young men on charges of having committed sodomy with a 17-year old named Jacopo Saltarelli, a goldsmith-apprentice who moonlighted as a prostitute. Homosexuality was tolerated in Florence, certainly among the upper classes, as long as one was discreet. Elsewhere in Italy, "the Florentine manner" was a by-word for gay sex; in Germany, known homosexual men were called *Florenzer.* Officially, however, sodomy was on the books as a capital offense, even in Florence; therefore, the hand of the authorities was forced if someone filed an official complaint in special drop boxes (known as *tamburi* or "drums") where citizens could anonymously denounce someone. On April 9, 1476, an anonymous letter accused Saltarelli of having engaged in "many wretched affairs" with a tailor named Baccino from Orto San Michele; a goldsmith named Bartolomeo di Pasquino; a certain Leonardo de' Tornabuoni; and Leonardo da Vinci. Leonardo must have been mortified. An intensely private person, he cared deeply about his appearance and his reputation. More importantly, the taint of sodomy carried the real possibility of depriving him of Church commissions. After a lengthy investigation, however, the judge decided to drop the charges on June 7. Some authors have detected the hand of Lorenzo' de Medici in this. One of the accused, Leonardo de' Tornabuoni, was possibly related to Lorenzo de' Medici's mother, Lucrezia de' Tornabuoni. That could certainly have motivated Lorenzo to intervene in the proceedings and bury the matter, so as to avoid severe embarrassment to his family. It would also have motivated him to keep Leonardo at arms' length.

[13] See Jean-Pierre Isbouts and Christopher Brown, *Young Leonardo*; p. 57-61

[14] Charles Nicholl, *Leonardo da Vinci: Flights of the Mind*; p. 384-385.

[15] Unfortunately, Ser Piero's information was out of date; when Leonardo got in touch with the Servites, they told him that they already had signed a contract with another artist, Filippino Lippi. Ironically, this was the same Filippino who only four years earlier had completed an *Adoration of the Magi* for the friars of San Donato in Scopeto, the painting that had originally been commissioned from Leonardo. Filippino was all too aware of the painful history. Upon hearing the news of Leonardo's interest in the Servite painting, he graciously bowed out of the contract.

[16] Vasari, Giorgio, *Le Vite de' più eccellenti pittori, scultori e architetti;* 1568 Edition.

[17] Copsey, Richard O. Carm., "A Carmelite Link to Leonardo da Vinci", from *The British Province of Carmelite Friars*, December 26, 2011.

[18] Some authors believe that the vicar is referring to is the *Burlington Cartoon,* now in the National Gallery in London, based in part on Paolo Giovio's comment that "the first thing he undertook [in Florence] was the design of an Altar-piece for the Annunciate; in this he represented the

little Jesus with his mother, St. Anne, and St. John. Leonardo rendered himself extremely popular among his countrymen by this performance, which was seen and applauded by the whole city." But modern research has shown that the *Burlington Cartoon* must have predated the drawing that Leonardo was working on in the spring of 1501.

[19] Pietro da Novellara, *Letter to Isabella d'Este, Marchioness of Mantua*, April 3, 1501. Archivio di Stato di Matova, Archivio Gonzaga, Mantua, E, XXVIII, b. 1103, c. 272.

[20] His reputation certainly hasn't been helped by the recent Showtime series *The Borgias*, which unfortunately has many historical inaccuracies.

[21] Some authors have argued that this is the first instance of a "modern" map, drawn from a bird's eye view, as is common with all maps today. The fact that Leonardo had, of course, no way of actually observing the town from altitude makes this achievement even more remarkable.

[22] Bramly, Serge, *Leonardo,* pp. 329-330.

[23] Zöllner, Frank, "Leonardo's Portrait of Mona Lisa del Giocondo," in *Gazette des Beaux-Arts,* 121 (1993), pp. 115-138.

[24] Gene E. Brucker, *Renaissance Florence*; p. 86.

[25] Beltrami, Luca, *Documenti e memorie riguardanti la vita e le opere di Leonardo da Vinci.* Milan, 1919; document 125.

[26] As Veit Probst has argued, that reticence was not all Soderini's doing, for the majority of the Signoria was opposed to the Arno scheme, in the belief that it was too costly, and the risk of failure too great. Nonetheless, Soderini continued to commission feasibility studies, mostly written by Machiavelli's secretary Agostino Vespucci, who eventually produced no less than 93 documents. See Veit Probst, *Zur Entstehungsgeschichte der Mona Lisa*; p. 32.

[27] Gene A. Brucker, *Renaissance Florence,* p. 86.

[28] The Mona Lisa Foundation, *Mona Lisa: Leonardo's Earlier Version*; p. 66.
[29] By comparison, when Maddalena Strozzi married Agnolo Doni in 1504, the dowry consisted of 1400 florins. Francesco himself made sure that in 1537, his grand-daughter Cassandra had a dowry of 1440 florins when she was about to be wed.

[30] The Bargello, an austere crenellated building built in the mid-13th century, is the oldest building in Florence. It served as the model for the Palazzo della Signoria, today known as the Palazzo Vecchio.

[31] Some authors have argued that the death of little Piera is the reason why the veil in the *Mona Lisa* painting is black, since the lady was still in mourning. But by 1502 Lisa had given birth to another little girl, who was alive and well when Leonardo undertook her portrait, therewith obviating the need to wear clothes of mourning. And second, the veil is not black (an effect produced by layers of varnish and soot), but transparent.

[32] The Latin text reads *...mutuum amorem et dilectionem dicti testatoris erga dictam Lisam eius dilectam uxorem.. et attento qualiter se gessit prefata domina Lisa erga dictum testatorem ingénue et tanquam mulier ingenua.* From the *Notarile antecosimiano* 7799, c. 6, Archivio di Stato di Firenze; reproduced in Pallanti, p. 71.

[33] What's more, Lisa had a sweet disposition. She bore her stepson, little Bartolomeo, so much love and devotion that no one could have guessed the child was not her own. Indeed, when Francesco died in 1538, Lisa designated Bartolomeo, rather than her own son Piero, as her representative with power of attorney.

[34] Veit Probst, "Rätselhafte Mona Lisa: Wer ist die geheimnisvoll lächelnde Dame auf Leonardo da Vincis Bild?" in *UniSpiegel*, University of Heidelberg, 2008.

[35] Martin Kemp and Giuseppe Pallanti, *Mona Lisa: The People and the Painting.* Oxford University Press, 2017.

[36] Claire Farago (Ed.), *Biography and Early Art Criticism of Leonardo da Vinci*; page 88.

[37] Ibid, page 88.

[38] Antonio de Beatis, "Account of the Visit of Cardinal Louis d'Aragon paid to Leonardo, at the Château de Cloux, October 10, 1517," in Delieuvin, Vincent, *Saint Anne: Leonardo da Vinci's ultimate Masterpiece;* p. 199.

[39] Edward McCurdy, *Life of Leonardo;* p. 114.

[40] I should, however, mention that Vasari claims that Raphael and Taddeo Taddei were good friends, and that Taddei "would have him ever in his house and at his table," so perhaps the proximity of Raphael's rooms in the Palazzo Taddei to the Giocondo home was purely coincidental.

[41] Codex Riccardianus 1207, fol. 47v-58r. Interestingly, Leonardo Dati served as Master general of the Dominican Order from 1414 until his death in 1425, residing at the same monastery of Santa Maria Novella where Leonardo da Vinci would create the cartoon for the *Anghiari* fresco. He was buried at the *Cappella Rucellai* in the same church, under a tombstone designed by Ghiberti.

[42] *Codex Urbinas Latinus* 6r-v (McM 36)

[43] It has been suggested that the four officers represent the four principal commanders in the battle: from left to right, Francesco Piccinino; Niccolò Piccinino; Ludovico Trevisan; and Giovanni Antonio Del Balzo Orsini.

[44] David S. Chambers, *Patrons and Artists in the Italian Renaissance.* Columbia, SC: University of South Carolina Press, 1971, pp. 147–8.

[45] Based on a report by Machiavelli's assistant Biagio Buonaccorso, in MS Machiavelli C 6.78; Biblioteca Nazionale, Florence; reproduced in Nicholl, Charles, *Leonardo da Vinci;* p. 359.

[46] For more information about the *Battle of Anghiari* project, please see the new study by Margherita Melani, *The Fascination of the Unfinished Work: The Battle of Anghiari.* CB Edizioni, 2012.

[47] Adding further to the mystery surrounding the *Anghiari* project, the *Tavola Doria* copy was stolen in 1940 and only recently emerged in a Japanese collection; as announced on December 3, 2012, the painting will now be exhibited in Japan and Italy on a rotating basis.

[48] *Kington, Tom (6 December 2011).* "Lost Leonardo Da- Vinci battle scene sparks row between art historians". *The Guardian, London.* Retrieved 12 March 2012.

[49] Fernando "the Spaniard", properly known as Fernando Yañez de la Almedina, would shortly thereafter return to his native Spain and execute a portrait of *St. Catherine of Alexandria* (1510), whose features betray the influence of the Earlier *Mona Lisa.* The painting is currently in the Museo del Prado in Madrid.

[50] A bill of receipt, discovered by Bertrand Jestaz in 1999 in the National Archives in France, specifies a payment of 2,604 lire—an immense sum—to "Salai, son of Pietro d'Oreno," in exchange "for the delivery to the king of several paintings." Salaì was well aware of King François's craze for Italian art, particularly works by Leonardo, and probably figured that any offer to the royal court would be gladly accepted. Vincent Delieuvin has suggested that this bill of sale suggests that Leonardo "had ceded title to his paintings [to Salai], doubtless as a partial early transfer of his inheritance." But such clearly contradicts the terms of Leonardo's will, which bequeathed this inheritance to Melzi, not to Salaì. See Isbouts, Jean-Pierre and Brown, Christopher H., *The Da Vinci Legacy*; page 121.

[51] "Salai's Probate Inventory, April 21, 1525," in Delieuvin, Vincent, *Saint Anne;* p. 282.

[52] Scailliérez, Cécile, *Leonardo da Vinci: La Joconde.* Paris: Musée du Louvre, Departement des Peintures, 2003.

[53] Pallanti, Giuseppe, *Mona Lisa Revealed: The True Identity of Leonardo's Model.* New York: Rizzoli, 2006.

[54] Rubin, Patricia Lee, *Giorgio Vasari: Art and History.* Yale University Press, 1995; p. 123.

[55] These terracotta sculptures and bronzes were the subject of a special exhibition at Florence's Bargello Museum on January 10, 2011, entitled *The Large Bronzes of the Baptistery: Giovanfrancesco Rustici and Leonardo.*

[56] Lomazzo, Gian Paolo, *Trattato dell'arte della pittura, scoltura et architettura* [Milano 1584] in *Scritti sulle arti* Vol. II, Roberto Paolo Ciardi, Florence 1974.

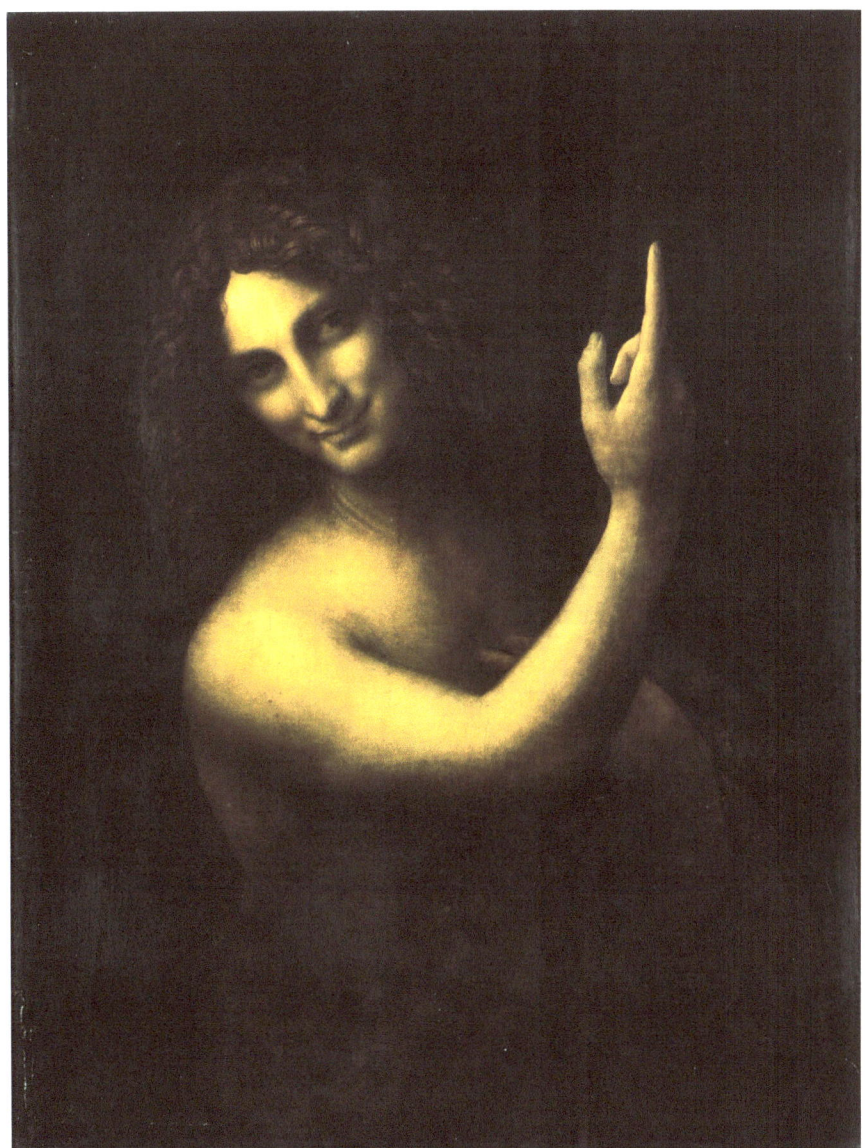

Fig. 26. Leonardo da Vinci, *John the Baptist,* ca. 1513-1516. This painting has only recently been recognized as a late autograph work by Leonardo.

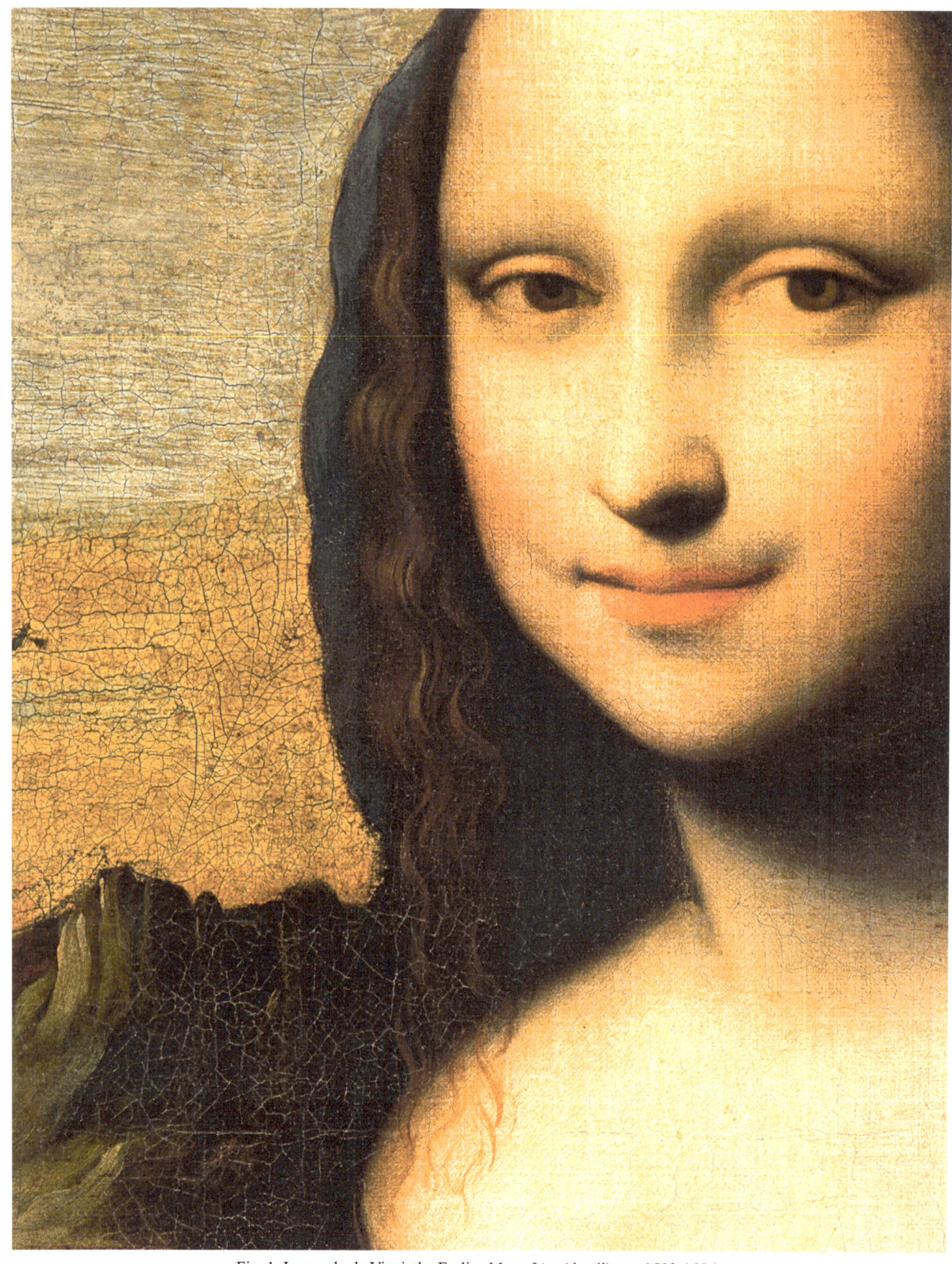

Fig. 1. Leonardo da Vinci, the Earlier *Mona Lisa* (detail), ca. 1503-1506.

The Scientific Attribution of the Earlier Mona Lisa

J. F. Asmus, Professor Emeritus
Department of Physics & Center for Advanced Nanotechnology,
University of California, San Diego

V. A. Parfenov, Professor
Department of Photonics,
St. Petersburg Electrotechnical University

A Fulbright Scholarship has been awarded for further research by the authors following
the publication of this paper, which has been extensively peer-reviewed.

Introduction

Traditionally, the purpose of using scientific tests in the authentication of paintings is to *exclude* a work or an artist if parameters are discovered that are inconsistent with known features of the artist's oeuvre. For example, the date may be wrong (e.g., by way of radio carbon dating), a pigment may be wrong (e.g., it may use a modern formula), or some form of an underpainting or sketch may be revealed that renders the authentication implausible (either through an X-ray or Infrared scan).

By contrast, this article will propose an original approach to identify the individual "fingerprints" of a particular artist by virtue of his brushwork, based on our previous publications in several peer-reviewed journals. This new procedure involves extracting luminosity histogram statistics of a painting in order to quantify its sfumato/chiaroscuro properties for either entire compositions or particular features (e.g., eyes, noses, or lips.) This novel approach can determine whether a work can indeed be associated with a particular artist, rather than be excluded from his or her generally accepted body of work.

In recent years, the use of *digital* images as part of the authentication process has grown considerably. Most of these methods serve as a means of studying the visual characteristics of an artist's brushstrokes. Until now, however, this information was limited to study paint layers and style. In developing our technique, however, we recognized that the act of applying paint is a highly individual process for each artist, since it can be characterized as a unique "fingerprint". How to extract and analyze this "fingerprint"? One way is to mathematically process ("or quantify") a digital picture with modalities such as the statistical method of a wavelet analysis; the support vector method; and the fuzzy clustering method, which are all used to analyze the brushwork technique.[1] In some cases, these methods are combined with analysis methods from other scientific fields, e.g. biometrics and medicine.[2] Our investigation, by contrast, proposes a new scientific method for the comparative analysis and authentication of paintings. This method employs intensity histograms of digital optical images, by way of identifying the unique "fingerprint" of the artist. This, for example, makes it possible to identify Leonardo's "fingerprint" as part of the authentication of the Earlier *Mona Lisa*.

Basic principles of histogram analyses in paintings

When creating a painting, an artist often applies a large number of brushstrokes to a canvas, a panel, or another form of support. The resulting painting surface thus acquires specific spatial and spectral characteristics that can be identified for the analysis of the individual painting technique of the particular master. The brushstrokes of each artist, as a rule, have a certain length and direction, as well as a viscosity of the paint particular to this master. They result from the texture of the brushes, the speed of the hand movements, the particular features of the color palette, as well as the pigment mixing techniques and the use of glazing.

In light of this, one possible way of studying the properties of an artist's painting technique is to analyze the histograms from digital images of the paintings. Any amplitude histogram (another name for the intensity histogram) of a digital optical image is a function (graph) of the statistical distribution of the image elements of various intensities, in which the horizontal axis indicates the brightness level and where the relative number of pixels with a specified brightness value are plotted on the vertical axis. These histograms from digital images of paintings can be considered the artists' "fingerprints", as noted above. This is motivated by the idea that histograms display a unique distribution of light and dark shading, reflecting the style of each master. In other words, the analysis of pictures with the use of histograms is a quantification of their *chiaroscuro*, meaning "light and darkness", or the technique of painting that is characterized by a sharp contrast of light and dark tones. This technique serves to convey contrasts—that are often quite dramatic—in a painting. The term *chiaroscuro* should thus be understood as the general character of the distribution of light and dark tones throughout any pictorial image. In the opinion of many art historians (including Kenneth Clark and Carlo Pedretti [3]), the analysis of the chiaroscuro feature plays an important role when comparing the paintings of different Masters, since in the process of creating the work each artist develops the dance of "shadows" that is particular to him/her, and that is a unique individual characteristic of his/her painting technique. Thus the

scientifically extracted histogram of the digital image of a painting can serve as the identity of an individual artist's "fingerprint".

As a rule, chiaroscuro is a result of the blending of the color saturation and albedo from one region of a painting to the adjacent zones. Under the traditional connoisseurship approach in the attribution of paintings, an art expert evaluates a picture visually (without any use of analytical methods). The properties of spatial blending and contrasts of light and shade are the main features that are taken into consideration to establish the authorship of the artist's works, and to isolate forgeries or copies. This visual impression is correlated in the expert's mind with his memory of impressions of similar authenticated works by the same artist. As a result of this comparison, the expert gives his/her —admittedly subjective—conclusion. Obviously, a scientific analysis of the intensity histogram in the digital version of a painting will allow experts to arrive at a more objective conclusion, using mathematically precise data.

Method of the analysis of pictures through intensity histograms

In terms of the technical aspects of a histogram analysis, in all typical formats of digital optical images the pixels have a range of 256 intensity levels (their values can vary from 0 to 255). Currently, many computer-based digital image-processing programs incorporate special functions that allow us to obtain reliable histograms. Using the histogram "intensity" option, we can then count and plot the number of pixels (in the whole image or an individual region) for each of the 256 intensity levels. The graphical dependence of the quantification (the number of pixels) on the intensity level is known as an amplitude or intensity histogram.

When paint pigments are blended uniformly, the luminosity of the picture image can vary widely (from bright-light to very dark tones). In this case, the gradient in the luminosity distribution of the individual pixels from the highest to the lowest intensity values will be uniform (there will be no discontinuities or abrupt transitions in the distribution of the histogram). It should be added that each intensity histogram is characterized by two basic mathematical parameters: mathematical mean and standard (mean-square) deviation. When analyzing the artists' brushstrokes, the most important characteristic from these two parameters is the standard deviation. Therefore, when a painting is being examined by means of a histogram analysis, one should not only compare the form of the distribution, but also take into account the value of this standard deviation. Paintings created by the same artist should obviously have a close similarity in terms of the painting technique, and consequently, their histograms should be similar to each other according to these two criteria. This is key to a comparative analysis of paintings based on a quantitative exposure of the artist's style through amplitude histograms. In order to obtain a more precise result when comparing histograms, we discovered that it is better to convert the color image to a grayscale (that is, to a black and white image). The results can be more accurate if a comparative analysis of the histograms is carried out in different spectral bands (separately in the red, blue, and green ranges).

We should emphasize that histogram analysis is a method of *comparative* analysis, i.e. comparing the painting under examination to others which have already accepted attributions. Of course, it is important to bear in mind that the painting techniques can change throughout an artist's life. Therefore, some differences in the characteristics revealed through histograms can be explained by the evolution of the artist's style and technique. It is also important to take into account that artists with little or no chiaroscuro technique may not manifest themselves in the individual histogram features of the digital images of their pictures.

As shown in a number of research studies,[4] works of masters with a very delicate painting technique most often have very distinctive features in the histograms. An excellent example is Leonardo da Vinci as he is well known for being the first to apply the technique of *sfumato* (from the Italian *sfumare*, meaning "to evaporate like smoke"). This term denotes a manner of painting that is marked by fine shading, which softens the outlines of figures and objects, and even allows the artist to convey the air that envelopes them. Recent research on Leonardo's art has revealed that this effect was achieved by applying brushstrokes with a thickness of several micrometres, and that the total thickness of the paint layer often did not exceed 30-40 micrometres. It follows that the use of histogram approach might be very useful for the analysis and authentication of paintings by Leonardo. It is also important to note that in portrait painting, histogram analysis is particularly effective when comparing facial characteristics. In other words, the focus of such a histogram analysis should be on parts of the paintings depicting human faces, for the face is the key element in the composition of a portrait. It is well known that great masters often involved their assistants and apprentices in the performance of their work. However, the depictions of the faces in portraits were, as a rule, executed by the masters themselves. Consequently, a histogram analysis of the facial images is the most reliable way to establish if works being compared belong to the hand of the same master.

All above mentioned issues have been taken into account in our studies of the Earlier *Mona Lisa*.

Comparative analysis of the Isleworth or Earlier *Mona Lisa*, Louvre *Mona Lisa* and other *Mona Lisa* portraits

The story of the analysis of the Earlier *Mona Lisa* by means of image processing techniques began in 1989, when one of the authors of this article, John Asmus, had concluded extensive and successful work on the attributions of Rembrandt self-portraits.[5] At

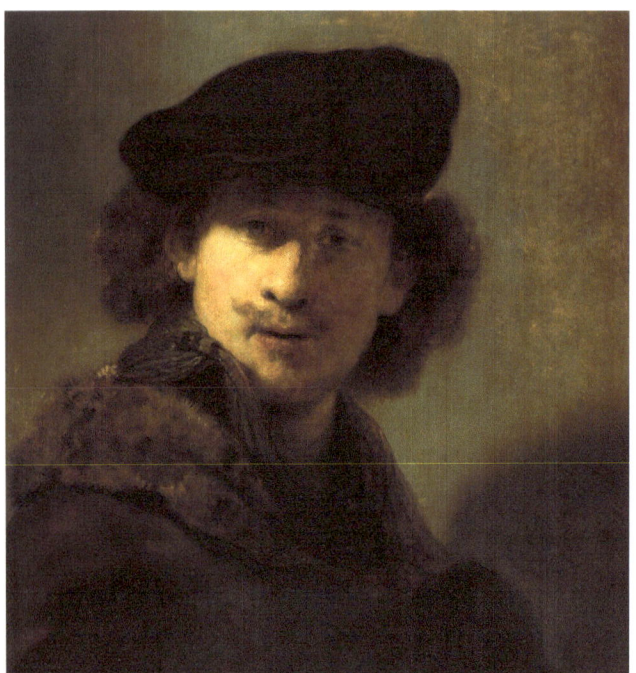

Fig. 2. Rembrandt van Rijn, *Self-portrait in a Velvet Beret*, 1634.

the instigation of Dr. Kenneth Clark, Dr. Asmus then received an invitation to study the Louvre *Mona Lisa* in depth. As part of this investigation, he spent a day alone with this famous artwork at the Louvre Museum in Paris, and carried out a computer "restoration" of the Louvre *Mona Lisa* that created an idea of the original appearance of the portrait without the dark yellow varnish and the craquelure webs that lie over the image.[6] This was soon followed by an invitation to examine the Earlier *Mona Lisa* in a similar fashion.

As demonstrated in other chapters of this monograph, the historical evidence shows that there were two distinct portraits of the *Mona Lisa*, though executed at different times and in different locations by Leonardo. One is an earlier, "unfinished" version (known as the Earlier *Mona Lisa*) with Lisa seated between flanking columns, which was executed in Florence c.1503-1506 for Francesco del Giocondo. It may presumably have been left with Salaì, Leonardo's servant, and is possibly listed in the inventory of his estate in 1525. A second finished version (i.e. the Louvre version), executed in Leonardo's post-1508

style without flanking columns, was probably executed in Rome c.1513-16 for Giuliano de Medici, and then taken to France, where it was seen by Antonio de Beatis in 1517. It was subsequently acquired by the French King Francis I in 1518. The aim of Professor Asmus' work was to determine scientifically whether these two painting were indeed painted by the same artist.

The first stage of the research involved a detailed study of digital images of both these Leonardo paintings. The proportions and arrangement of the key elements in the composition of both paintings showed that the Earlier *Mona Lisa* could not be a copy of the Louvre painting since the pictures differ significantly from each other: not only in terms of the proportions of the images but also in many other fundamental matters of construction. In addition, their main axes (the axes that can be aligned along the eye line (horizontally) and the hairlines section (vertically) do not coincide (see Figure 3).

However, the first results from the intensity histograms of both paintings were quite astonishing. The character of the distribution and the main parameters of the histograms (mathematical mean and standard deviation) in the areas of the face were almost identical in both pictures (Figure 4). Consequently, if the histograms of the digital images are the "fingerprints" of their authors as scientifically demonstrated and validated in the experience with the Rembrandt portraits, we can draw the conclusion on the basis of the experimental data that the faces of the Earlier *Mona Lisa* and the Louvre *Mona Lisa* would most likely have been created by the same artist.

In order to further substantiate this conclusion, we decided to develop a histogram analysis of digital images from the most famous copies of the *Mona Lisa*. These include: 1. The *Mona Lisa* from the Prado Museum in Madrid (Spain), considered to be the earliest copy of the Louvre *Mona Lisa*; 2. The *Mona Lisa* from the National Museum of Art in Oslo

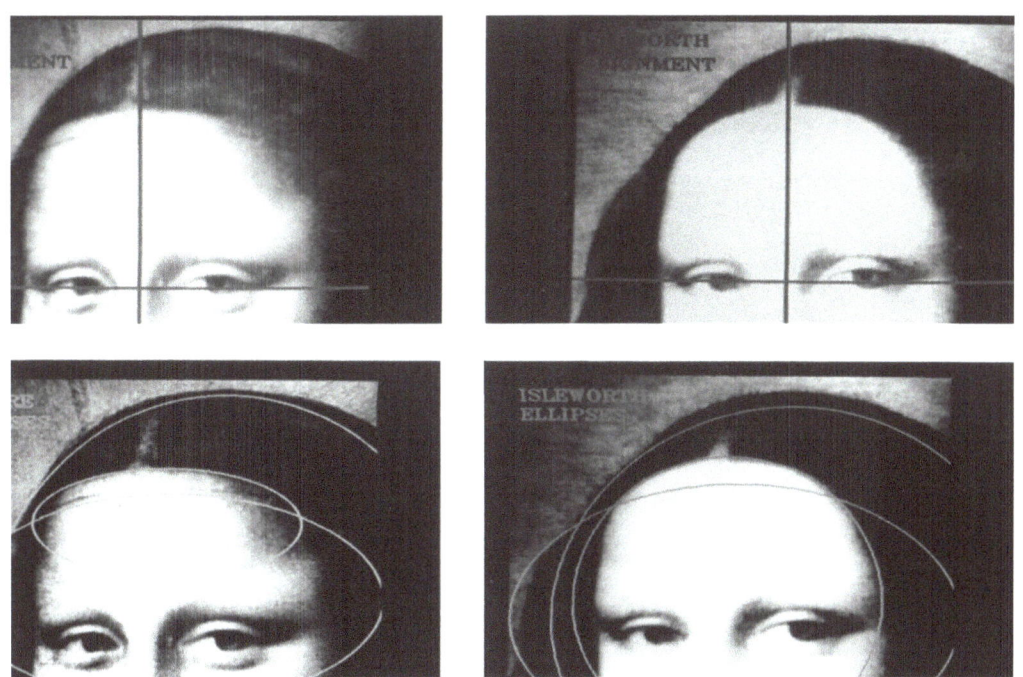

Fig. 3. Comparison of geometrical features of images of the Louvre *Mona Lisa* (left) and "Earlier *Mona Lisa* (right)

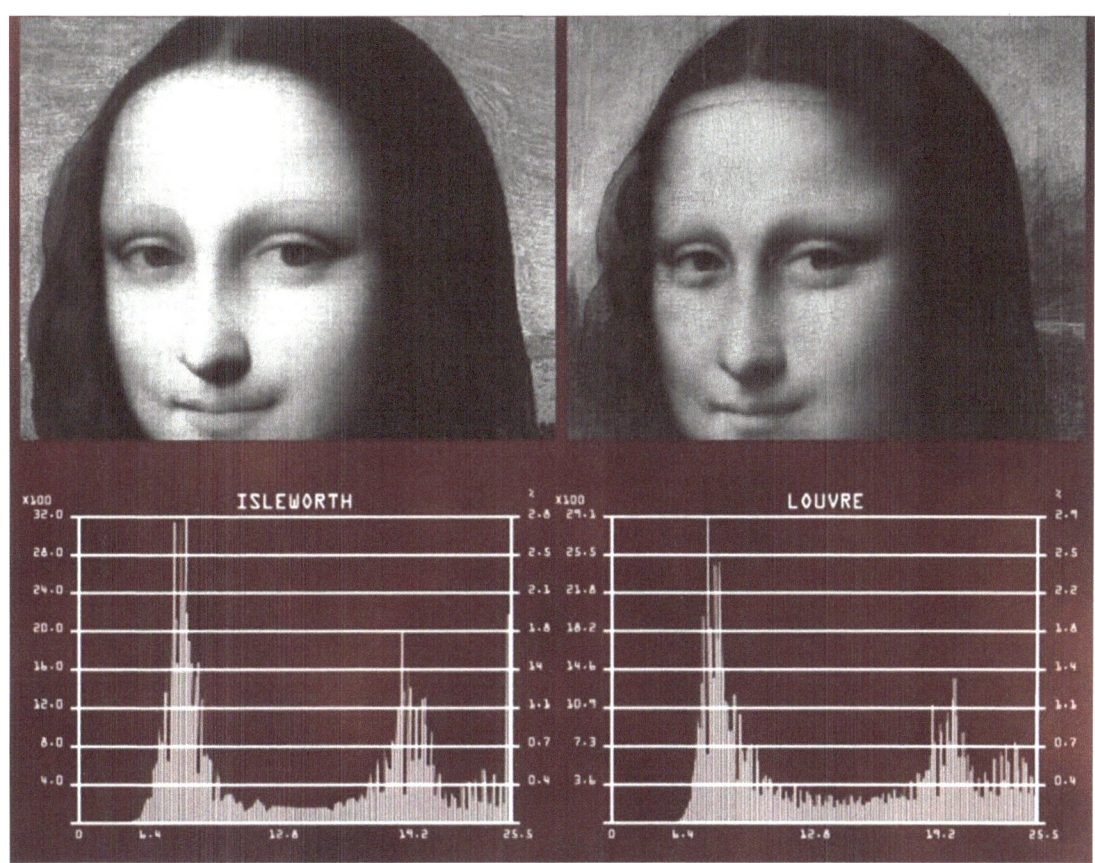

Fig.4. Histograms of digitized images of the Earlier *Mona Lisa* (*left*) and Louvre *Mona Lisa* (right)

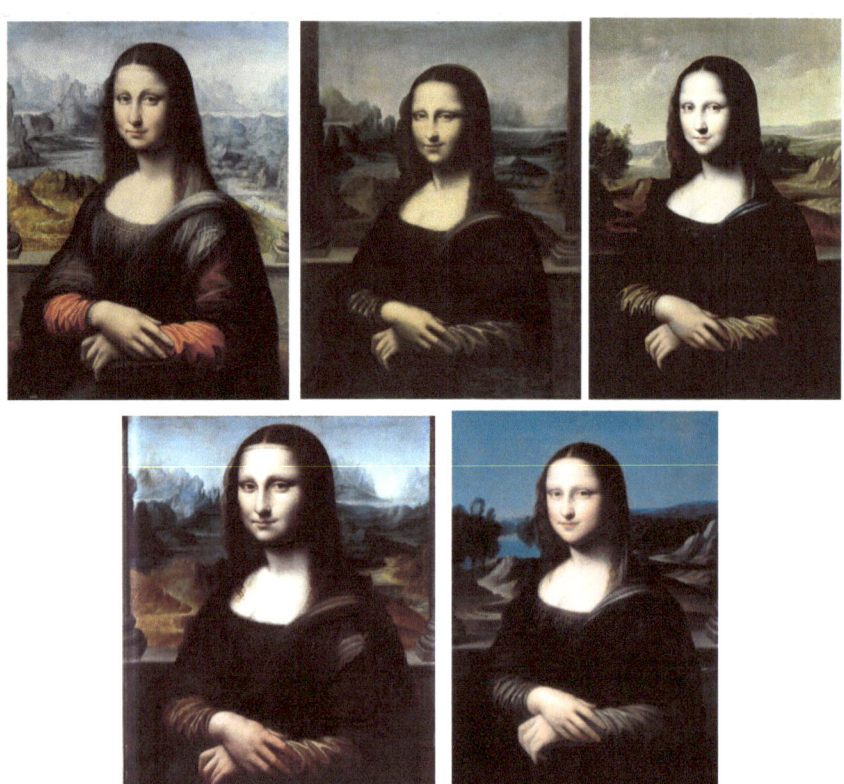

Fig. 5. From left: the Prado *Mona Lisa*, the Walters *Mona Lisa*, the Flemish *Mona Lisa*, the Reynolds *Mona Lisa* and the Oslo *Mona Lisa*. The histograms show that they all have significant differences from the histogram of the Louvre *Mona Lisa*.

(Norway), dating from the 17th century; 3. The *Mona Lisa* from the Walters Art Museum in Baltimore, MD, attributed to Simon Vouet (1590-1649); 4. The Reynolds *Mona Lisa* (now in a private collection in the UK) and 5. The *Mona Lisa* by the Flemish school (also in a private British collection) dating from the 16th and 17th centuries, respectively. These portraits are shown in Figure 5.

The data comparison shown in Figures 4 and 6 demonstrates that the histograms of the digital images of all the copies are distinctly different from the histograms of both the Louvre *Mona Lisa* and the Earlier *Mona Lisa*. These differ not only in the distribution characteristics of the histograms, but also in their basic parameters. This significantly distinguishes the Earlier *Mona Lisa* from copies of the *Mona Lisa*. However, in order for the attribution to be even more accurate, we also compared the histograms of the individual features of the faces in all the

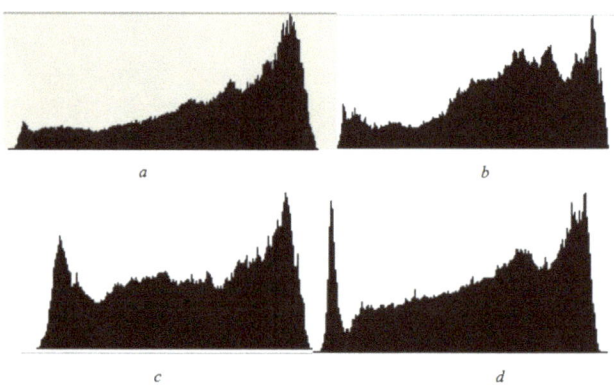

Fig. 6. Histograms of digitized images of the Louvre *Mona Lisa* (*a*) and its copies: with The National Gallery (Oslo) (*b*), with The Walters Art museum (*c*) and with Prado museum (*d*)

According to Morelli, studying the details of the art form allows us to reveal the specific character of the individual style of each master. Morelli was convinced that the artist's personality manifested itself in small details, since both the artist and the imitator displayed the individual features of their

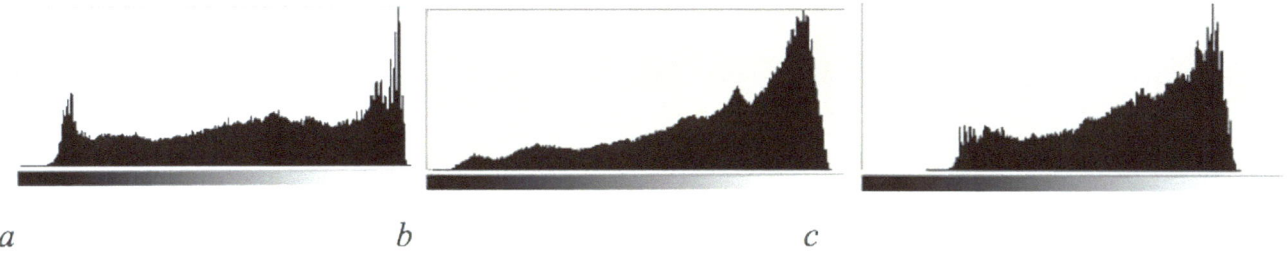

Fig. 7. Histograms of digitized images of Reynolds *Mona Lisa* (*a*), Louvre *Mona Lisa* (*b*) and Earlier *Mona Lisa* (*c*) in green spectral bandwidth

painting technique by a natural stroke, rather than in a neat signature. This is due to the fact that while the artist is painting details, he becomes relaxed and acts intuitively. Consequently, an analysis of the individual parts in paintings with a similar composition may reveal distinctions in the techniques of different artists most clearly.

In addition, a comparison of the histograms of the images of all the above-mentioned works was carried out in different spectral bands (in the blue, green, and red ranges). Some of these histograms are shown in Figure 7.

As can be seen from the graphs in Figure 7, there is a very good correlation between the histograms of the Isleworth *Mona Lisa* and those of the Louvre *Mona Lisa*. This similarity becomes particularly remarkable if the histograms of these two portraits are superimposed on each other (see Figure 8). By contrast, the comparisons of the histograms from

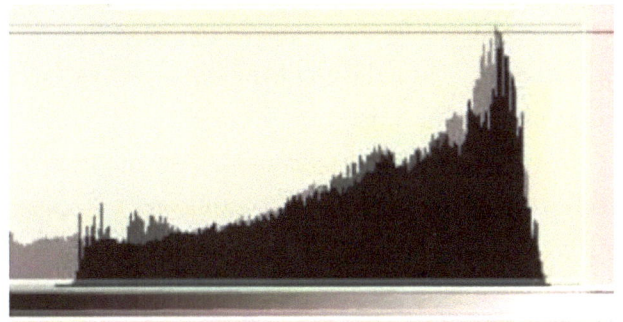

Fig. 8. Result of matching of histograms of digitized images of faces (in the field of nose) on the Earlier *Mona Lisa* and Louvre *Mona Lisa* (background is histogram of Earlier *Mona Lisa*)

the Louvre *Mona Lisa* and its copies in similar studies indicate many apparent differences. The same result is demonstrated in a 3D-diagram (Figure 9). It shows the normalized values of the standard deviation of the histograms of the Louvre *Mona Lisa* (LML), the Earlier *Mona Lisa* (EML), the copies from the Prado museums and the Oslo museum, and the copy executed by the Flemish painter. On the three axes in the diagram, the values of the standard deviation of the histograms from all these pictures in the regions of the nose, mouth and eyes are plotted. The graph clearly displays that the Louvre *Mona Lisa* and the Earlier *Mona Lisa* have the best correspondence in the standard deviation.

Thus, based on the results of careful retracted studies of digital optical images of the Earlier *Mona Lisa* and Louvre *Mona Lisa* paintings, as similarly demonstrated and validated in the work on Rembrandt self-portraits, we can conclude with full confidence that the faces in both works were created by the same artist.

Characterizing the spatial modulation of Leonardo's chiaroscuro by means of overlay of *Mona Lisa* optical images

It is obvious from Leonardo's writings that he took modulation and blending very seriously. The main advantage of the histogram approach is that it allows one to generate digital luminosity histograms to numerically display this very unique distribution of light and dark in Leonardo's art globally. As we discussed, we performed our analyses on prominent

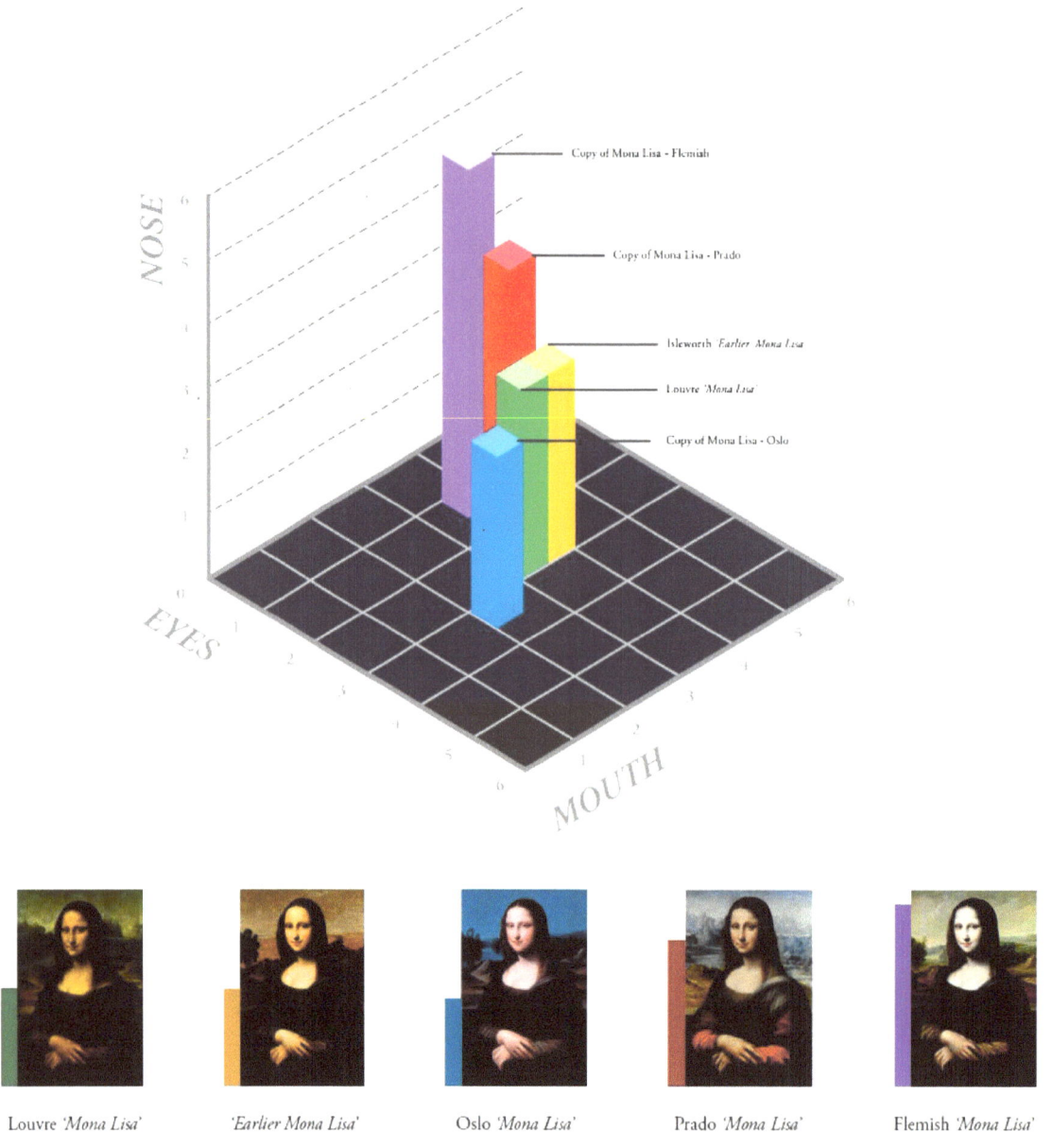

Fig. 9. 3D-plot of the statistical variances of three regions (eyes, noses, and mouths) of five *Mona Lisa* paintings
(Louvre and Earlier versions as well as the Oslo, Prado, and Flemish copies)

local regions of studied paintings, such as the eyes, nose, and mouth.

However, to remove any possible bias in our conclusions, we decided to carry out an additional analysis of optical images of *Mona Lisa* portraits by means of their chromatic overlays. It was our expectation that these displays would facilitate the visualization of Leonardo's unique chiaroscuro as opposed to that of other artists and copyists. If our hypothesis is correct, it may give us very convincing further arguments for a reliable attribution of the Earlier *Mona Lisa* and the Louvre *Mona Lisa* as the works of the same artist.

In astronomy, medical diagnostic imaging, and many other sciences, it has been customary to compare and contrast two images by means of color-coded overlays. For instance, one image may be displayed in red, whereas a comparative image may be displayed in green. One can digitally superimpose semitransparent versions of such pairs. For such a hypothetical image pair, an overlay would appear yellow in areas where conformal images are comparable in luminosity, while red or green, respectively, is used when one or the other of the images is brighter. In other words, the appearance of red, green, or yellow on such a composite overlay reveals regions where intensity gradients (such as chiaroscuro) match or diverge. We produced such chromatic overlay pairs (scaled in proportion) between the faces by Leonardo in contrast to those of other artists with the hope of revealing (graphically) unique hand/eye chiaroscuro gradients associated with particular portrait features, such as the eyes, noses, and lips.

Indeed, our study shows that the red and green images are merged in regions of comparable intensity and contrast to recreate the original flesh tones. For regions where chiaroscuro gradients diverge spurious optical tints are revealed. Our research fully confirmed these assumptions, and as a result of careful analysis of these overlay images, we can conclude that the chiaroscuro of the image of the Earlier *Mona Lisa* is much closer to the chiaroscuro of the Louvre *Mona Lisa* than the overlays of all other ones (see Figure 10 – 12).

From our point of view, this set of overlays is one additional confirmation that both the Earlier *Mona Lisa* and the Louvre *Mona Lisa* were created by the same artist—and perhaps even more compelling confirmation than the histogram data.

Conclusions

Our research resulted in obtaining an original set of experimental results that form substantive evidence for the attribution of the Earlier *Mona Lisa* to Leonardo da Vinci. To summarize:

1. There is an almost identical matching in the distribution of histogram data in the images from both the Earlier and the Louvre *Mona Lisas* (including eyes, noses and mouths); by contrast, the histogram data in

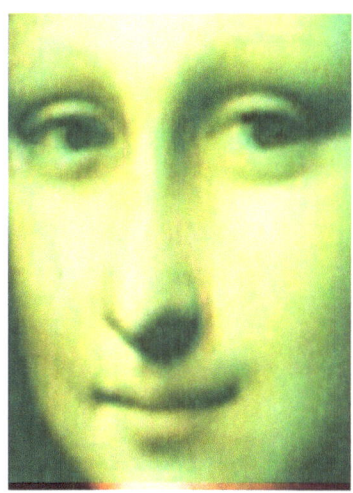

Fig. 10. Overlay of images of the Louvre *Mona Lisa* and Earlier *Mona Lisa*

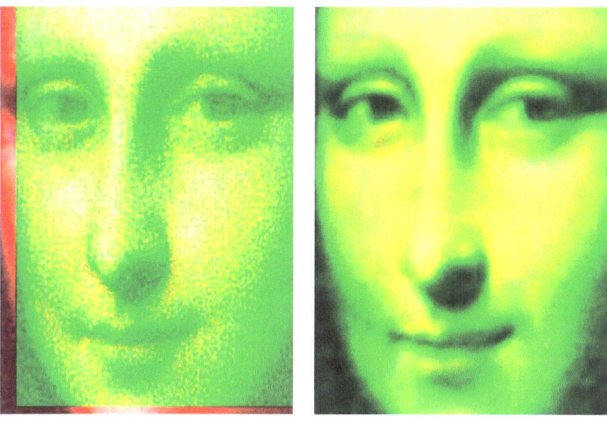

Fig. 11. Overlay of images of the Louvre *Mona Lisa* with the Oslo *Mona Lisa* (left) and with the Prado`s copy of *Mona Lisa* (right)

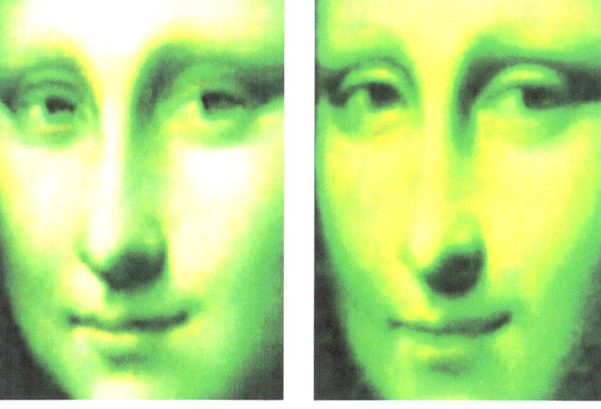

Fig. 12. Overlay of images of the Louvre *Mona Lisa* with the Reynolds copy (left) and the Walters copy (right)

comparison with other *Mona Lisa* portraits are quite different.

2. The chiaroscuro of the Earlier *Mona Lisa* image is much closer to the chiaroscuro of the Louvre *Mona Lisa* image than images of all other paintings.

3. In addition, we developed and verified a new method of comparative analysis of histograms of images of the Earlier and Louvre *Mona Lisas* by using different spectral bandwidths (red, green and blue). These furthermore confirm the findings in (1) and (2) above.

Taking all the above into consideration together with the results of all the other traditional tests carried out on the Earlier *Mona Lisa* painting, we can now confirm with 99% probability, i.e. practical certainty, that the faces of Earlier/Isleworth and Louvre *Mona Lisas* were painted by the same artist.

About the Authors

John Asmus has been an authoritative Research Physicist at the Institute for Pure and Applied Physical Sciences, at the University of California, San Diego since the early 1970s. Prof. Asmus and his team developed specialized equipment to assist the city of Venice, Italy, in cleaning and restoring many of its invaluable marble statues. Through laser holography, and NDT (Non Destructive Testing), holographic interferograms could reveal hidden defects in artwork. Based on some of this work, Prof. Asmus was approached to try and determine if any remains existed of Leonardo's '*Battle of Anghiari*' fresco under Vasari's subsequent murals, in the Palazzo Vecchio in Florence. In 1976, he and his team designed, built and tested a 1 MHz ultrasonic digital imaging system with an automated stepping-motor-controlled transducer scanner, and the following year ultrasonically mapped

the masonry strata beneath the Vasari paintings. Subsequent work by others has also been performed, but if anything remains of Leonardo's extraordinary work, it is out of sight for the present. Prof. Asmus was also commissioned to 'clarify' the Louvre '*Mona Lisa*', to see what it could look like without cracks and the brown 'smoggy atmosphere'. One of the discoveries made as a result of this test from the mid-1980s was that Leonardo had originally painted the female image with a necklace, and had subsequently painted it over. Ten years after first questioning the validity of the discovery, the Louvre's own new X-rays confirmed the existence of the necklace. A few years later, Prof. Asmus performed an independent investigation of the '*Isleworth Mona Lisa*', as the '*Earlier Version*' was known at that time, and that is how the painting is referred to in his reports, which are presented in the foundation's book.

Vadim Parfenov was born in St.Petersburg on August 12, 1962. He graduated from St. Petersburg State Polytechnic University in 1985. He received his PhD degree in 2002 (specialty – "Quantum electronics"). In 1985-2007 he worked at the Research Center "S.I.Vavilov State Optical Institute" (SOI), where he was involved in research into the development of lasers for various applications (including scientific, industrial and defense). In 2008 he was appointed to the permanent position of Associate Professor at St. Petersburg State Electrotechnical University. For the past 10 years his research has focused on the use of laser and opto-electronic techniques in Cultural Heritage preservation. He pioneered the practical use of laser cleaning and 3D laser scanning in art conservation in St.Petersburg, where he has had numerous collaborative works with leading museums, including The State Russian museum, The Hermitage museum, The museum-preserve "Tsarskoye Selo" and The State museum of Urban Sculpture. He has also collaborated with The State Tretyakov Gallery in Moscow in the use of 3D laser scanning for documentation and replication of artworks. He was the first to introduce the non-contact replication of outdoor monuments in Russia based on use of 3D laser scanning and CNC milling. Dr. Parfenov has been involved in numerous conferences and seminars since 1986, both in Russia and abroad. In 2014 he became a member of the Permanent Scientific Committee of LACONA (Lasers for Artwork Conservation). He has published numerous scientific papers and several books.

References

[1] See, for example, B. Mandelbrot, *The fractal geometry of nature*, W. H. Freeman, New York, NY, 1982; S. Lyu, D. Rickmore, and H. Farid, "A digital technique for art authentication", in *Proceedings of the National Academy of Sciences*; 101 (49), pp. 17006–17010, 2004; M. Shahram, D. G. Stork, and D. Donoho, "Recovering layers of brushstrokes through statistical analysis of color and shape: An application to Van Gogh's Self-portrait with grey fell hat", in D. G. Stork and J. Coddington (Eds.), *Computer image analysis in the study of art*, 6810, pp. 68100D–1–8, SPIE/IS&T, Bellingham, WA, 2008; and lastly, S. Jafarpour, G. Polatkan, E. Brevdo, S. Hughes, A. Brasoveanu, and I. Daubechies, "Stylistic Analysis of Paintings Using Wavelets and Machine Learning," *Proceedings of the European Signal Processing Conference* (EUSIPCO), 2009.

[2] Friedman T., Lurie D. J., Shalom A. "Authentication of Rembrandt's Self-portraits through the use of facial aging analysis," in *The Israel Medicine Association Journal*. 2012.Vol. 14, P. 591–594.

[3] K. Clark, *Leonardo da Vinci*. Cambridge: Cambridge University Press, 1952. C. Pedretti, *Leonardo: A Study in Chronology and Style*. Berkeley: University of California Press, 1973.

[4] Asmus J. F. "Spectral and Spatial Statistics of Raphael Paintings," in *Applications of Digital Image Processing XVII*, 1994. doi: 10.1117/12.186550.

[5] Asmus J. F. "Computer Image Studies of Rembrandt Self Portraits," in *Human Vision III*. 1992. Vol.1666, P.436-445.

[6] Asmus J.F., Bernstein R., Dave J.V., Myers H.J. "Computer enhancement of the Mona Lisa," in *Perspectives in Computing*. 1987. Vol. 7, P. 11-22.

[7] Asmus J. F. "Computer Studies of the Isleworth and Louvre Mona Lisas," in *Optical Engineering*. 1989. Vol. 28, No. 7. P. 800–804.

[8] G. Morelli, *Kunstkritische Studien über italienische Malerei*. Leipzig. 1890-1893. Bd. 1-3.

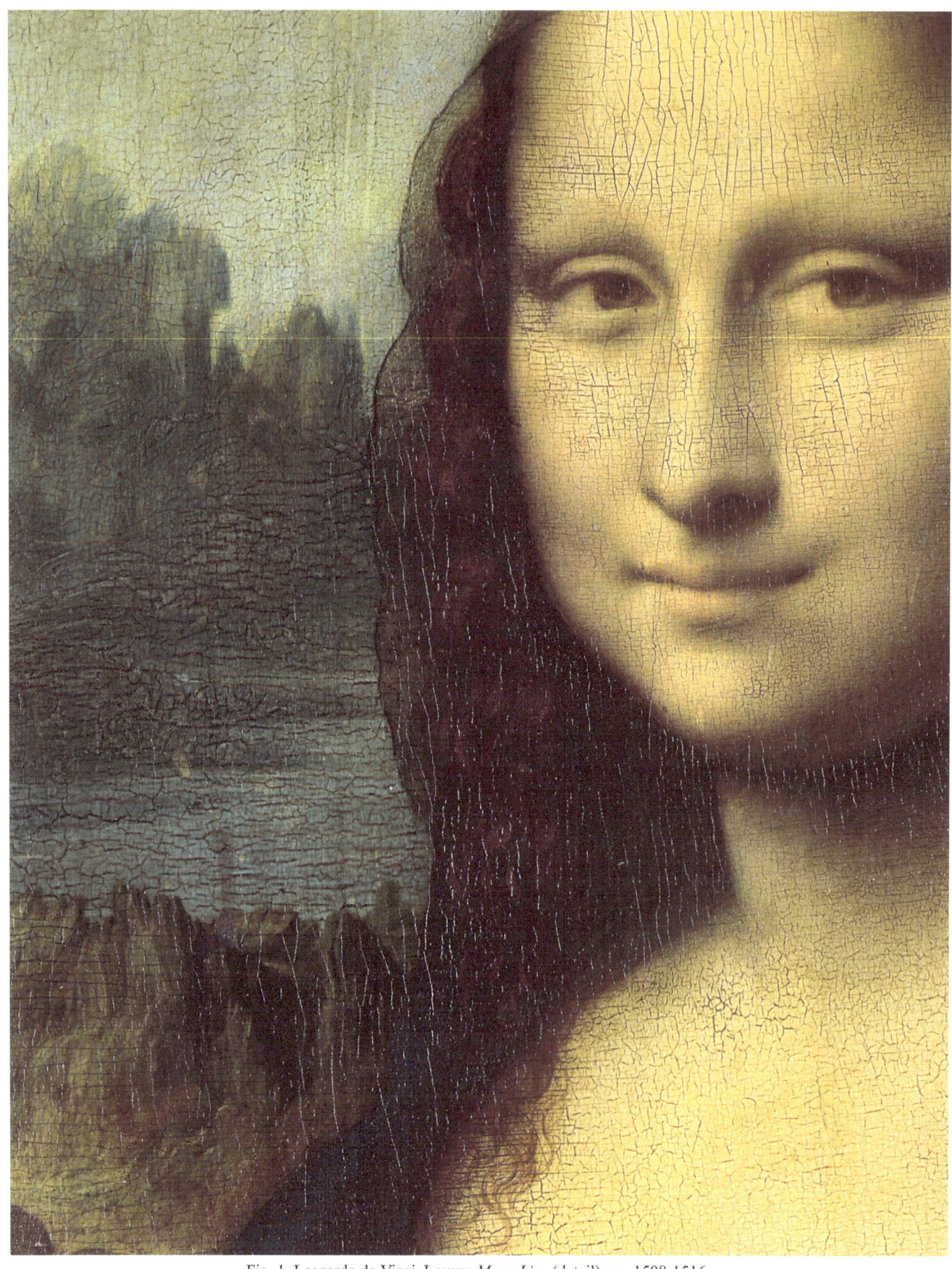

Fig. 1. Leonardo da Vinci, Louvre *Mona Lisa* (detail), ca. 1508-1516.

The Two Mona Lisas

Gérard Boudin de l'Arche
Art Historian, Author

There is now hardly any doubt that Leonardo Da Vinci painted two portraits of the spouse of the Florentine silk merchant, Francesco del Giocondo. However, if the provenance of one of those portraits, the Louvre *Mona Lisa*, has never been lost, it has not been quite the same for the other, which for the moment we shall call the X *Mona Lisa*. Has this version disappeared, like the *Leda and the Swan*, or is it hidden in some private collection? This is the question that was asked in an essay entitled *Au temps où la Joconde devint Monna Lisa 1503-1513* ("When *La Joconde* became the *Mona Lisa* 1513-1513")[1], and in the documentary film *la Joconde: à la recherche du tableau perdu* ("The *Mona Lisa*: the search for the missing painting"), released in December of 2018.

But before we go any further, what evidence do we have that there were indeed two portraits of Lisa Maria Gherardini, the wife of Del Giocondo, as painted by Leonardo Da Vinci? The witnesses and historical documentation give us a lead. Taken together, their considerations make it a certainty.

Vasari

Let us begin with the painter Vasari who, in his book *The Lives of the Artists* (published in Florence in 1550 and again in 1568) wrote: *Prese Lionardo a fare per Francesco Del Giocondo il ritratto di Mona Lisa sua moglie: e quattro anni penatovi lo lascio imperfetto laquale opera oggi è appresso il Re Francesco di Francia in Fontanableo* ("Leonardo undertook to execute, for Francesco del Giocondo, the portrait of *Monna Lisa*, his wife; and after toiling over it for four years, he left it unfinished; and the work is now in the collection of King Francis of France, at Fontainebleau.")[2] This account by Vasari gives us three important details:

1. The painting is definitely a portrait of Mona Lisa, the wife of Francesco del Giocondo.
2. The painting was unfinished in 1550.
3. In that same year it was at the palace of Fontainebleau in France, the property of King Francis I, who had died just three years earlier.

This means that the portrait could only be the one that is exhibited today in the Louvre, for which the provenance was never lost. The problem is, we know that this same portrait was perfectly finished in 1517, thanks to another, earlier and more reliable witness.

Antonio de Beatis

We owe this account to Antonio de Beatis, the secretary of Cardinal Louis d'Aragon, who visited Leonardo in Amboise on October 10, 1517. De Beatis described this visit in a diary known as *Itinerario*, today in the National Library of Naples. On page 76, he wrote that Leonardo showed them three paintings, amongst which was *Uno di certa donna firentina facta di naturale ad instantia del quondam Magnifico Juliano de Medici* ("a certain Florentine lady, done from nature at the behest of the late Magnificent

Giuliano de Medici.")[3] The two other paintings were described as one of "John the Baptist" and "one of the Madonna with the child, seated on the lap of Saint Anne." All three are described as *perfectissimi*, i.e. perfectly finished. From this document we can conclude that:

1. The "certa dona firentina" could only be "Lisa del Giocondo."

2. The client was no longer Francesco del Giocondo as stated by Vasari 30 years later, but Giuliano de Medici, the youngest son of Lorenzo the Magnificent, who was in fact the patron of Leonardo da Vinci from 1513 to 1516, during the period when the Medicis had been evicted from power in Florence.

3. This painting was certainly perfectly finished, contrary to what Vasari will state 30 years later!

Vespucci

A third account may allow us to discover what truly happened. We only learned about this very recently. It is the discovery of a handwritten note in the margin of a book of Cicero (*Epistulae ad familiares,* published in Bologna in 1477), which belonged to Agostino Vespucci, secretary to the Signoria of Florence, and the assistant of Machiavelli. This book was discovered by Armin Schlechter in 2005 during a reclassification of ancient publications in the Heidelberg Library. The handwritten annotation in Latin states: *Apelles Pictor, Ita Leonardos Vincius facet in omnibus suis picturis, ut enim caput lise del giocondo et anna matris virginis, videbimus quid faciet de aula magnii consilli, de qua re convenit iam cum vexillofero, 1503 8.bris* ("The painter Apelles. So does Leonardo da Vinci in all his paintings, like for the face of Lisa del Giocondo and Anne, the mother of the Virgin. We will see what he will do for the Hall of the Great Council as planned with the Gonfaloniere, October 1503").[4] This note confirms that:

1. In October of 1503, Leonardo Da Vinci was already painting the face (*caput*) of Lisa del Giocondo, at the same time that he was working on the St. Anne.

2. The portrait was not made at the request of Giuliano de Medici, who on that date was far from Florence, having been chased from the city with his family some 10 years earlier.

3. The portrait was painted at the request of the husband, Francesco del Giocondo, as described by Vasari nearly 50 years later, who omitted (perhaps purposely?) the actual date.

4. If, as indicated by Antonio de Beatis, Giuliano de Medici indeed ordered a portrait of Lisa del Giocondo, such could only have taken place 10 years later, on his return to Florence.

Accordingly, we conclude that there must have been two paintings of Lisa del Giocondo, painted "from life" (according to Leonardo) and that there is therefore a difference of age of about ten years between the two portraits.

Raphael

Thanks to the very comprehensive holdings of the Florentine State Archives, we know that Lisa del Giocondo, née Lisa Maria Gherardini, was born on June 15, 1479 on the Via Sguazza, Florence. In October 1503, she was therefore 24 years old, which means that ten years later she was 34 years old. Those 34 years correspond to the face of the Louvre portrait. In addition, we have a sketch by Raphael from 1504, based on Leonardo's portrait of 1503.

Here, we clearly see a Mona Lisa who is younger than the sitter of the Louvre portrait. This must therefore represent the Earlier *Mona Lisa*, painted by Leonardo when Lisa Maria was only 24 years old.

In sum, we may conclude that the Louvre *Mona Lisa* has to be the portrait ordered by Giuliano de Medici from Leonardo in 1513, when Lisa del Giocondo was already 34 years old. That portrait was the one admired by Antonio de Beatis and Cardinal d'Aragon in October 1517, who remarked on its perfectly finished condition. That same portrait

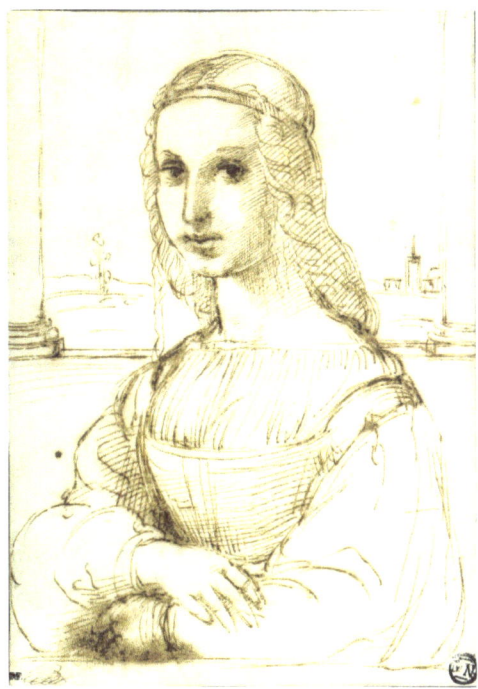
Fig. 2. Raphael, *Portrait of a Young Woman*, 1504.

was then sold to Francis I in 1518. Therefore, the description by Vasari in 1550 in *Lives of the Artists* cannot relate to that portrait, because at that time it had been in France for more than 30 years, and Vasari had never traveled there. What's more, the Louvre portrait lacks eyebrows, which Vasari specifically remarks upon.

But we can also arrive at another question. There has to be a reason why a man would ask an artist to paint the portrait of a woman. On reason could be because he was a very loving husband (for example, the portrait of 1503) or because he was a lover wishing to have the portrait of a beloved mistress (the portrait of 1513). To answer this question, we must follow the evidence. One theory is that in 1513, Lisa Maria del Giocondo had become the mistress of the new ruler of Florence, Giuliano de Medici, who was known for womanizing. If that's true, she was not the loyal wife described by Francesco Del Giocondo in his testament!

The X *Mona Lisa*

This question also brings us to the identification of the X *Mona Lisa* painting. We know from the evidence described above that:

1) The *Mona Lisa* was about ten years younger than the Louvre *Mona Lisa*

2) The painting must have been unfinished (according to Vasari)

3) It must include the columns seen and sketched by Raphael

Historians have identified at least nine *Mona Lisa* versions or copies painted in the 16th century that could fit these criteria. These paintings are:

1) The St. Petersburg *Mona Lisa*
2) The Prado *Mona Lisa*
3) The Baltimore *Mona Lisa*
4) The Epinal *Mona Lisa*
5) The Thalwill *Mona Lisa*
6) The Lord Brownlow *Mona Lisa*
7) The Flemish *Mona Lisa*
8) The Oslo *Mona Lisa*
9) The Isleworth/Earlier *Mona Lisa*

The 6 first examples can be put aside because they present a background which is identical to the Louvre version. Since the Louvre version is indisputably an original work by Leonardo, the others can only be copies of the Louvre portrait and not the X *Mona Lisa*. There thus remain the last three, nos. 7, 8 and 9. The Flemish *Mona Lisa*, no.7, is disqualified because it does not include the columns sketched by Raphael. As for the remaining two, numbers 8 and 9, one seems to be the copy of the other. For example, there is the same cluster to the right of the face representing a reflection of trees in water. However, one is more complete (the Oslo *Mona Lisa*). The back lists the date of 1525 in Roman figures, which is 6 years after the death of Leonardo. It is attributed to Bernardino Luini,

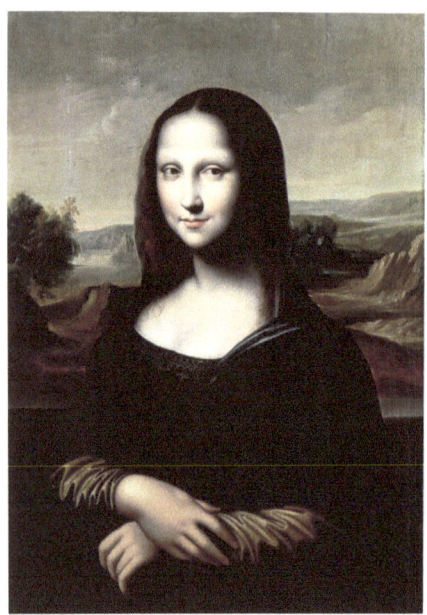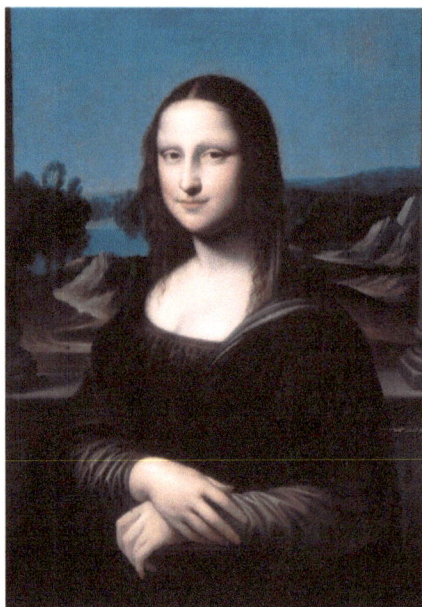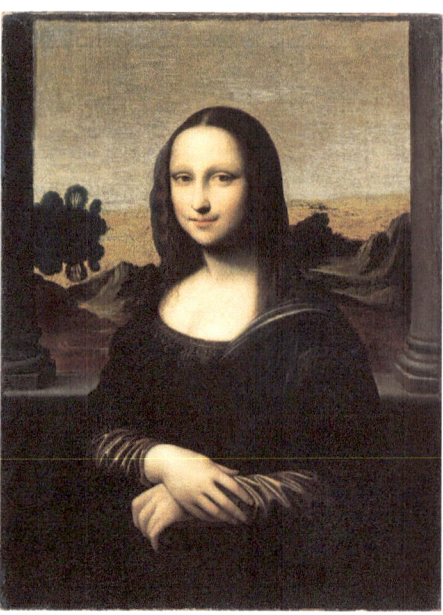

Fig. 3. The Flemish *Mona Lisa* (16th century); the Oslo *Mona Lisa* (17th century); and the Isleworth *Mona Lisa* (early 16th century).

a talented painter of Lombardy, who was familiar with Leonardo, and who would never have made a copy of a copy! He could only have copied the original, which he may have seen at Vaprio when visiting Francesco Melzi, Leonardo's last pupil who brought it with him, in 1520, as part of the inheritance given by Leonardo.

The last remaining option is thus the Isleworth *Mona Lisa*. Is it the portrait ordered in 1503 by Francesco del Giocondo from Leonardo da Vinci? A close observation shows that:
1) She is about ten years younger and has eyebrows as described by Vasari, which are not present in the Louvre painting.
2) The painting is unfinished (as described by Vasari).
3) The Raphael columns are clearly included.

This is all without taking into account the inimitable brushstrokes of Leonardo, which are clearly evident. There is for many, however, one serious issue: this painting was painted on canvas, while it is known that Leonardo painted on wood panel. However, this problem can be overcome. In fact, before coming to Florence in April 1500, we know that Leonardo was in Venice at the end of 1499 and the beginning 1500. At that time, the custom of painting on canvas as practiced in the Low Countries was being introduced through Venice to Italy. It is difficult to believe that Leonardo would not have tried out this method, particularly since the portrait was executed for a simple merchant, rather than a prince. Indeed, Leonardo specifically describes the use of canvas in his *Treatise on Painting*.

There are three points that remain to be clarified:
1) Why did Vasari mix up the two paintings? Was it his ignorance, or was it done on purpose?
2) Where did Leonardo (who only painted from nature) find his inspiration for the countryside depicted in the background of the Louvre painting, to the right of the portrait—including the topographical error of different levels between the lake at left and the lake to the right?
3) Why and for what reason are the eyebrows not present in the Louvre *Mona Lisa*?

Conclusion

Giorgio Vasari was a very well-known personality in Florence, and a protégé of the Medicis. Among others, he designed the loggia near the Ponte Vecchio over the Arno. Vasari was a contemporary of Lisa del Giocondo, who retired to the convent of Saint Orsola. But he was also acquainted with Francesco Melzi, whom he visited at Vaprio in preparation for his publication of *Lives of the Artists*. It is possible that he was aware of a putative liaison between Giuliano de Medici and Mona Lisa, based on rumors that may have been circulating in Florence. In order to avoid scandal falling upon the family of Mona Lisa, he may have purposely confused the two paintings, even though one was copied from the other. With this stratagem the duality was eliminated, and so the Louvre *Mona Lisa* was attributed to Francesco del Giocondo, the husband. If it wasn't for the comment by Leonardo as noted by Antonio de Beatis, the secret would have been kept in spite of the obvious contradictions.

The Isleworth *Mona Lisa* is certainly the painting first described by Vespucci in his handwritten note. It is also the painting copied by Bernardino Luini in 1525 in Vaprio and seen by Vasari before 1550. The painting was brought to England around 1750 (under circumstances that are still to be discovered) by the young Thomas Benedictus Marwood after his "grand tour" in Italy; since then the trace has never been lost.

About the Author

Gérard Boudin de l'Arche was raised in Italy but educated in his native country of France, where he studied law, political science and economics. Later he taught economics at "Sup de Co Marseille" (a French business school). He then undertook a professional in real estate in both France and the United States. His interests pushed him to explore two new avenues. The first was theoretical physics, about which he published three essays (*Relativity dead end*, 2009; *A divine game of dice*, 2010; and *Up to the border of space and time*, 2015). Secondly, he started exploring secrets and myths of history about which he published three other essays: *In search of the Odyssey* (2005); *In search of Atlantis (*2012*);* and, most recently, *In search of*

Monna Lisa (2017). He has also produced a film on the story of the two Mona Lisa paintings entitled *la Joconde: à la recherche du tableau perdu* ("The Mona Lisa: the search for the missing painting").

References

[1] Gérard Boudin de l'Arche, *Au temps où la Joconde devint Monna Lisa 1503-1513*. Omnibus Editions December, 2017.

[2] Vasari, Giorgio, *Le Vite de' più eccellenti pittori, scultori e architetti;* 1568 Edition.

[3] Antonio de Beatis, "Account of the Visit of Cardinal Louis d'Aragon paid to Leonardo, at the Château de Cloux, October 10, 1517," in Delieuvin, Vincent, *Saint Anne: Leonardo da Vinci's ultimate Masterpiece;* p. 199.

[4] Probst, Veit, "Rätselhafte Mona Lisa: Wer ist die geheimnisvoll lächelnde Dame auf Leonardo da Vincis Bild?" in *UniSpiegel*, University of Heidelberg, 2008.

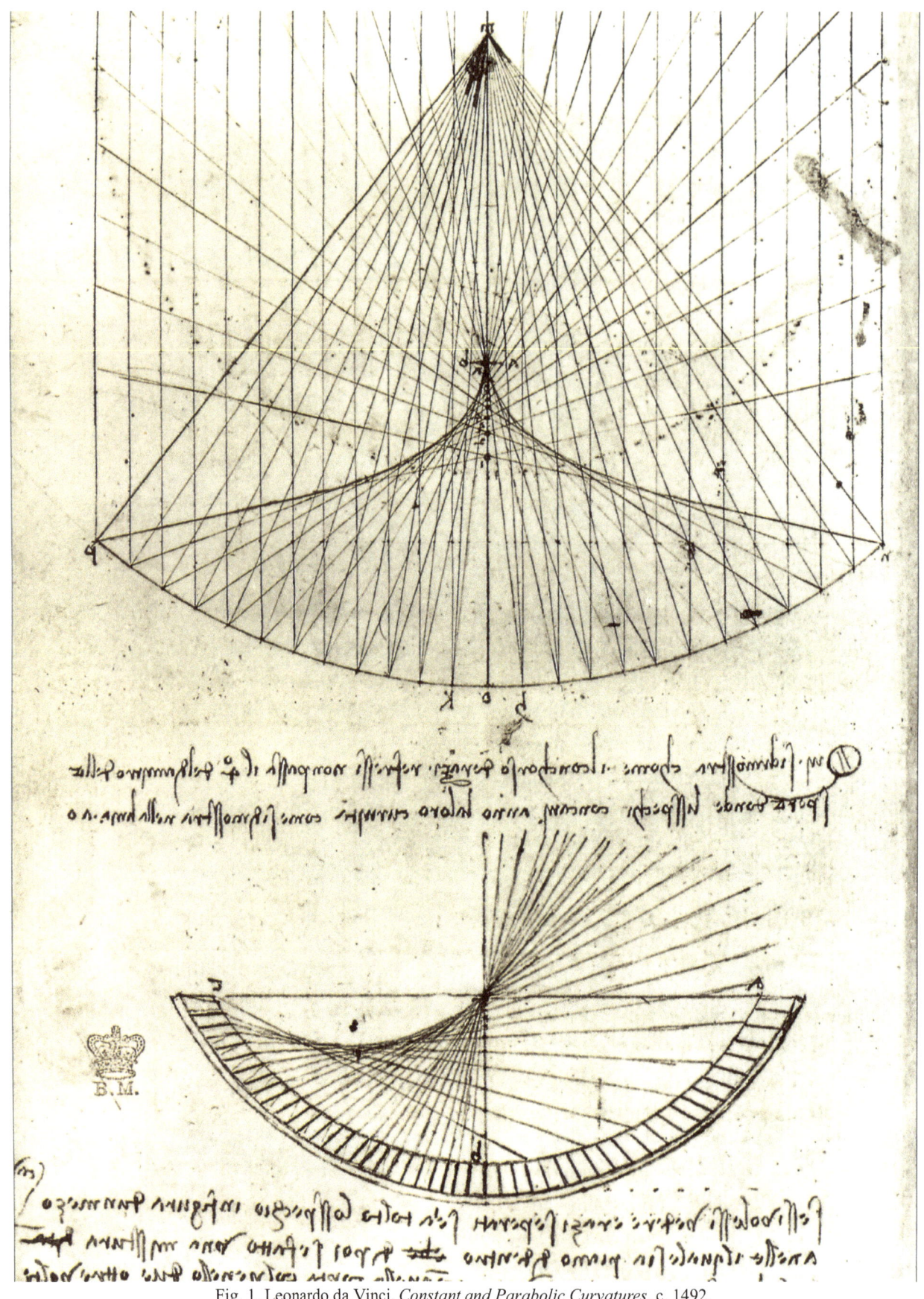

Fig. 1. Leonardo da Vinci, *Constant and Parabolic Curvatures*, c. 1492.

Leonardo da Vinci's Use of Perspective in the Mona Lisa Portraits

Albert Sauteur
Painter, Mathematician and Art Theorist
Payerne, Switzerland

The previous chapters have made the argument that Leonardo painted not one, but two versions of the *Mona Lisa*: the so-called Earlier *Mona Lisa*, dated 1503-1506, and the Louvre *Mona Lisa*, dated 1508-1515. This article will argue that when Leonardo da Vinci began painting the Earlier *Mona Lisa*, he used a monocular perspective, with only one vanishing point. The following excerpt from his *Treatise on Painting* exemplifies this idea:

> Perspective is nothing but the vision of a scene behind a flat and transparent glass, on which we mark all the objects which are on the other side of this window: they can be connected by pyramids with the center of the eye; and these pyramids are intercepted by said glass.

However, after steady experimentation, Leonardo discovered the limits of this concept and developed a more nuanced approach. As he wrote:

> Among [the] painters, there are those who look at the works of nature by windows or other transparent sheets and net, and they transfer them there on transparent surfaces, and then trace the contours according to the rules of proportionality, enlarging and then filling these chiaroscuro outlines by demarcating the location, extent and shape of the shadows and forms. But this must only be praised in those who are able to reproduce these natural effects with imagination, and use these means only to enhance their work and not to deviate in any way from the proper imitation of the object with exact verisimilitude. It is necessary to fault this invention when those who use it do not know how to apply it without thinking about themselves, because by their laziness they destroy its spirit and cannot produce anything good.

In the process, Leonardo developed the so-called *binocular perspective*: the attempt to depict nature as actually perceived by both eyes. As this article will show, this is particularly evident in the artist's depiction of the *Mona Lisa* in the Louvre, thus establishing a unique relationship between the Earlier *Mona Lisa* and the Louvre version.

A Comparison of the Panels

To begin with—and as previous authors have already noted—the size of the Earlier *Mona Lisa* is larger than that of the Louvre version. However, while the space around the Earlier version is larger, the size of the character in relationship to that space is smaller. Conversely, the figure in the Louvre portrait is smaller,

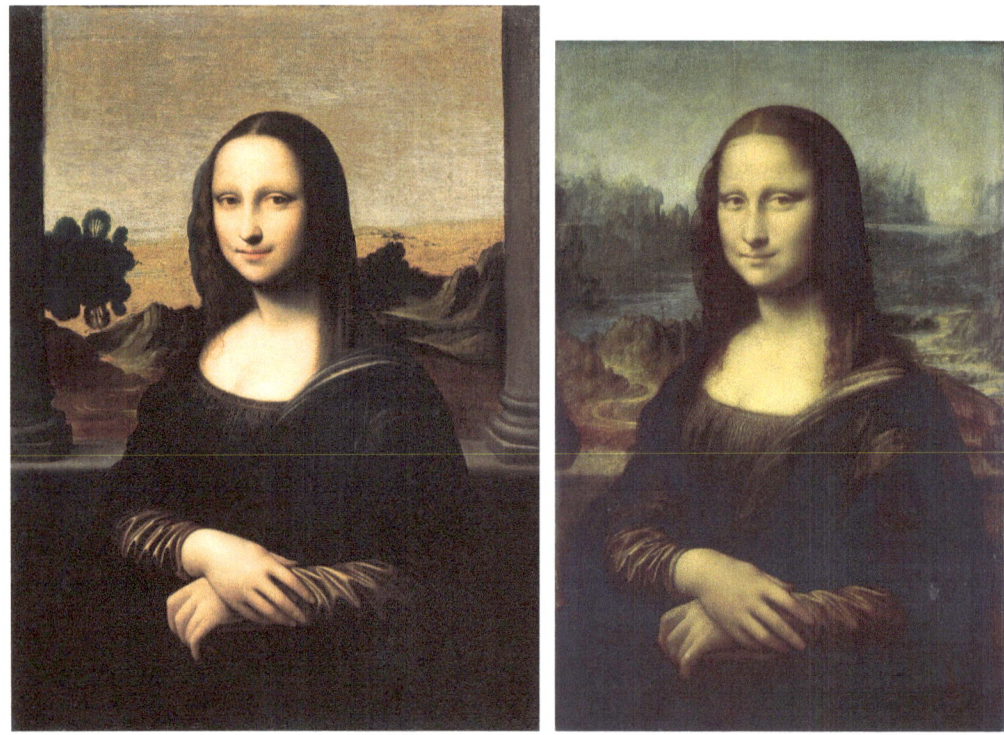

Fig. 2. The Earlier *Mona Lisa* (64,5 cm x 86 cm) and the Louvre *Mona Lisa* (53,3 cm x 79,2 cm).

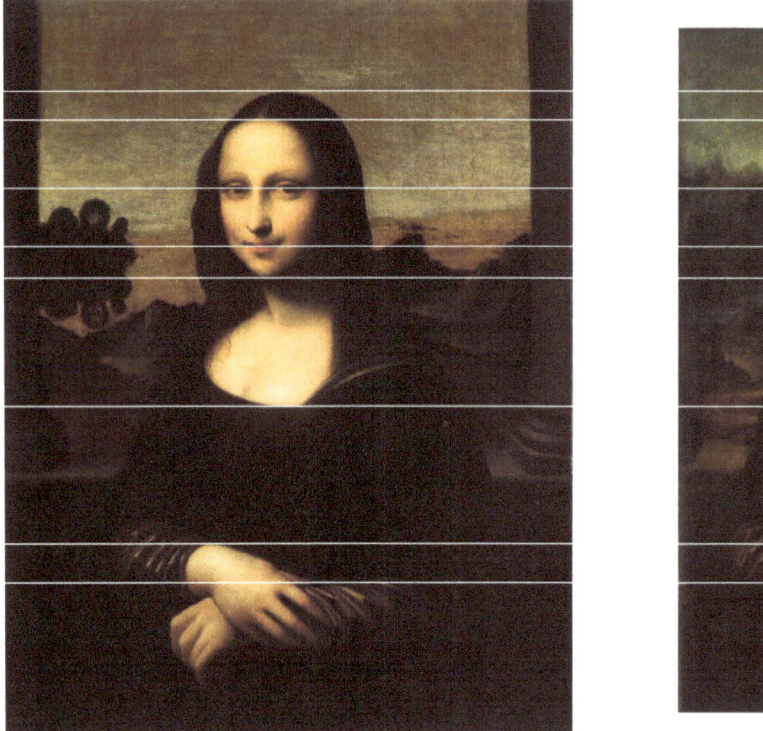
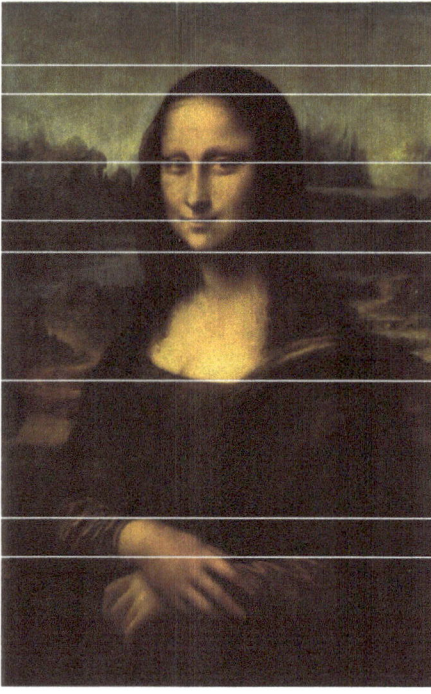

Fig. 3. The Earlier *Mona Lisa* and the Louvre *Mona Lisa*. The latter has been digitally reduced by 10% to allow for a proportionate comparison of the models.

but the character is larger in proportion to the space around her.

Horizontal Comparison Of Models

If we ignore that ratio for a moment, we will note that proportionally, the characters are virtually identical (please note: the painting of the Louvre *Mona Lisa* in this image is reduced by 90% to allow the comparison of models on the same scale).

Vertical Comparison of the Models

On the other hand, a vertical comparison of the two models shows that that the eyes of the Louvre *Mona Lisa* are placed in closer proximity to each other than the Earlier version. This is the first indication that Leonardo could have painted the Louvre portrait in accordance with binocular vision (a video explaining this theory can be seen at www.albertsauteur.ch/film).

Monocular Vs. Binocular Perspective

All of these distinctive features can be explained by the theory of monocular vs. binocular perspective, as shown in the diagram below. In a monocular vision of traditional perspective (left), the space A x A, shown in gray in the diagram, will be projected proportionally when seen through a glass wall A 'x A'. In a binocular vision, however (right), the red space A x B, observed through the glass wall, expands horizontally. That means that for this space to be reproduced in its entirety, it must be compressed horizontally (B) in order to fit the painted surface. This will inevitably result in some form of proportional distortion.

Why is this significant? The answer is that the different spacing of the eyes in both paintings can be explained by the fact that when Leonardo painted the Louvre *Mona Lisa* a decade or so later than the Earlier version, he had progressed to the use of binocular vision. This may also explain why the two columns of the Earlier *Mona Lisa* do not appear in the Louvre painting, except for their base. To illustrate

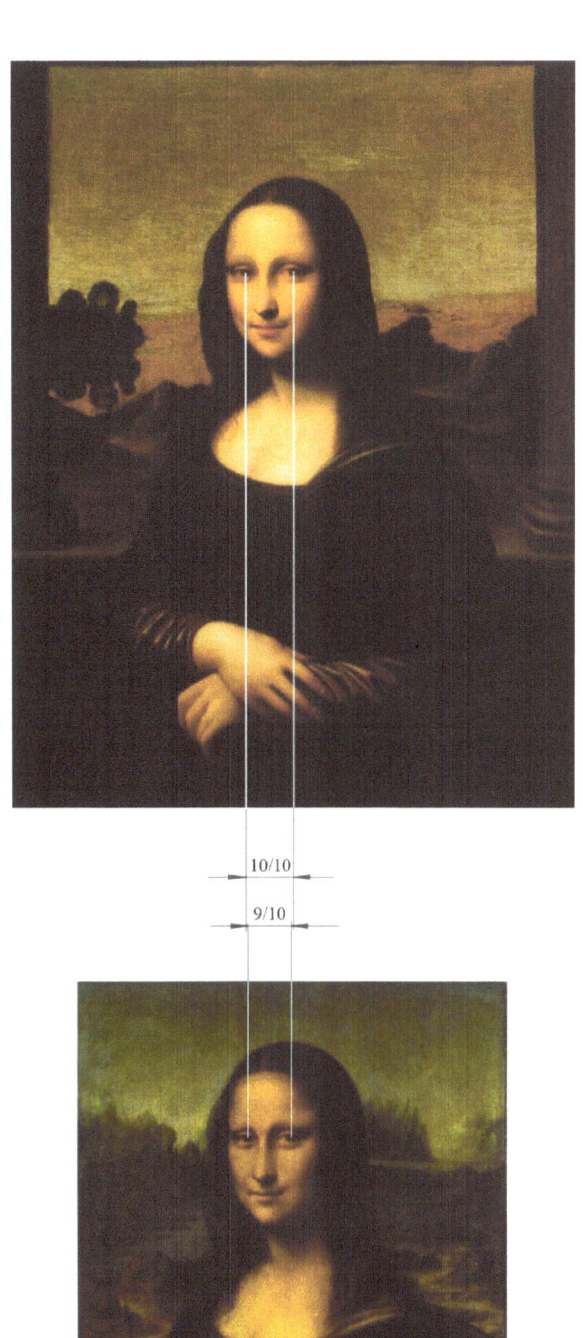

Fig. 4. A comparison of the two *Mona Lisa* portraits shows that the eyes in the Louvre version are closer together.

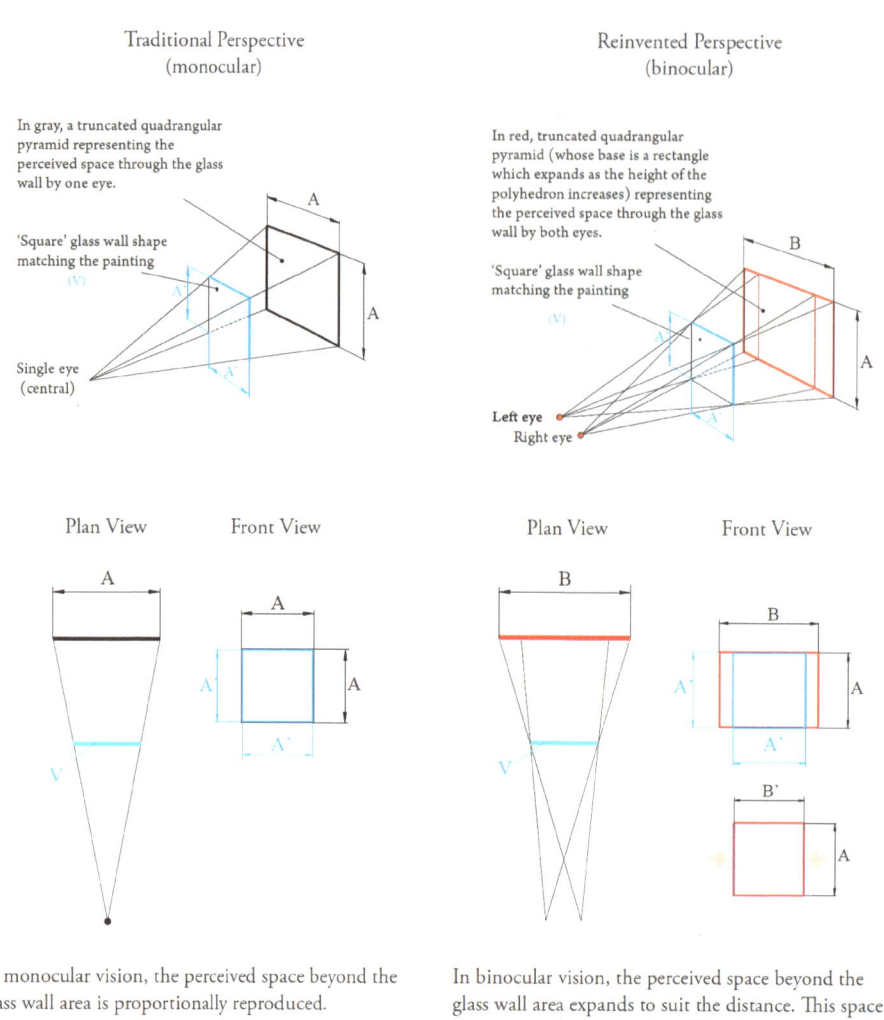

Traditional Perspective
(monocular)

In gray, a truncated quadrangular pyramid representing the perceived space through the glass wall by one eye.

'Square' glass wall shape matching the painting

Single eye (central)

Reinvented Perspective
(binocular)

In red, truncated quadrangular pyramid (whose base is a rectangle which expands as the height of the polyhedron increases) representing the perceived space through the glass wall by both eyes.

'Square' glass wall shape matching the painting

Left eye
Right eye

Plan View   Front View

Plan View   Front View

In monocular vision, the perceived space beyond the glass wall area is proportionally reproduced.

In binocular vision, the perceived space beyond the glass wall area expands to suit the distance. This space is compressed horizontally in B' so that it can be fully shown in the painting. This results in a deformation.

Fig. 5. Traditional Perspective vs. Reinvented Perspective

this, the graphic in Figure 6 shows the Louvre portrait superimposed over that of the Earlier *Mona Lisa*. This composite image clearly shows that the bases of the columns of Earlier version, highlighted by a yellow line, do not appear in the frame of the Louvre painting. In other words, in a monocular vision, we have a narrower field of view than in binocular vision.

If, on the other hand, one compresses the Earlier *Mona Lisa* horizontally (gray arrows) until the bases of the columns are superimposed over those of the painting of the Louvre (here in orange), one sees that the separation of the eyes corresponds to that of the *Mona Lisa* of the Louvre, with striking precision (Fig.3).

Subtle Correlations

Another important factor may corroborate the hypothesis that Vinci would have intuitively painted the Louvre *Mona Lisa* in accordance with the binocular vision: the vanishing points of the bases of the columns are consistent with my theory of binocular perspective. The experiment described in Figures 7-9 demonstrates this.

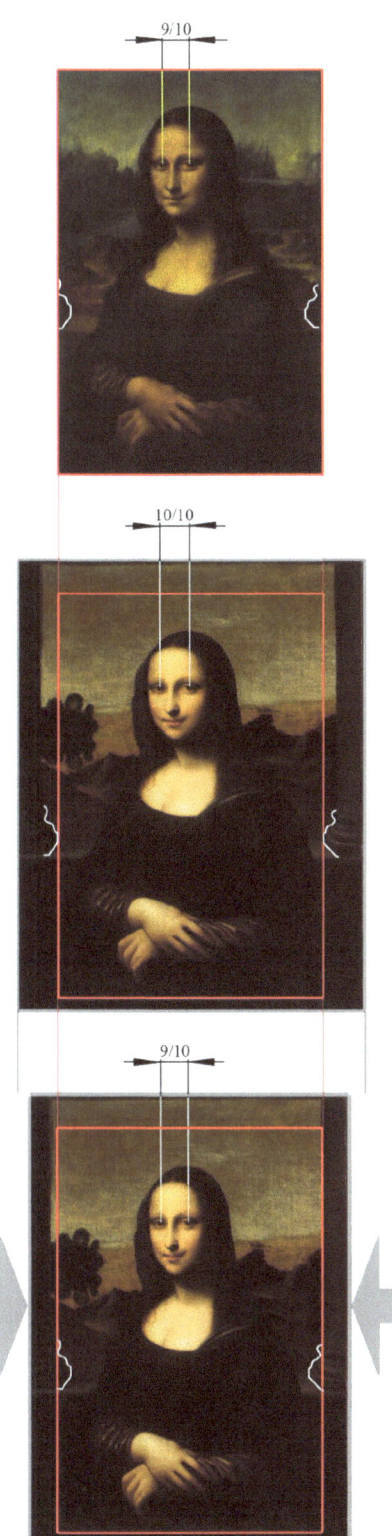

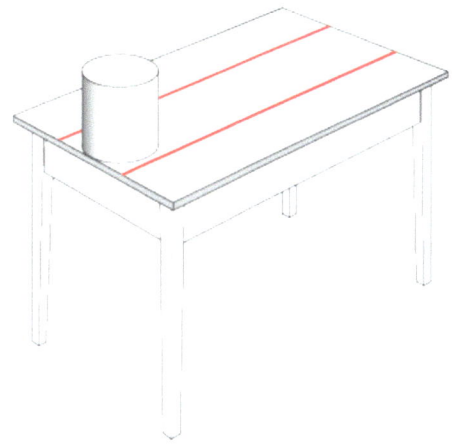

Fig. 7. A cylinder placed at the end of the table represents the bust of the *Mona Lisa*. It is placed between two parallel lines that recall the edges of the bases of the columns.

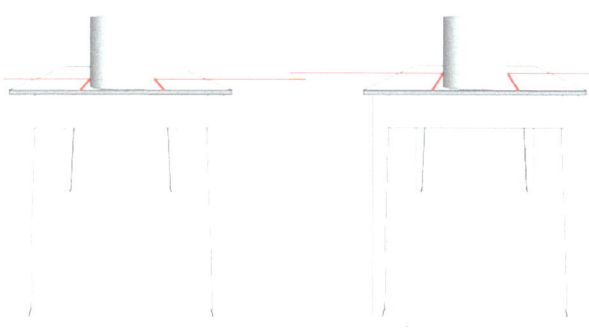

Fig. 8. The location of the plane where the vanishing lines disappear at the rear of the cylinder is farther removed in binocular perspective.

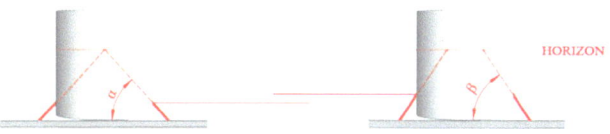

Fig. 9. As a result, the angle of binocular creep is more open (β> α). These angular differences of the vanishing lines are clearly shown in the two paintings representing the *Mona Lisa*.

Fig 6. If the Louvre *Mona Lisa* and the Earlier *Mona Lisa* are superimposed (b), the bases of the columns (highlighted by the white line) do not appear in the red frame that matches the Louvre *Mona Lisa*. If, on the other hand, the image of the Earlier *Mona Lisa* is compressed until her eye spacing matches that of the Louvre version (c), the bases of the columns appear in the painting like the Louvre *Mona Lisa* with striking accuracy.

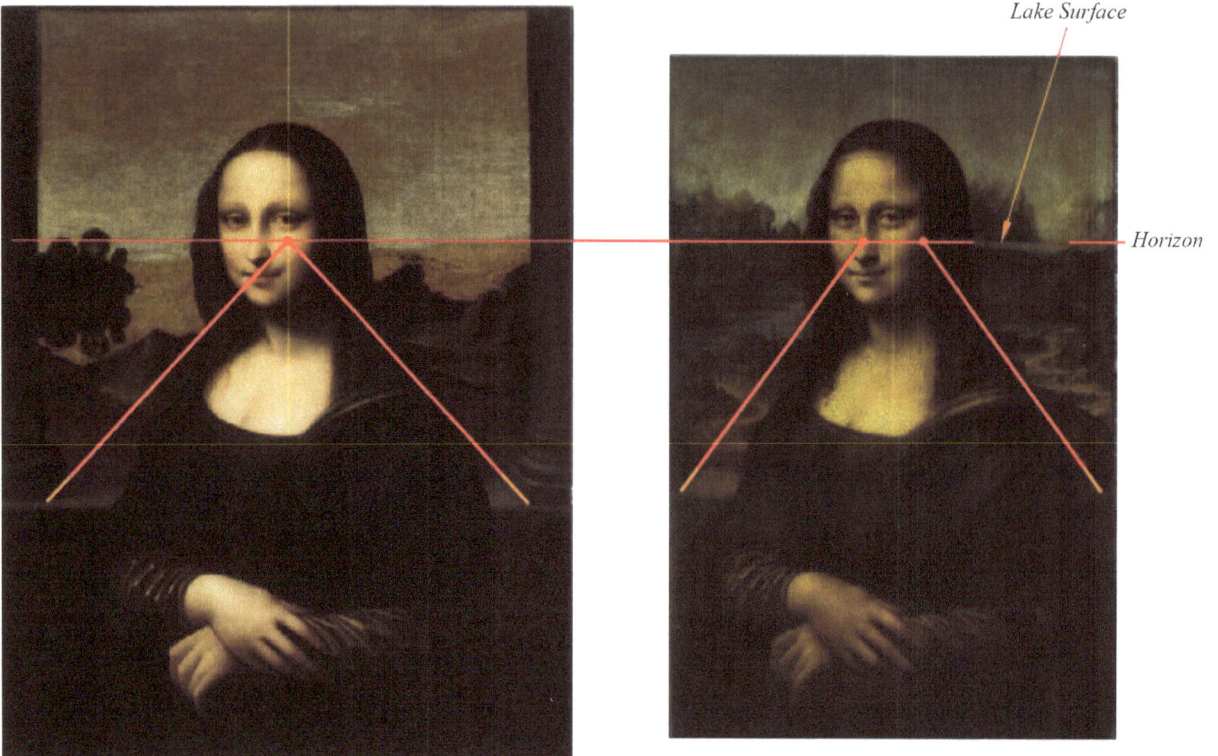

Fig. 10. Vanishing points in the Earlier and Louvre *Mona Lisa*.

In the Earlier *Mona Lisa*, the confluence of the monocular vanishing lines, defined by the bases of the columns, determines the traditional vanishing point, and establishes the horizon. In the Louvre version, the binocular vanishing lines generated by the bases of the columns meet in a point located at the same horizon. Moreover, this horizon corresponds to the surface of the lake located to the right side of Lisa's head. These correlations, which complete the horizontal compression of the image, allow us to think that such subtle refinements in both paintings can only be the product of a brilliant mind such as Leonardo's.

About the Author

Albert Sauteur was born in Saint-Martin (Fribourg-Switzerland) on March 28, 1950.

His practice as an artist has enabled him to redefine the concept of linear perspective and the way that every human being, with two eyes, perceives three-dimensional space. This has produced several experiments that allow the viewer to see the incredible and vertiginous complexity of the representation of our perception of the real. The artist has presented his discovery of the binocular perspective through articles including one of the most widely read national journals in Switzerland (Migros Journal), conferences including *The Reinvented Perspective* at the Palace of Discovery, Paris (2011); *Five Centuries After Vinci - The Discovery of Binocular Perspective*, WIPO, Geneva (2011) and at the University of Friborg, Switzerland (2014). In addition, his art has been exhibited at prestigious venues such as ETH, Zürich (2004), the United Nations (2006) and the Louvre Museum, Paris (2008). His website is www.albertsauteur.ch.

References

[1] André Chastel (2203). Leonardo da Vinci: Treatise on painting. Ivry-sur-Seine, calmann-lévy, 2003), p.123.

[2] Ibid, pp. 209-210.

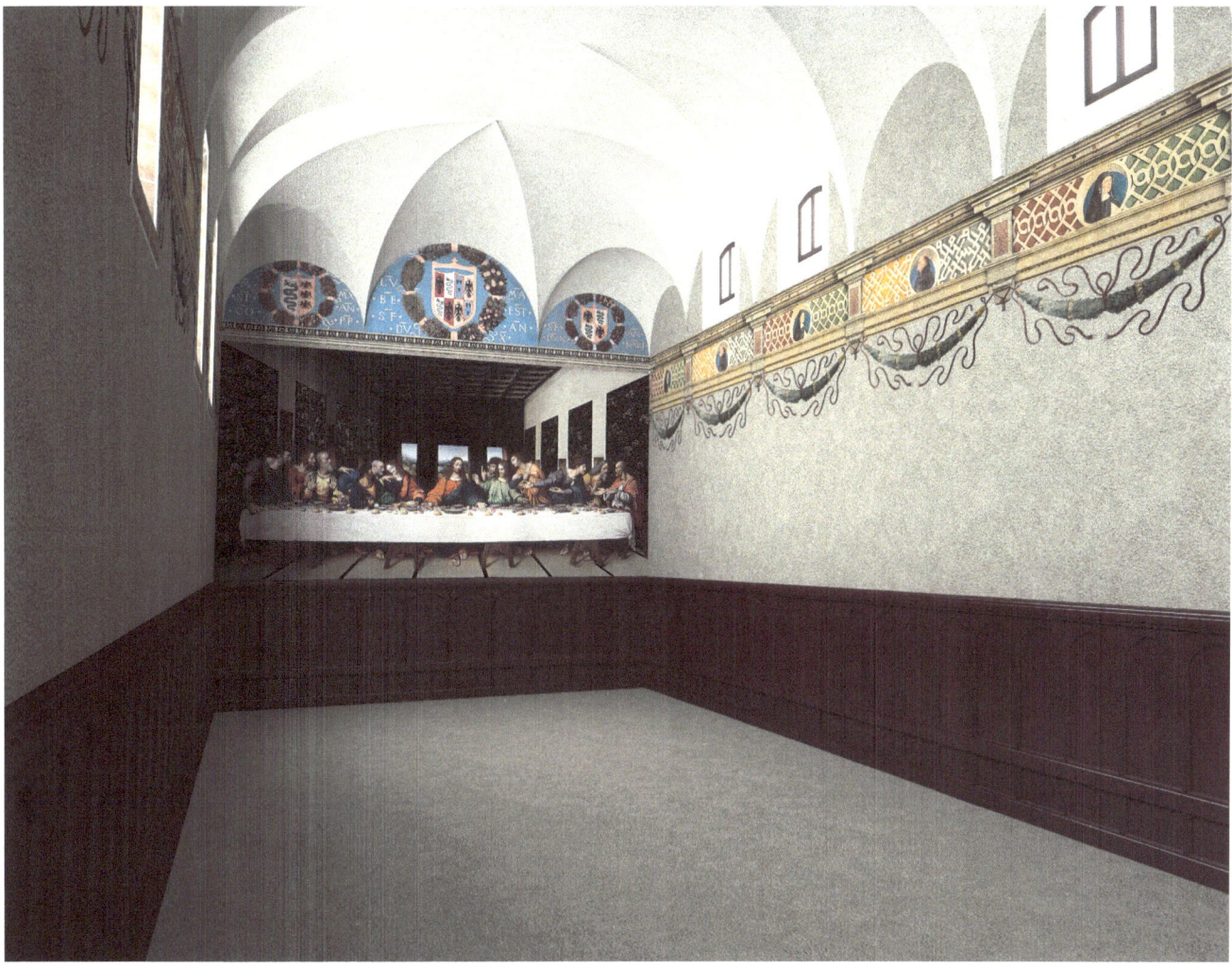

Fig. 11. A modern reconstruction of the refectory, the *Cenacolo*, with Leonardo's *Last Supper* (1495-1499) in the Santa Maria delle Grazie in Milan. Here, Leonardo arrived at another unique solution to traditional Quattrocento perspective. Since the mural was as large as the northern wall of the refectory, and with a space as deep as the refectory itself, there was no single point that could convincingly serve as the vanishing point at eye level. In response, Leonardo placed the vanishing point some fourteen feet *above* the natural eye level of visitor standing in the hall, placing it near Christ's right ear. As a result, the deep projection of the painting appears as an entirely plausible suggestion of depth, no matter where one stands in the refectory.

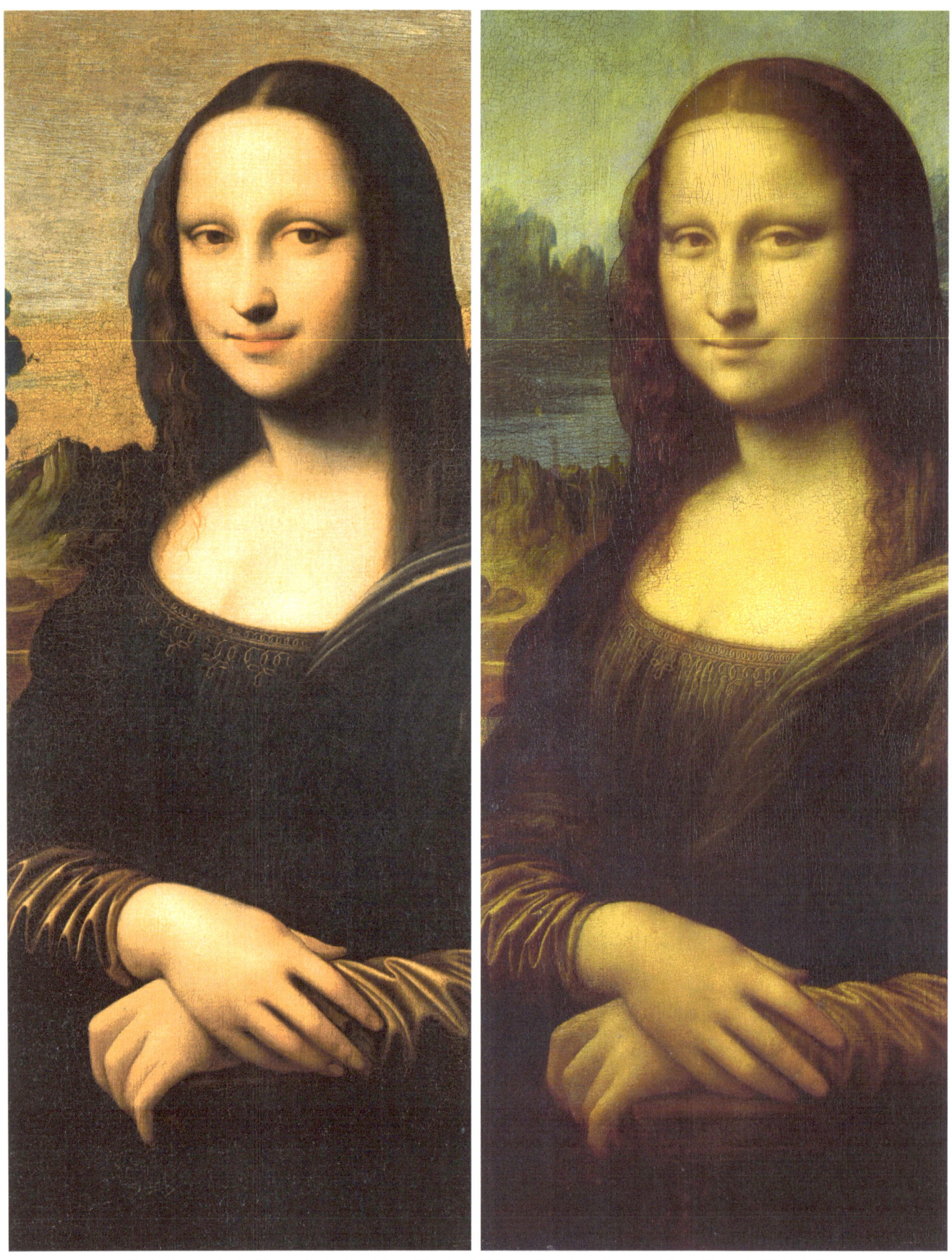

Fig 1. Leonardo da Vinci, the Earlier *Mona Lisa* (c. 1503-1506) and the Louvre *Mona Lisa* c. 1508-1516).

A STUDY OF CONTRASTS:
The Isleworth and the Louvre versions of the Mona Lisa

Átila Soares da Costa Filho
Art History Professor in Renaissance and Contemporary
Painting, Philosophy and Sociology.

Among about sixty alleged *Mona Lisa* portraits spread around Europe, the United States and Japan, one seems to stands out: the Isleworth *Mona Lisa* or Earlier *Mona Lisa*, an oil-on-canvas work that is slightly larger (84.8 x 64.8 cm) than the celebrated version of the Paris Louvre (78.8 x 53.3 cm), which is also older. Basically, the two paintings are similar and, at first, draw attention to the fact that the model from the first version is younger and more alluring.

The most reliable reports about the Isleworth painting go back to the eighteenth century, when it was acquired from its unknown Italian owner and brought to Great Britain, where it would be part of an aristocrat patrimony in Somerset for almost two centuries. It was later acquired by William Hugh Blaker, curator of the Holburne Museum of Art in Bath, a connoisseur and acclaimed art collector, who brought it to his home in Isleworth, a suburb of west London in 1913. During the First War, for safety reasons, the painting was sent to the United States. Many years later, after its return to Great Britain, the British art collector and publisher Dr. Henry F. Pulitzer became the new owner of the work. Pulitzer is the author of a major study about the painting, probably published in 1966 under the title *Where is the Mona Lisa?* (the work presents no exact references for its publication year). After his death in 1979, the painting became the property of his companion, Elizabeth Meyer. When she passed away in 2008, the portrait passed into the hands of its current owners.

Lisa, the young 'Gioconda'

The character of the Earlier *Mona Lisa*, in Dr. Pulitzer's opinion, was the real Mona Lisa ("mona", which in old Italian is a contraction of *ma donna*, meaning "lady"), a woman about 11 years younger than the figure portrayed in the Louvre, who would have been about 34 years old at the time the Louvre portrait was completed. The model, called Lisa del Giocondo (previously, Lisa Gherardini), was the wife of a wealthy Florentine silk merchant called Francesco di Bartolomeo di Zanobi del Giocondo. While sitting for the portrait, she wore what appears to be a thin mourning veil covering her head, perhaps because her little daughter had passed some time earlier; something that is less clear in the later version. Indeed, the later Louvre version depicts a lady who could be a mistress of Giuliano de Medici, Costanza D'Avalos, also known as "Gioconda," whose composition allegedly used the same design scheme of the previous version. In that interpretation, the term "Gioconda," or "smiling," does not have anything to do with the name del "Giocondo", and instead refers to the smile in the Louvre version. Other researchers have claimed that the true identity of *La Gioconda* is Isabella Gualanda (another mistress of Giuliano), or Isabella d'Este; or even Cecilia Gallerani (the model for *Lady with an Ermine*, today in Cracow), who were all known figures in Italian society at that time.[1]

A controversial theory

One of the most traditional sources about the *Mona Lisa,* the book by the Italian Renaissance artist and biographer Giorgio Vasari,[2] could decisively put an end to this controversy. However, Dr. Pulitzer questions the text's validity when he argues that Vasari never saw the *Mona Lisa* that is today in the Louvre, since he was only four years old when Leonardo took the portrait to France. As we know, Vasari never visited that country. Nevertheless, Vasari is able to describe the painting in detail, with features that match the characteristics of the Isleworth *Mona Lisa,* which was then perhaps in the possession of Francesco Del Giocondo. The latter may even have been his friend.

In addition, the distinguished chronicler Gian Paolo Lomazzo wrote about the painting in his 1584 book, in which he clearly distinguishes between two works: the "Gioconda" and the "Mona Lisa."[3] Also, the secretary of Cardinal D'Aragon, Antonio of Beatis, took notes of a conversation that the cardinal had with Leonardo at the latter's home in Cloux, France, in 1517, which suggest that the work in the Louvre was ordered by Giuliano of Medici (see above my reference to Costanza). Pulitzer also cited other evidence:

1) One of the specialists called to examine the *Gioconda* after it was stolen from the Louvre in 1911, Prof. Commendatore Lorenzo Cecconi, authenticated the Isleworth version in London as a Leonardo autograph.

2) John Eyre, also an art connoisseur, wrote in his publication *The Two Mona Lisas* (1924) that the hands and face in the Isleworth version were unquestionably painted by Leonardo.

According to a 1914 article in *The Century Magazine,* written by Walter Littlefield, another version, the newly-restored *Mona Lisa* or *Gioconda Velata* in the Prado Museum (Madrid) had originally been acquired by Charles I of Spain to rival the original portrait owned by King François I of France. This claim was seen as legitimate at the time, but the growing glamorization and mystique of the Paris version were gradually blurring the importance and legitimacy of the Prado version. Today, the most accepted interpretation is that Francesco Melzi, Leonardo's assistant, painted the Prado *Mona Lisa,* albeit under Leonardo's supervision as attested by numerous *pentimenti.*

The Prado *Mona Lisa*

The background of the Prado version – once black – was removed in 2012, revealing a landscape similar to the Louvre's version. However, it has been posited by some that these two portraits (from the Prado and the Louvre) actually represent the same sitter, with the Spanish version being the first. If that is true, it would deprive the Louvre's version of its original status. To sustain the thesis, these authors argued that the Louvre *Mona Lisa* looks older because of the aged varnishes and craquelures that turned her into a woman of middle age.

The problem with this theory is that, if this is true, then everything that has been written and discussed during the last centuries about old paintings should be discarded, since all of them went through the same aging processes, thus making it impossible for specialists to understand the real age of any portrait. Moreover, these effects only become noticeable when the model's face is seen up close. Thus, we must conclude that craquelures and related effects never had such an impact as to confuse youth with maturity. If the model of Paris appears to be older than her cousin in Prado, the reason is that it was intended that way, even if they are based on the same cartoon. Therefore, the youthfulness of the *"Velata"* or Prado version would corroborate the *"Isleworth",* since evidence suggests that the Prado version emerged from the same original.

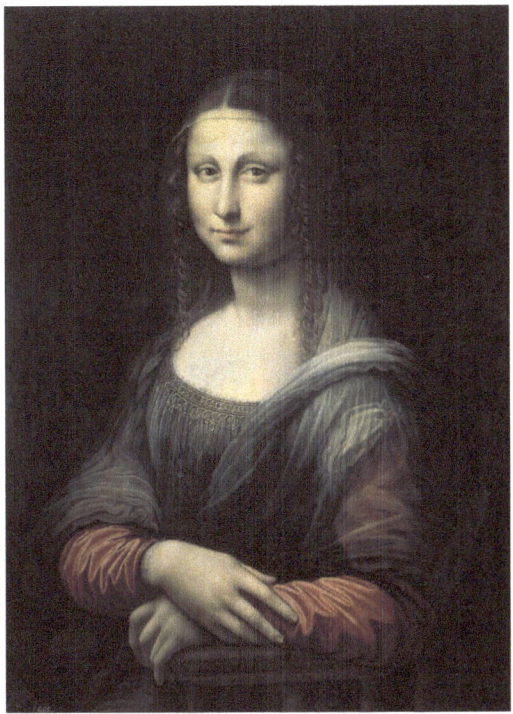

Fig. 2. Salaì (?), the Prado *Mona Lisa* (c. 1513-1515), before the 2012 restoration.

Fig. 3. Salaì (?), the Prado *Mona Lisa* (c. 1513-1515), after the 2012 restoration.

Discussions and Further Evidence

Henry Pulitzer argued that scholars have a tendency to reject anything that is unprecedented, since this forces them to reconsider many of their assumptions. Theories developed across the length of a career could thus be invalidated. From the days of Pulitzer to this day, the Isleworth has become the subject of a comprehensive effort to show that it is indeed a da Vinci autograph; and, moreover, that it depicts the same woman as in the Louvre version – as will be confirmed in future studies. To this end, much evidence has been gathered from different scholars, many of whom are represented in this monograph.

A number of tests were performed on the Isleworth version (as documented in the Appendix to this book), including ultraviolet light, radiocarbon dating and measurements of spectrometry by gamma-ray, which concluded that the painting was executed at some time in the beginning of the sixteenth century. In 2005, further tests showed that the pigments used in the painting were indeed available in Florence at the time of Da Vinci. In addition, it was found that the treatment scrupulously followed Leonardo's prescriptions in his *Trattato della Pittura*. For example, the pigments chosen for the painting primer (a combination of ochre-red, light brown and calcite - CaCO3, as was customary in the High Renaissance, and quartz) are the same or similar to the primer of his other works. All of these tests would support the theory that the Isleworth portrait is an authentic Leonardo and that its model is the young Lisa del Giocondo, *née* Gherardini, who was 11 to 12 years younger than the model in the Louvre's version.

In 2005, this theory received considerable reinforcement by the discovery at the University of Heidelberg in Germany of notes by a secretary of Niccolò Machiavelli, Agostino Vespucci, dated to 1503. According to this document, the author had witnessed Leonardo working on the portrait of Lisa del Giocondo. Note that today, much of the academic world agrees that the Paris *Mona Lisa*, for more specific technical reasons, was mainly executed at

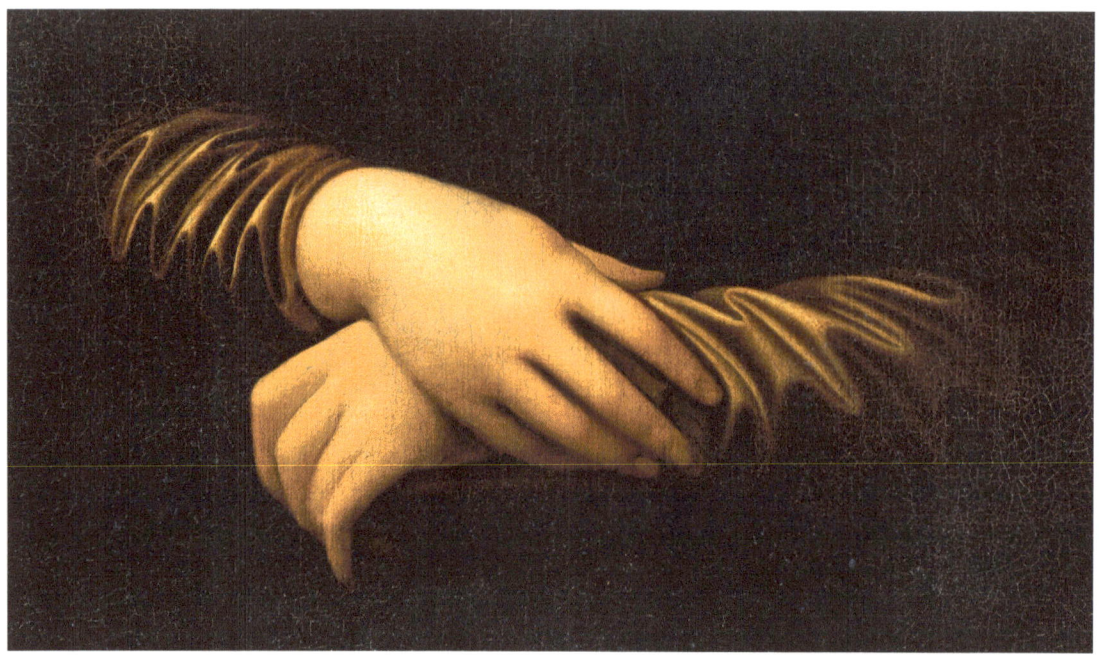

Fig. 4. Leonardo da Vinci, The Earlier *Mona Lisa*, ca. 1503-1506; detail of the hands.

some time after 1508. The argument that the Isleworth version could not be an original because it was painted on canvas rather than wood (which at the time was the most popular support), is pointless. For example, the *Madonna de Benoit*, today in Hermitage, Saint Petersburg, is a painting over canvas authenticated by virtually every Leonardo expert. There are other important reasons to believe that Leonardo would have painted on canvas.

If we accept that Leonardo was a genius, open to any and all types of innovations and experiments – including those pertaining to his art – then it is no surprise that he would be interested in using new techniques and substituting the popular poplar support for something new. This fascination with experimental techniques is the reason for the disaster that struck his second most famous work, *The Last Supper* in the Santa Maria delle Grazie, Milan, which has severely deteriorated due to an unreliable tempera technique. This is a curious thing about Leonardo scholarship: when Leonardo is unsuccessful with a new experiment, it is routinely accepted as his responsibility. Yet, in the case of the Earlier *Mona*

Lisa, where his work was executed perfectly, why not give him the credit? Leonardo wrote extensively on the subject of using a canvas in his *Trattato della Pittura*, published posthumously in 1651.

As documented in this volume, many scholars identify the Earlier and the Louvre portraits as depicting the same person. One of their strongest arguments is the description by secretary Antonio de Beatis during his visit to Leonardo's manor in France. This meeting took place in 1517, when the secretary documented Leonardo's comment that one of the paintings presented by the artist was a portrait of "a certain Florentine lady, done from life at the request of the late Magnificent Giuliano Medici." Given the date, we can only conclude that this is referring to the Louvre version, since it would soon belong to the French royal collections with *The Virgin and Child with Saint Anne* and *Saint John the Baptist*, also mentioned by De Beatis.

Marks of the Renaissance

The composition and execution of the Isleworth painting, including the hands and face of the sitter, are manifestly Leonardesque, and these elements must certainly have been executed by him. The main elements of the composition conform to the master's drawing style. Furthermore, the head, neck, and bases of the columns indicate the brushstrokes of a left-handed artist like Da Vinci. The ethereal atmosphere seen in the Louvre version is also recognizable here, through the use of an incipient *sfumato*, thus lending the composition an aura of mystery. It is not an exaggeration to say that no other version or copy of the *Mona Lisa* (either by collaborators or late followers) has the same quality of style and pictorial principles of the Master. By contrast, the simple treatment of the rest of the composition, such as the background landscape, seems to point to the work of an assistant. Leonardo's taste for details, such as his interest for natural themes, also seems to corroborate this thesis.

In addition, the Isleworth version places Lisa between two Greek columns – an obvious Renaissance element – that does not exist in the Louvre version, save for a glimpse of the bases, but these columns are definitely present in a sketch made in 1504 by Raffaello Sanzio, who was present in Leonardo's studio while the latter worked on the Earlier *Mona Lisa*. It is worth noting that recent examinations have shown that the *Mona Lisa* in the Louvre never had its sides trimmed, though that procedure was commonplace at the time (and in subsequent centuries) in order to fit a picture into a previously prepared frame.

Furthermore, the Isleworth also follows the use of the "golden section", as is the case in some other authenticated works of Leonardo (*The Annunciation* in the Uffizi in Florence, or the *Mona Lisa* in the Louvre). Widely used during the Renaissance, the golden section is a geometric resource for creating mathematical compositions in art, first discovered in antiquity, using the principle of intersecting axes. Thus, the artist can, through subdivision of the image into several rectangles, produce a series of major and minor forms that would flow to infinity. This in effect guides our vision spiral, resulting in a transcendent order in space, as it would in nature.

From a geometric point of view, the Goldblatt Thesis is of particular interest for the construction of the Isleworth portrait. Maurice H. Goldblatt was an expert and art critic at the beginning of the twentieth century who was particularly interested in unmasking *Mona Lisa* fakes. His thesis posits that only Leonardo's originals had the mouth line of a feminine smile drawn in an arc of a circle, which when extended, would touch the external corner of one or both eyes. It also suggests, in the case of the heads of Leonardo's models (such as the *Mona Lisa*), that its outline is "the arc of another circle two times the diameter of the first circle."

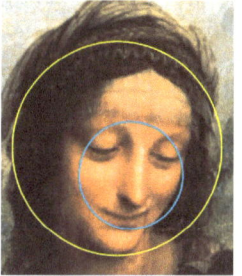

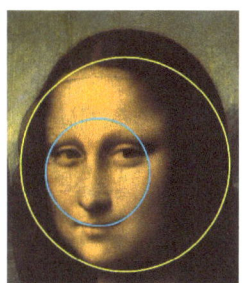

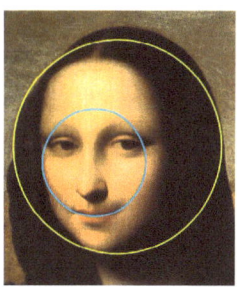

Fig. 5. The Goldblatt Thesis illustrated with a detail from Leonardo's *Virgin and Child with St. Anne* (1503-1516); the Louvre *Mona Lisa* (1508-1516) and the Earlier *Mona Lisa* (1503-1506).

The *Sfumato*: 3D without glasses

Even though the technique known as *sfumato* is closely associated with oil painting, Leonardo Da Vinci is not its creator, as is commonly thought. The Italian term means "gone up in smoke", "smoky", or "evaporated", since that is what used to happen with brush marks on a painting: they virtually disappear. Da Vinci, however, applied *sfumato* with a new *glacis*, a technique that involves the application of an oil layer mixed with a minimum amount of colored pigment over a white primer. This produces a thin layer of ethereal colored tones. Such a procedure allows light, when passing through this "veil", to penetrate into the bottom of the painting and then reflect back to the viewer. The multiple shade tones in Leonardo's later works are actually successive applications of those layers. Adding such pigmentations, one on top of the other, thus results in an effect of vibrant constancy.

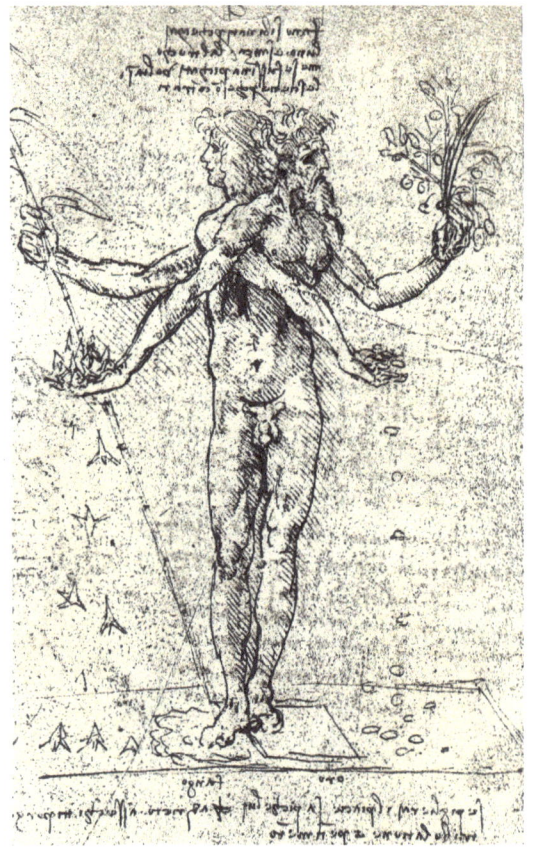

Fig 6. Leonardo da Vinci, *Allegory of Pleasure and Pain,* ca. 1480.

This glazing technique in the sfumato appears only in the later works of the artist, i.e. after 1510; quite possibly, the Louvre *Mona Lisa* is the first instance in which it was used. Some evidence for this can be drawn from recent findings by Mady Elias of the French National Center for Scientific Research, and by the multispectral digitization tests performed by Pascal Cotte of Lumiere Technology.[9]

Sfumato was used in post-medieval art with the purpose of creating a supernatural atmosphere. It gave the composition a new sense of depth in a world used to flat imagery, thus producing a more naturalistic representation. Hence, it is not difficult to imagine the reaction of those who first witnessed the impact of these effects, that were perhaps not dissimilar to the fascination of the modern public with 3D or I-Max movies.[10]

Given Leonardo's interest in optical and nature studies, and their multiple dimensional implications, this technique became an essential feature of his late artistic production. This may be the reason why De Beatis, following his meeting with Leonardo and the Louvre *Mona Lisa* in 1517, described the work as *perfect* and *looking alive*. For the audience of th late fifteenth and sixteenth centuries, the realism of this treatment must have been shocking.[11]

Philosophical Implications

An important Renaissance factor in the Earlier *Mona Lisa* is Leonardo's keen interest in the search for the question of duality, or the phenomenon of "opposites" demonstrating the contrasts in things. This idea was first formulated by Heraclitus of Ephesus (c.535-475 B.C.E.) in his thoughts on the cosmos. Also, studies of Fibonacci and the golden ratio, including the strength of symmetrical balance, would exert a strong influence on Leonardo's aesthetic and compositions. There are several examples of how da Vinci, as artist-designer, was drawn to the contrast of opposites.

One is the drawing of two mythical ladies using

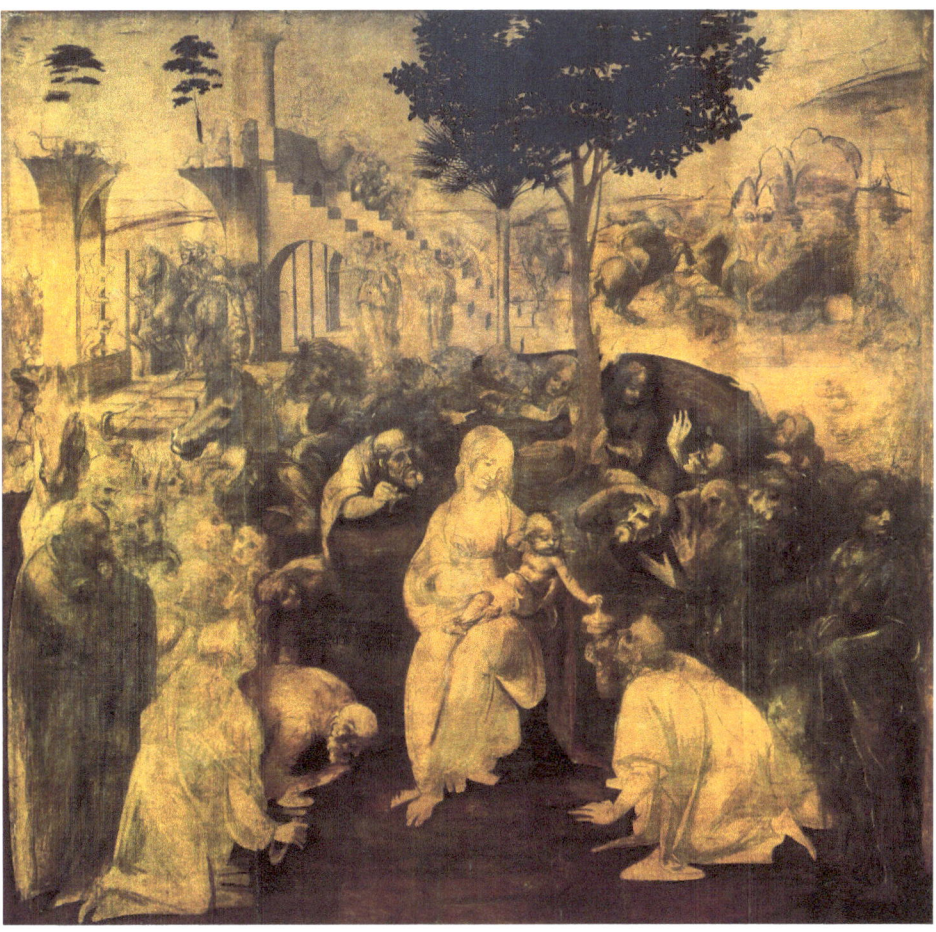

Fig 7. Leonardo da Vinci, *Adoration of the Magi,* ca. 1481-1482.

a "magical" mirror,[12] including references to ancient symbols for alchemy and hermeticism (control of the natural elements). One of the women in this scheme is presented with a young face, and another, an old one. The theme of *vanitas*, of the transience of man was a constant in the philosophies and the occult during the Middle Ages and the Renaissance, continuing in Romanticism and Expressionism. Another drawing known as the *Allegory of Pleasure and Pain* from 1480 sees two male figures – one young, and one old – that emanate from the same body. It illustrates the corollary of pain in the pursuit of pleasure, and vice versa: a contrast of opposites.

Another example where this idea is manifest is the oil on panel painting of *The Adoration of the Magi*, today in the Uffizi in Florence, begun in 1481 and left unfinished from 1482. Here, we see a group of young people around a carob tree[13] in the background, while a group of seniors surround the main scene in the foreground. The theme of the visitation by the Magi is taken from the New Testament, affirming their recognition of the divinity of Jesus. The carob tree and wild honey are described in the Bible as the diet of John the Baptist, the patron saint of Florence, while living in the Judean desert. In Renaissance Italy, this tree became a spiritual symbol of prophets, and an object of veneration for those interested in Gnosticism (including John the Baptist's role in the Christian universe).[14] Gnosticism and Neo-Platonic thought circulated in the more lettered Italian circles at the time, of which Leonardo – to judge by many of his drawings and notes – was certainly aware.[15]

My point is that the contrast of opposites so prominent in Leonardo's work may serve as an

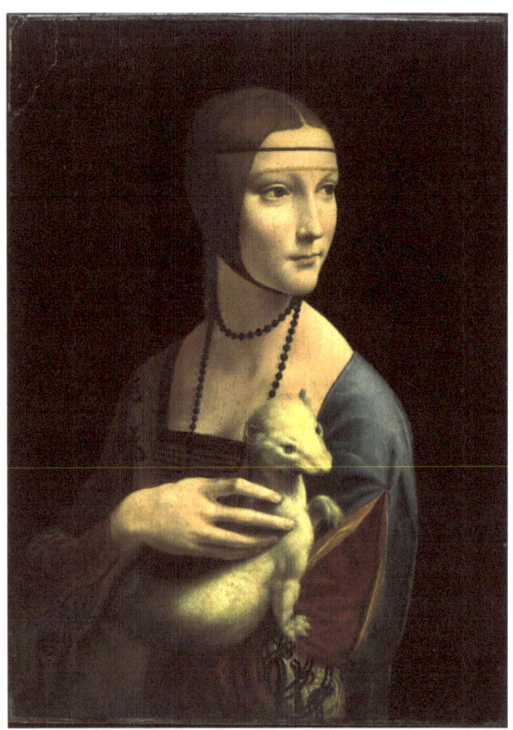

Fig 8. Leonardo da Vinci, *Lady with an Ermine,* ca. 1489-1490.

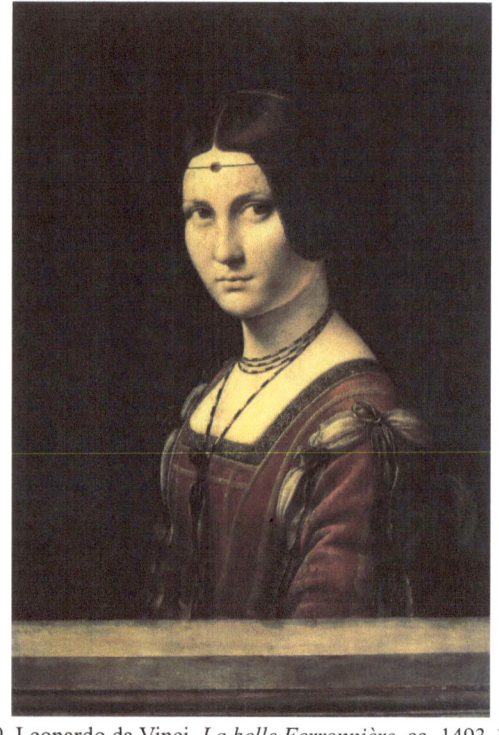

Fig 9. Leonardo da Vinci, *La belle Ferronnière,* ca. 1493-1494.

analogy for our discussion of the two *Mona Lisa* portraits. The Earlier *Mona Lisa* is essentially a younger counterpoint to the classic version in the Louvre. This idea also clarifies the relationship of the earlier version to the later one: to provide a visible representation of a rejuvenated *La Gioconda*. The beauty of the lips of young Lisa Gherardini intensifies the contrast between the two versions – a younger woman versus an older one. At the turn of the fifteenth to the sixteenth century, using such provocative reddish hues in a mature woman would have raised eyebrows. Indeed, an in-depth study of the original colors used in the *Gioconda* of the Louvre demonstrate that her lips were not much different than they look today. The same is true for the *Mona Lisa* in the Prado.

For Leonardo, therefore, the *Mona Lisa* in Louvre served as the polar opposite of the Earlier *Mona Lisa*. That counterpoint allows him to reflect on the invisible reality, the bigger reality, in which the opposites orchestrate the movement of history and all of Creation.

The youth of the supposedly most recent muse

Another point of evidence in favor of authenticating the Isleworth version as an autograph is shown by the sheer verisimilitude of Lisa Gherardini's face. No wonder, then, that it would become a signal reference point for works by his followers. De Predis, Boltraffio, D'Oggiono, Salai, Luini, and Giampietrino are some of the disciples that tried to use Lisa's face in various portraits – including those of androgynous males.

Inevitably, this raises the question: since Leonardo himself painted not only the image of Lisa del Giocondo but also of other women, why would this become such an important hallmark? We already know his portraits of Ginevra de' Benci, of Cecilia Gallerani in *Lady with an Ermine,* of Bianca Sforza in *La Bella Principessa,* of Lucrezia Crivelli in *La Belle Ferronière,* and of Isabella d'Este in the famous drawing, which are all strong examples of how Leonardo could endow a portrait with a life of its own. But I believe that with Lisa, Leonardo felt the need to develop something of much greater visual power: a treatment so direct and realistic that it could dispense with the normative conventions of Quattrocento portraiture. Unlike the Louvre version, we have no problem accepting that the Earlier *Mona Lisa* represents a living person, a real character in the form of the young Lisa del Giocondo anno 1503. Apart from Leonardo's use of geometry, this painting has every claim to be an aesthetic and social turning point in the depiction of women in Renaissance society.

Of the opposing forces, the equilibrium

The Burlington Cartoon, also known as *the Virgin and Child with Saint Anne and Saint John the Baptist*, (1499-1500) is a drawing of charcoal and white chalk on paper, now at the National Gallery of London. It reveals an apocryphal scene: the young Mary is seated with her mature mother. Both characters have a strong physical resemblance to Lisa Gherardini as both a young woman[16] (the Earlier *Mona Lisa*) and a mature woman (the Louvre's version), respectively.[17] The Louvre museum has the painting that would eventually emerge from the London drawing: *the Virgin and Child with Saint Anne*. There, the similarity between the facial traits of Jesus' grandmother with those of the *Mona Lisa* leaves little doubt that a single sitter served as the model for both portraits. However, due to the change in angle and inclination of the Virgin's head in the Louvre painting, that resemblance is not immediately obvious. Indeed, no document has even been found about the identity of this model. What we may assume is that Mary may be a rejuvenated version of Saint Anne, perhaps modeled on the historical character of the "young" Lisa Gherardini.[18]

The Heir

The attempt to identify the young Mary in the London drawing could prompt a comparison with Lisa as depicted in the Earlier *Mona Lisa*. Yet, the angle at which the characters' heads are shown, both in the painting and the cartoon, make such a comparison

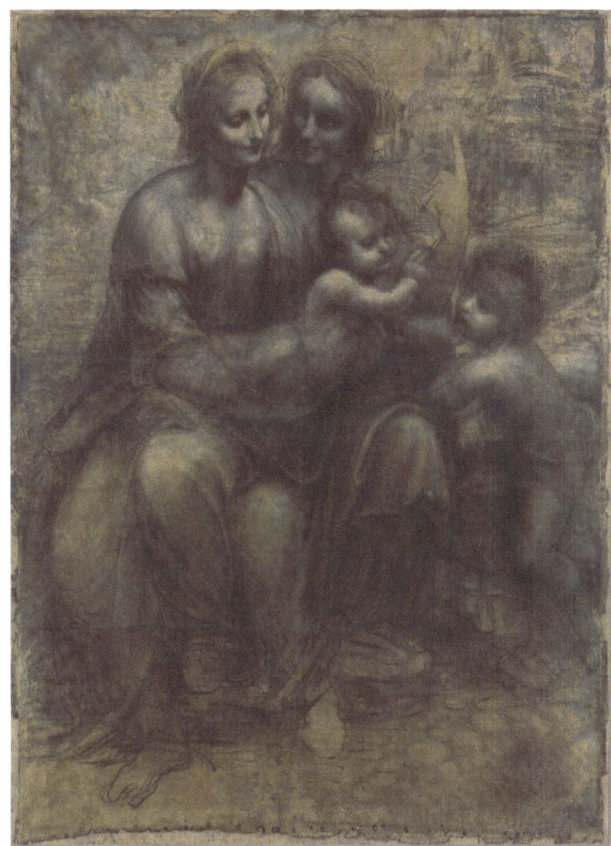

Fig 10. Leonardo da Vinci, *Saint Anne, Mary, Jesus and John* (the Burlington Cartoon), ca. 1499-1500.

more difficult. We should also remember that the Burlington Cartoon was probably drawn in 1499 or 1500, whereas the Earlier *Mona Lisa* followed three years later. But the work of one of Leonardo's students might provide an answer us. That pupil is Francesco Melzi. Unfortunately, not much is known about this great friend and assistant of the elderly Leonardo, but the trust Leonardo would place in this young man of Milanese origin allowed Melzi to preserve much of Leonardo's paintings, drawings, notebooks – including anatomic studies - and sketches, in addition to a rich legacy of writings. If today we know much about da Vinci's life, that surely is due to Melzi.

Around 1520, this artist painted *Vertumnus and Pomona*, today in Gemäldegalerie in Berlin. The subject is taken from Ovid's *Metamorphoses*: Pomona was the goddess of fruit, while Vertumnus was the god of transformation, who could change himself into

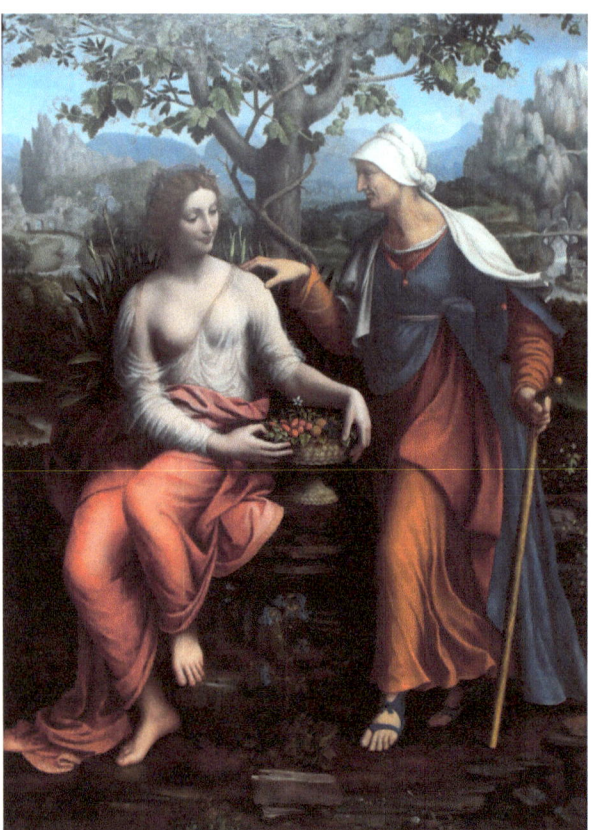

Fig. 11. Francesco Melzi, *Vertumnus and Pomona*, ca. 1520.

allegory. There are two versions of this painting: one at Hermitage in St. Petersburg, and another at the Virginia Museum of Fine Arts. Another version in the Borghese Gallery in Rome shows *Flora* in a slightly different pose that owes much to the Early *Mona Lisa*, apart from a minor difference in arrangements and clothing. In 1525, Luini would paint a *Ritratto di Donna*, inspired by Melzi's *Flora*.[19]

One more example of Francesco Melzi's dependence on the younger Lisa in the creation of his characters is *Pluto and Persephone*. Though it is very likely that this painting was executed by one of his followers, the figure of Persephone is another adaptation of the Columbina figure.[20]

These examples show the enduring influence of the Isleworth *Mona Lisa*, even though the influence may not be explicit at first glance. In all of these works, the characters are of young women, rather than mature figures. This is true for the majority of works by *Leonardeschi*, which all appear to be inspired by the younger version of *Gioconda*, rather than the aged and stained version of Louvre. Perhaps this would finally explain the meaning of the often heard expression of the *Mona Lisa* as "*la donna più bella del mondo*"...

whatever he wanted. One day, frustrated by Pomona's constant indifference, Vertumnus decided to disguise himself as an old woman in order to seduce her. In Melzi's painting, that produced an opportunity to once again see the iconography of opposites: Vertumnus is shown as an elderly figure, in contrast to Pomona, who is young and beautiful. Melzi's model is the Virgin Mary in Leonardo's *Burlington Cartoon*. In that same year, another famous pupil, Bernardino Luini, also took advantage of Leonardo's cartoon for his *Holy Family* (Pinacoteca Ambrosiana of Milan).

The same contrast of opposites is also present in Melzi's painting of *Flora*, goddess of Spring (1517 - 1521). Also known as "*Columbina*", a reference to the flower held by the character, this Flora is poised between death and resurrection: the columbine in her left hand and her bare breast represent fertility, while the anemones in her lap suggest death and resurrection, possibly injecting a Christian theme in this pagan

Conclusion

The famous smile of the *Mona Lisa* in Paris has gained an almost sacred character, as evidenced by the endless "pilgrimages" to the Louvre. Her figure has become synonymous with the greatness that the human race is capable of, as John F. Kennedy famously said during the portrait's tour of the United States in 1963. As such, this feature would appear to supplant all its other achievements: she is sensitivity and solidity personified.

But the Earlier *Mona Lisa* is not that much different: the sovereign pose and enchanting smile are also evident in this version, thus exemplifying the ideal portrait of humankind at the dawn of Modernity.

LEONARDO DA VINCI'S MONA LISA: NEW PERSPECTIVES

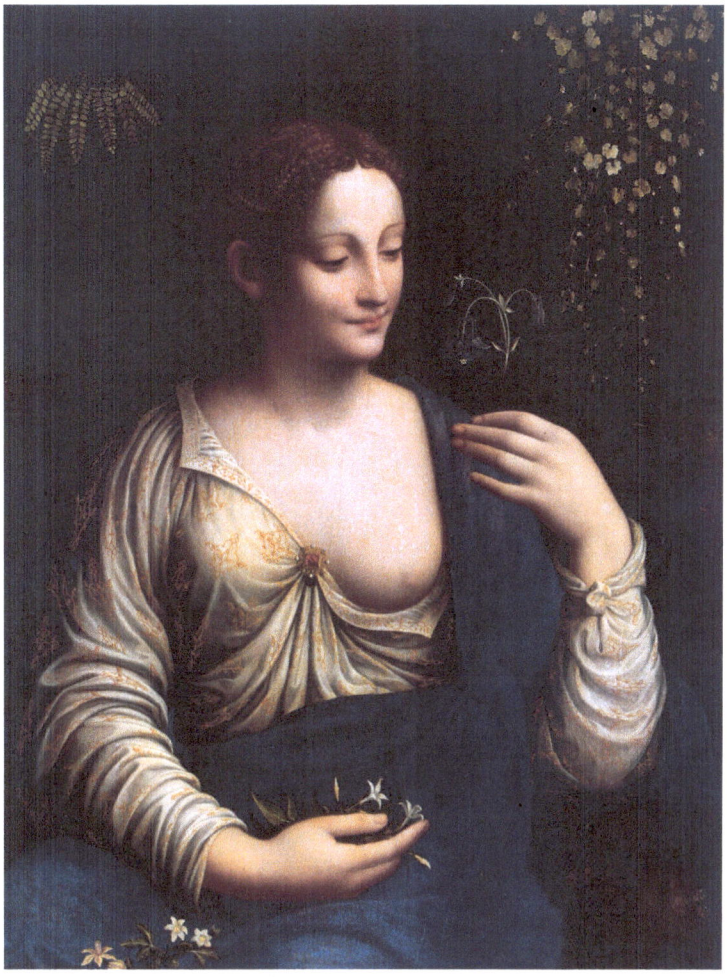

Fig. 12. Francesco Melzi, *Flora* (also known as *Columbina*), ca. 1520

The countenance of this young woman captures the essence of humanity with all her majesty, challenging whoever looks at her. It shows how art can serve as a great ally of nature, since our species is also the work of God's art. It marks the moment when humankind acquires that unique restlessness and speculation of the modern age—or what the theologian Paul Tillich calls its "last unquietness", testifying to its transforming vocation.

About the Author

Born in 1973 in Rio de Janeiro, Átila Soares graduated from the Industrial Design program at the Pontifical Catholic University of Rio de Janeiro and obtained postgraduate titles on History, Philosophy, Sociology, Art History and Anthropology. Some of his greatest influences have come from the ideas of the medievalist Jean Delumeau, the semiologist Umberto Eco and the historians Peter Burke and Ivan Gaskell. He has focused his research in the Arts (Medieval, Renaissance and Baroque), particularly of Portugal, Spain and Italy. Among others, he has already analyzed the authenticity of works of art in private collections, including Leonardo da Vinci, Rafael Sanzio, Pieter Bruegel, El Greco, the Swiss Rococo artist Jean-Étienne Liotard and Francisco de Goya. He is a contributor to the journals *Leituras da História* and *Historia Catarina*. One of the leading Renaissance experts in Latin America, Soares is the author of a study about the Renaissance painter Sandro Botticelli and the co-author of *A Jovem Mona Lisa* and *Leonardo E O Sudári*.

References

[1] As well as, perhaps, Bianca Giovanna Sforza (daughter of Ludovico, il Mouro), or some Spanish courtesan, among other contenders.

[2] Leonardo, apparently, never left any note about the portrait.

[3] Lomazzo, Gian Paolo, *Trattato dell'arte della pittura, scoltura et architettura* [Milano 1584] in *Scritti sulle arti* Vol. II, Roberto Paolo Ciardi, Florence 1974.

[4] These tests were conducted by, among others, Professor Hermann Kuhn, Munich – pigment analysis; the Swiss Institute for Art Research, Zurich - pigment analysis; Editech (Dr. Mauricio Seracini), Florence - pigment and support analysis; Lumiere Technology (Pascal Cotte), Paris – Multispectral Digitization; Professor Alfonso Rubino, Italy – geometrical analysis; The Mona Lisa Foundation, Zurich - visual, spectral and mathematical analysis; The University of Oxford, Research Laboratory, UK – radiocarbon dating; The Swiss Federal Polytechnic Institute (ETH) (Prof. Hans-Arno Synal), Zurich – radiocarbon dating; and Professor John Asmus, University of San Diego, California – scientific studies about reflections, brushstroke identification, and spectral and spatial comparative analysis. Lastly, the results of thirty-five years of intensive research recently became available at the website (http://monalisa.org), and at the release of the book *Mona Lisa - Leonardo's Earlier Version,* published by The Mona Lisa Foundation

[5] See *La Belle Ferronnière, The St. Anne* and the *Mona Lisa* in the Louvre. In respect to the last one, Asmus would say spectral similarities indicated an origin from the same palette.

[6] This would be like saying, five hundred years from now, that scholars of the cultural history of the Twentieth Century will refuse to admit that Tom Hanks may be the same actor from *Philadelphia,* or *Saving Private Ryan,* only because he was also the protagonist of the most popular comedies of the 1980s.

[7] Antonio de Beatis, "Account of the Visit of Cardinal Louis d'Aragon paid to Leonardo, at the Château de Cloux, October 10, 1517," in Delieuvin, Vincent, *Saint Anne: Leonardo da Vinci's ultimate Masterpiece;* p. 199.

[8] Do not confuse this technique with that one of his first works, executed before the development of this new version of "vitrification".

[9] Cotte also examined the Earlier *Mona Lisa* between 2010 and 2011, concluding that there is nothing that could indicate that it is not, indeed, from the hand of Leonardo da Vinci.

[10] 1838 was the year of the invention of the stereoscope by the British physicist Charles Wheatstone, and 1922 saw the release of the first 3D movie in the History: *The Power of Love,* an American feature film directed by Nat G.Deverich.

[11] That level of sophistication in the execution of a painting, as initiated by Leonardo, was so novel that Watelet (and M.Robin) wrote in their *Dictionnaire des Arts de Peinture* (1790): "*Alors le glacis est un moyen efficace de perfection pour l'art, et un remede aux défauts échappés dans la première couche*".

[12] According to a later interpretation, mirrors were used by French troops during François I's invasion of Milan in 1499.

[13] And not "grasshoppers", as an erroneous interpretation of *Vulgata* suggests.

[14] Leonardo would have been fascinated to know of the 2010 discovery of antimatter or the "God Particle" – an idea whose existence, in theory, had long been accepted in physics. Antimatter has an electrical charge of an opposing pole to "ordinary" matter, which, once joined to the respective matter, ends up destroying its opposite element. The discovery was made by the CERN Large Hadron Collider, located in France and Switzerland. It produced a trillionth of a gram of antimatter, which survived only 16 hundredth of a second before annihilating its correspondent matter, exactly as scientists had predicted.

[15] The idea that there is something archetypical about this concept is provided by a sequence in the film *Unbreakable* (2000) by M. Night Shyamalan. In the plot, the character of Samuel L. Jackson, Elijah Price, suffers from a disease called Lobstein disease (or Type I osteogenesis imperfecta) that renders human bones extremely fragile and prone to fracture. According to the logic of the astute Price, there must be someone with the opposite pathology, a carrier of an unbreakable bone structure, and this is obviously the character of David Dunn, played by Bruce Willis.

[16] Hence, the *Earlier Mona Lisa,* the counterpoint to the classic version of Paris, adds to the iconographic work of the opposites created by Leonardo. Its contrast to the Louvre version is more than clear: general aspects of the portrait itself reveal to us the evident representation of a rejuvenated *La Gioconda.*

[17] Nevertheless, thematic about this imagined encounter between saints were something the artist would reveal being a big concern of his until the end of his life.

[18] It is interesting to note that with regards to the Saint Anne with the Virgin in Louvre, the way they are intertwined, strikes us as a shapeless mass in which is hard to notice to whom belong each limb. That would be one more reinforcement of the idea of the unity of opposites.

[19] Concerning the *Flora* in the Hermitage, there is a curious episode related to the apparition of a wax bust, attributed to Da Vinci, at the beginning of the nineteenth century. That work resembled another work of a Roman school of the eighteenth? century, which was part of Pontow collection (Mannheim), with the difference that the first appears to be much older. It was found in the antiquary of Murray Marx, London, in 1907 by a German art scientist, Dr. Max J. Friedländer, who was convinced of its value due to quality– indicating it to be a work from antiquity. The path from there to glory was short: it was acquired by the Kaiser-Friedrich Museum (Berlin State Museums), and authenticated by the renowned director Wilhelm von Bode. Later on, it was found to be a fraud executed by sculptor Richard Kockl Lucas. *The Times* had

already decided to expose the sculpture
to the world that same year. Even being a
fake, the bust – as confirmed posteriorly
by Lucas' son, already 80 years old-, had
as inspiration the young *Flora* by Melzi.
The arms are in the same position (though
partially mutilated) in both sculptures (and
inclination) in each one of three versions
(S. Petersburg, Rome, and Mannheim)
- in fact, these gestures make them a
Leonardesque model. And, a comparison
of these sculptures' faces clearly show
us the influence of the young Lisa del
Giocondo as the model. Considering the
age of infant Jesus in a *cartoon*, the Virgin
Mary would be about eighteen years.

[20] The painting was auctioned by Sotheby's
in New York in 2007

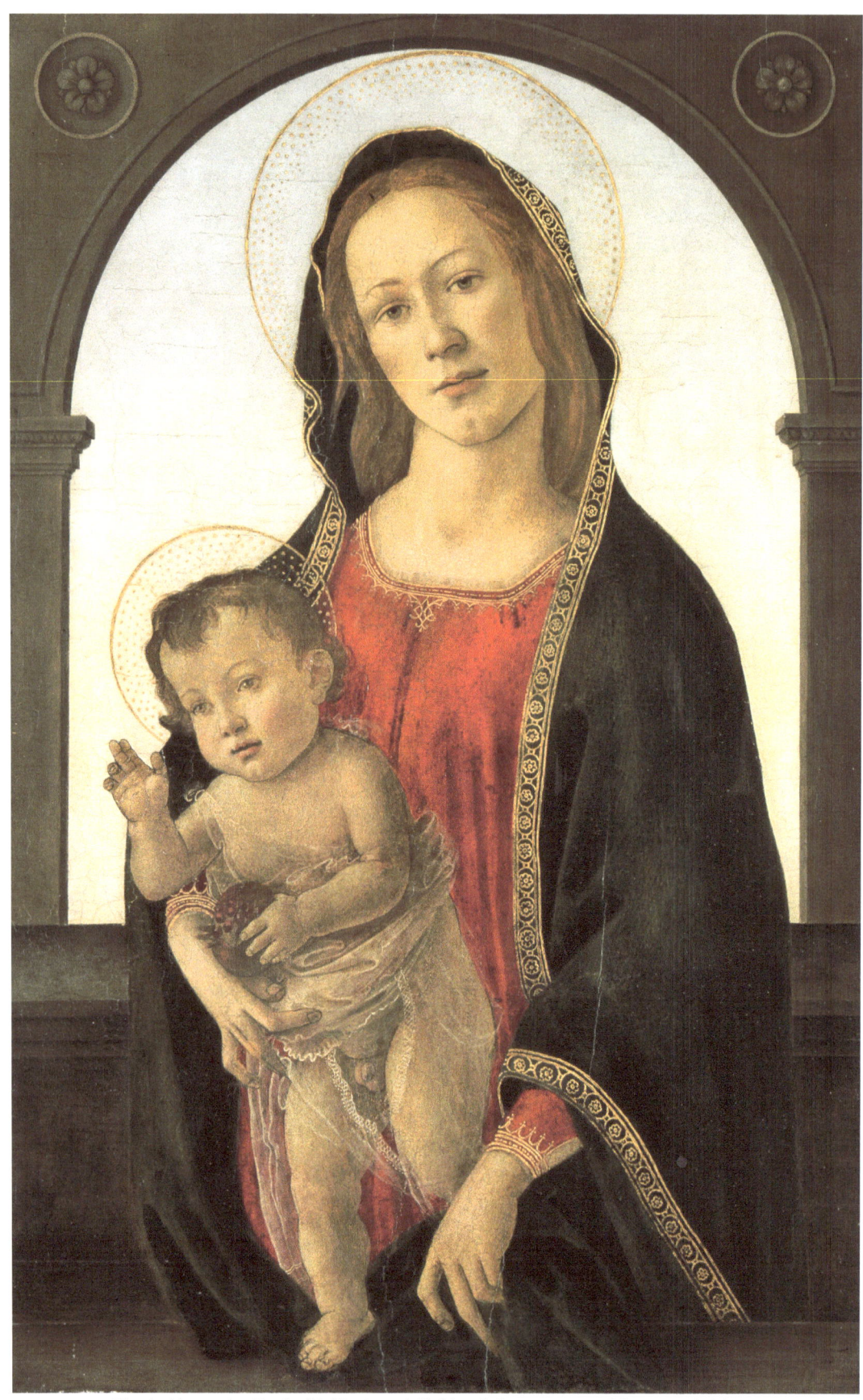

Fig. 1. Alessandro Botticelli, *Virgin and Child with Pomegranate*. Oil on wood, 1480s.
Purchased from Hugh Blaker by Gwendoline and Margaret Davies in 1920.

Hugh Blaker and the Old Masters

The Connoisseurship of the Man Who Discovered the Isleworth Mona Lisa

Prof. Robert Meyrick
Head of Department, Aberystwyth University
Ceredigion, Wales

When in 1913 Hugh Blaker purchased the canvas that would become known as the *Isleworth Mona Lisa*, and later the Earlier *Mona Lisa*, he was in little doubt he had discovered a "sleeper". That beneath the dirt and discoloured varnish lay a genuine and important work of art which had been overlooked by the art market and forgotten by art historians. Blaker was convinced it was not, as most assumed, one of the many copies of Leonardo's masterpiece. It was, he argued, a likeness of Madonna Lisa Gioconda which predated the iconic Louvre portrait, was executed in the master's studio and was, in its main part at least, by Leonardo da Vinci himself. [Fig. 1] It is 'a very delightful thing,' he wrote in January 1914, 'showing the colors mentioned by Vasari' and 'much larger than the Louvre picture. The background is entirely different, unfinished as Vasari stated ......'[1]

The evidence and expert opinion published by Blaker and his step-father John Eyre appeared to corroborate his conviction, however Blaker never sold his *Mona Lisa*. When he died in 1936 it was among some six hundred artworks at his home in Old Isleworth, a small village on the river Thames ten miles west of central London. In his later life it had been nigh impossible for him to make a living from the trade of paintings, due to the worldwide economic recession that followed the Wall Street Crash in October 1929. Blaker found himself in a 'veritable storm of suffering' – misunderstood, unappreciated,

frustrated, living on financial handouts, unable to settle even his butcher's account. He even lacked a proper suit of clothes to attend the private view of his loan exhibition of French paintings at the Whitechapel Gallery, London, to be opened by the French ambassador. Yet he was surrounded by artworks nowadays worth millions that he was unable to sell or, more accurately, was unwilling to sell for what he felt were derisory sums. 'No one wants me,' he wrote in his journal. The 'forced horror of living on the arts was but a snare and a delusion. I loved every picture I ever possessed. Every love was torn from me. When I sold, I sold my very soul.… Now, I am denied that privilege.'[2]

As well as dealer in Old Masters, Blaker was at times a painter, journalist, art critic, museum curator, playwright, poet, collector and indefatigable supporter and promoter of modern art. He came to regret that he had not been blessed with a single-mindedness of vision that could have enabled him to succeed in his calling as artist. "The cause of my failure to "make good" in any single branch of knowledge," he wrote,

> "is that I have too many interests. Had I been isolated in my youth at a time when there was demand for artistic expression, I should have been an artist of repute. I was dumped into a generation which did not care a damn for art – apart from popular art. I just happened. I was an Old Master, born centuries late."[3]

Blaker even suggests that he stumbled into art dealing after failing to become successful as an artist:

> "For fifteen years I wept and cried to the wanton god of art. For fifteen years my soul was withered like the grass in Autumn. The fifteen years I wandered as a soul in trance. I awoke to find myself little better than a blasted dealer in things I loved of yore."[4]

Today Blaker is all but forgotten; his significant contribution to the course of art history in Britain during the first half of the twentieth century has gone largely unrecognized. Advancing our understanding of the personal, professional and institutional forces that shaped Blaker as artist, critic, dealer and collector has presented significant challenges. His house and studio, archives and artworks were piecemeal dispersed or discarded over eighty years ago. Consequently, he has been excluded from the art historical canon due largely to a paucity of information and lack of awareness of his many achievements.

Aside from his journal entries selected and edited for publication in *Apollo* magazine by his friend, artist and one-time business partner Murray Urquhart (1880-1972), few of Blaker's personal papers and business records have survived.[5] There are no stock books relating to his purchases, offers and sales, though some extant correspondence with dealers and clients provide insights into his buying and selling of art. There are also his letters to the press, articles for periodicals, and books such as *Points for Posterity*, a handbook for social historians published in 1910 which 'paints a detailed portrait of its author: passionate, open minded yet opinionated, at times cynical and always radical.'[6] Two bound volumes of Blaker's hand-written journals spanning 1931-1936 recently came to light as well as a folio containing photographs of artworks from Blaker's stock. Among the photographs is a list in Blaker's hand that itemises key artworks in his inventory together with their likely sale value.

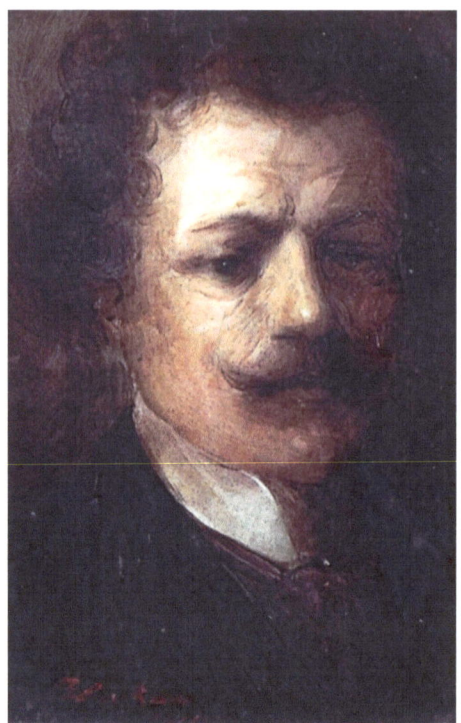

Fig. 2. Hugh Oswald Blaker, *Self-portrait*, 1906, Oil on panel.

It includes paintings by El Greco (£800), Vermeer (£1,200), Tintoretto (£600), Rossetti (£500), Burne-Jones (£600), Turner (£750), van Musscher (£700), Reynolds (£3,000), Bronzino (£800), Goya (£800), Massys (£4,000)[7], Hals (£12,000)[8], Berchem (£800)[9], Beechey (£3,000), Gainsborough (£4,000), Greuze (£3,000), and Holbein (£12,000). The attributions were Blaker's own.

Foresight, courage and capital

Hugh Oswald Blaker was born December 13, 1873 in Worthing, Sussex. His father Robert Charles Blaker (1836-1896) was a Master Builder, surveyor and contractor employing some thirty-two workers. After a privileged English public school education, Hugh Blaker trained in art in Worthing, London, Antwerp and Paris. He returned to Worthing in 1893 where he worked from a studio above his father's office. He eked out a living as artist. At age eighteen he began contributing ink drawings – 'amusing without being vulgar' – to *Comic Cuts*, a magazine for boys and girls.[10] Without success he entered oil paintings such as *Regatta Day* (1893) to Royal Academy of Arts summer exhibitions.

Robert Blaker died in 1896. His widow Jane married John Eyre two years later and the couple relocated to Teddington, near London. Hugh Blaker took studios in South Kensington, London but soon moved in with his mother when he found himself in financial straits. In the 1901 Census, Blaker identified himself as 'artist and author.' He had ventured into journalism that year with 'American Politicians', a sardonic 10-page debut essay for *The Westminster Review*.[11] He contributed two articles about National Gallery acquisitions – 'Bargains in Paint' and 'Fortunes in Paint' – to *The English Illustrated Magazine* in 1905.[12] Therein Blaker reveals an early interest in the art trade, collecting practices and an awareness of the fluctuating value of Old Master paintings. The articles foretell not only of a profession as dealer in Old Masters but collector of Modern British art. "If one had the necessary foresight, courage and capital," he wrote,

> "one could with a few thousand pounds
> build up the basis of a large fortune.…
> It is quite certain that the works of
> many of the men who are painting
> today (and which could be secured
> very cheaply) would be magnificent
> investments. But (always the "but") the
> question is, who are these Old Masters
> in embryo?"[13]

Blaker saw no distinction between his study of Old Masters and his admiration for the Moderns. In a letter to *The Saturday Review*, he expressed outrage at "the wholesale condemnation of the Post-Impressionist exhibition" staged by Roger Fry at the Grafton Galleries. As someone "brought up on the standards of the Old Masters," he failed to understand how "sincere, creative endeavour, based on tradition"

could "appear strange and uncouth." He points to the "tradition and experience" that informed Manet and Cézanne, and the genesis of their works in sixteenth and seventeenth century painting.[14]

In need of a regular income, Blaker took on the role of Curator at the Holburne Museum in Bath in July 1905. David Davies (1880-1944), later Lord Davies of Llandinam, Montgomeryshire, served as his guarantor. Since 1895 Blaker's sister Jenny Louisa Roberta Blaker (1869-1947) – who preferred to be known as 'Jane' – had been governess to Lord Davies' sisters Gwendoline Elizabeth Davies (1882-1951) and Margaret Sydney Davies (1887-1963). When the sisters came of age and inherited their share of the fortune amassed by their grandfather, the entrepreneurial industrialist David Davies 'Top Sawyer' (1818-1890), Jane Blaker remained at Plas Dinam as companion to their stepmother, Mrs Edward Davies. It was on a visit to Plas Dinam in 1910 that Blaker met Murray Urquhart who had been engaged by David Davies to paint the hunt. Urquhart and Davies had been friends since their years at Merchiston Castle School near Edinburgh. Davies's younger sisters were already forming an art collection with Hugh Blaker's counsel. Urquhart described him as the 'architect and inspirer' of the sisters' enterprise.[15] It has been pointed out that as advisor and intermediary, it was Blaker's 'taste that influenced the sisters in the formation of their renowned collections of nineteenth-century French art that they bequeathed to the National Museum of Wales, Cardiff' in 1952 and 1963.[16] Blaker was able to make useful contacts in the London artworld through his dealings on behalf of the sisters. He wrote to Gwendoline in July 1910 to thank her for the 'great pleasure' and 'great favour' of representing her at the salesrooms. As well as being of 'great interest' to him personally, it was doing him 'a lot of good in the picture world.'[17]

Blaker invited Ayerst Hooker Buttery (1868-1929) of the National Gallery's conservation department

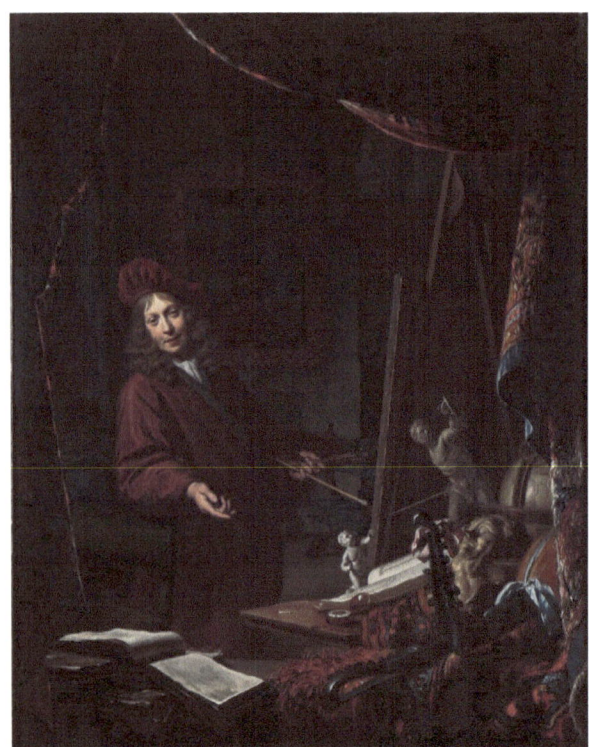

Fig. 3. Michiel van Musscher. *Self Portrait*. Oil on canvas, 1679.
Purchased by Hugh Blaker at Christie's on May 31, 1918.

to Bath to undertake a reclassification of Holburne
Museum's 258 Old Master paintings. Together they
concluded eleven to be *Very Good*, thirty-three to
be *Good*, fifty-nine to be *Fair*, and 155 to be *Bad*.
They consigned 125 paintings to the cellar. The
exercise provided Blaker considerable experience
and a new-found confidence in the evaluation of old
paintings. After the reappraisal of the collection was
completed, however, he appears to have lost interest
in his curatorial responsibilities. Blaker pursued other
interests as artist, writer, and advisor to the Davies
sisters. His frequent requests for leave of absence were
denied and he was ever in conflict with the Museum's
Trustees. It has been suggested that '[t]he rift between
them surely must have widened further with the
publication of his book *Points for Posterity* in which
he expressed his contempt for Trustee-controlled
institutions,' listing 'what in his opinion were shameful
errors and misattributions on the part of museum
officials.'[18]

Having to justify his every decision to a Board of
Trustees stifled Blaker. He resigned his position at the
Museum in July 1913. As Urquhart later points out,
connoisseurship had "claimed him and all his ener-
gies."[19] Blaker continued to frequent the salesrooms
bidding on behalf of the Davieses as well as for himself. He relocated from Bath to Old Isleworth, where
he lived with his mother and John Eyre.

Hoping for a capture

Though not a wealthy man, Blaker began to make
something of a name for himself in the London art
markets. Since his £37.10s quarterly salary at the
Holburne had never enabled him to indulge his passion
for Impressionist and Post-Impressionist paintings, he
started to look ahead of the dealers and bought works
by contemporary English or French artists such as
Harold Gilman, Walter Sickert, Maurice de Vlaminck
and Amedeo Modigliani. He scratched a living from
the profits accrued by playing the art market to speculate in Old Master paintings. In 1908, describing his
feverish bidding at auction for a Turner watercolour,
a journalist for *The Times* described Blaker as "one of
the greatest collectors of the day." In journal entries,
Blaker regularly boasted of the speculative purchases
he had made at auction. In November 1913, he acquired a possible Velázquez at Christie's for £25, "dirt
and all."[20] In May 1915 he picked up a version of Alessandro Botticelli's *Virgin and Child with Pomegranate*
at the same auction rooms for £105. And "in front of
'em all" he bought a Holbein portrait for £67 in June
1915.[21] These were the kind of ventures that Blaker
could typically afford.

Almost certainly Blaker would have needed to
borrow to have the funds to purchase or co-finance
the acquisition of his *Mona Lisa* in 1913, which he
discovered in the collection of a 'Somerset nobleman'.
Elizabeth Davies of Plas Dinam, to whom his sister
was now a Lady's Companion, may well have loaned
Blaker the capital in full or in part. She had been

generously provided for by her late husband.[22] In a journal entry of November that year, Blaker imagined how with capital he "could speedily make a fortune;" he longed for the day when "all eyes but [his] own will be shut to some masterpiece." He writes of scouring the auction houses "hoping for a capture" in order to clear the "£2,500 debt to Mrs Davies" which was "ever present' on his mind."[23] That she helped Blaker buy his *Mona Lisa* explains why on June 30, 1924 Eyre dedicated "to Mrs Edward Davies" a copy of his second book *The Two Mona Lisas* "with the author's compliments." Though Blaker had been engaged in buying or negotiating for artworks on behalf of her step-daughters Gwendoline and Margaret, and occasionally for their brother David, there is no other evidence to suggest Elizabeth Davies ever called on Blaker to negotiate acquisitions on her behalf.

Blaker was forty years old when he bought his *Mona Lisa* in late 1913. He recorded in his journal that it was "probably done in the master's studio" and was "more beautiful than the Louvre picture." If only he could "overcome that prejudice which states that everything is a copy which happens to resemble the *Mona Lisa*," he expected "it should fetch a big price."[24] Therein lay the challenge. Without scientific corroboration and a suitable provenance which was so important at that time, it is difficult enough to get any painting authenticated. How was Blaker to convince some art experts that there was another, earlier version of the most famous painting in the world, since likely none of them was aware of the background history which is now available? [25]

Although Blaker's extant papers make frequent reference to the artists, dealers, collectors and critics with whom he came into contact, nowhere does he make mention of his interactions with painting conservators. This is unusual given the hundreds of Old Master as well as eighteenth and early nineteenth century British paintings that passed through his hands over four decades.

In 1910, Sir Daniel Tupper, new owner of the Doric House, Bath, commissioned Blaker to restore *The Inroad of Turks upon Scio*, a 33 x 16 foot fresco painted in 1825 by Thomas Barker (1769-1847). According to *The Times*, the sandstone construction of the Neo-Classic house and picture gallery on Sion Hill had caused "one of the most important works of this character in the country" to dull and flake from damp and mildew. After the removal of dirt, Blaker consolidated the remaining paint with mastic varnish and undertook "a good deal of repainting on the affected parts." As a reporter for *The Times* points out, the "style and technique of the original are imitated to such good purpose that it is impossible to discriminate between the repainted portions and the old work."[26] Blaker had no qualms about restoring historic artworks. He was convinced that his natural abilities as a draughtsman, combined with his training in London, Paris and Antwerp, and his close study of old paintings, qualified him as the best person for the job.

In the same year he purchased his *Mona Lisa*, Blaker wrote to artists' colourmen Winsor and Newton. The artwork still bore no trace of repainting, nor was there the 'slightest lowering of tone' when compared with the old pigment against which the 'colours were exactly matched at the time.'[27] In a letter to *The Times*, Blaker joined a debate concerning the authenticity of a Breughel painting *The Bird Trap* on display at an exhibition of Flemish works at the Royal Academy of Arts. He compared it to a similar picture that he had sold to Paris antiquarian and collector Gaston Neumans. Blaker claimed he had 'removed the old varnish' for himself and made a close study of Breughel's handling of paint.[28] A recent condition report by a top expert team in the field, shown in the Appendix, confirm that Blaker's *Mona Lisa* has very few minor retouches and few small restorations only in the background area, and is in excellent original condition.

In his 1915 *Monograph on Leonardo da Vinci's Mona Lisa* published simultaneously by Grevel's in London and Schribner's in New York, John Eyre persuasively interconnects historical evidence with opinion and conjecture to convince readers that Leonardo was author of an earlier version of the *Mona Lisa*. He claims that writing the book was motivated by the judgement of a 'great connoisseur' who considered that "the Isleworth *Mona Lisa* can genuinely be ascribed to Leonardo da Vinci."[29] It is the "unequivocal opinion of one of the greatest of living judges of the works of the Old Masters," Eyre begins,

> "one who, to my knowledge, bought at public auction, during the years 1913 and 1914, eight old masterpieces, at nominal prices, most of which, when cleaned, bore initials or signatures, and of which one was a Rubens, that was sold afterwards for eighty times its auction price, through the

agency of one of the greatest of European art authorities. Yet all these pictures had passed, unrecognised, under the close scrutiny of home and foreign experts of repute, and of dealers the most astute." [30]

Though it "appeared almost hopeless to attempt to shake what some experts held, which decreed that the Louvre picture was the one and only version of Leonardo's world-famous portrait," Eyre was "convinced there was at least good ground for investigation."[31] We should bear in mind that all of these efforts were without knowledge of the recently discovered historical documents which serve to corroborate Eyre's arguments in no uncertain way.

During World War I, Blaker sent his *Mona Lisa* to Boston for safekeeping, while Eyre journeyed to New York with paintings by Botticelli and Holbein for the attention of American industrialist, financier and art

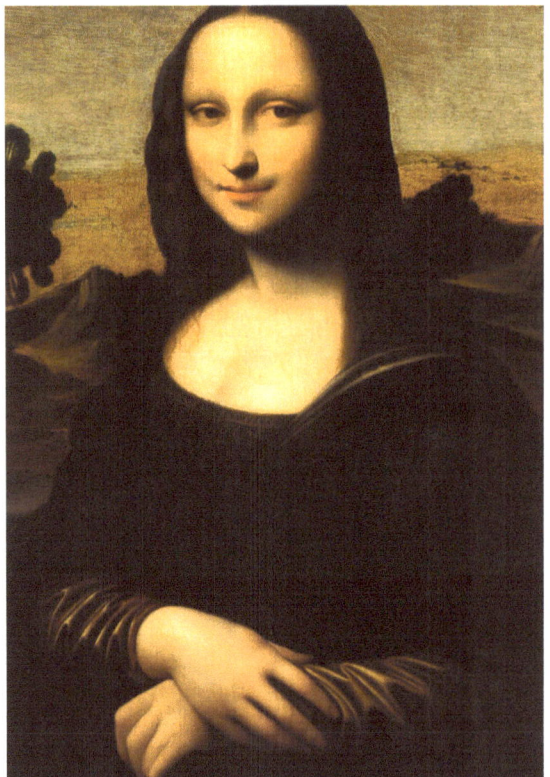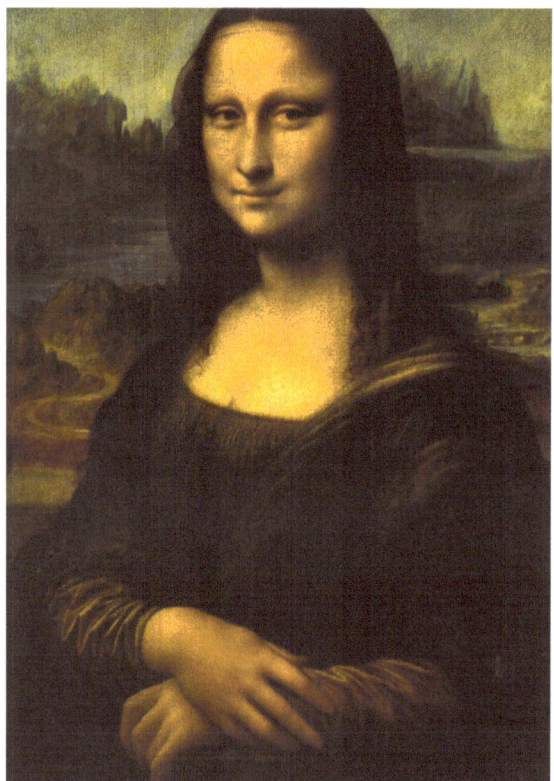

Fig. 4. Leonardo da Vinci, The Isleworth *Mona Lisa*. Oil on canvas, ca. 1502, and the Louvre *Mona Lisa*. Oil on wood, ca. 1508-1516.

collector Henry Clay Frick.[32]

It was a perilous time to be making a transatlantic crossing. British waters were occupied by German U-boats. The White Star Line *SS Arabic* was sunk 19 August and in May that year, the British liner *RMS Lusitania* was torpedoed off the south coast of Ireland. Among the 1,200 passengers to perish was Irish-born art collector Sir Hugh Lane who was returning from New York with a consignment of Old Masters in the hold. Yet Blaker was anxious for the safety of his Mona Lisa and in great need to make some sales of his other treasures. His mother had died a month earlier; her Estate was valued at just £9.9s.6d. Blaker was also in the process of suing Bond Street fine art dealers Thomas Agnew's for the unpaid commission he felt was owed him for introducing to them Thomas Gainsborough's *Portrait of Anne Horton, Duchess of Cumberland*. That law suit ended up before a special jury of the King's Bench Division. Blaker lost and was ordered to pay costs.[33] Consequently Blaker had much riding on both the sale of New York paintings as well as the publication of *Monograph* to convince sceptics that his Mona Lisa discovery was a genuine Leonardo with a good chance of later sale.

Drawing for their book on "the small amount of incontrovertible and contemporaneous evidence,"[34] Blaker and Eyre present a logical and skilfully articulated sequence of arguments in order to convince the artworld that the Isleworth *Mona Lisa* was not a copy of the Louvre *Mona Lisa* but an earlier painting by Leonardo of the same sitter. Densely packed and meticulously annotated "facts and contemporaneous evidence" are brought together in an attempt to "break down a tradition of such long standing"[35] that the Louvre *Mona Lisa* is the one and only version painted by Leonardo. Eyre and Blaker contend that Leonardo painted two versions of the *Mona Lisa* "both of superlative intrinsic merit."[36] Their fundamental reasoning has to this day been used in support of a positive attribution of the painting, enhanced with new and more substantial evidence.

Urquhart reminds us that Blaker "had an unfailing sense of quality in his judgement of pictures and this sense was his one sure guide." He did not consider necessary "the laborious examination with a magnifying glass of the whole surface of a canvas."[37] As a trained artist, Blaker was well qualified to provide detailed technical descriptions of the painting for *Monograph*, including the canvas and stretcher, the brushwork, glazing techniques, and palette of colours. Blaker also shunned independent scientific scrutiny. The chemical analysis of pigments, the microscope, X-ray and ultraviolet testing for evidence of repainting were all available at that time. Nor did he elicit independent opinion, save for quoting the Budapest-born, Vienna-educated, London-domiciled art critic and historian Paul George Konody (1872-1933) who, when writing for the *New York Times*, described the features of the Isleworth *Mona Lisa* as more delicate and "far more pleasing and beautiful than in the Louvre version."[38]

Eyre reasoned that it was "almost a principle" of Leonardo to commence two versions of every painting.[39] As someone who often wrote of his own failure to succeed in any one branch of endeavour, Blaker would have empathised with the multi-talented Leonardo who hardly ever was able to complete a painting. Eyre points out that Vasari is corroborated by Fra Pietro da Nuvolaria, Vice-General of the Order of Carmelites in Florence, who after his April 1501 visit to Leonardo's studio wrote to his friend Isabella d'Este, Marchesa of Mantua that Leonardo and his pupils were painting two portraits.[40]

Great significance was attached by Eyre to a 1504 ink drawing now in the Louvre Museum by Italian painter Raphael Sanzio da Urbino (1483-1520). Made after a visit to Leonardo's studio, Raphael's drawing of the painting shows Lisa Giocondo flanked by two columns. Since there are no columns – and never were – on the Louvre *Mona Lisa*, this was presented

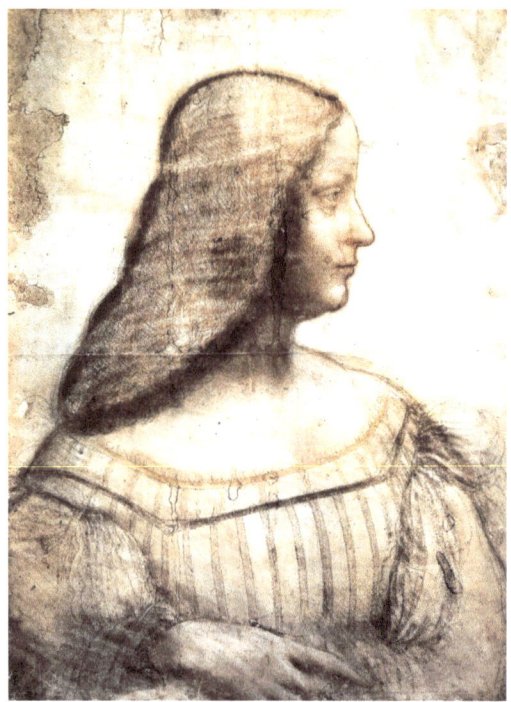

Fig. 5. Leonardo da Vinci, *Portrait of Isabella d'Este*,
c. 1499-1500.

as evidence that Raphael had seen for himself the
Isleworth *Mona Lisa* in the master's studio.[41] Blaker
and Eyre believed the Louvre *Mona Lisa* to be
Leonardo's second version of the sitter, began in
Florence in 1500 and completed – as was Leonardo's
painting of *St Anne* – at Cloux near Amboise in France
sometime after 1516.[42] They were "convinced that the
face, the bust and hands of the unfinished Isleworth
Mona Lisa are from Leonardo's brush and from none
other."[43] On October 10, 1517, some months before
his death, Leonardo showed the painting to Luigi
d'Aragona (1474–1519), Cardinal of Aragón. The
Cardinal's secretary Antonio de Beatis described
the occasion in his travel journal noting 'one picture
of a certain Florentine lady painted from life to the
order of the late Magnifico Giuliano de' Medici', a
ruler of Florence.[44] Eighteen months later the artist
was dead and the *Mona Lisa* seen by Giuliano di
Lorenzo de' Medici was inherited by Leonardo's pupil,
the Milanese painter Francesco de Melzi (*c*.1491-
1568/70), who sold it along with *St Anne* to King

Francis I (1494-1547). It eventually entered the Louvre
collection.

Blaker and Eyre believed that the unfinished
painting – the Isleworth *Mona Lisa* –was given to
Lisa Giocondo's husband Francesco. It had been
commissioned by the Giocondos soon after the
death of their only daughter in 1499. "The ineffably
calm, steady gaze from the beautiful eyes, and the
sweet, sad, forced smile," wrote Eyre, speak "not of
coquettishness, not of cunning, not of intrigue, but
of that calm resignation born of deep sorrow, which
appeals and touches the human heart, and which
represents all that is great, heroic, and ennobling in
life, and all that Leonardo so much admired."[45]

The authors acknowledged that the Isleworth
painting did not have a complete pedigree at that
time and that this was problematic because of its
importance in the art world. Blaker and Eyre knew
all too well that only an incontrovertible provenance
would convince artworld sceptics of the painting's
authenticity. Yet Blaker persisted with the narrative
that he had bought the canvas in Bath from "a
Somerset nobleman" who – for reasons unclear, but
probably for not wanting to be in the spotlight– wished
to remain anonymous. Purchased by an ancestor in
Italy as an original by Leonardo in the late eighteenth
century, he was told, the painting had since hung in the
family's "old Manor house in Somerset."[46] This was
as much as Blaker disclosed. We don't know if he ever
revealed how he came to know about and subsequently
purchase the painting, or how much he paid.[47]

Eyre took the painting to Italy during November
and December 1922 where at the Grand Hotel, Rome
he showed it to artist Lorenzo Cecconi, picture
conservator and curator of the Accademia di San
Luca; Corrado Ricci, President of the Institute of
Archaeology and History of Art; Ludovico Spiridon,
a prominent Italian collector; the Maltese sculptor
Antonio Sciortino, Honorary Director of the British
Academy of Arts in Rome; Arduino Colasanti,

Director General of the Department of Antiquities and Fine Arts; as well as the painter and art historian Giulio Cantalamessa, Director of the Borghese Gallery.[48] Their opinions were totally in favour of a Leonardo attribution of the painting. In the ten years that had passed since *Monograph* appeared, Blaker and Eyre had become considerably more experienced at eliciting expert opinion.

Hugh Blaker died in 1936, after which Urquhart and Jane Blaker cleared her brother's Isleworth houses in 1936. Together they organized a selling exhibition *Drawings Selected from the Collection of the Late Hugh Blaker* at the Leicester Galleries, London in March 1937. Jane returned to Gregynog Hall (where she now lived with Gwendoline and Margaret Davies) with paintings from his collection, artworks by her brother, his library, diaries and archives. "I am making headway slowly," she wrote to her younger brother Cyril in Melbourne, Australia. "I have sent pictures of lesser value to two auction rooms … but I do not expect much result…. I still owe £2,000!! £1,000 to the Davieses! The other amount consists of a big overdraft at the Bank, death duties and the remaining debts of dear H.B. – so many pictures and nothing else."[49] She described his journals – some entries from which were transcribed by Gregynog's Agent, Thomas Hughes – as "a hotchpotch of every subject and, of course, much that has happened in the art world."[50] Urquhart inherited Blaker's library, journals and correspondence when Jane died in 1947.

The following year, in accordance with the Jane Blaker's wishes, Urquhart organised a second exhibition at the Leicester Galleries of works from her late brother's collection. Income from sales was to be shared between the Blakers' nephew and niece in Australia. While most of the 102 paintings, drawings and sculptures found new homes, the Isleworth *Mona Lisa* was not sold at that time. Nephew Hugh Herbert Blaker stayed with Murray Urquhart in early 1950 and visited Gregynog Hall to wind up his aunt's Estate.

It remains a mystery what happened to the unsold Isleworth painting between the close of the Leicester Galleries exhibition in 1948 and 1962 when it was purchased by the Austro-Hungarian, London-based art connoisseur, collector and publisher Henry F. Pulitzer.[51] He states that he sold his Kensington home and much of his art collection to raise part of the asking price.[52]

'Lovely hens who would not lay'
Blaker had neither savings nor inheritances. He lived modestly. His only income – the profits accrued from picture sales – he re-invested in the speculative purchase of Old Masters or new paintings for his own collection of Modern British and French art. Loans from friends or arranged bank overdrafts regularly funded new acquisitions. Although his art dealership never offered him security, he loved what he was doing and he managed to sustain a living as long as

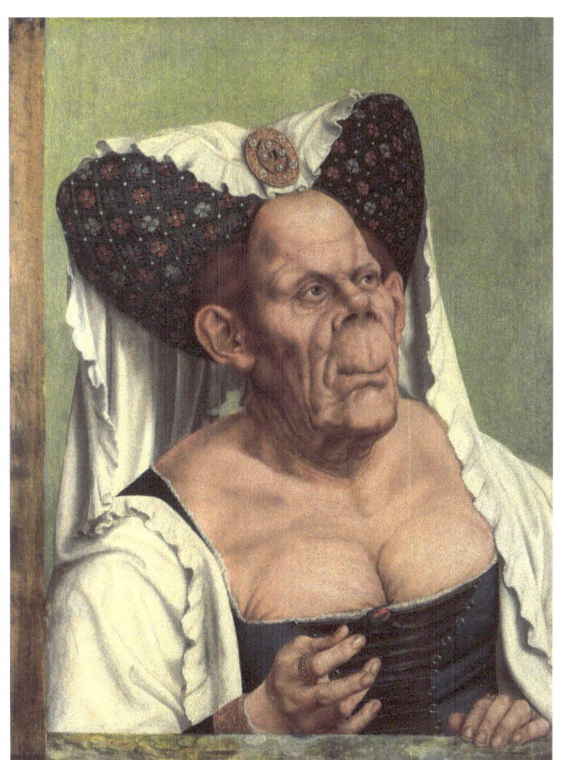

Fig. 6. Quinten Massys, *A Grotesque Old Woman*. Oil on wood, 1525-30. "The title of the ugliest portrait in the world," Blaker wrote, who purchased the work at auction in 1918. "But what a masterpiece. I simply love her."

the markets remained strong. In a journal entry dated January 14, 1935, he wrote:

> "All my 'lovely chickens', my pictures, were just as nothing in time of financial stress. In the past, although I had to part with them, they laid me hundreds, sometimes thousands, per cent in pounds sterling. Much as I hated selling every hen, such was preferable to finding every hen on my hands, sterile. Although fate decreed that I should become nothing but a loathsome dealer in pictures, the decree was worse when I was left with lovely hens who would not lay. Every hen I ever bought I bought because I loved. But I was left with my loves. Truly an ideal state of existence if you don't have to eat. But no man can live on love." [53]

Blaker lacked financial resilience. Art dealing only ever seemed bring him "tortures, agonies, mortgages, overdrafts, [and] loans." [54] He was no stranger to financial crisis. His father Robert Blaker, who had been a successful builder and long "associated with the commercial life of Worthing," was declared bankrupt in 1888 when Hugh was a schoolboy. As *The Worthing Gazette* reported, "the extreme mental anxiety consequent upon the unfavourable position of his affairs was really the originating cause of his fatal illness" in May 1896.[55] That his "rich and smug" uncle Frederick Blaker refused to help his father "in bankruptcy, when a thousand or two would have bound brother to brother" meant the family was forced to live in reduced circumstances.[56] Hugh's older brother Robert Ernest Blaker went to sea as an apprentice and met with a terrible accident when he fell from a ship's rigging. Sister Jenny went into service as governess in 1895, and their youngest brother Cyril emigrated to seek his fortune in the goldfields of Western Australia.[57] By Hugh Blaker's own admission, he was not himself good in money matters. On April 3, 1900, not long after he had moved into his mother's

Teddington home, a petition for bankruptcy was filed against him. On May 29 he appeared at the Court House, Kingston, Surrey where he was charged under Sect 4-1 (G) of the Bankruptcy Act 1883.[58] He landed in court the first time he tried to invest on the stock market just months before he acquired his *Mona Lisa*. He was unsuccessful in his law suit against Bath stockbrokers Hawes and Brown, whom he claimed had mismanaged his Malacca rubber shares.[59] "I am temperamentally incapable of keeping accounts, both for others and myself in regard to Income Tax," he wrote to his brother Cyril.[60] He lost deposits on works when he could not meet the balance[61] and on occasion resigned himself to heavy losses: "Lord Lee consented to give me £2,500 for the Flemish picture *Portrait of a Lady* for which I had paid £4,500 at Christie's. This was mania indeed in the wilderness of the slump. I blessed that £2,000 loss as a heaven sent gift." [62]

It had not always been thus. With all his money invested in the Isleworth *Mona Lisa*, which must have been a hefty amount, and in "desperate straits" following the Hawes and Brown law suit, Blaker still managed to purchase a seventeenth-century canvas at Sotheby's "in front of all the "experts" British and Foreign." It was his first successful gamble. In May 1914, he wrote, that it is

> 'a lovely portrait of Elizabeth Brant by Rubens; from his own hand! Price, dirt and all £68. The great experts can't see through varnish and dirt, thank Heavens! Berlin Bode vouches for it, and M. Kappel, the German collector buys it for £4,000.'[63]

Blaker was now regularly inviting eminent scholars to provide expert opinion to corroborate his attributions and he remunerated them for their services. As he explained to painter, critic and former Director of both the Tate Gallery and Wallace Collection, Dugald Sutherland MacColl (1859-1948), "many would-be collectors are afraid to trust their own judgement."[64]

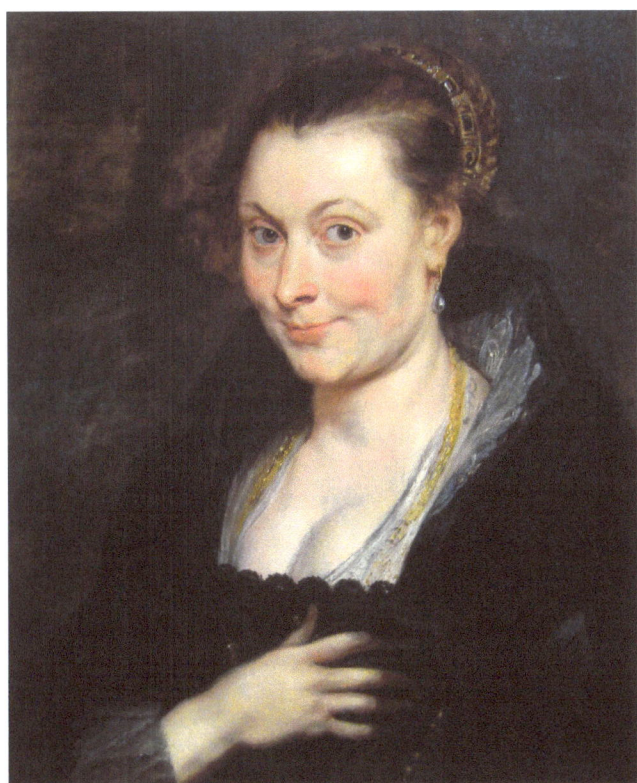

Fig. 7. Peter Paul Rubens, *Portrait of Isabella Brant.*
Oil on wood, c.1620-25.

On September 22, 1915, Eyre had departed Liverpool on the American Line steamship *St Paul* bound for New York.[68] In the hold were the Boston-bound *Mona Lisa* and two paintings for Frick's inspection, the Holbein portrait and *Virgin and Child with Pomegranate* by Alessandro Botticelli recently acquired at Christie's for £105 from the collection of the late Professor Jackson, Fellow of Worcester College, Oxford. Modelled on the central figures of Botticelli's 1485 San Barnaba Altarpiece of in the Uffizi Gallery, Blaker was expecting to make £16,000 from its sale.[69]

Blaker did not have the conventional training expected by his profession. He believed that his art training furnished him with the skills, judgement and insight necessary to assess and ultimately authenticate paintings. He thought his fine art training was far more valuable to him than the formal training in art history

Wilhelm von Bode was an eminent art historian and Director of the Kaiser Friedrich Museum in Berlin. Not only did he confirm Blaker's attribution, he brokered the sale of the Rubens portrait to Berlin grain merchant and financier Marcus Kappel (1839-1919). Kappel collected Dutch, Flemish and German paintings under the guidance of Bode who also advised on the hang of artworks at Kappel's Tiergartenstrasse home. Blaker received the cheque 'just three days before the outbreak of the Great War.'[66]

One year later, his *Mona Lisa* was shipped to America for protection. 'Owing to the war, and thanks to the kindly courtesy of the Directors of the Boston Museum of Fine Arts,' wrote Eyre,

> "the Isleworth masterpiece is now in their Gallery in Boston, USA, out of harm's way and in safe keeping, beyond the reach of either cannon-belching culture, the false philosophy of force, or the cardinal virtue of aggression."[67]

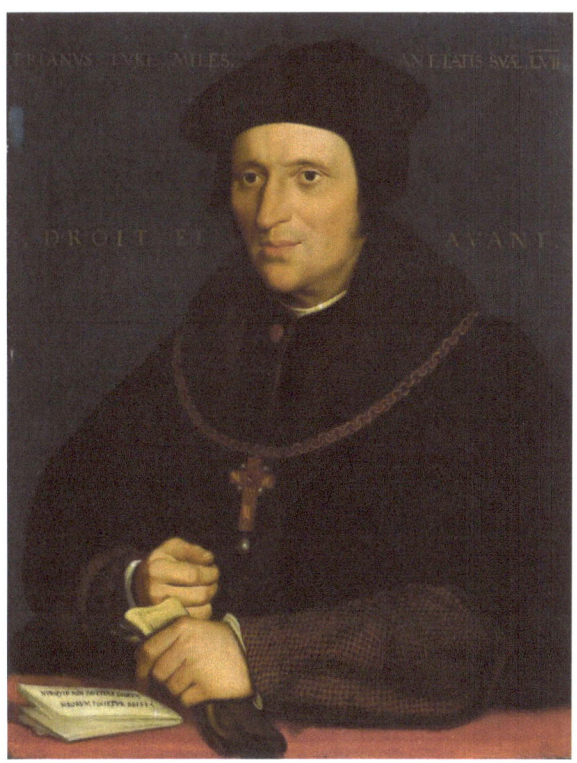

Fig 8. After Hans Holbein the Younger. *Portrait of Sir Brian Tuke.* Oil on wood, c.1616. It was purchased by Blaker in June 1915 for £67, and taken to the United States later that year together with the Isleworth *Mona Lisa.*

that was normally expected of gentlemen-dealers. He gained experience by visiting galleries and salerooms, handling and scrutinising artworks, and studying their materials and technique. He undertook research and discussed the merits of a painting with esteemed museum professionals rather than fellow dealers. Scholars gathered to debate a painting was a theme to which Blaker often returned in his own art practice. In his letters to the press, Blaker rebuked those with an "indifferent critical faculty." He distinguished between those who "study pictures" and those who "study the history of pictures," those who considered themselves "experts by reason of their biographical and historical study of art and artists."[70] He was concerned that "historians, art detectives and archaeologists" paid no attention to the "intrinsic qualities of a work of art." The ultimate test, he argued, should be that of artistic merit.[71] Connoisseurship, he believed, "required long experience, a great love of the subject, constant study, and a technical knowledge of painting and drawing as factors for determining the authenticity of pictures."[72] He felt that "English judges of the Old Masters" were best informed on account of 'the constant stream of pictures which pass through the London sale rooms.'[73]

Throughout the 1910s and 1920s Blaker speculated on numerous Old Master as well as eighteenth and nineteenth century British paintings. He bought and sold wisely. There were some artworks that made him a considerable profit, others for which experts were unwilling to corroborate his attribution, and those with which he was unwilling to part. Paintings by Velazquez, El Greco, Hals, Massys, Manet, Constable, La Tour, Wilson, Reynolds, Gainsborough, Millet, Corot, Whistler and Turner were at times in his possession. Many are now housed among the world's greatest collections: at London's Tate Gallery and National Gallery, the Norton Simon Museum in Pasadena, National Museum of Wales, the University of Oxford's Ashmolean Museum, the Art Institute of Chicago, Cleveland Museum of Art, British

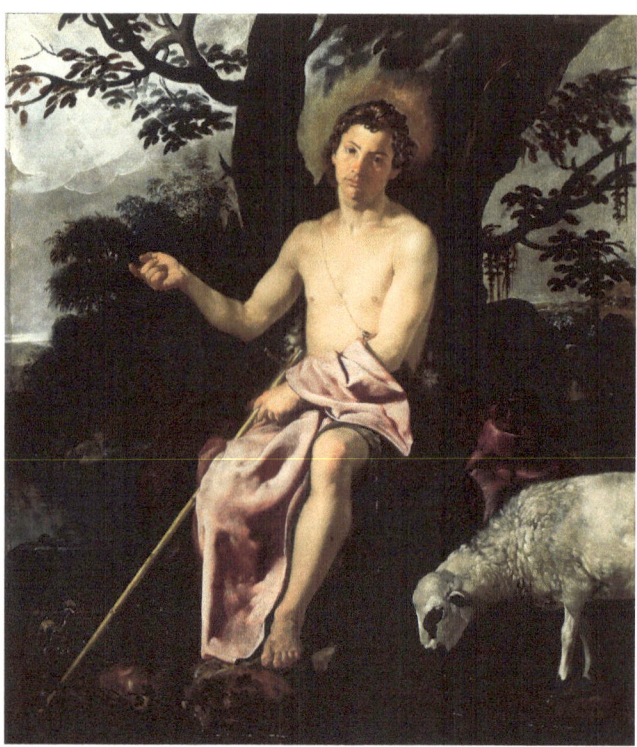

Fig. 9. Attributed to Diego Velázquez (1599-1660). *Saint John the Baptist in the Wilderness*. Oil on canvas, c.1622. Originally identified as a work by the school of Zurbarán, Blaker purchased it in 1921, believing it was actually a work by Velázquez from his late Seville period.

Museum, and Louvre Museum.

'Art, at once my heaven and my sin, played me false.'

The economic downturn of the late 1920s had not only affected the art market but also curbed Blaker's spending. By 1934 he had conceded that: "Art, at once my heaven and my sin, played me false."[74] Since it was not a good time to be buying and selling pictures, he concentrated on touring his already significant personal collection. In 1928 he staged an exhibition of 192 works *Modern British Paintings and Drawings from the Hugh Blaker Collection* at the Whitechapel Art Gallery, London. It subsequently toured the provinces through the agency of the Art Exhibitions Bureaux.

No longer trading in artworks, Blaker returned to painting as well as writing poetry, plays, letters

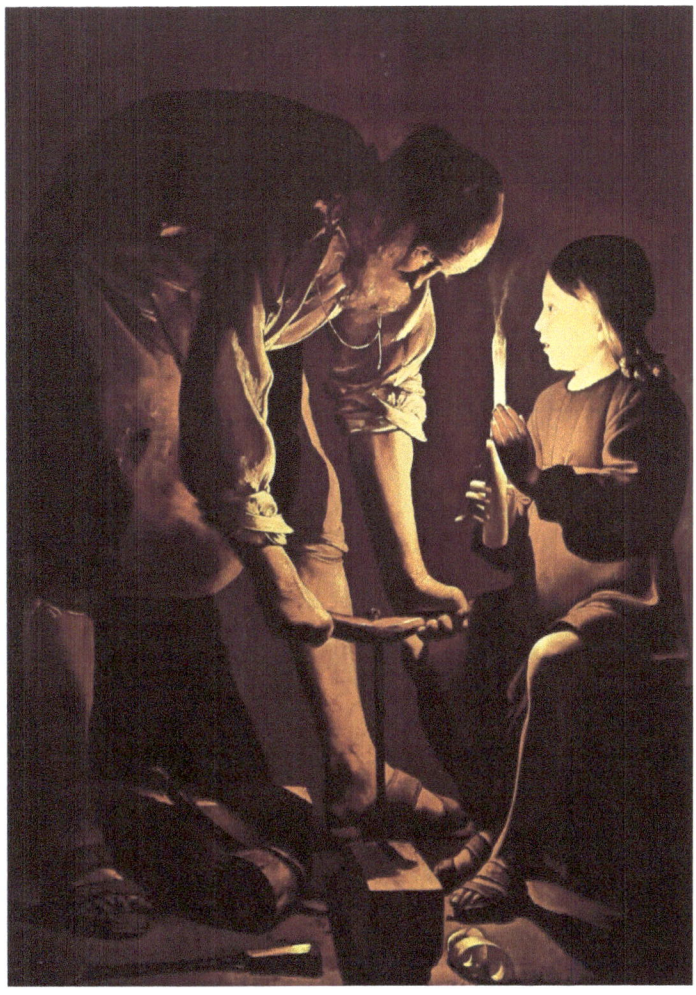

Fig. 10. Georges de La Tour, *St Joseph the Carpenter*. Oil on canvas, 1645.

to the press and recording his private thoughts in his journals. He navigated 'the sylvan waters of the Thames' on the *Daumier*, "a real tub of a boat" which he moored on the river opposite his house. He cruised toward the city as far as Chelsea and in the opposite direction from Isleworth to Oxford. Preferring "the Thames to proffered gain as critic," he moored overnight at Hurley where he made drawings, painted and penned his verse.[75] His only published play, *Woman Triumphant: A Comedy*, was published by Grant Richards, London in 1935.

Blaker's experiences with the Isleworth *Mona Lisa* as well as paintings by Botticelli, El Greco Hals, Holbein and Velázquez reveal much about collecting and connoisseurial practice in the early twentieth century. His successes and disappointments tell us

that the conclusions he reached could only be as good as the limited evidence and knowledge available at that time. Any anomaly or exception to accepted convention and not properly understood or explained – like his *Mona Lisa*, for example, being unusually painted on canvas – would inevitably raise questions of genuineness or exceptions to the rule at that time. Blaker judged works of art by what he saw and by what he knew. If conservation treatment offered new insights, or the discovery of long lost documents provided new knowledge, then there were fresh judgements to be made and different conclusions to be reached about the dating, provenance or authorship of a work of art.

We learn from Blaker's practice that knowledge advances. A figure group Blaker assigned to Dutch painter Gerard van Honthurst (1592-1656) was recently discovered to be a master work by French Baroque painter Georges de La Tour (1593-1652). It was sold to art dealer Percy Moore Turner (1877-1950) by Jane Blaker in March 1937 for £50, together with two nudes by John Constable at £10 each and Edouard Manet's *Marine a Berck: Bateaux de Peche et Pecheurs* at £20. All four were gifted by Turner to the Louvre Museum in 1948. La Tour's 1645 canvas *St Joseph the Carpenter* was subject of a 2016 monograph and exhibition by Louvre curator Dimitri Salmon. As in the case of the Isleworth *Mona Lisa*, Blaker remains amongst the early owners.

Blaker's experience also demonstrates that what was believed as reliable today may well be different tomorrow when the truth about a painting's history and nature are known and properly appreciated. Authentication is restricted by the limits of our knowledge at the time. Though it is now widely accepted the Isleworth *Mona Lisa* is neither copy nor counterfeit of the Louvre version, a number of questions had remained open—many of which, we trust are addressed in this monograph. Many genuine artworks have gone without full recognition for many years. It was just such a sleeper that Blaker believed he had discovered in the Isleworth *Mona Lisa.*, and time has already demonstrated that he was correct on so many occasions.

About the Author

Robert Meyrick is Head of the School of Art at Aberystwyth University's School of Art and Keeper of the School of Art Museum. He trained in fine art and art history and now writes on 20th-century British art, the history of printmaking, and the visual culture of Wales. Through building and working with collections and archives at Aberystwyth, often working closely with the artists themselves or their heirs, his research involves original investigation and improved insights into the work of lesser known British artists and collectors. In 2001 he was invited to become an Honorary Fellow of the in 'recognition of his services to the art of printmaking in Britain'. Robert's research is disseminated though the publication of books, catalogues raisonné and articles, as well as curated exhibitions. Robert has staged exhibitions for museums and galleries throughout the UK. His retrospective exhibition of paintings by the Welsh artist Christopher Williams was shown at the National Library of Wales throughout this Summer and his exhibition of prints by Sydney Lee RA can be seen at the Royal Academy of Arts in London next Spring. In addition to his numerous monographs, he has regularly contributed chapters for books, journals and catalogues. He has toured exhibitions of paintings by Hugh Blaker and published widely on Blaker's activities as artist, advisor and collector, most notably his 2004 article for the Oxford University Press Journal of the History of Collections – 'Hugh Blaker: Doing his Bit for the Moderns'.

1 Blaker qtd. in Urquhart, *Apollo*, p.294-5.

2 Blaker *Journal* 22 January, 1934.

3 Blaker *Journal* 25 February 1932.

4 Blaker *Journal* 29 August 1935.

5 All attempts to discover the original journals have to date failed. See Meyrick OUP 2004.

6 Meyrick OUP

7 Possibly this is Joos van Cleve (1485-1540) *St Jerome in his Study* (oil on panel, 607 x 467 mm), purchased by Blaker as a Quentin Matsys for 600gns at Christie's, London 18 July 1924 (Lot 110) from the collection of HRH The Princess Royal. Sold by Blaker at Christie's, London 8 July 1927 (Lot 107) as a Quentin Matsys for 700gns to Sir William Berry, later 1st Viscount Camrose (1879-1954).

8 Sold by Blaker to Margaret Davies in December 1920, £9,000. Bequeathed by Margaret Davies to National Museum of Wales, Cardiff in 1963. Now ascribed Portrait of a Lady, 17th Century Netherlandish.

9 Possibly this is *Italian Landscape* (oil on canvas, 1210 x 1950 mm), ex-collection King George III of England, purchased by Blaker 22 March 1918. By 1937 it was with the Antwerp dealer Sam Hartveld. It passed hands several times until 3 January 1942 when purchased by Adolf Hitler. Now held by Museum de Lakenhal, Leiden.

10 Blaker *Journal* 3 October 1931.

11 Blaker 'American Politicians' The Westminster Review January 1901, pp.15-24.

12 Blaker 'Bargains in Paint' *The English Illustrated Magazine* May 1905, pp.102-109; Blaker 'Fortunes in Paint' *The English Illustrated Magazine* November 1905, pp.105-114.

13 Blaker 'Bargains in Paint' *The English Illustrated Magazine* May 1905, p.103.

14 *THE POST-IMPRESSIONISTS*. Blaker, Hugh Saturday review of politics, literature, science and art; Jan 7, 1911; 111, 2880; British Periodicals pg. 17.

15 Urquhart, *Apollo*, p.293.

16 Meyrick OUP

17 Blaker, letter to Gwendoline Davies, July 21, 1910, National Museum of Wales, Cardiff.

18 Meyrick, R. Hugh Blaker: doing his bit for the Moderns. etc. Blaker's small volume *Points for Posterity* was published in 1910. The typed manuscript, entitled *Hints for Historians*, is now with Blaker's descendants in Australia.

19 Urquhart, *Apollo*, p.293.

20 Blaker qtd. in Urquhart, *Apollo*, p.294. He believed *Boy with a Flagon* to be a Velázquez of about 1618. He sold it to Margaret Davies for £800 in April 1920.

21 *Journal*, op. cit. (note 3), (17 April 1921), p. 295.

22 Rhyl Record and Advertiser, 12 November 1898. On his death in 1898, the gross value of Edward Davies's personal estate was estimated to be £1,206,311. 7s. 11d.

23 Blaker *Journal* November 1913, transcribed extracts by T. W. Hughes, Gregynog Agent. Private Collection, Wales, UK.

24 Ibid.

25 'Dark, dismal and uninteresting' on its discovery by Blaker, the painting 'was so covered with dirt and varnish that all its intrinsic beauties were completely hidden.' Until, that is, his *Mona Lisa* was 'thoroughly cleaned.'

26 'Thomas Barker's Fresco at Bath' *The Times* 5 November 1910, p.12; *The British Architect* 11 November 1910, p.237.

27 Hugh Blaker, letter to Winsor and Newton, March 20, 1913. Winsor and Newton published Blaker's testimonial within an advertisement printed on the back cover of Charles Holmes' *The Art of the Book* (London: *The Studio*, 1914).

28 Blaker 'Judgement on Old Masters' Letters to the Editor *The Times* 26 May 1927, p.12.

29 *Monograph*, Foreword.

30 Ibid, Foreword.

31 Ibid, Foreword.

32 Blaker letter to Henry Clay Frick. November 7, 1915. Frick archives

33 In his claim for commission, Blaker appeared before Justice Darling and a special jury of the King's Bench Division. He brought action against Old Bond Street fine art dealers Thomas Agnew and Sons to recover £1,000 guineas he believed was owed to him for introducing the respected dealer Lockett Agnew to Thomas Gainsborough's 1766 portrait of Anne Horton, later Duchess of Cumberland. Blaker claimed to have obtained 'verbal assurance that he would receive the usual commission of 10 per cent if they purchased the picture'. They subsequently acquired it from Henry Anson Horton of Catton Hall in south Derbyshire for 10,000 guineas. Agnews denied any such liability and that he painting had been acquired by them as a consequence of Blaker's introduction to the vendor. After hearing the evidence, Justice Darling felt there was no case for the jury, judged in favour of the defendants and Blaker was ordered to pay costs. Robert Frederick Colam K.C., acting for the plaintiff described Blaker as a former museum curator 'skilled in pictures' who had 'previously introduced pictures' to Agnews and 'received commission for them'.... 'In 1909 he "introduced" a Vandyke to the defendants, and was paid £600 as commission on the purchase price of £6,000.'

34 *Monograph*, Foreword.

35 Ibid, p.1.

36 Ibid, p.3.

37 Urquhart, *Apollo*, p.293.

38 Konody *The New York Times* February 15, 1914 qtd. in *Monograph*, p.4.

39 Ibid.

40 Ibid.

41 *Monograph*, p.X.

42 Ibid, p.35.

43 Ibid, p.21.

44 Ibid.

45 Ibid, p.42.

46 Ibid, p.3.

47 He had possibly promised never to disclose this information when making the acquisition.

48 Their opinions and written testimonials are published in *The Two Mona Lisas*, pp. 34-39.

49 Jane Blaker letter to Cyril Blaker. February 28, 1937. Private Collection, Australia. By the time of her death in 1947, Jane Blaker had repaid half loan to her brother from the Davies. Her Will states 'My debts include any balance that may be outstanding at the. date of my death of a loan of £1,000 made by the Misses Gwendoline Elizabeth and Margaret Sidney Davies of Gregynog Hall, Newtown, Montgomeryshire, to my brother Hugh Blaker (deceased) and secured on his Collection of modern pictures which was bequeathed to me as sole beneficiary under his Will. The balance outstanding at the date hereof is £500.'

50 Writing to Rollo Charles, Keeper of Art at the National Museum and Gallery of Wales, 20 March 1961, Urquhart states: 'When his sister died in 1947 I was sole Executor, and had the task of dispersing Blaker's collection of some 600 pictures. I was also bequeathed his large library and his diaries and letters.' Fifty-four works were sold from the 1948 exhibition and among the clients were Cartwright Hall Art Gallery, Bradford (J. F. Millet, *La Couseuse*), York Minster (Charles Ricketts, *The Crucifixion*) the Tate Gallery (Mark Gertler, *The Teapot,* 1918, Harold Gilman, *Woman on the Sofa*, 1910), British Council (William Roberts, *The Stockbroker's Clerk*, 1920), Arts Council (William Roberts, *The Gypsy Girl*, 1925-6) and Sir Kenneth Clark (Alphonse Legros, *Le Manège*). See M. Urquhart (Introduction), *Catalogue of an Exhibition of Selected Paintings, Drawings and Sculpture from the Hugh Blaker Collection* Leicester Galleries (London, 1948). The works on paper were transferred to Aberystwyth (whilst the oil paintings remained on display at Gregynog). This is the largest public collection of Blaker's work. Other examples may be found at the University of Wales Gregynog, the National Library of Wales, National Museum and Gallery of Wales, Worthing Museum and the British Museum. *Hugh Blaker: Artist, Connoisseur and Curator 1873 – 1936*, an exhibition of seventy oil paintings, watercolours and drawings was researched and curated by Robert Meyrick in 1991. It toured Gregynog Festival Exhibition No.2, Gregynog Hall, Newtown, 1991, National Museum and Art Gallery of Wales Cardiff, 1992, Holburne of Menstrie Museum and Art Gallery, Bath, 1993, and the Catherine Lewis Gallery, U. W. Aberystwyth, 1995 – 1996. See R. Meyrick, *Hugh Blaker*, exh. cat. University of Wales (Aberystwyth, 1991) and J. Stather, 'Hugh Oswald Blaker 1873-1936', unpublished MA dissertation (University of Wales, Aberystwyth, 1990).

51 Pulizter too sought expert opinion and rekindled the debate when in 1966 he privately published his book, *Where is the Mona Lisa?*

52 Pulitzer had been considering the purchase for some time and only when he had the help from a partner could he finally make the purchase. In 1950 Urquhart must 'have still been in the process' of disposing pictures, he wrote, but 'the Estate was never discussed in any detail because my lack of knowledge and perhaps his reticence.'

53 Blaker *Journal* 14 January 1935.

54 Ibid.

55 'Death of Mr R. C. Blaker', *The Worthing Gazette*, 13 May 1896, p.5.

56 Blaker *Journal* 19 February, 1936; corroborated *Morning Post*, 11 August 1888, p.6.

57 Hugh Herbert Blaker. Letter to the author. Undated, 2002.

58 *The London Gazette* 24 April 1900; 1 May 1900.

59 "Law Report, June 20." *Times* [London, England] 21 June 1913: 23. *The Times Digital Archive*. Web. 24 Nov. 2018.

60 Hugh Blaker letter to Cyril Blaker, June 9, 1935. Private Collection, Australia.

61 In August 1910 he agreed to pay £200 for Jean-Louis Forain's *En Police Correctionale* and *Le Palais de Justice* at the International Society exhibition but lost his £40 deposit when he failed to raise the capital. Blaker qtd. in Urquhart, *Apollo*, p.294.

62 Blaker *Journal* 14 January 1935. In a journal entry dated, September 1, 1924, qtd. Urquhart, Blaker writes that he 'picked up with Sampson an early Holbein at the sale of Lord Darnley's pictures: a supposed portrait of a lady by Antonio Mor. Convinced it is a Holbein. *Nous verrons*. Price 4,200 guineas.'

63 Blaker qtd. in Urquhart, *Apollo*, p.295.

64 Blaker letter to D. S. MacColl, February 26, 1929. MacColl Papers, University of Glasgow Special Collections GB0247 MS MacColl B217.

65 See Sven Kuhrau: The art collector in the Empire. Art and representation in the Berlin private collector culture. Ludwig, Kiel 2005. Blaker had bought the oil on panel portrait of Rubens' wife just a few weeks earlier from the sale of property belonging to the late Welsh Conservative Member of Parliament Joseph Russell Bailey, Baron Glanusk (1858-1899), at Christie's April 29, 1914. It remained part of the Kappel Estate until 1947 when it sold through New York dealers to Cleveland Museum of Art.

66 Urquhart 'Hugh Blaker Collector' *The Hugh Blaker Collection* Catalogue (London: Leicester Galleries, March 1948)

67 *Monograph*, p.46.

68 'Names and Descriptions of British Passengers embarked at the Port of Liverpool, *SS St Paul*, 22 September 1915.

69 Henry Clay Frick Papers, Series II Correspondence The Frick Collection/ Frick Art Reference Library Archives.

70 Blaker 'Tests for Old Masters' Letters to the Editor *The Times* 31 January 1929, p.17.

[71] Blaker *Burlington Magazine* vol.48, no.275, Feb.1926, p.111-112.

[72] Blaker 'Judgement on Old Masters' Letters to the Editor *The Times* 26 May 1927, p.12.

[73] Blaker *Burlington Magazine* vol.48, no.275, Feb.1926, p.111-112.

[74] Blaker *Journal* 22 January, 1934.

[75] Blaker *Journal* 24 January 1936.

[76] 'A la Lumière d'un Chef-d'Oeuvre Le Saint Joseph Charpentier de George de la Tour' 3 July – 2 October 2016 staged by the Musée du Louvre and Musée départemental Georges de La Tour, in Vic-sur-Seille.

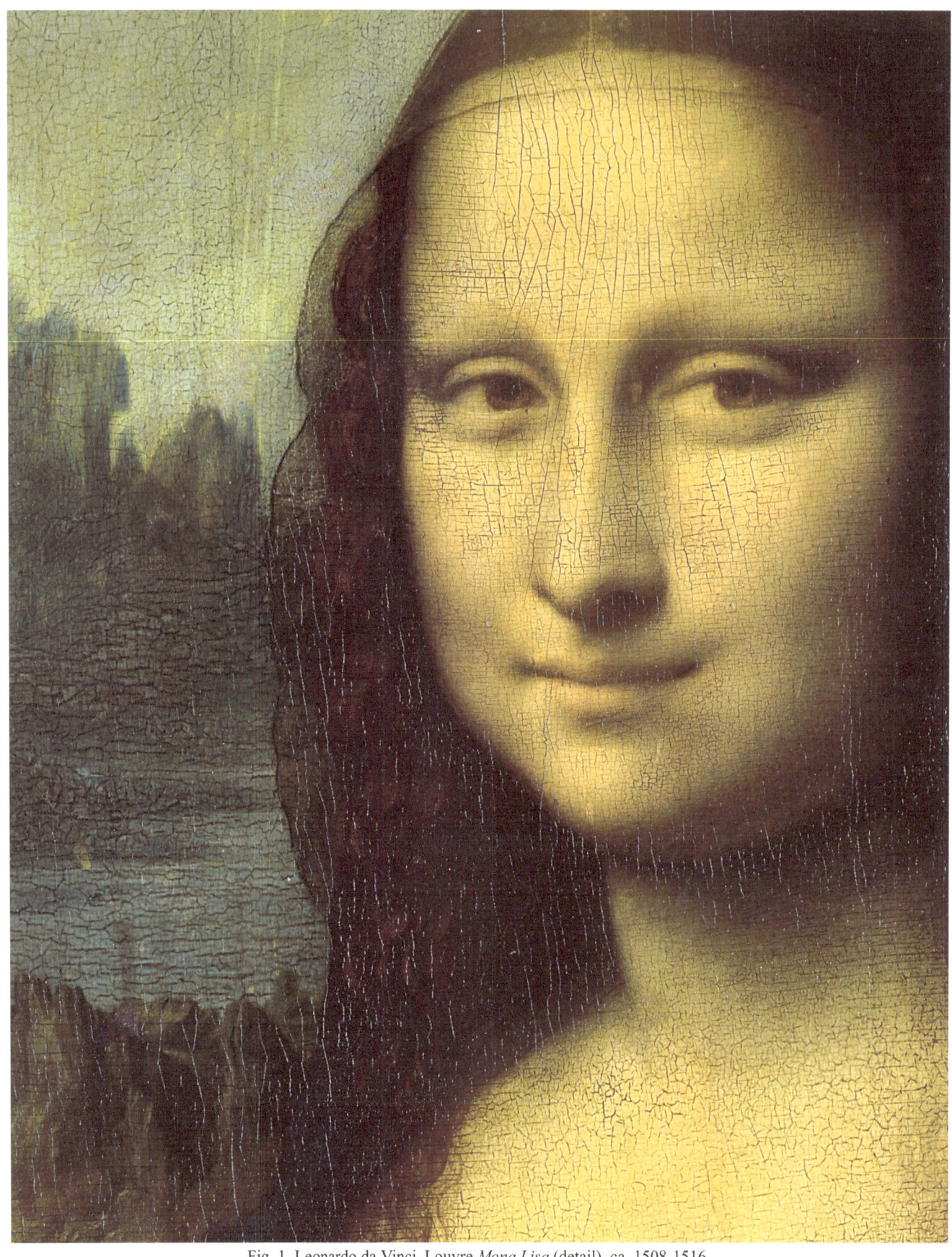

Fig. 1. Leonardo da Vinci, Louvre *Mona Lisa* (detail), ca. 1508-1516.

THE LOUVRE MONA LISA, BUT FOR WHOM?

Prof. Jean-Pierre Isbouts
Fielding Graduate University
Santa Barbara, CA

In his 2012 publication on Leonardo's painting of the *St. Anne, the Virgin and Child*, Louvre curator Vincent Delieuvin asked, "A Saint Anne, but for whom?" The same question could be posed with regards to the Louvre *Mona Lisa*, if we accept the argument from the scholars in this monograph that the Louvre painting is Leonardo's second version of this portrait. The obvious corollary to this question is: but why would Leonardo *want* to paint another portrait of an otherwise unknown Florentine lady? True, he and his studio had produced several versions of his paintings, but these invariably involved sacred art, including portraits of Madonna's and other saints (such as Saint Anne), which enjoyed broad popularity throughout Italy and France. What commercial value could there be in the development of *another* portrait of a woman who was neither known nor recognized outside the immediate orbit of the Giocondo family? After all, this was not a famous personage such as Isabella d'Este. This was a Florentine housewife, pure and simple; a lovely woman, to be sure, but not a subject that would have any obvious appeal to a buyer outside the Giocondo circle.

We cannot leave our discussion of the Earlier *Mona Lisa* without addressing this urgent issue, for without examining Leonardo's motives for producing two versions, we can never hope to settle the matter (as ambitious a goal as that may be). And here we find, as in the case of Delieuvin's discussion of the *St. Anne*,

that the documentation is once again ambiguous. If we assume that the Louvre *Mona Lisa* cannot be the result of Francesco del Giocondo's commission of 1503, for all the reasons we discussed in previous chapters, then who or what prompted Leonardo to paint it?

As we saw, the primary evidence for the identification of the patron is provided by Antonio de Beatis, the secretary of the cardinal who visited Leonardo in Amboise in 1517. "In one of the suburbs [of Amboise], His Eminence and we others went to visit M. Lunardo [*sic*] Vinci," de Beatis wrote, "(a) Florentine, over LXX years old, of the most excellent painters of our times." The secretary added that Leonardo is not just a painter, because "he has also written on the nature of water, on diverse machines and other subjects, according to what he says, an infinite number of volumes, all in vernacular, which if they are to be published, will be beneficial and very delightful." Here is a clear attestation of Leonardo's notebooks, which soon would pass into the diligent hands of Francesco Melzi and thus—at least in part—into posterity.

"It is true that we can no longer expect anything further from him," de Beatis continued, "because he has been struck by a paralysis on his right side"— which suggests that Leonardo had suffered a stroke. Indeed, he continued, "M. Lunardo can no longer work with colors as he was accustomed"—confirming that Leonardo was, as of 1517, no longer able to paint in oils—but "he continues to do drawings and to teach others." In fact, the de Beatis added, "he has trained a Milanese disciple who does quite good work"—no doubt referring to Melzi, which would suggest that by this date, Salaì had already returned to Milan.

The greatest praise, however, was reserved for the three paintings that Leonardo had installed in his home:

> One of these was of a certain Florentine lady, done from life at the behest of the late Magnificent Giuliano de Medici. The other of Saint John the Baptist, young, and one of the Madonna with the child, seated on the lap of Saint Anne, all absolutely perfect.

As we saw in a previous chapter, the comment that all three paintings were "all absolutely perfect" (*tucti perfectissimi*) clearly indicates that the works had reached a high level of finish, which clearly contradicts Vasari's comment that the *Mona Lisa* that *he* saw was "unfinished." But most intriguing is Leonardo's declaration that the portrait of this "certain Florentine lady" had been done "from life at the behest of the late Magnificent Giuliano Medici" (*Uno di certa donna firentina facta di naturale ad instantia del quondam Magnifico Juliano de Medici*). The words "done from life" either suggest that Leonardo told his visitors that he had used a live model; or by contrast, that the lifelike realism of the portrait struck de Beatis as a work that could only have been made "from nature." Which of these two possibilities is correct, we may never know.

But Leonardo's claim that the work was done at the request of his patron in Rome, Giuliano de Medici, raises quite another question. What did Leonardo mean with "at the behest" of Giuliano? Did Giuliano commission him to undertake the work, perhaps because his brother, Pope Leo X, continued to ignore Leonardo and instead favored artists such as Raphael and Michelangelo? Was this second *Mona Lisa* therefore a consolation prize of sorts, to maintain Leonardo's standing as an artist at the papal court? Or did Giuliano explicitly wish to have a portrait made of "a certain Florentine lady?" And if that is the case, why did Leonardo not identify her?

In the introduction to this monograph, we discussed several theories that argue that the Louvre *Mona Lisa* is not M(ad)onna Lisa at all, but rather, a portrait of one of Giuliano's mistresses, such as Pacifica Brandano or possibly Costanza d'Avalos. This theory was originally posited as early as 1914 by A.C. Coppier in *Les Arts*, and endorsed by Ludwig Goldscheider in his da Vinci biography of 1943. Josephine Mariotti found that As we saw, this hypothesis was then boosted by a series of multispectral images taken by the French scientist Pascal Cotte, and published in 2015. Cotte claims that these scans reveal the image of a lady underneath the *Mona Lisa*, which looks strikingly different than the final portrait. But why would Leonardo dutifully paint a portrait of his patron's mistress, only to cover it up with a painting of an entirely different lady? Indeed, mere months after Giuliano's death in 1516 (which could have ended to the commission to paint his mistress), Leonardo was on his way to France with a *Mona Lisa* portrait that by then was virtually complete.

The strong similarity between the Earlier *Mona Lisa* and the Louvre *Mona Lisa*—in terms of composition, though not in terms of likeness—must suggest another scenario. That both may have been derived from the same source drawings or cartoon is evidenced by the almost identical application of the golden rule, as John Asmus and Vadim Parfenov argued in their chapter. So clearly, the two works are related, though key differences—in terms of their size, as well as features such as the columns and the landscape—suggest that they are *not* a copy of one another. It would perhaps be more apt to say that both are variations on a common theme. But if that is

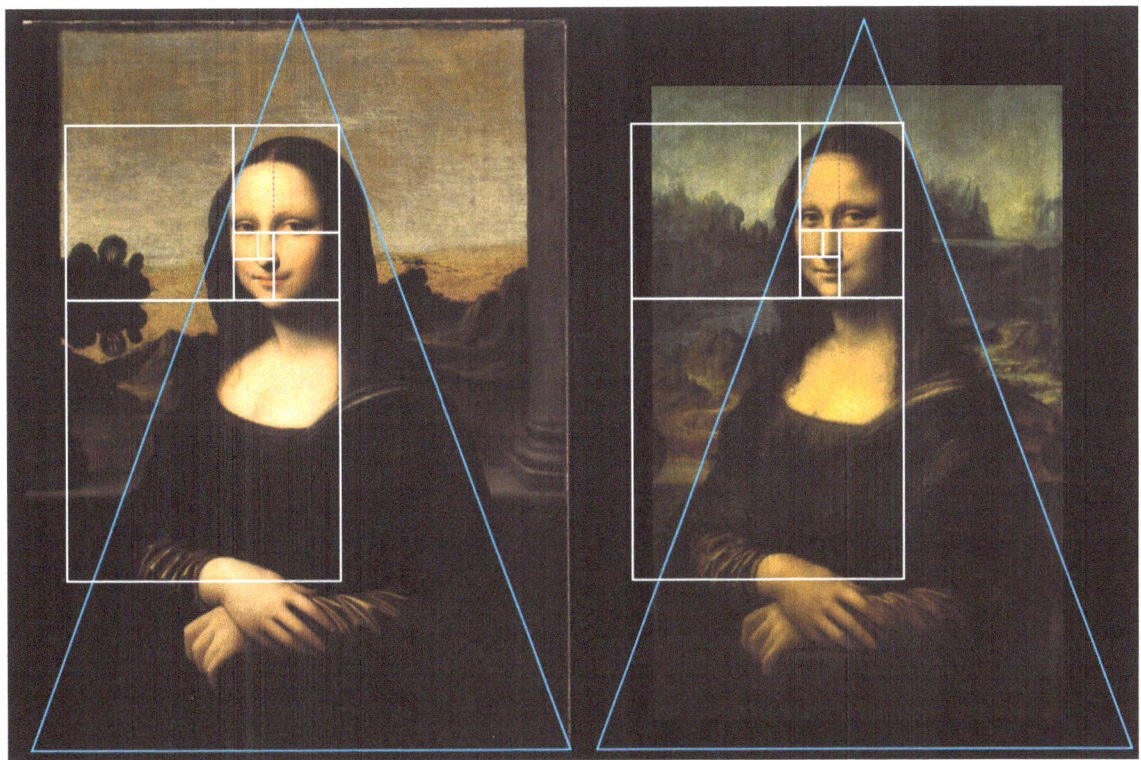

Fig. 2. Use of the "Golden Rule" in both the Earlier *Mona Lisa* and the Louvre *Mona Lisa*.

true, then the question still remains: what prompted Leonardo to do so?

Of all the hypotheses that rise to the surface, there are two theories that appear to have some merit. One is the idea first proposed by John R. Eyre, an art collector and the father-in-law of Hugh Blaker, who discovered the Earlier *Mona Lisa* in a Somerset manor in 1913. In his 1922 book, Eyre argues that Leonardo's patron, Giuliano de Medici, played some role in the Medici government in Florence from September, 1512 to October, 1513. During that sojourn (when Leonardo was in Milan, save for short visits to Florence) Giovanni may have been invited to visit the home of Francesco del Giocondo, and seen the Earlier *Mona Lisa* with his own eyes. It is conceivable that the painting made a deep impression on Giovanni, particularly since, as Eyre wrote, it "is a work of transcendent beauty, with the most exquisite eyes that ever an artist's brush gave life to." This then would have filled Giovanni with the desire to own a copy of this painting, and to commission Leonardo to produce such at the earliest opportunity.

This is a plausible theory, for it would solve a few problems. One, it would explain why Leonardo referred to the second *Mona Lisa* as "a certain Florentine lady" without specifically identifying her, because she was a merchant's wife, without any title or credit that would be of any interest to his visitors. Two, it may also be the reason why Giuliano sought Leonardo out to begin with, and offered him a position at the papal court under his personal patronage in 1513. And three, the choice for this portrait, even if it depicted a mere daughter of impoverished gentry, would still have some emotional value. After all, Lisa was a Florentine like Giuliano himself, and perhaps a reminder of the beauties that the city was renowned for—in contrast to Rome, which in the early 16th century was a rather unsophisticated medieval village where thieves and brigands roamed freely at night.

The problem with this interpretation, however,

is that the motive for painting the Louvre *Mona Lisa* would be entirely Giuliano's, rather than Leonardo's. The great care that Leonardo invested in creating this painting, including the development of a new and strikingly beautiful background, suggests otherwise. Put differently, the Louvre *Mona Lisa* cannot be a mere version of the Earlier portrait, because it has so many ideas that reach back across the arc of Leonardo's life as an artist. It is, quite simply, a summary of all the things that preoccupied him throughout his career, including his scientific studies of optics, atmosphere, geography, anatomy, human psychology and human emotion. What's more, it is difficult to believe that Leonardo could have produced such a seminal work in the relatively short span of his stay in Rome, particularly given the slow pace of his creative process, and the fact that in 1515 he apparently suffered a major illness. That year, he wrote to Giuliano: "I was so greatly rejoiced, most illustrious Lord, by the desired restoration of your health, that it almost had the effect that my own illness left me ['*male mio da me s'è fuggito*']. This disposition could very well have been the stroke that de Beatis would allude to two years later. Significantly, in 1515 Giuliano married Filiberta, daughter of the Duke of Savoy; her nephew was none other than François, the *dauphin* of France, who had just succeeded Louis XII. The king even invested Giuliano with the title of *Duc de Nemours*, a prosperous region in the Île-de-France, which drew him even closer to the French royal orbit. In preparation for this marriage, Raphael was charged with painting Giuliano's portrait, so that the bride could see for herself what her intended looked like. The Duke's pose is reminiscent of that of the *Mona Lisa*, except that his gaze is turned to something outside the picture frame. The original portrait is now lost, but a copy has survived and is now in the collection of the Metropolitan Museum in New York.

All these factors suggest that the Louvre *Mona Lisa* was begun much earlier, possibly during the same

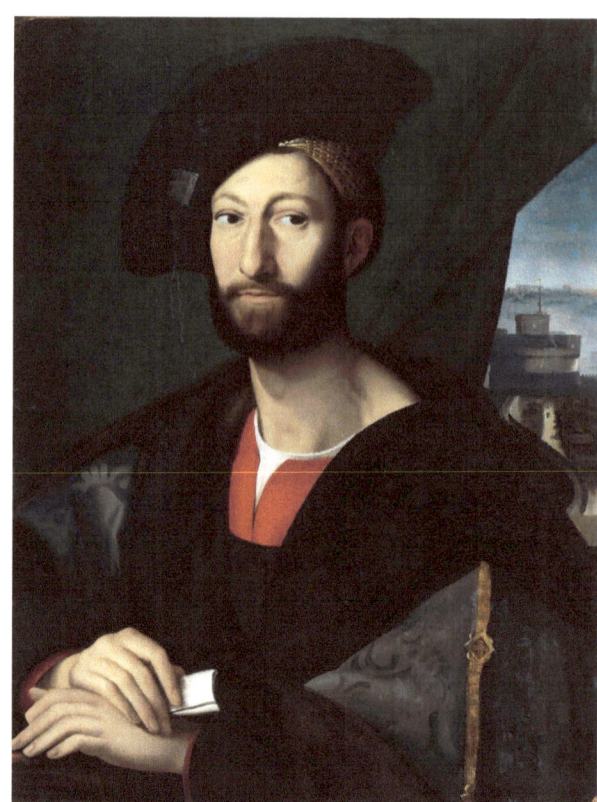

Fig. 3. Anonymous Artist, *Portrait of Giuliano de' Medici*, after an original by Raphael, ca. 1515.

time that the *St Anne* was beginning to take form. That would put us in the second Milanese period from about 1507 or 1508 onwards.

This idea is attractive for several reasons. To begin with, both the *Mona Lisa* and the *St Anne* use poplar panels that were prepared with an unusual double strata of gesso: a *gesso grosso* or "dense" gesso, which was composed of calcium sulphate; and another layer known as *gesso sottile* or "fine gesso," using rehydrated gypsum. In both paintings, moreover, the segments of the sky extend under parts of the landscape and even the figures, unlike the traditional Renaissance convention of limiting these passages to areas visible to the beholder. This use of seamless transitions between background landscape and the sky above was a fundamental part of Leonardo's art theory, as described in this *Treatise on Painting*:

"The boundaries that separate one
body from another are of the nature of

mathematical lines, not of real lines. The end of any color is only the beginning of another, and it ought not to be called a line, for nothing interposes between them, except the termination of the one against the other, which being nothing in itself, cannot be perceived, therefore the painter ought not to make it pronounced in distant objects."

Moreover, both paintings give us an unimpeded view of the vista beyond the figures, thus creating a visual bond between foreground and background that serves to enhance the overall monumentality of the figures. In both works, the landscape is strikingly different from the gentle flowing hills of Tuscany. In fact, Leonardo divides this vista into two levels: a realistic depiction of nature in the foreground, and a more fantastic view of jagged Alpine peaks in the background. These spectacular mountain vistas are reminiscent of the foothills of the Alps that could be observed north

of Milan, at a distance of only half a day's march. In producing these awesome panoramas, Leonardo applied his theory of aerial perspective, which specifies that progressively distant objects will appear more bluish, "by means of the great quantity of air that interposes between the eye and such mountains." Thus, Leonardo wrote, "it is easy to determine the distance of different objects by the differences of the air."

The idea that the Louvre *Mona Lisa* would have been painted in the same timeframe as the *St Anne* would also explain the resemblance between the sitter of the Louvre portrait and the face of Mary in the *St Anne*, which suggests that Leonardo could have used the same model. But this doesn't solve the essential problem of *why* Leonardo would want to paint a second version of the *Mona Lisa*. A *St Anne* had a commercial value, anywhere in Europe. But what value was attached to a portrait of an unknown sitter?

The answer, I believe, may be found in a curious event that took place in the autumn of 1507, after Leonardo had been formally appointed in Milan as

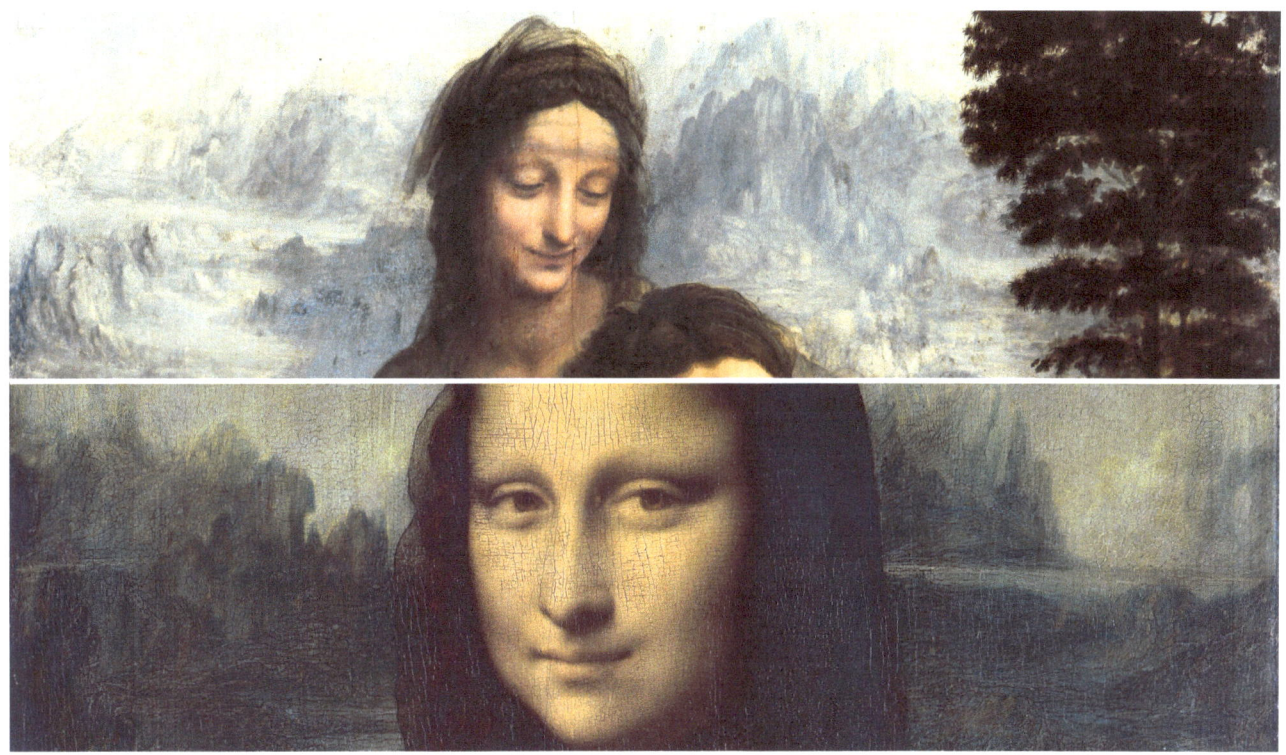

Fig. 4. Comparison of the far background in the *St Anne* (top) and the *Mona Lisa* (bottom).

the painter and engineer to the French king, Louis XII. As it happened, his uncle Francesco had died a few months before. The terms of his will, however, stipulated that Leonardo was to receive his property near Vinci, as we saw in a previous chapter; Leonardo may even have visited that property in late 1504. Unfortunately, his half-brothers—the legitimate children of Ser Piero—were evidently not satisfied with excluding Leonardo from his father's inheritance. They now vowed to deny him his uncle's estate as well. A suit was filed with the court in Florence, based on the flimsy notion that when both Piero and Francesco were still alive, the childless Francesco had promised Ser Piero to give his entire estate to his (legitimate) nephews. Perhaps the half-brothers were aware of the bad blood that now existed between Leonardo and the *gonfaloniere*, Piero Soderini, because of Leonardo's failure to complete the *Battle of Anghiari*. If so, they may have figured that a Florentine court would have very little sympathy for the master in Milan.

This time, Leonardo vowed to fight. He had been powerless when his share of his father's estate was taken from him, but he would not sit idle and be deprived of his inheritance from his uncle as well. And so Leonardo found himself in the uncomfortable position of having to go back to Florence, just when his reputation in the city was at its lowest ebb. But he hedged his bets. Just before leaving Milan, he personally supervised the lavish decoration of the city for the triumphant entry of King Louis, complete with triumphal arches, sacred tableaux, ballets, masques and dances. The king was charmed.

Soon thereafter, Leonardo retraced his steps to the city of his youth, this time only accompanied by Salaì. To move back into his apartment at the Santa Maria Novella was obviously out of the question, for he had no intention of continuing to work on the *Anghiari* fresco. Fortunately, a wealthy patron of the arts, Piero di Braccio Martelli, invited him to stay in his palazzo on the Via Larga. Leonardo gratefully accepted; after all, he expected his stay to be short, a few weeks at most.

But things did not go as planned. One of Leonardo's half-brothers, Ser Giuliano, had followed his father in the legal profession and now vowed to pursue the case with vigor. The matter dragged on, motions were filed, witnesses were consulted. It soon became obvious that the republic was in no hurry to give Leonardo what he wanted. Eventually, Leonardo had little choice but to impose on the goodwill of his French patron, King Louis. The monarch was happy to oblige. On July 26, the king fired off a note to the Signoria, urging that "this lawsuit be brought to a conclusion in the best and swiftest rendering of justice possible." The letter referred to Leonardo as '*nostre peintre et ingénieur ordinaire*', which left no doubt that the master was now considered an official member of the French royal court.[12] In other words, an injustice against him would be considered a slight against the kingdom of France itself. This missive was followed by another letter by Charles d'Amboise, warning the Signoria that Leonardo's absence from Milan had been granted "with the greatest reluctance," given that he was working on a "painting very dear to the king."[13] Elsewhere, I have suggested what kind of painting the king was referring to: a large-scale copy of the *Last Supper*, painted by Leonardo's assistants under his supervision, and executed on canvas so that it could be easily transported back to France.[14]

The pressure from the French court in Milan had its effect. Soderini himself assigned a new judge to the case, with the directive to conclude the matter by November of 1507. But no one was particularly surprised when the case dragged on into 1508. If revenge is a dish best eaten cold, Soderini certainly knew how to savor it. The upshot of this unexpected delay, soon stretching to six months, is that it placed Leonardo in a very unique and unfamiliar situation: *he had nothing to do*. Most of his assistants, his paintings, his notebooks and sketches were in his studio in Milan. He was, quite simply, marooned in Florence, at the mercy of a hostile Florentine government.

Never one to be idle, he remembered his old notebooks and manuscripts at the Ospedale di Santa Maria Nuova, the same institution where he had also banked his savings. He decided to use this respite to try to organize this large cache of papers. As he wrote on the first folio:

> Begun at Florence, in the house of Piero di Braccio Martelli, on the 22nd day of March 1508. And this is to be a collection without order, taken from many papers which I have copied here, hoping to arrange them later each in its place, according to the subjects of which they may treat. But I believe that before I am at the end of this [task] I shall have to repeat the same things several times; for which, O reader! do not blame me, for the subjects are many and memory cannot retain them [all]."[15]

Leonardo's Anatomical Studies

Eventually, Leonardo took rooms with his friend and former classmate in Verrocchio's workshop, Giovanni Francesco Rustici, and assisted him in the development of bronze figures for the Florence Baptistery. Soon, however, another opportunity beckoned: to continue his anatomical studies by performing dissections at the Ospedale di Santa Maria Nuova. Leonardo's interest in such studies had been kindled in the workshop of Verrocchio, who set great store by teaching his pupils the importance of understanding human anatomy. Verrocchio may have used drawings by the Pollaiuolo brothers, Piero and Antonio, who were one of the first artists to conduct dissections on male cadavers so as to better understand the movement of limbs and bone, and the flexing of muscle under skin. Leonardo's interest then deepened during his first Milanese period,

when he probably carried out his first dissections in preparation for the various poses of his Apostles in *The Last Supper.* Vasari claims that until then, the mysteries of human anatomy "had been wrapped in the thick and gross darkness of ignorance," but this is not entirely accurate. Though various papal bulls had tried to proscribe dissections over the centuries, the use of autopsies was fairly widespread, particularly by medical faculties of universities such as the University of Bologna, an early center of anatomical research. However, the cadavers used for such dissections were universally male, and usually involved executed prisoners or the poor. "By law only unknown and ignoble bodies can be sought for dissection," the physician Alessandro Benedetti wrote in 1497, just ten years before Leonardo's arrival at the Ospedale in Florence; "[people] from distant regions without injury to neighbors and relatives."[16]

What's more, the purpose of these anatomical experiments was not only to improve medical practice, but also to settle long-running disputes about natural philosophy. As Sara Taglialagambia writes, "Up to the first half of the Sixteenth century the anatomical notions were fragmentary and yet not completely organized, since anatomy was still seen as a practical exercise through which the rules of the art of medicine could be shown, without bringing developments in the morphological and physiological sectors."[17] For Leonardo, too, the early experiments with dissections were essentially practical in nature.

But after 1507, beginning with his enforced stay in Florence, that interest changed. Always the consummate empirical scientist, he wanted to understand the intricate mechanisms by which the human body, that "wondrous machine," actually functioned. He knew he had to tread carefully, not only to avoid running afoul of the Signoria but also because he knew he had to conduct his autopsies while the corpse was still fresh, before decomposition despoiled the organs. As a result, he would sometimes roam the hospital like the grim reaper incarnate, looking for prospects. In a note to himself, dated late 1507, he described how during one of those perambulations he had come across an old man, clearly within a hair's breadth from death. Leonardo sat down at his bedside, whereupon the patient told him he was over a hundred years old and never had an illness; only old age and "feebleness" had got him in the end. "And thus," Leonardo later recalled, "sitting on a bed in the hospital of Santa Maria Nuova in Florence, without any movement or sign of distress, he passed from this life." A few hours later, he was under Leonardo's knife. "I carried out an autopsy to determine the cause of such a calm death," he continued, and discovered it was a result of the "insufficiency of blood and of the artery supplying the heart and other lower members"—a condition we now know as arteriosclerosis.[18] Leonardo was the first to discover heart disease.

Increasingly, however, he was drawn to the most elusive of all human mysteries: the origin of life. How was human life created, and how did it develop through its nine-month gestation? To investigate this, he needed to dissect female cadavers, even though legally this was still out of bounds. Firstly, a woman's chastity was a highly prized virtue in the Middle Ages; a dissection would expose her most intimate parts to the eyes of strangers, compounding the grief of her relatives with shame. And second, matters of conception and procreation were jealously guarded by the Church. Even in the early Cinquecento, this is where Church doctrine still held sway. To open a woman's body and explore the secrets of her womb might bring one in conflict with Church teachings, and thus expose oneself to charges of heresy. Indeed, the only known anatomical study of a pregnant woman at the time was a crude and largely inaccurate illustration in the medical tract *Fasciculus medicinae* (1491), known as "*the Gravida.*"

For Leonardo, however, the mystery of

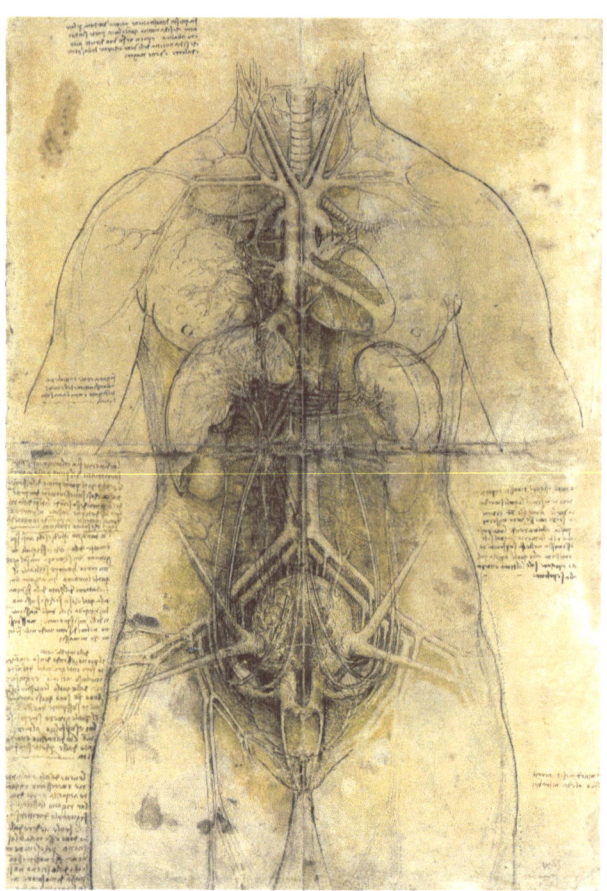

Fig. 5. Leonardo da Vinci, *Anatomical study of a woman*, ca. 1508-1510.

motherhood was the ultimate frontier. Thus, under cover of darkness, he began to perform dissections of female bodies. In 1510, this would ultimately produce the red-chalk drawing at Windsor of 1510 that is the first detailed, scientific anatomical study of an adult woman. He then continued his dissections after his return to Milan, at the University of Padua, where he worked alongside a young anatomist named Marcantonio della Torre. Among others, Leonardo correctly identified the uterine artery, as well as the vascular system of the cervix and vagina. From there he ventured into embryology, and discovered that the uterus is a single chamber, contrary to contemporary belief that it comprised several compartments so as to accommodate more than one fetus.

These discoveries on the origins of human life fascinated him. It fulfilled an ambition first articulated in Milan, to understand "the conception of man" by studying "the form of the womb, and how the child lives in it, and to what stage it resides in it, and in what way it is given life and food." In the process, Leonardo produced the first complete inventory of the female body in human history—developing, in effect, a vocabulary of anatomical illustration that is still relevant in modern medicine today.[20]

In my view, these anatomical studies gave further impetus to Leonardo's lifelong fascination with womanhood—not as sexual beings, but as mothers, as paragons of grace and unstinting, nurturing love. The root of this desire was very likely his traumatic experience of being separated from his mother at age five, without the polar balance of a strong and loving father figure. And while it may well have stymied his sexual development in puberty, it also endowed him with a lifelong yearning to capture the elusive ideal of a motherhood—graceful, loving, eternally young and beautiful—in his art. This focus found an early outlet in the motif of the Madonna, a theme that dominates

Leonardo's oeuvre and would grow in importance in the later stages of his life, culminating in his last great masterpiece, the *Saint Anne*. That work is a study of motherhood *par excellence*, for it overlays one maternal bond—that of Anne and Mary—over another—that of Mary and her child Jesus, thus creating an unprecedented level of complexity in both an aesthetic and psychological sense. How to represent this unique interrelationship of human emotions became the subject of a series of sketches that vividly illustrate how Leonardo grappled with the idea.

It may also have rekindled the memory of Lisa del Giocondo. For Leonardo, Lisa may have embodied all the qualities that Leonardo identified with motherhood: youth, beauty, kindness, and love, vividly exemplified by the birth of her son Andrea in December of 1502. Very likely, Lisa's figure still bore the traces of that recent pregnancy when she posed for Leonardo in early 1503. This may explain why Leonardo took care to depict her glowing skin and the fullness of her breasts, further accentuated by the arabesque

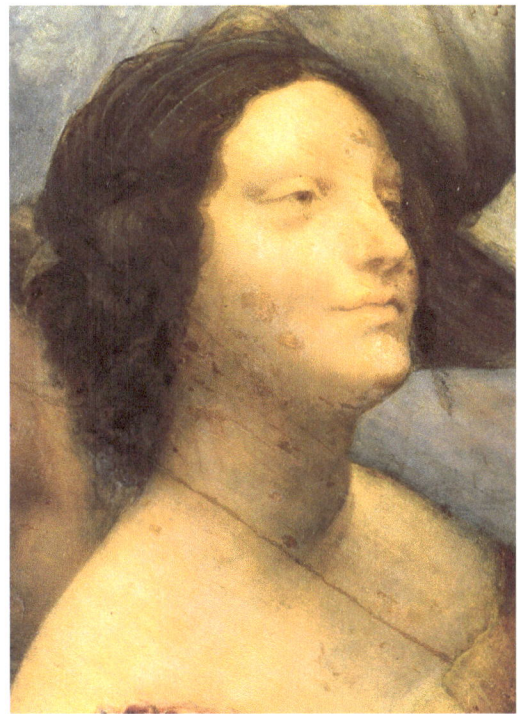

Fig. 6. Leonardo da Vinci, *St. Anne, Virgin and Child*: detail of Mary (tilted for comparison), ca. 1508-1515.

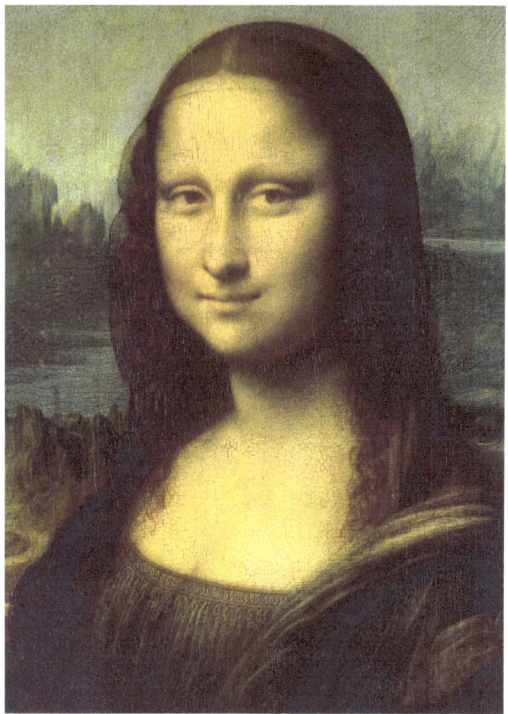

Fig. 7. Leonardo da Vinci, Louvre *Mona Lisa* (detail), ca. 1508-1515.

ornamentation of her dress.

If, as many historians believe, the Louvre portrait originated around 1508, then as we saw earlier, it is difficult to argue that it was commissioned by Giuliano de Medici. As of the summer of that year, Leonardo was back in Milan. For that reason, it is unlikely (though not impossible) that he used Lisa again as his model, who was nearing 30 at that time; her countenance and figure, having had five pregnancies, were probably not unlike the portrait that slowly materialized on Leonardo's easel. But Lisa was in Florence, whereas Leonardo was working 200 miles away, in Milan.

My point is that the Louvre painting is no longer a *portrait* in the strict sense of the word; it is no longer a likeness of Lisa, or any other sitter for that matter. Instead, I believe the Louvre *Mona Lisa* is a meditation on the mystery and unflinching love of motherhood—a Florentine Madonna made flesh. That is why it is not at all surprising that the features of this *Mona Lisa* and that of Mary in the *St. Anne* are so similar; Leonardo may simply have used the same model because to him, they represented the same motif, the same idea of complete and utter devotion.[21]

The same fascination with the enigma of human conception also led him to a very different treatment of the female: the *Leda and the Swan*, a work that is only known from copies, since Leonardo's original has been lost. The story of Leda is told in Ovid's *Metamorphoses*. One day, the Greek supreme god Zeus fell in love with the beautiful Leda, wife of King Tyndareus of Sparta. Zeus proceeded to seduce her in the guise of a swan. As a result of this encounter, Leda conceived and bore two sets of twins, each delivered in an egg shell: Helen and Polydeuces, children of Zeus; and Castor and Clytemnestra, children of her husband Tyndareus.

Considered a rather risqué subject in the Quattrocento, the motif would become highly popular in the Cinquecento, for it enabled artists such as

Michelangelo and Correggio to depict the passion of human intercourse using the swan as a proxy. Leonardo did not go that far; his earliest drawings (such as the study in the Devonshire Collection in Chatsworth) show the nude Leda receiving a chaste kiss from the swan. The final composition, known only from copies by *Leonardeschi*, shows Leda in classic *contrapposto*. While her torso is turned towards the swan, her thighs are facing the beholder, and her gaze is turned the other way, towards the four infants at her feet. This composition was already in place as early as 1504, as evidenced by a drawing by Raphael from that year. Remarkably, the erotic quality that would soon be attached to the theme is mostly lacking. Instead, Leda is depicted as a loving mother whose attention is entirely absorbed by the birth of her children as they scramble out of their broken eggshells. *Leda* means 'woman'; she is the *Ur-Göttin* or "Earth Goddess" whom the Romans called Gaia. In Greek mythology, she gave birth to the cosmic egg that ultimately produced human life. Both the *Leda* and the *Saint Anne* are therefore similar in a sense that they explore the mystery of motherhood from two different angles: a pagan perspective on the one hand, and a Christian view on the other.

Seen in this context, Leonardo's desire to try to produce a *contemporary* portrait of the quintessential mother begins to make sense. He no longer had the original portrait of Lisa del Giocondo, for as we saw, that was duly delivered to the man who commissioned it, Francesco del Giocondo, in 1506. But presumably, Leonardo did have the drawings and sketches he had made of Lisa at that time, which is how he was able to largely reconstruct the original composition. That also means that he *could* have recreated Lisa's original countenance, if he had wished to do so.

But the point is, he didn't. This second painting was no longer meant to be a likeness but "the portrait of an idea," in the words of Erwin Panofsky.[23] Indeed, infrared reflectography scans taken by the Louvre

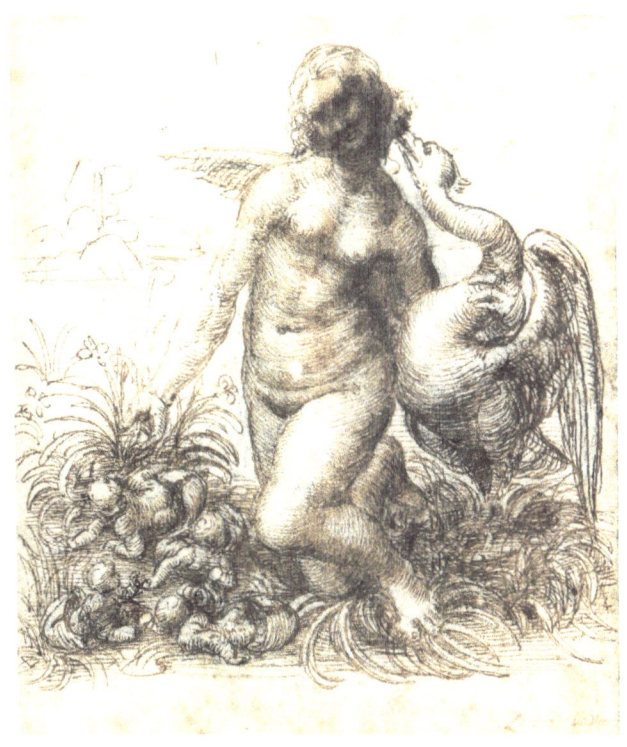

Fig. 8. Leonardo da Vinci, *Study for the Leda and the Swan*, ca. 1503-4; Chatsworth.

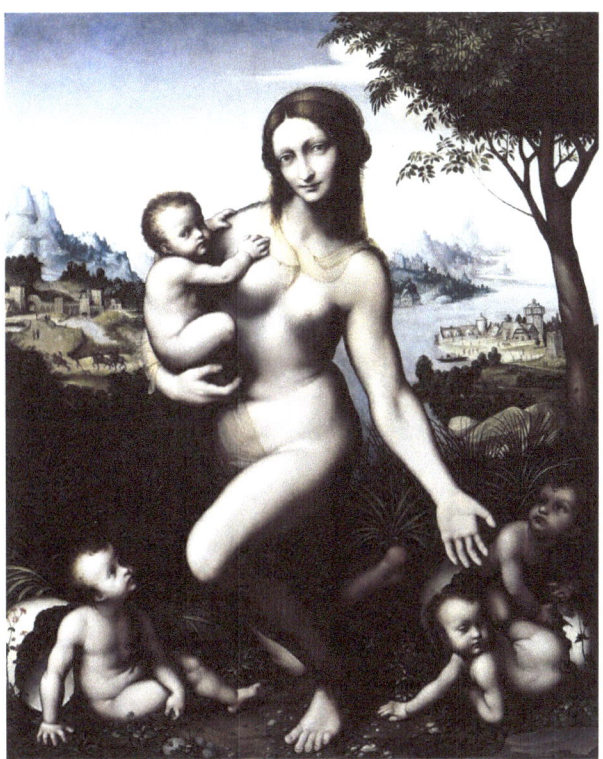

Fig. 9. Giampietrino, *Leda and the Swan*, ca. 1506-10.

show that Leonardo made many changes to the face, moving from a "square" countenance with heavy features and thick cheeks to a more slender, oval shape.[24] He also allowed the locks of hair to freely tumble onto Lisa's shoulder, as in the case of the Earlier version, but then decided to cover some of the strands under her veil. The left hand originally gripped the end of armrest tightly, before Leonardo decided to release the hand and allow the fingers to curl more playfully. The position of the index finger of the right hand underwent some variations as well.

The panel Leonardo chose for the portrait was smaller than the canvas he used for the Earlier version: 79 cm by 53 cm, or 31 by 20.8 inches, which was still wider than his other portraits. What's more, the rear of the panel is unusually smooth, which has led curators to speculate that Leonardo deliberately chose the outer face of the plank so as to avoid convex warping.[25]

In both portraits, the chair is placed in a small loggia, framed by a low wall topped by a cornice,

which looks out over the countryside. But the loggia columns of the Earlier version (which also appeared in the Raphael drawing of 1504) are all but missing in the Louvre portrait; here, we only see a fragment of their bases. Interestingly, whereas the left column in the Earlier version casts a soft shadow on the top of the balcony balustrade, no such shadow is present in the Louvre portrait. Much has been written about the "disappearance" of these columns, both in this monograph as well as the Leonardo literature. In my view, the decision to dispense with this (essentially North European) motif of "screening" the sitter is entirely in character. As Daniel Arasse has argued, the arc of Leonardo art shows that the artist progressively renounced architectural space in order to associate his figures more clearly with the nature that they inhabit.[26] This process began with the *Last Supper,* where the relationship of the figures and the architectural interior is ambiguous, and continued with his subsequent work, including the *Battle of Anghiari* and ultimately the *St Anne*, where any reference to an architectural frame is abandoned altogether. When seen in this context, the columns of the Earlier version may have seen a needless interference in the close harmony between figure and panorama that Leonardo was trying to achieve. It also enabled him to create a uniform tonal effect across all living elements, both human and nature, using thin, barely tinted layers of sfumato.

The idea that the Louvre *Mona Lisa* could have originated around the same time that Leonardo began the oil version of *St Anne*, at some point after 1508, may be corroborated by his letter to the French governor of Milan, in which he announced his imminent return to this city. The date of this letter, of which several drafts were found in Leonardo's *Codex Atlanticus*, is uncertain, but most authors believe a range between 1508 and 1510 is most likely. In this letter, Leonardo writes that "I am almost at the end of my litigation with my brothers," and that therefore "I expect to find myself with you this Easter." What's more, he promises "to bring with me two pictures of Our Lady, of different sizes, which have in my own time been brought almost to completion for our own most Christian King, or for whomsoever Your Lordship pleases." The reference to "*due quadri di due Nosstre Donne di varie grandezze*" was modified in a later draft to "*due quadri di Nostra Donna che io o comincate e olle ne tempi che mi sono avanzati condote in assai bon porto,*" or "two pictures of Our Lady, which I have begun and have in my own time brought almost to completion."[27]

It is almost certain that one of these two paintings is the *St. Anne*, a hypothesis supported by Vincent Delieuvin.[28] I would argue that the other portrait is the Louvre *Mona Lisa*, precisely because in depicting this allegorical depiction of motherhood, he was guided by his iconographic ideal of the Madonna, honed since the days in Verrocchio's workshop. One clue that could strengthen this putative relationship between the Louvre *Mona Lisa* and Leonardo's Madonna

repertoire is the robe that is thrown, toga-like, over her left shoulder. This same attribute is worn by Mary in the *Burlington Cartoon*; in the *Saint Anne*; and in the Landsdowne *Madonna of the Yarnwinder.* Another link is the *guarnello*, the thin, gauzy veil that covers the sitter's hair and neck. Such a transparent veil, made of white silk or linen, was worn by Italian women to signal that they were expecting, or to protect their modesty when they found themselves compelled to nurse in the company of others. For that reason, in the Middle Ages the *guarnello* became an attribute of the Virgin Mary, as evidenced by countless Quattrocento paintings. And finally, what both Mary in the *St Anne* and the sitter of the Louvre *Mona Lisa* have in common is their enigmatic smile—a smile informed by the unique power of a woman to produce human life. This may be the reason why Marcel Brion called the Louvre *Mona Lisa* "*la dernière grande peinture religieuse qui ait* été *peinte*"—"his last great religious painting."[29]

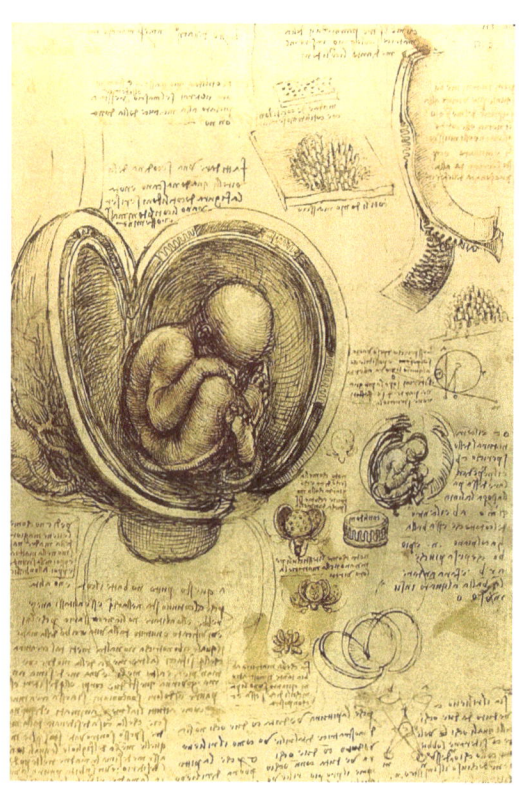

Fig. 10. Leonardo da Vinci, *Anatomical study of an embryo*, 1508-1510.

The idea that Leonardo's second *Mona Lisa* is an effort to capture the mystery of human creation also explains the primordial, Genesis-like mountain range in the background; it serves to illustrate the tremendous life-giving power of God's creation. This analogy between the human and the divine is suggested by Leonardo's comment that "though human ingenuity may make wondrous inventions and machines, it will never devise an invention more beautiful, more simple and more direct, than Nature; because in her invention nothing is lacking, and nothing is superfluous."[30] In the same breath he marveled at the "soul of the mother, which first constructs within the womb the shape of man, and in due time awakens the soul that is to be its inhabitant." To quote Herman Colenbrander, Leonardo was interested "not only (in) the external beauty of the world…. but also the inner structure and the *forze spirituali*, the powers that determine the outward shapes of reality."[31]

Lastly, the explicit reference in Leonardo's letter that he would bring both paintings "for our own most Christian King, or for whomsoever Your Lordship pleases" clearly shows that both works were not being developed for any particular patron, or in response to any particular commission. Though their compositions may have been informed by earlier works—in the case of the *Mona Lisa*, the portrait of Lisa del Giocondo; and in the case of *St Anne*, the commission for the Annunziata altarpiece—in their final iteration they became the product of Leonardo's genius, and his genius alone. Indeed, that these were works primarily undertaken for Leonardo's own benefit is underscored by the fact that they were never delivered to a putative patron. Instead, Leonardo took them with him wherever he went, from Milan to Rome, and finally from Rome to Amboise. As he wrote in his letter, these works had been begun "in his own time," on his own initiative, and were therefore not yet complete. However, he was gracious enough to offer them to Louis XII, his benefactor in Milan, just as several

years later he would be careful to credit Giuliano de Medici as the "instigator" of these works, since they were completed under his patronage. In this, as in so many other things, Leonardo revealed his talent as the consummate courtier, with skills that had been honed at the court of the mercurial Ludovico Sforza.

If it is true that in its ultimate iteration; the portrait in the Louvre was informed by Leonardo's lifetime preoccupation with the mystery of motherhood, or the *"expression parfait de l'eternal féminin,"*[32] then this would explain why he kept both the Louvre *Mona Lisa* and the *Saint Anne* with him through the last chapter of his life. Both are a meditation on the mysterious ways in which the divine reveals itself to man. They are the expression of the mind that, having studied the secrets of nature, must conclude that there are limits to what human reason can achieve.

References

[1] As Josephine Rogers Mariotti writes, virtually all experts –including Carlo Pedretti, Kenneth Clark, Martin Kemp, Pietro Marani and Carlo Vecce – agreed that the Louvre *Mona Lisa* must stylistically be dated to a period well after 1503. See Josephine Rogers Mariotti, *Monna Lisa: La 'Gioconda' del Magnifico Giuliano*. Firenze: Ediziono Polistampa, 2009; p. 47.

[2] Rather than 70, Leonardo was actually 65 at the time, though with his flowing beard and long hair, he may have looked older to his visitors.

[3] Antonio de Beatis, "Account of the Visit of Cardinal Louis d'Aragon paid to Leonardo, at the Château de Cloux, October 10, 1517," in Delieuvin, Vincent, *Saint Anne: Leonardo da Vinci's ultimate Masterpiece;* p. 199.

[4] Josephine Rogers Mariotti, *Monna Lisa: La 'Giocanda' del Magnifico Giuliano*; p. 14.

[5] A.C. Coppier, "La joconde est-elle *le* portrait de Monna Lisa?" in *Les Arts,* January 1914, pp. 2-9. Ludwig Goldscheider, *Leonardo da Vinci*. London and New York, 1943.

[6] John R. Eyre, The Two Mona Lisa: which was Giocondo's picture? London: J.M. Ouseley & Son, 1922; pp. 18-19.

[7] Draft of a letter to Giuliano de' Medici, 1351; in Richter, Jean Paul, *The Notebooks of Leonardo da Vinci*; p. 407.

[8] Mohen, Jean-Pierre et al., *Mona Lisa: Inside the Painting*; p. 56.

[9] Leonardo da Vinci, *Treatise on Painting*; Rigaud translation, 1835; nr. 264.

[10] Some have tentatively associated this landscape with the Alpe di Campione; see, for example, https://alpedicampione.it/cartografia/.

[11] Leonardo da Vinci, *Treatise on Painting*; Rigaud translation, 1835; nr. 138.

[12] Letter from Louis XII to the Signoria of Florence, July 26, 1507

[13] Charles d'Amboise, *Letter to the Signoria of Florence*; Milan, August 15, 1507. Archivio di Stato di Firenze, Responsive originali, 30, fol. 164.

[14] Jean-Pierre Isbouts and Christopher H. Brown, *Young Leonardo: The evolution of a revolutionary artist*. New York: St. Martin's Press: 2017; pp. 176-186.

[15] Richter, Jean Paul, *Scritti Letterari di Leonardo da Vinci*, Part 1: p. 12

[16] Ibid, p. 12.

[17] Sara Taglialagambia, *Leonardo & Anatomy*; p. 26.

[18] Leonardo da Vinci, folio RL 19027, Royal Library at Windsor Castle, UK.

[19] Kenneth Clark, *Leonardo da Vinci*; 1228lr, Q1 12r

[20] Bambach, Carmen. "Anatomy in the Renaissance". In *Heilbrunn Timeline of Art History*. New York: The Metropolitan Museum of Art, October 2002.

[21] It's rather implausible to think that the project was completely divorced from whatever Leonardo was supposed to be doing for the Servite friars in 1501, since they were paying for Leonardo's upkeep— and that of his entourage—all through these months. What is more likely is that the *Saint Anne* was on Leonardo's mind when he received the commission for the Servite monastery, possibly as a result of conversations with the King, and that what eventually emerged from his mind was not what the friars were expecting. This would explain the discrepancy in size, as well as the fact that Leonardo "kept them waiting a long time" before finally showing a life-size cartoon. The maestro may have figured that all would be forgiven once the friars saw a fully executed rendering, confident that its sheer beauty would placate them. And as Vasari tells us, that's exactly what happened. As soon as Leonardo finished his full-length design, using wash and silverpoint to render the drawing in painterly detail, his hosts were overwhelmed. Not only were they overwhelmed, but they enthusiastically organized a "public exhibit" of the finished drawing, which had people lining up around the block—perhaps the first public exhibition of a work by Leonardo da Vinci: "When it was finished, men and women, young and old, continued for two days to flock for a sight of it to the room where it was, as if to a solemn festival, in order to gaze at the marvels of Leonardo, which caused all those people to be amazed."

[22] Some scholars insist that Leda and the Swan never existed as an autograph work, but the plethora of copies and the clearly *Leonardesque* use of sfumato strongly suggests that a Leonardo original did exist.

[23] Erwin Panofsky, *Idea: A Concept in Art Theory*. New York: Icon, 1968.

[24] Bruno Mottin, *Reading the Image,* in Ibid., page 70.

[25] Elisabeth Ravaud, "The Mona Lisa's Wooden Support," in: Mohen, J.P. et al, *The Mona Lisa: Inside the Painting*. New York: Abrams, 1999

[26] Daniel Arasse, *Léonard de Vinci, Le rythme du monde*. Paris: Hazan, 1997; p. 314.

[27] Leonardo da Vinci, "Draft of a letter to Charles d'Amboise." *Codex Atlanticus*, fol. 872 recto; Bibliotheca Ambrosiana, Milan.

[28] Delieuvin, Vincent, "*Saint Anne: Leonardo's Ultimate Masterpiece*. Exhibition catalog.Paris: Musée du Louvre; 2012; p. 130.

[29] Marcel Brion, *Léonard de Vinci,* génie et destinée. Paris, Michel, 1952; pp. 467-469.

[30] Edward McCurdy (ed. and trans.) *Leonardo da Vinci's Notebooks*, 1906; bk. 1

[31] Herman T. Colenbrander, "Hand in Leonardo's Portraiture," in Carlo Pedretti (Ed.), *Achademia Leonardi Vinci*, Volume V, 1992: p. 37.

[32] "The perfect expression of the eternal woman." S. Reinach, *Bulletin des Musées* II; 1909: pp. 17-32.

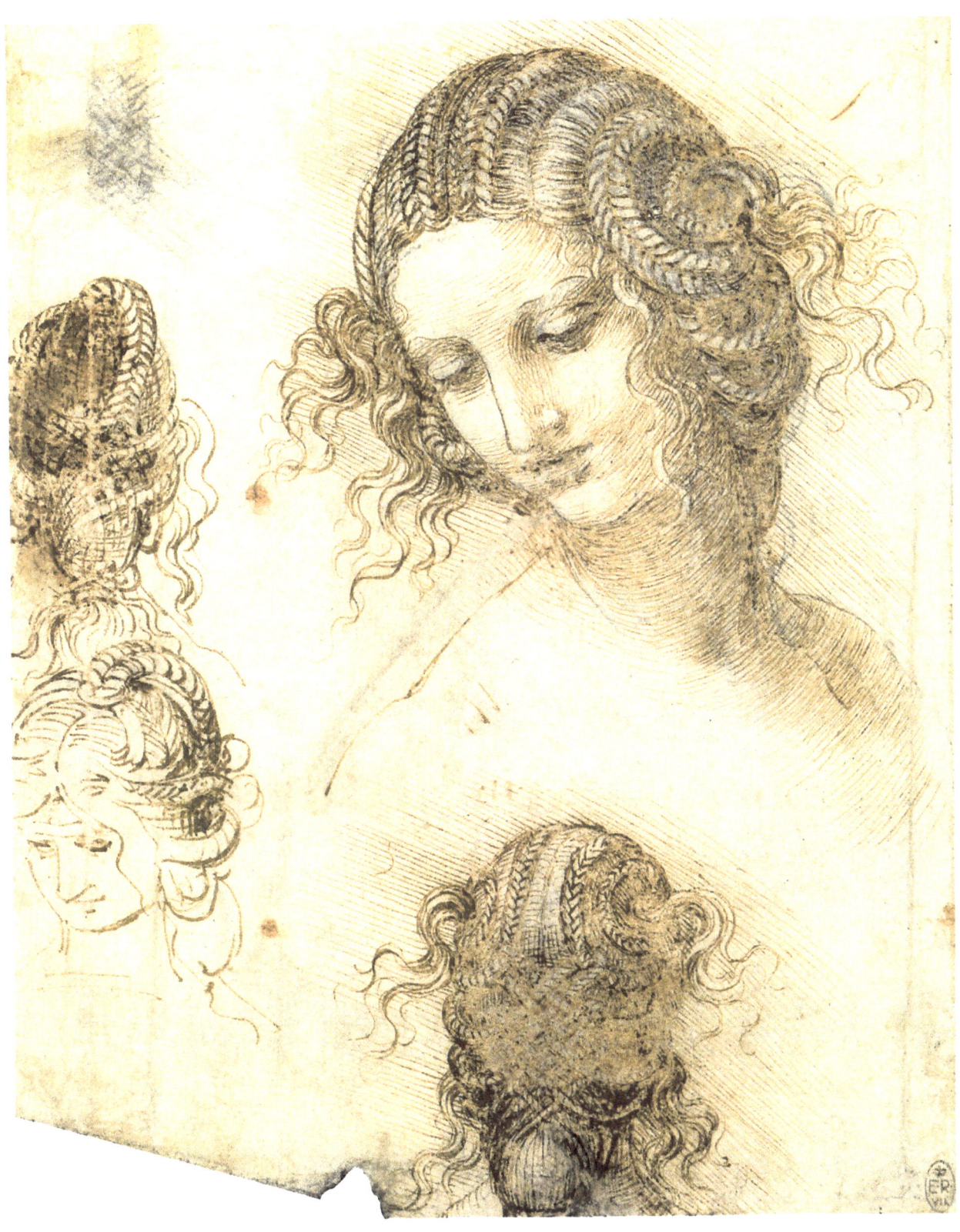

Fig. 11. Leonardo da Vinci, *Study for Leda and the Swan*, ca. 1505-1506.

THE LOUVRE MONA LISA, BUT FOR WHOM?

151

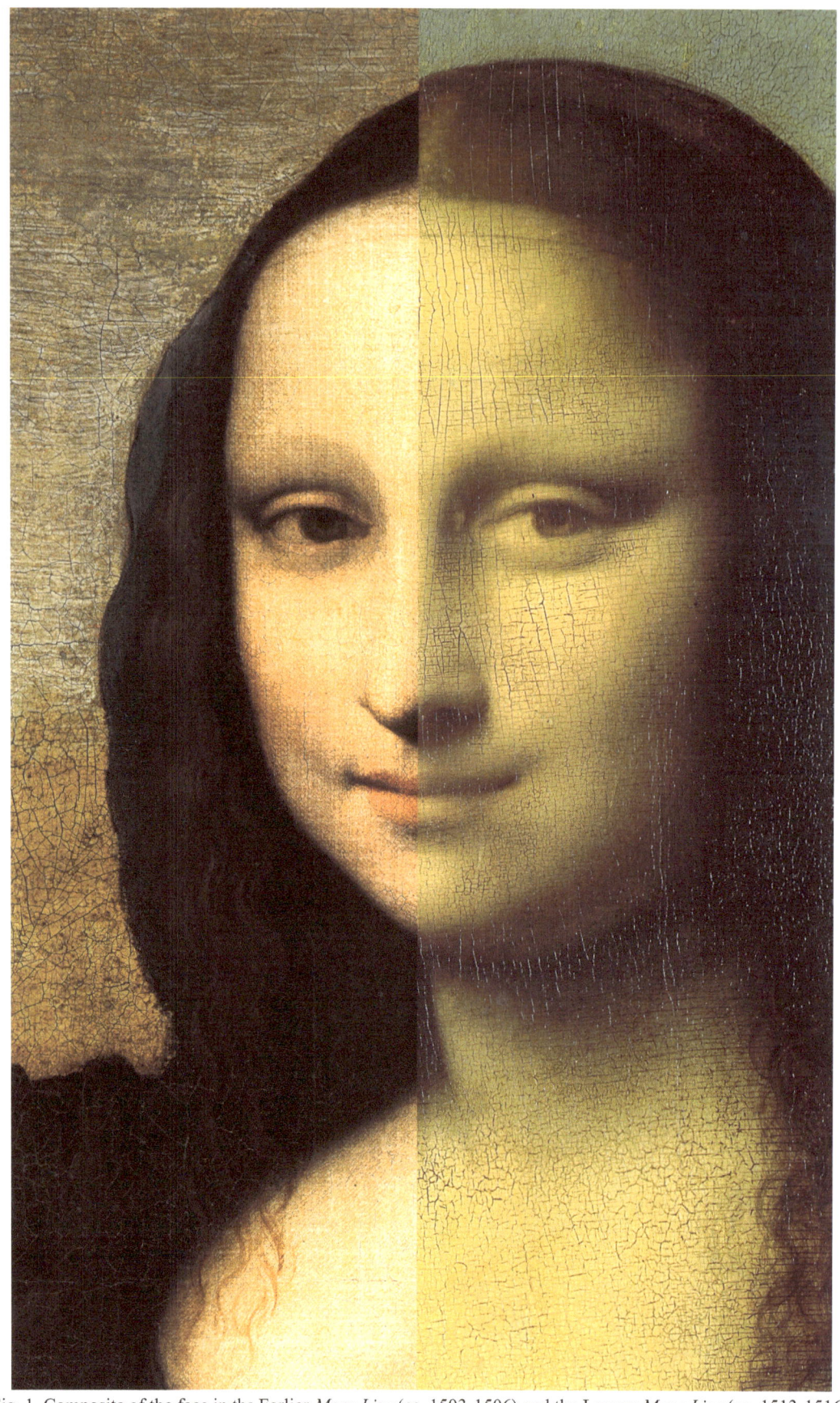

Fig. 1. Composite of the face in the Earlier *Mona Lisa* (ca. 1503-1506) and the Louvre *Mona Lisa* (ca. 1513-1516).

152

An Experimental Regression of the Louvre Mona Lisa

Joe Mullins
Professor in Art Forensics, Specialist in Human Face Aging
Washington, D.C.

Previous chapters have argued that Leonardo da Vinci began the Louvre *Mona Lisa* during his second period in Milan and continued to work on the portrait during his sojourn at the papal court in Rome. These authors also posit that Leonardo must have based this second *Mona Lisa* on his earlier drawings, and possibly his cartoon, of the likeness of Lisa del Giocondo as she appeared in 1503. This is the only way to explain the almost exact match between the two figures, even though the paintings themselves differ in terms of size and composition. At the same time, virtually all authors in this monograph recognize that the figure in the Earlier *Mona Lisa* is much younger than the more matronly appearance of the sitter in the Louvre portrait, notwithstanding the fact that both share some common facial traits.

If this is true, then this argument has two outcomes: either Lisa del Giocondo sat for Leonardo again, probably in Florence; or Leonardo deliberately "age-progressed" her in his later portrait, as he imagined she would appear some 11-12 years later. As previous chapters have shown, the suggestion that Lisa posed for Leonardo a second time is not attractive for a variety of reasons.

A deliberate progression would therefore seem to be the more likely conclusion. In this, Leonardo would have deployed his understanding of human anatomy and experience as a portraitist to create a more "aged" version of his model, and thus produce an idealized portrait of the quintessence of motherhood.

Such a progression challenge would not at all be beyond his genius, and his desire to test the limits of what he could achieve. In order to advance this hypothesis, I embarked on a forensic experiment for The Mona Lisa Foundation, which as far as I know has never been tried before in an art historical context. The parameters of the project were clear: assuming that the Earlier *Mona Lisa* was painted c.1503-06, and assuming that the Louvre *Mona Lisa* was executed c.1513 - 1516, this would present an age difference between the two portraits of roughly 11-12 years. Using the *Mona Lisa* of the Louvre as a 'base', I set out to do the reverse of what Leonardo intended, namely, to 'regress' the age of the sitter in the Louvre portrait to what she might have looked like 11-12 years earlier.

If successful, this test would tell us a few things. First, it could determine the likelihood that both paintings essentially use the same model, but painted about 11-12 years apart. Second, it would show to what extent the Louvre *Mona Lisa* is based on the Earlier *Mona Lisa*.

There are many competent forensic artists who are experienced in 'progressing' the age of a person's picture, usually on behalf of police and law-enforcement departments or security organizations. The purpose of such progression is to identify and locate long-term missing and exploited children. But

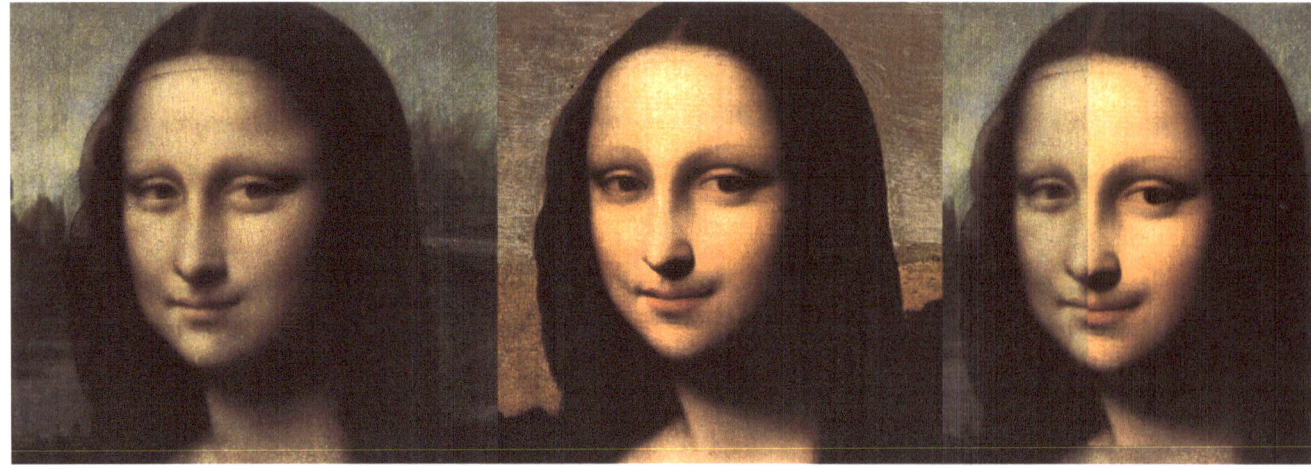

Fig. 2. The Louvre *Mona Lisa* (left), the Earlier *Mona Lisa* (center), and a composite of the two (right).

a 'regression' –i.e. the attempt to reconstruct what a person looked like at an *earlier* age— involves different skills, accumulated after years of professional experience.

It is important to emphasize that when I began the regression project, I was not aware of the possibility that Leonardo painted another, *earlier* version of the *Mona Lisa*. The Foundation was careful to withhold that information from me, in order to maintain the scholarly integrity of the project. I was only given a high-resolution photograph of the Louvre *Mona Lisa*, and asked to see what the sitter might have looked like some 11 or 12 years earlier.

I proceeded to convert the image of the Louvre *Mona Lisa* into a digital photograph, and technically manipulated it to produce what in my opinion was an image of what the model would have looked at least a decade younger. This phase of the experiment was concluded when I sent the Foundation the regressed image in digital photographic form.

Immediately thereafter, Phase 2 began. This is when the Foundation disclosed the existence of an Earlier *Mona Lisa*, and sent me high-resolution scans along with some historical data. It was at that point that I was able to compare, for the first time, the image of the regressed version of the Louvre portrait with the

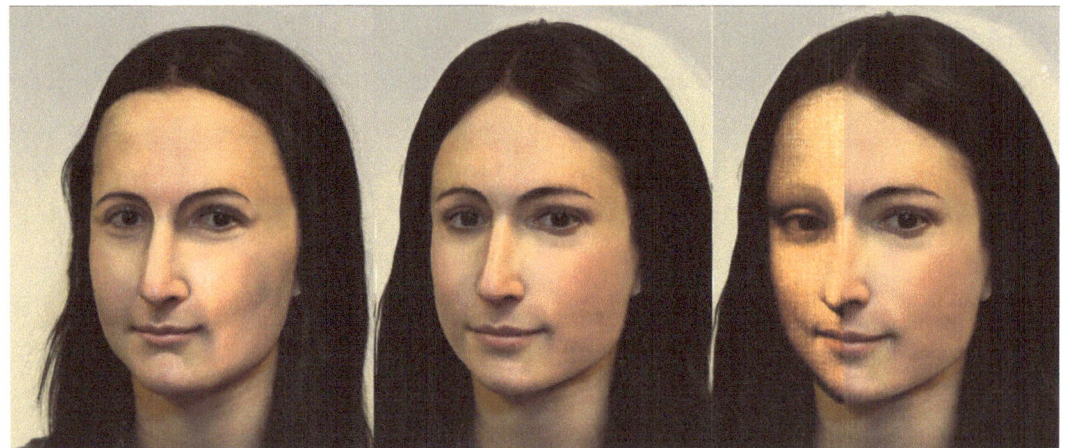

Fig. 3. The Louvre *Mona Lisa* regressed by about 6 (left) and 12 years (center) during Phase 1. The 12-year regression is then compared with the Earlier *Mona Lisa* in a split image (right) during Phase 2.

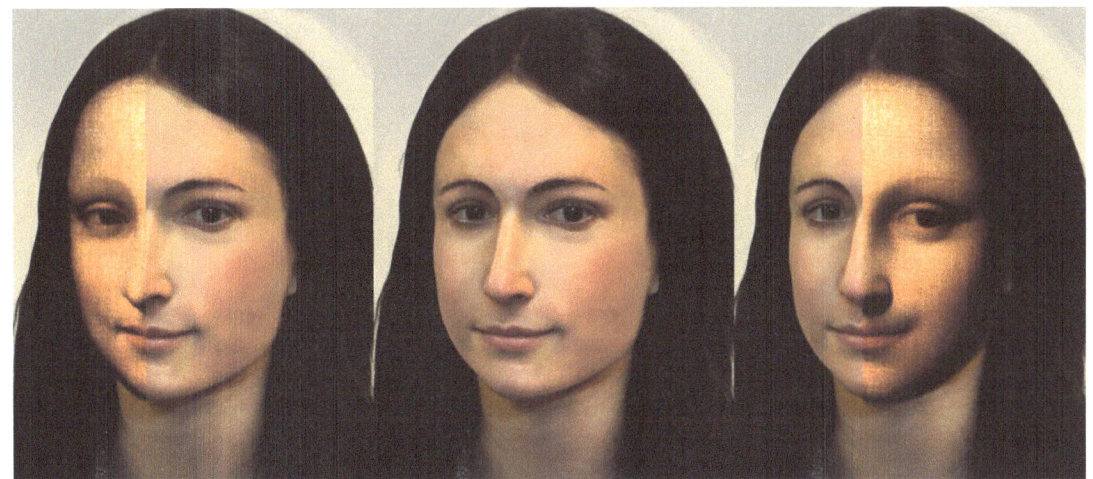

Fig. 4. The 12-year regressed image of the Louvre *Mona Lisa* (center) compared with the Earlier *Mona Lisa* (left and right). The facial resemblance is striking.

Earlier *Mona Lisa*, and analyze them together. The results are quite stunning. They lend further credence to the identification of Lisa del Giocondo as the model in both paintings, even if the Louvre version is the result of progressive aging.

This evidence also confirms the hypothesis that Leonardo would have used material from the Earlier *Mona Lisa* as a model for the Louvre painting. It also suggests that the painting must have been executed between 1513 and 1516, during Leonardo's residence in Rome. This is further supported by the fact that the glazing technique of the Louvre painting was only developed after 1508, and the fact that the Prado *Mona Lisa* was executed at the same time.

About the Author

Joe Mullins is one of the world's foremost Forensic Imaging Specialists, and is based in Washington D.C. Mr. Mullins has a degree in Fine Art from the Savannah College of Art & Design, and a degree in Fine Art and Graphic Design from James Madison University. He has received extensive training in this specialization, including in Advanced Facial Reconstruction at the University of Oklahoma, in Digital Facial Reconstruction at the University of Dundee, Scotland, and in Forensic Facial Imaging at the headquarters of the Federal Bureau of Investigations, Quantico, VA. Mr. Mullins currently does consulting work for the F.B.I. and other law enforcement agencies; and he teaches Facial Reconstruction at the New York Academy of Art; at George Mason University, Fairfax, VA, and at the Art League., Alexandria, VA. He is the author of the article on 'Age Progression and Regression', in the newly published book 'Craniofacial Identification'.

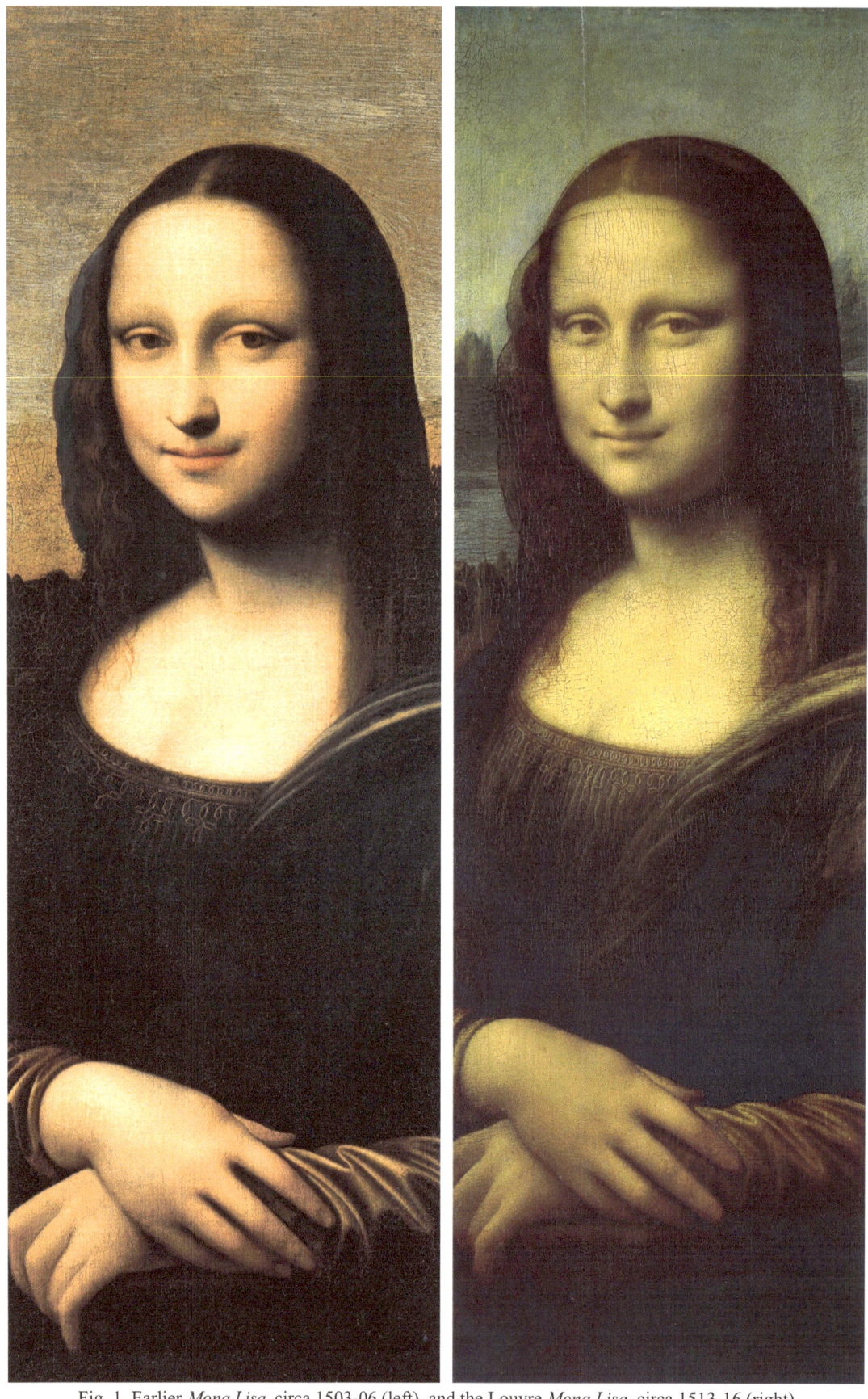

Fig. 1. Earlier *Mona Lisa*, circa 1503-06 (left), and the Louvre *Mona Lisa*, circa 1513-16 (right)

TIME TRAVEL, PATTERN RECOGNITION & THE SCIENTIFIC METHOD; LEONARDO'S EARLIER & LATER MONA LISA

Jason Halter
Art Historian, Researcher and Lecturer
University of Michigan

"O Time! Consumer of all things; O envious age! Thou dost destroy all things and devour all things with the relentless teeth of years, little by little in a slow death. Helen, when she looked in her mirror, seeing the withered wrinkles made in her face by old age, wept and wondered why she had twice been carried away." *Leonardo da Vinci.*

Two paintings were executed by Leonardo da Vinci portraying a Florentine woman, identified by the artist and chronicler Giorgio Vasari, in his *Lives of the Most Excellent Painters, Sculptors, and Architects*, as Lisa Gherardini, wife of the silk merchant Francesco del Giocondo, friend of Leonardo's father Ser Piero da Vinci. The first of these paintings, entitled here the Earlier *Mona Lisa*, was executed on canvas with paint pigments of the period and linseed oil binder, and was being worked on in 1503, according to several records at the time. Its background was never completed, nor was it delivered, in my opinion, to its presumed client, but instead traveled with Leonardo and his studio until close to the end of his life.

The second painting, begun in 1513 for the artist's then-patron, Giuliano de' Medici, is slightly smaller in overall size, painted on a prepared wood panel, and was executed using the medium that the artist preferred, oil on poplar panel. While the overall composition of the painting differed intentionally, the most striking difference in each painting is the age of its subject, Mona Lisa, as she came to be called. In fact, Leonardo was so adept at recognizing, observing and recording the usually imperceptible subtleties of nature and aging life, the gradual transformation of appearance in the complex human structure over time, that it is suggested here that he took the opportunity, deliberately with the commission for Guiliano de' Medici, to paint the Louvre *Mona Lisa*, using the young sitter, Lisa Gherardini, with her ideal beauty and inimitable nature as his starting point, or inspiration. As a result, he thereby demonstrated with these two painted images, executed over a ten-year time lapse, how time may be rendered with the representation of ideal beauty, this example of beautiful mortality.

Comparing the painting of the Louvre *Mona Lisa*, and by referencing the image of the live painting of Lisa Gherardini in the Earlier *Mona Lisa*, Leonardo was the first scientist/artist in the history of painting to demonstrate with this dual portrait opportunity how to depict the aging of an individual over 10 years. As Professor Jean-Pierre Isbouts adds, in reference to another work by Leonardo, a work entitled *La Belle Ferronière*, "The almost photographic realism of the portrait", which we also see in the Earlier *Mona Lisa*, is at once captivating, but also alarming in its clarity

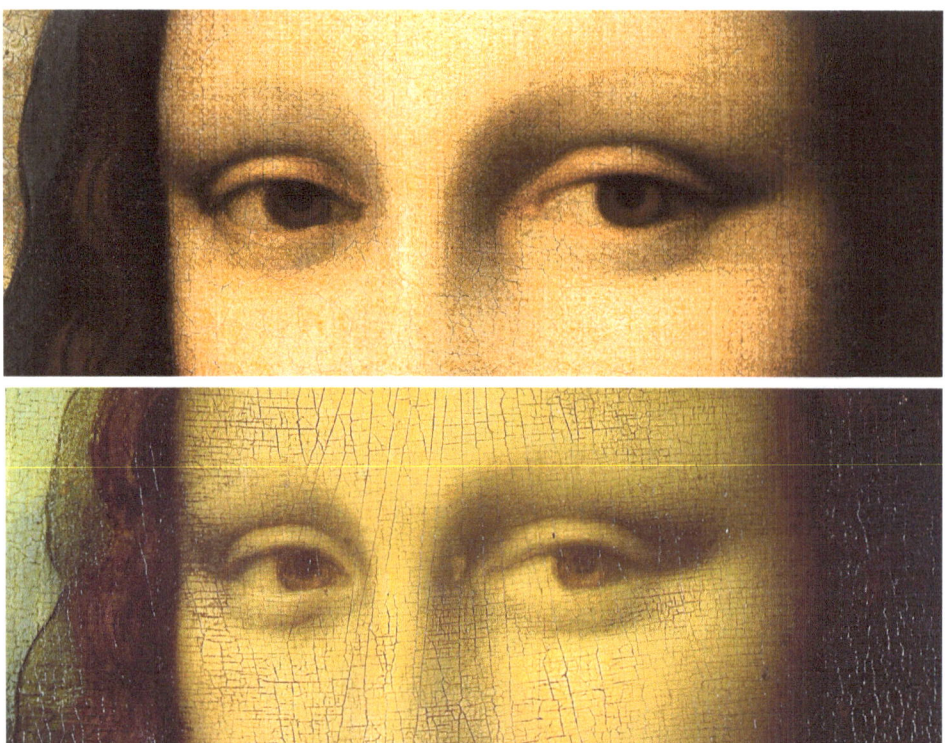

Fig. 2. Details of the eyes in the Earlier *Mona Lisa* and the Louvre *Mona Lisa.*

and pure presence.[1]

The sense that she is real, that the painting has captured a snapshot moment, stays with one long after having seen her in person. It is this snapshot accuracy with which Leonardo is able to measure his Louvre *Mona Lisa* against and alongside the Earlier painting. The experiment, rendered with different pigments, support, and with his expert ability to separate the portraits by the same amount of time, visibly and perceptibly, was in actuality the period between their first appearing on a painted surface.

In the visage of both portraits of a once unknown Florentine woman, there appears a palpable similitude, in a myriad of features, from her all-knowing smile to her eyes that incredibly follow you when you gaze at her. It's as though she gains more from the stare than the viewer, as if she is seeing deeper than the depth perceived in her own beautiful brown eyes.

These eyes with their marble-like translucent brown glow are magnificent, and no matter where you stand, she looks at you in the same way, as if to have a dialogue with you. This magical effect, like the Louvre *Mona Lisa,* can only be by Leonardo.[2] This was my immediate experience as I approached the painting for the first time. Upon reflection of this incredible dynamic, I experienced the Earlier *Mona Lisa* in the same intimate space, with a visual effect that is both real and remarkably perceptible.

Just as Leonardo once said that the eyes are the 'windows of the soul', so too do Lisa's eyes in both the Earlier and Louvre versions show an indescribable depth and beauty in their gaze, while peering as if by magic more deeply into one's own self. Only an artist of this enormous talent, indeed only a scientist with such acute abilities of observation and execution as Leonardo could conceivably undertake to create these two portraits—using the same patterns, geometries and exacting natures, while building into them advances in optics, nuances and the temporal confluence to render in them, this exquisite subtle expression of the passage of time.

There is little doubt that Leonardo da Vinci

intended to codify his innumerable writings from his notebooks to create a full *Treatise on Painting*. According to his friend and contemporary, the great mathematician Luca Pacioli, sections of this *Treatise* were completed by 1498, while Leonardo and his atelier were ensconced in the Castello Sforzesco in Milan. Even during this period, when Leonardo was commissioned to paint the *Last Supper*, it seems his passion and attention were devoted to science, engineering, and an incredibly wide range of esoteric studies. These included mathematics, anatomy, and the theretofore unexplored nature of how the human body worked, how it moved, and more amazingly, how it saw, perceived and processed reality. These were areas that had never been fully explained by any science, let alone by an artist, and the blending of Leonardo's scientific approach to study, coupled with his expansive philosophical breadth, was matched in prowess by his extreme artistic ability in painting.

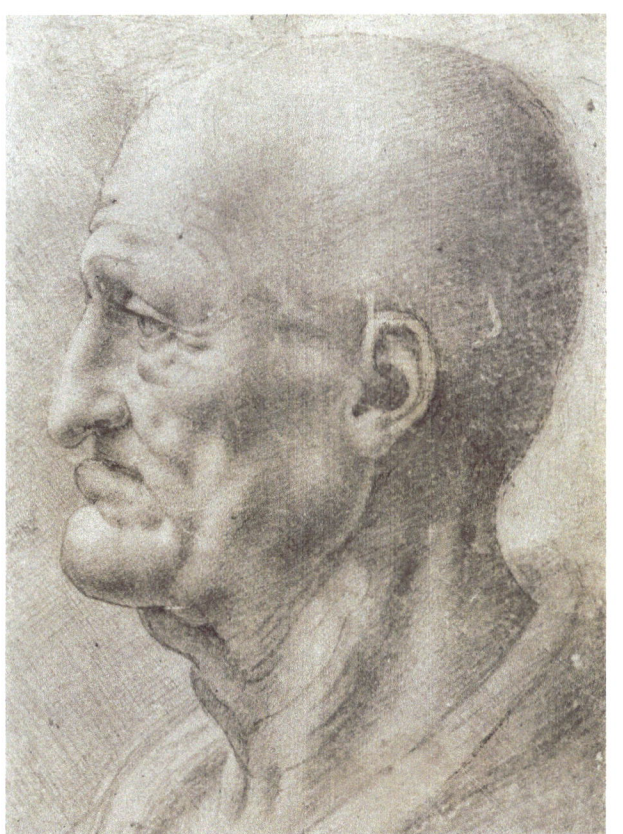

Fig. 3. Leonardo da Vinci, *Drawing of an Old Man in Profile*, ca. 1492-1494.

Would this treatise on painting also have included instruction on how to render time through portraiture? And would he not have constructed this experiment with two paintings that represent the ideal beauty in a mortal human, our Florentine lady, as opposed to a painting of a Madonna, whose age would never change? Would a debate of this nature even have been appropriate due to its subject matter? Leonardo was a true visionary, and with hundreds of years in advance of the invention of photography, it seems apparent that he imagined how it could be conceived in still portraiture, to represent such an elusive subject as time and aging. Given his genius and ability, the age differential of the two *Mona Lisas* are clear evidence of this plausible experiment.

Painting was therefore a critical tool for Leonardo to express what he saw as an act of recording nature, or encapsulating something so elusive as the passage of time. The means by which Leonardo was able to fully express his observations of the human condition, this pure scientific method, *painting*, became the measure by which he would experiment with time in painting the Louvre *Mona Lisa*. In this way, he was employing the Earlier *Mona Lisa* as his methodological control, and by extension, time traveling to distinguish the two Lisas, the younger a portrait of a silk merchant's wife, and the Louvre version as a pictorial future tense.

Of her extraordinary beauty and inherent mystery, the Earlier *Mona Lisa* is in essence the exemplar of beauty and ideal youth. Lisa was neither Mary, the mother of Jesus Christ, nor one of Ludovico Sforza's mistresses. She was also not the powerful Isabella d'Este, Marchioness of Mantova, from the Duchy of Ferrara, who numbered among the many that implored Leonardo to paint them during his life. Lisa was rather, in the words of Frank Zöllner, "Not just the likeness of a real person, but also, the embodiment of an ideal."[3]

With approximately ten years separating the Earlier and Louvre *Mona Lisas*, da Vinci used his superior skills as a painter, combining his thorough scientific understanding of the human body and its subtle muscular nuances, to intentionally prove the thesis of how everything was in flux, indeed of the potential of rendering a discernible time differential. The Louvre *Mona Lisa*, the portrait likely commissioned in 1513 by Guiliano de' Medici, was perhaps the same Lisa Gherardini who, once the painting was executed, appeared discernibly older. With this commission and opportunity, therefore, it would be plausible that Leonardo could not only depict a second painting of the now famous subject of the Florentine *madonna*, but that the opportunity to render her likeness through the lens of time was a demonstrable scientific application of all that Leonardo had witnessed in his many studies of anatomy.

Apparently, Leonardo was deeply interested in anatomical studies in the period from 1506 onwards, and he highlighted his interest in the consequences of aging on the body, in particular with drawings of a man's face at different ages. Regarding the vast number of drawings that Leonardo made from humans and animals, both drawn from life and from his indelible observations and recordings from his experiments dissecting deceased bodies, his acuity and representational ability was deeply profound.

His detailed observations and recordings in drawn and written form aimed to achieve a deeper understanding of the mysterious workings of the human and animal body previously unknown to the world. He took note of motion and movement, the subtle differences that became studies of typology and universality, and was able to discern the most subtle qualities that comprise the human condition, seeing and describing the young and the old, beauty from ugliness, athleticism and musculature in all its forms. As he wrote, "though human ingenuity may make various inventions, it will never devise any inventions more beautiful, nor more simple, nor more to the purpose than Nature does; because

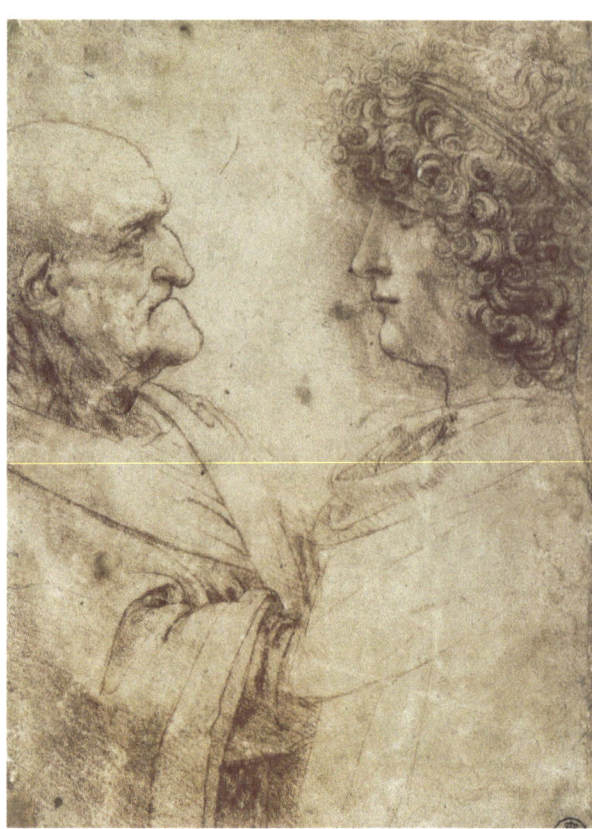

Fig. 4. Leonardo da Vinci, *Profiles of an Old Man and a Youth*, ca. 1495.

in her inventions nothing is wanting, and nothing is superfluous…"[4]

From the portions we have of the still extant notebooks, we see instructions on sketching figures and portraits, the position of the head, of the light and on the face, general suggestions for historical pictures, how to represent the differences of age and sex, and of representing the emotions, among many, many other notated and illustrated observations. The breadth and scope of his study was as tremendous as his ability to blend disciplines. The application of theory to practice was no less impressive as we again perceive these subtle differences in the Earlier and Louvre *Mona Lisa*, that allow us to see a younger live sitter, and in the decade forward, an older, more serene projected lady.

Hence with the Louvre painting, the second of the same subject, and with a decade having passed, Leonardo married the twin pursuits of scientific theory and exacting artistic expression in a culminating example of two paintings, that for the first time in the history of painting pictorially articulate the aging process. Interestingly, the Louvre *Mona Lisa* bore not only the younger Lisa's resemblance, but also something that experts have speculated is a curious blend of the artist's own making.

Vasari suggests that Leonardo's assistants commented they could see some of the Master in the face of the Florentine lady, the subject of the *Mona Lisa* paintings. And if this were so, then with the Louvre *Mona Lisa*, painted ten years later, it makes sense that Leonardo would execute this portrait showing flux, gravity and time. As Leonardo wrote a second time in his notebooks, 'O Time! Consumer of all things, and O envious age! by which all things are devoured…' In addition to the sitting model Lisa, as well perhaps of Leonardo's own self-image, some experts have even suggested that the spirit evoked in the image of the Louvre *Mona Lisa* could even be that of Caterina, Leonardo's mother.

The Louvre *Mona Lisa* was executed during the last decade of Leonardo's life, a period of renewed painting activity, in which a number of documented works were begun while he was still in Rome, and which he brought to his final home in France, at the manor house at Cloux. Likely accompanying Leonardo, in addition to his assistants Salaì and Francesco Melzi and his possessions, paintings sketches and notebooks, was a growing sense of finality, of self-reflection, and the solitude that the advance of one's elderly years naturally brings. If Leonardo had intentionally wanted to depict aging as a visible expression in a portrait, especially one whose subject was the ideal of beauty, then the satisfaction he would also gain from looking at the face of Lisa in his last years, would be many-fold increased if in some way, he was also looking in at his mother. Irrespective of who the ultimate

inspiration was for the Louvre *Mona Lisa*, in addition to the Earlier *Mona Lisa*, it is possible that both these portraits remained with Leonardo until close to the time of his death, in May of 1519; 500 years ago.[5]

Leonardo's extraordinary skills of looking, seeking, observing and then recording, and the instructional way that his notation guided both himself and later readers through the described outcomes, made Leonardo the greatest authority of the known world in his time, as well as the definitive 'pure scientist' of any age. As Sigmund Freud once said of him, "He was like a man who awoke too early in the darkness, while the others were all still asleep." The light he shed on the world of the Renaissance was therefore the perfect marriage of art and science, and the demonstration of age and of passing time with the Earlier and Louvre *Mona Lisas* is one of the most compelling expressions of a pure scientific approach from theory to practice.

In 1417 the Italian scholar and early humanist Poggio Bracciolini, who was also an extraordinary book hunter, made an astounding discovery in the Benedictine library at Fulda, in Germany. It was the book/poem entitled *De rerum natura* ("On the Nature of the Universe"), long considered lost, by the Roman author Lucretius. According to Stephen Greenblatt, "The core of Lucretius' poem is a profound, therapeutic meditation on the fear of death."[6] It was an Epicurean homage to "the stuff of the universe… an infinite number of atoms moving randomly through space, like dust motes in a sunbeam, colliding, hooking together, forming complex structures, breaking apart again, in a ceaseless process of creation and destruction."

As a humanist and ever-inquisitive scientist, surely Leonardo must have known of *On the Nature of the Universe*. Perhaps he even had a vernacular translation in his library. And surely he must also have intuited that all was in flux, that all things moving as atoms in the universe are in motion, hence the fluid nature of our selves and of the transformation during the passing of time's relentless advance. And perhaps he endeavored in his own way, to show in painting, that it could be possible to render time.

Quoting from the translated Latin by Ronald Melville, from Lucretius' *On the Nature of the Universe*, in Book Two;

> Matter, for sure, is not one solid mass
> Close packed together. We see that everything
> Diminishes, and through the long lapse of time
> We note that all things seem to melt away
> As years and age withdraw them from our sight.
> And yet the sum of things stays unimpaired.
> This is because when particles are shed
> From a thing they diminish it as they leave it,
> And then increase the object that they come to.
> They make the one grow old, the other flourish,
> But do not linger there. The sum of things
> Is thus forever renewed, and mortals live
> By mutual interchange by one another...

Indeed, it is a "Time Travel".

About the Author

Jason Roy Halter is an art historian, renaissance scholar and senior design architect. He is a senior lecturer at the Haliburton School of Art & Design, visiting research scholar at the University of Michigan, and has held positions as Adjunct Professor at the University of Toronto, Adjunct Associate Professor at the University of British Columbia, Sessional Lecturer at the University of Waterloo, and Graduate Fellow and Researcher at Syracuse University, Florence, Italy.

References

[1] Jean-Pierre Isbouts and Christopher H. Brown, *Young Leonardo: The Evolution of a Revolutionary Artist.* New York, N.Y: Thomas Dunne Books, 2017; p.86

[2] German researchers recently conducted an experiment widely reported in the media concluding that the "Mona Lisa effect" is incorrect and only a myth. However, they made a fundamental mistake using a screen monitor instead of the original painting. The phenomenon works only with the original painting and never with any replicas, copies, photo or screen images etc. It is the unique Leonardo "magic".

[3] Frank Zöllner, *Leonardo da Vinci: The Complete Paintings.* New York, N.Y.: Taschen, 2003; p. 245.

[4] H. Anna Suh (Ed.), *Leonardo's Notebooks - Writing & Art of the Great Master.* Black Dog & Leventhal, 1886; p.197.

[5] Apparently they ended up with Salai from whom Francis I acquired the Later *Mona Lisa* in 1518 (Ref. Treasury Receipt) and the Earlier *Mona Lisa* noted in the inventory of his estate (Ref. Estate List 1525).

[6] Stephen Greenblatt, *The Swerve: How the World became Modern.* New York, N.Y.: Norton & Company, 2012; p.5.

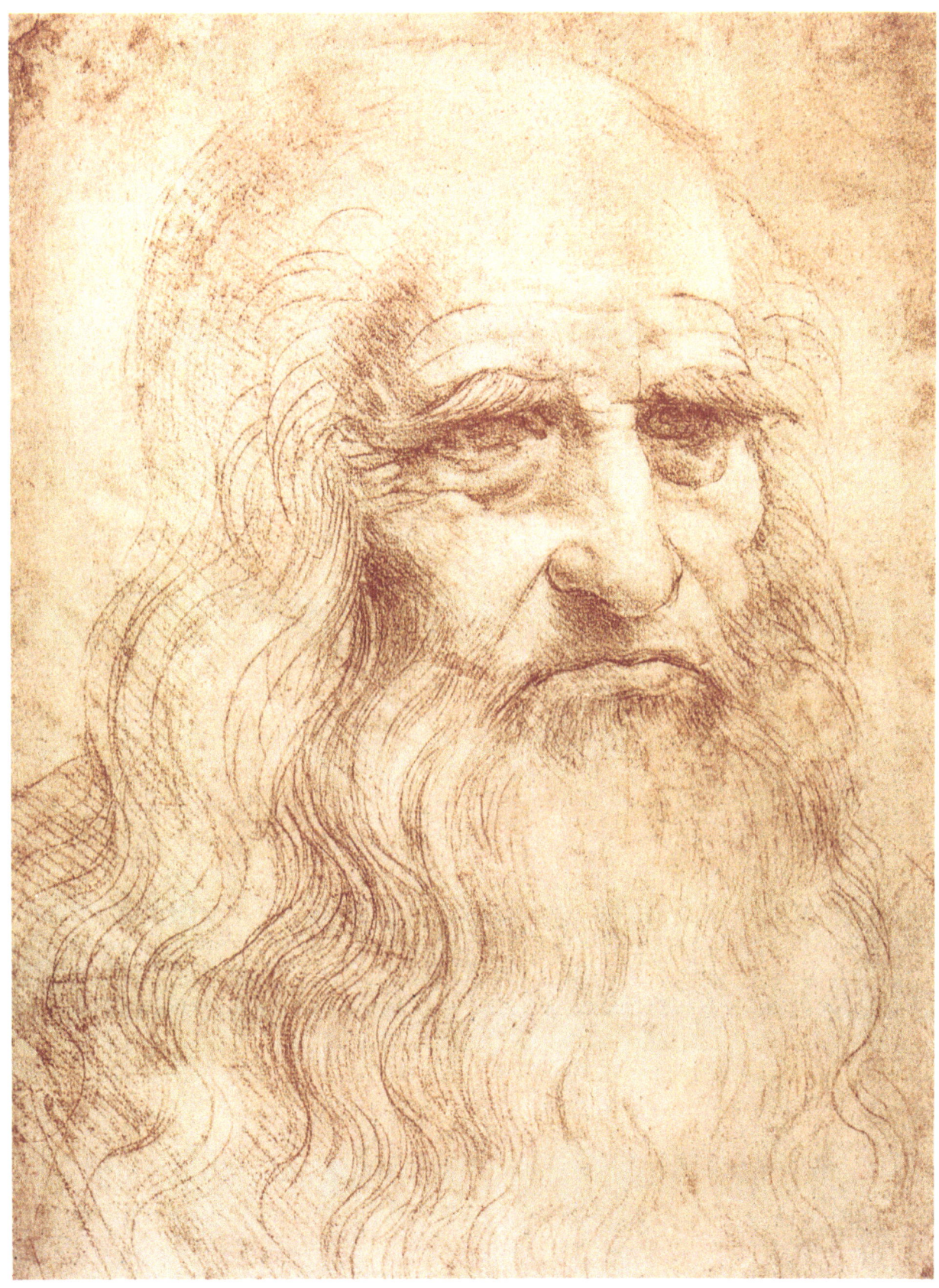

Fig. 5. Leonardo da Vinci, *Self-portrait,* red chalk, ca. 1519.

APPENDIX:
SCIENTIFIC EXAMINATION OF THE EARLIER MONA LISA PAINTING

The following tests and scientific studies of the Earlier *Mona Lisa* painting were undertaken by various independent experts in their respective fields and first published by The Mona Lisa Foundation. These results are reproduced here with permission at the instigation of the Editor as a helpful guide to the reader. The conclusion is contributed by the Editor.

The Lining

It is a common technique with very old paintings on canvas to reinforce the original support by attaching it to a new second canvas or lining. This process not only strengthens the original support, but assists greatly in the overall preservation of the picture. In the case of the Earlier *Mona Lisa* this attachment was executed by means of a glue mixture: a combination of flour paste, gum and Venetian turpentine as plasticizer. In certain lights, this produces a slightly uneven surface – a difficulty later overcome by the subsequent process of hot table-wax lining.

A technical examination of the painting shows that the original canvas was very slightly trimmed when it was attached to the lining, but the raw edges of the original paint have not been touched. The lining is a manufactured fabric of uniform plain tabby weave, with an average count of 14 threads per cm for the warp, and 14 threads per cm for the weft. This is the canvas now visible on the back of the work. It was attached to the stretcher with nails. As there are no holes from prior nails in the lining, one can surmise that the present stretcher was put into use when the painting was lined. The pattern of the canvas appears slightly wavy along some edges, due to irregular degrees of tautness when it was attached to the original stretcher.

The Stretcher

This is the wooden frame upon which the canvas has been made taut. The one seen at the back of the Earlier *Mona Lisa* today is a replacement for the original stretcher. The corners of the lining canvas have been cut back to correspond with the original canvas, the edges glued and then trimmed on the stretcher. This likely would not have been the case if this was the original wooden framing stretcher. The lining is now fixed according to the actual dimensions of the painting, and the wooden wedges inserted at the four corners give the canvas maximum tension.

The Ground

The base ground layer is composed of a combination of red-brown ochre and calcite, with some grains of quartz. This color as a base, allows to bring out a sense of warmth across the whole painting, where the colors are predominantly earth-tones on the hand-woven canvas. Significant in the painting's inherent beauty is the conspicuous lack of any strong polychromatic color: all the elements are in organic harmony, and help to accentuate the gorgeous skin tones. Part of the reason for this is the reddish-brown undercoating.

Dating: Gamma Spectroscopy

A 210Pb measurement was taken by gamma spectroscopy on a lead white sample. This test is valuable in identifying the nature of lead-white, which can indicate if the artwork was executed more than

250 years ago. If the carbon content is completely decayed, the work was executed more than 250 years ago. To detect the presence of 210Pb radioisotope, the Lead White sample 7 was analyzed with a Gamma Spectrometer for 278 hours, with a high resolution and low noise detector GX-HP Ge (ORTEC). A Radioisotope is considered totally decayed when 12 t1/2 are passed. The data shown in the chart below indicate that all 210Pb isotopes present in the sample analyzed were completely decayed. Since 210Pb has a t1/2-20.4 years, materials in the sample examined are certainly more than 250 years old, a dating which may go back to the early 16th Century. The materials with Pb in sample 7 are three: in the priming [$2PbCO_3 – Pb(OH)_2$]; in the minium [Pb_304]; in the upper gray layer and in the white layer, of lead white, cinnabar and carbon black.

	Mass (mg)	Activity (Bq/g)
P 1307-11 (sample 7)	0,001	0,000

Carbon Dating

'Carbon Dating' (or 'Radio Carbon Dating') procedures can be a valuable tool in the art world for the complicated purpose of dating paintings. This is a radiometric dating method using naturally occurring radioisotope carbon -14 (14c) to determine the age of carbonaceous and other organic material, as far back as about 60,000 years. Though carbon dating is not conclusive as a test taken by itself, it can confirm a spread of years before which a painting could not have been executed. In general, carbon dating tests provide a window of years, which can be quite large. Other than the probability percentages of certain years within the window, there is no way to know the likelihood of each year.

A recent example which demonstrates this exercise was undertaken among other tests on the vellum support for *La Bella Principessa*, a work subsequently authenticated by Martin Kemp and others, as being an autograph work by da Vinci. The result of that test gave "a 95.4% probability of a bracketed date of AD 1440 – 1650." Obviously this 210-year spread cannot establish a Leonardo attribution. However, the test does date the vellum support itself, just not the actual artwork on it.

As previously described, the original handmade canvas of the Earlier *Mona Lisa* has been relined on a much later machine-made canvas. The original painting and canvas cover the entire facing surface, but hardly any of the original canvas folds around the sides of the existing stretcher. However, a very small but acceptable sample of the original canvas was sacrificed and extracted for radio carbon dating from a zone located on one edge.

This test yielded a dating of the canvas between 1492 and 1652, with a higher probability in the earlier part of that period. This date range is a standard and is one that is typically expected for dating results of paintings executed in the early 1500s. This test confirms that the canvas used in the Earlier *Mona Lisa* can indeed be from the period during which Leonardo would have painted it, and fits with the chronology documented by Giorgio Vasari and the 1503 date confirmed by Agostino Vespucci. Professor Hans-Arno Synal, of the Swiss Federal Institute of Technology, Zurich on reviewing the results of the test, states: "It is therefore clear that materials, which would have been originating at the turn of the 16th Century, would certainly give a similar radiocarbon age as the final result we have now achieved."

Retouches & Restoration

Minor restoration work to the paint surface of the background took place in the 20th Century, likely between 1926 and 1966. The retouching did not involve any of the important areas or sections such as the figure, hands or lower columns, but fortunately was concentrated in some areas of the sky above the

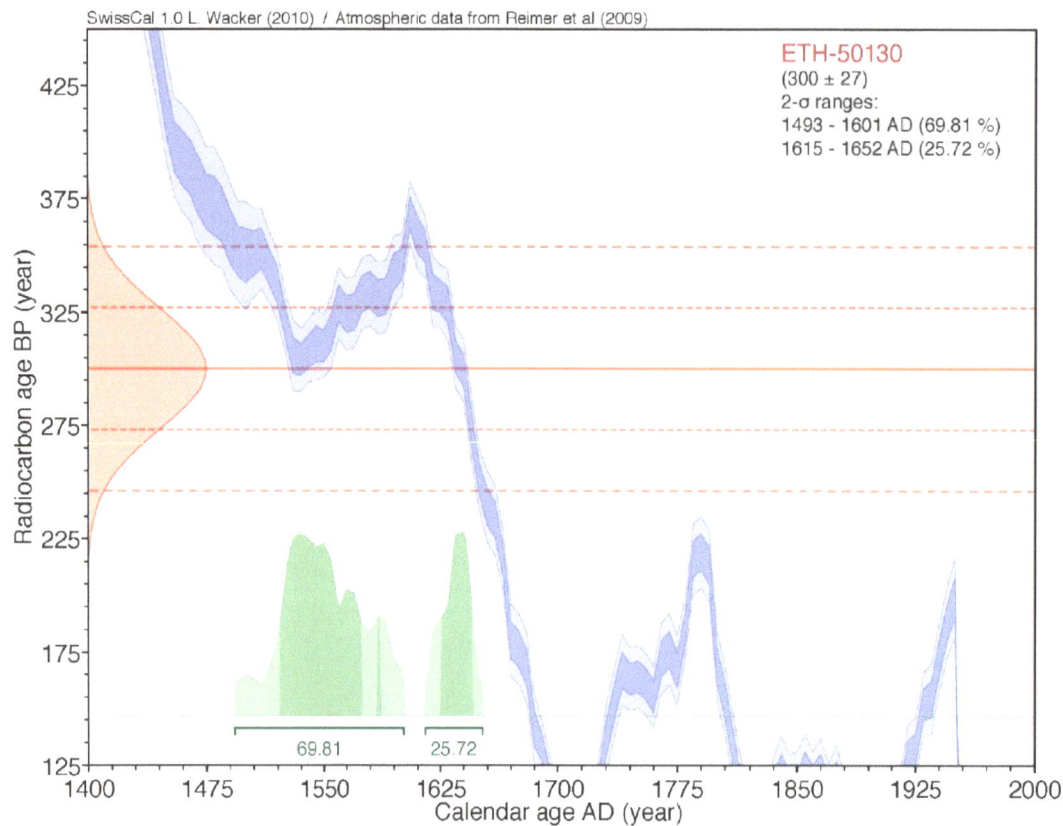

SwissCal 1.0 L. Wacker (2010) / Atmospheric data from Reimer et al (2009)

ETH-50130
(300 ± 27)
2-σ ranges:
1493 - 1601 AD (69.81 %)
1615 - 1652 AD (25.72 %)

Fig. 1. Results of the CD14 test dating the Earlier *Mona Lisa*.

trees, and on the right-hand side above the faded hills. During those procedures, it seems that some definition in the distant landscape was reduced due to possible over-cleaning. The tree to the viewer's left appears as if falsely enlarged due to the missing blue lake beneath it. The painting was always in an unfinished state as described by Vasari. The Oslo *Mona Lisa* from the National Museum, Oslo shows the lake, tree reflection and sky as astutely copied by the artist.

Ultraviolet Light Examination

Prior to the recent introduction of such sophisticated technology as ultra-high-resolution multi-spectral cameras, the Earlier *Mona Lisa* underwent numerous traditional procedures. Ultraviolet photography can be used to observe the colored fluorescence characteristics of the pigments in the paint, and can help to identify them or differentiate between them. Any efficiency in ultraviolet light illumination will depend upon the

phenomenon known as fluorescence that occurs on the surface of the painting. Regarding the background, there are two areas on the left of the painting, and various smaller areas on the right, that fluoresce less than the adjacent paint. This could indicate some slight retouching or restoration to the original paintwork in those areas. In addition, some parts that appear slightly hazy in the fluorescence indicate the possibility that additional varnish may have been applied over the retouched spots. A subsequent scientific analysis of the pigments in 2005 verified that some areas of the painting carried more varnish than others.

X-Ray Examination

X-rays are absorbed by the white that contains lead and other dense pigments. They do not reveal pigments not containing lead, but they do show the sum of dense paint of all the superimposed layers. In an early examination of the painting, no other image was discernible below the surface image. In fact, the X-ray plates showed almost all the surface details, including the figure, the balustrade, and the columns with the bases. Only the background was not present, likely due to the amount of lead white. In a later 2005 examination, the X-radiography revealed the order in which the painting was executed. First the figure and columns, then the sky, and finally, the landscape. In an X-radiography detail of the head, the barely radiopaque materials used to paint the hair were outlined by the more radiopaque materials used in the sky.

2010 Multispectral Examination

Pascal Cotte of Lumiere Technologies in Paris conducted extensive spectral analyses of the painting using cutting edge equipment and methods that have been used to examine the Louvre *Mona Lisa* and other Leonardo paintings, as well as to authenticate recent attributions to the master. A summary of the 2010 results of the analyses conducted on the Earlier *Mona Lisa* are:

• All pigments used were common on Leonardo's palette, and were available at the beginning of the 16th Century in Florence.
• The painting has some clear underdrawings, by the columns and elsewhere, signifying that it is not a direct copy of anything, and clearly an original work.
• No handprint or fingerprint could be identified; a similar result as that for the Louvre *Mona Lisa*.
• No traces were found of the glazing techniques developed only later by Leonardo during his 'Second Milanese Period' (1506-13). The earliest known use of these techniques can be found in his famous cartoon: *The Foetus in the Womb* c.1510. The Louvre version, by contrast, displays them, especially to demonstrate shadows and give the appearance of a three-dimensional effect to the eye.
• The lady's right elbow is resting on the arm of the

chair, below which are very fine details, similar to the Louvre version that cannot be seen by the naked eye and likely only known to the artist. Mr. Cotte confirms that the artist was likely the same for both paintings.
• Apart from obvious differences with the Louvre version, such as the columns, and the ages of the sitters, there are clearly many other small variations in what may appear at first glance to be the same: the embroidery knots, the sleeves, etc.

Mr. Cotte confirmed that the scientific analysis undertaken with the Lumiere Technology multispectral camera fails to show any result that could indicate that the Earlier *Mona Lisa* was not painted by Leonardo. In a 2015 documentary aired on PBS in the United States, Mr. Cotte stated the following concerning the Earlier *Mona Lisa*: "If we analyse the pigments, all the pigments are OK. So the Carbon dating is OK. The varnish is OK. The binder is OK. So technically, everything is OK."

Analysis of the Pigments

Two series of analytical probes were effected on the painting primarily in order to identify the complete range of pigments and other media used, as well as to help ascertain some of the techniques he employed in the preparation of the canvas support, and the application of the base, ground and paint layers. The results not only identified the pigments and other material, but also pointed to the sequence in which sections of the work were undertaken. Dr. Hermann Kuhn's nine probes were taken in June 1977, and it was in June 2005, exactly 28 years later, when Dr. Maurizio Seracini dated the results of his further 10 probes. Except for his first probe, which goes to the lowest base layer, Dr. Kuhn's report primarily specified the surface pigmentation in each case. Dr. Seracini's probes identified the pigment material in every layer of each probe.

Naturally, there cannot be any direct comparison

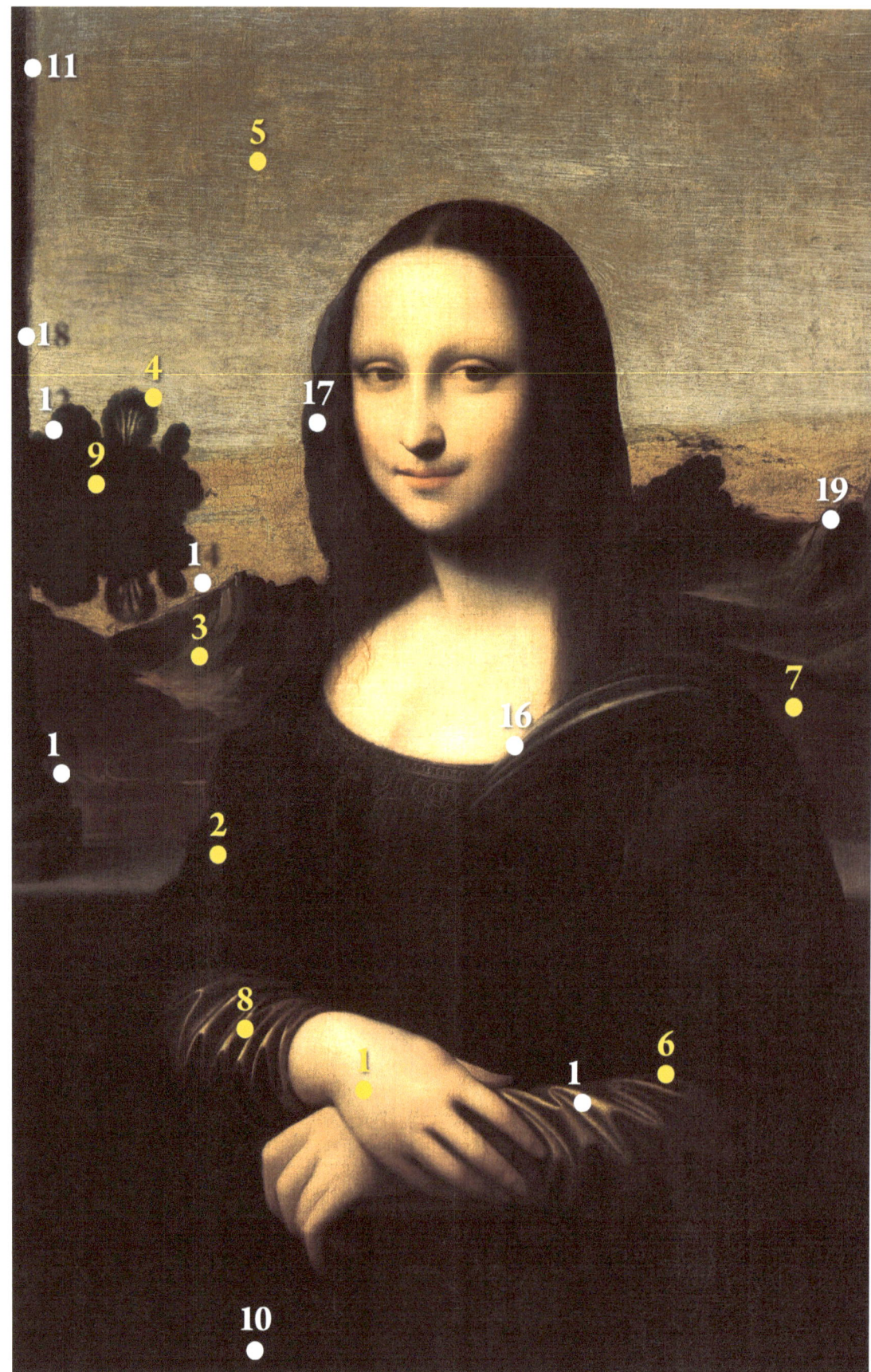

Fig. 2. Key to the probe samples taken from the Earlier *Mona Lisa*.

LEONARDO DA VINCI'S MONA LISA: NEW PERSPECTIVES

between the results, as each probe was taken from a different part of the painting.

Probe Tests by Dr. Hermann Kuhn

Probe #1: Flesh pigment. The lowest layer is a red to red-brown base that is composed of red-brown ochre and calcite, and includes a few bigger grains of quartz. There is a subsequent grey layer of base consisting of calcite, lead white and bone black. This is covered by the flesh layers which contain lead white, calcite, a few grains of black vermilion, zinnober* (HgS – Mercury sulphide), vermilion, and yellow ochre. [*Editor's note: this is what Leonardo refers to as dry cinnabar]

Probe #2: Dress, brown pigment. On analysis it was found to contain brown iron-oxide of manganese umber, vegetable black, lead white, calcite, and red lacquer.

Probe #3: Mountain, yellow highlight pigment. Two tests were made on the yellowish to green-brown layer that contained the total of pigments present. It contained vegetable black (powder of charcoal), smalt, blue copper pigment apparently made artificially with copper blue - called veriter, azurite in little traces, transparent yellow, brown and red grains of iron oxide (burnt green, earth or earth sienna), yellow lacquer, calcite, lead white, and a large quantity of uncolored glaze.

Probe #4: Tree, green pigment. Large grains of blue pigment in a yellowish brown binding. The analysis shows azurite in large quantities, smalt, and grains of lead white. The impression of green is given by an unidentified yellow (vegetable pigment). On reanalysis of this unidentifiable yellow it was found that there are not any yellow pigments except the presence of impurities of iron oxide.

Probe #5: Sky, pigment. Two paint samples were taken from different areas of the sky. Under magnification it is revealed that the two samples contained calcite, lead white, and a large amount of smalt, which has a fine grain and a very pale color. A large part of the pigment looks colorless.

Probe #6: Dress, light brown pigment. The following components were found: brown iron oxide of manganese-umber, yellow ochre, lead white, little traces of red lacquer, and bone black.

Probe #7: Left background, red-brown pigment. It contains a mixture of yellow and red iron oxide (ochre and earth sienna), vegetable black, smalt, calcite, lead white, green earth, and artificial copper blue called veriter.

Probe #8: Dress fold, yellow highlight pigment. Contained lead white, calcite, yellow lacquer, yellow iron oxide (ochre), and vegetable black.

Probe #9: Left tree, dark green pigment. Over a grey-blue layer is a layer containing large grains of smalt and azurite, plus little traces of lead white, and calcite. The very dark tone is caused by an overlaying brown layer – (vegetable pigment), originally yellow-aged and/or yellowed varnish.

Probe tests by Dr. Maurizio Seracini

Probe #10: Dress Layer 1: Red ground of earth pigments, natural ochres, lead white, minium, bone black, carbon black, smalt. Layer 2: Grey layer priming of lead white, calcite, carbon black, and granules of red ochres. Layer 3: Layer of carbon black, lead white, and umber. Layer 4: Dark grey layer of carbon black, umber, and lead white. Layer 5: Thin grey layer of calcite, and carbon black. Layer 6: Dark layer of calcite in a rich binding medium. Layer 7:

Carbon black, calcite and lead white. Layer 8: Varnish Layer 9: Glaze of carbon black. Layer 10: Layer of varnish. Layer 11: Layer of low-fluorescent varnish. Probe #11: Edge of pillar Layer 1: Red ground matrix of earth pigments, incl. lead white, minium, particles of carbon black, and bone black. Layer 2: Grey priming layer of lead white, calcite, and carbon black. Layer 3: Lead white and partly-decoloured smalt.

Probe #12: Tree Layer 1: Red ground of earth pigments, lead white, minium, particles of smalt. Layer 2: Grey priming coat of lead white, calcite, carbon black, granules of red ochre. Layer 3: Lead white and decoloured smalt-blue. Layer 4: Azurite and lead white. Layer 5: Varnish.

Probe #13: Mountain Layer 1: Red ground of earth pigments, lead white, minium, particles of carbon black, and bone black. Layer 2: Grey priming coat of lead white, calcite, and carbon black. Layer 3: Thin brown layer of lead white, calcite, and carbon black. Layer 4: Green-blue pigments, plus brown-green layer of lead white, earth pigments, and umber. Layer 5: Double layer of varnish.

Probe #14: Edge of tree Layer 1: Red ground of earth pigments, lead white, minium, particles of carbon black, and bone black. Layer 2: Grey priming coat of lead white, calcite, and carbon black. Layer 3: Brown layer consisting of lead white, carbon black, calcite, earth pigments, and traces of smalt. Layer 4: As 'layer 3' above, plus azurite. Layer 5: Decolored smalt, lead white, and earth pigments. Layer 6: Green/yellow layer of earth pigments, yellow lake, plus green/blue pigment. Layers 7-9: Three layers of varnish.

Probe #15: Sleeve Layer 1: Red ground of earth pigments, lead white, minium, particles of carbon black, and bone black. Layer 2: Grey priming coat of lead white, calcite and carbon black. Layer 3: Light

brown layer consisting of lead white, calcite, earth pigments, particles of umber, and yellow lake. Layer 4: Beige layer of lead white, calcite and earth pigments. Layer 5+: Several layers of varnish.

Probe #16: Chest Layer 1: Red ground of earth pigments, lead white, minium, particles of carbon black, and bone black. Layer 2: Grey priming coat of lead white, calcite and carbon black. Layers 3 and 4: Two layers of white, consisting of lead white, vermillion, and a few granules of carbon black. Layer 5+: Several layers of varnish.

Probe #17: Hair Layer 1: Red ground of earth pigments, lead white, minium, particles of carbon black, and bone black. Layer 2: Grey priming coat of lead white, calcite and carbon black. Layers 3 and 4: Two layers light brown, of lead white, earth pigments, umber, and bone black. Layer 5: Particles of decolored red lake. Layer 6: Several layers of varnish.

Probe #18: Pillar Layer 1: Red ground of earth pigments, lead white, minium, particles of carbon black, and bone black. Layer 2: Grey priming coat of lead white, calcite and carbon black. Layer 3: Brown layer of lead white, calcite and earth pigments. Layer 4: Black layer of lead white, carbon black, and earth pigments. Layer 5: Paint layer – color unspecified. Layer 6: Brown layer of calcite. Layer 7: Black layer of carbon black, small quantities of lead white, calcite and earth pigments. Layer 8: Thin layer of brown organic material. Layer 9 +: Several layers of varnish.

Probe #19: Landscape Layer 1: Red ground of earth pigments, lead white, minium, particles of carbon black, and bone black. Layer 2: Grey priming coat of lead white, calcite and carbon black. Layer 3: Brown layer of decolored smalt, lead white, and earth pigments. Layer 4: Green layer of lead white, earth pigments, green/blue pigment, and granules of smalt.

Layer 5: Organic brown glaze. Layer 6: Thin layer of lead white, and earth pigments. Layer 7 +: Several layers of varnish.

The results of the foregoing analyses indicate that all the pigments that were found were readily available at the beginning of the 16th century.

A recent BBC documentary suggested that none of the probes had extracted a sample from the face, and that perhaps the face had been repainted in the 20th Century. However, both Kuhn and Seracini decided that no face probe should be made because it could mark the painting's most important feature, and because the flesh pigments were obviously similar all through. Cotte also confirmed that all pigments were correct, including the face. Therefore, the BBC suggestion has no base in fact, since all pigments are carbon-decayed (indicating an age of more than 250 years). Furthermore, an expert report on the condition clearly states that the face section of the painting shows absolutely no signs of either repainting or retouching.

Conclusion: The *Mona Lisa* Palette

A comparison of the pigments used in the two original *Mona Lisas* brings interesting results. Lead white, for example is an important constituent of both. Regarding the Earlier *Mona Lisa*, both Dr. Kuhn and Dr. Seracini found lead white in every single probe, including the grey second ground coat. The Louvre report on their *Mona Lisa* states simply that lead is present everywhere in the form of lead white. Other pigments that are common to both paintings include azurite, blue copper, vermilion, umber and even smalt. In fact, both pictures feature significant amounts of earth pigments such as the various ranges of siennas, ochres and umbers; natural enough for a time before the development of artificial pigments. There are variations as to how black pigments are referred.

Burnt umber, an earth-tone used in both paintings,

has wonderful mineral properties: "One may therefore suppose that natural burnt-umber, or an earth pigment rich in manganese oxide, plays an important part in achieving Leonardo's famous sfumato effect. The relative absence of cracks in the shadows of the face can be related to the drying properties of this pigment, which no doubt originated from Umbria, a region that is also famous for the quality of its earthenware." Traces of smalt were found exclusively in the background landscape of the Earlier *Mona Lisa* and in other parts of the Louvre version. Its popularity on artist's palettes increased in the second half of the 16th century; however according to senior scientists at the Centre de Recherche et de Restauration des Musées de France, the use of smalt in easel painting was well known, though to a more limited extent, in the second half of the 15th Century. Pascal Cotte of Lumiere Technology in Paris, who has examined the Louvre's *Mona Lisa* as well as *Lady with the Ermine* and the Earlier *Mona Lisa* concurs with the Louvre that smalt was well in use at the beginning of the 16th Century.

A problem that many artists of that time had to face was the lack of ready availability of the pigments they required. Grinding minerals and earth-pigments with the correct media, to the right consistency and shade was a laborious and therefore expensive process. Many of these pigments "being imports as far as color-merchants in the principal art centers of Italy, the Netherlands, France and England were concerned, were expensive and not always so readily available. Consequently, we can imagine that artists were eager to learn of any man-made pigments that could serve as alternatives to the traditional palette."

In Leonardo's *Treatise*, there is a reference to "a diluted veil of dry cinnabar." This is present on the Earlier *Mona Lisa*, noted as 'zinnober', in a probe of one of the flesh tones, but is not mentioned for the Louvre *Mona Lisa*. That painting shows a small amount of vermilion in some of the flesh tints, as does the Earlier *Mona Lisa*. Leonardo cited red lac (or lake) as the correct pigment for shadows and light areas. Again, both paintings show traces: on the face of the younger woman, and on the hands of the Louvre *Mona Lisa*.

In other chapters of his *Treatise*, Leonardo frequently refers to the use of lake, or red lake, particularly for flesh tones: *L'incarnatione fara biacca, lacca, e giallolino: l'ombra fara nero, e majorica, e un poco di lacca, o vuoi lapis duro* ("The flesh colour may be made with white, lake, and Naples yellow. The shades with black umber, and a little lake; you may, if you please, use black chalk").

In summary, the results of these tests, scientific studies, and pigment analyses are consistent with a work of Leonardo Da Vinci at the beginning of the 16th century in Florence, Italy.

References

[1] The Mona Lisa Foundation, "Leonardo Da Vinci's Earlier Mona Lisa", 5th Edition 2018 (pp.84-96).

[2] In December 2015, it was reported that Cotte had found a hidden portrait underneath the surface of the painting using reflective light technology. The portrait was claimed to be an underlying image of a model looking off to the side. Having been given access to the painting by Louvre in 2004, Cotte spent ten years using layer amplification methods to study the painting. According to Cotte, the underlying image may be Leonardo's original Mona Lisa. However, Cotte himself admits this is only a hypothesis, and many of experts oppose this idea. Furthermore the image he proposes does not conform to either Vasari's description, Vespucci's account nor Raphael's depiction of Lisa.

[3] *Secrets of the Mona Lisa*, BBC documentary, hosted by Andrew Graham-Dixon; December 9, 2015.

[4] Mohen, Jean-Pierre, et al., *Mona Lisa: Inside the Painting*. Paris: the Louvre Museum, 2006.

[5] Ibid.

[6] Fleming, Stuart, "An Evaluation of Physico-chemical Approaches to Authentication," in *Authenticity in the Visual Arts*; 1975.

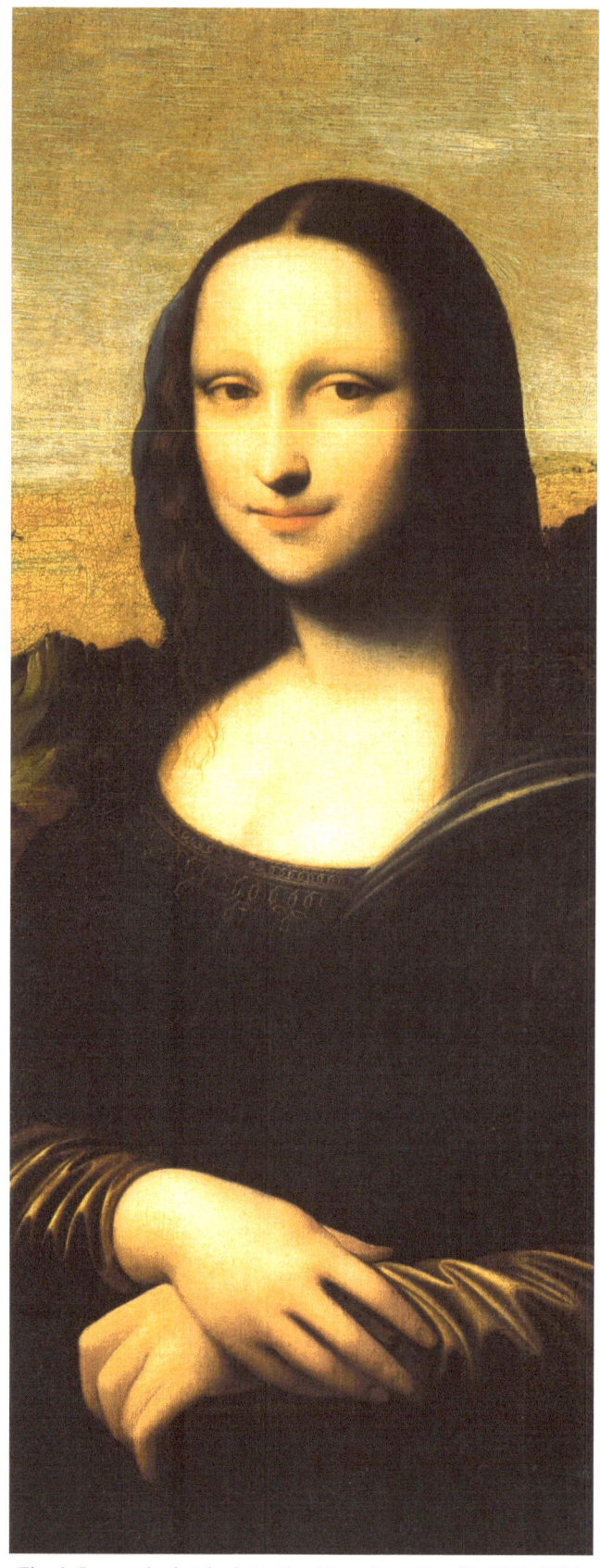

Fig. 3. Leonardo da Vinci, Earlier *Mona Lisa* (detail), 1502-1506.

SELECT BIBLIOGRAPHY

LEONARDO DA VINCI, GENERAL BIOGRAPHIES AND ANTHOLOGIES

Arasse, Daniel, *Léonard de Vinci, Le rythme du monde*. Paris: Hazan, 1997.

Baskins, Wade, *The Wisdom of Leonardo da Vinci*. New York: Barnes & Noble, 2004.

Bramly, Serge, *Leonardo: The Artist and the Man*. New York: Penguin, 1994.

Brion, Marcel, *Léonard de Vinci, génie et destinée*. Paris, Michel, 1952.

Clayton, Martin, *Leonardo da Vinci: A Singular Vision*. Exhibition catalog, Queen's Gallery, Buckingham Palace. New York: Abbeville Press, 1996.

Delieuvin, Vincent, *Saint Anne: Leonardo's Ultimate Masterpiece*. Exhibition catalog. Paris: Musée du Louvre; 2012.

Farago, Claire J. (Ed), *Leonardo da Vinci, Selected Scholarship: Leonardo's Projects, c. 1500-1519*. Taylor & Francis, 1999.

Forcellino, Antonio, *Leonardo: A Restless Genius*. Cambridge, Polity Press, 2018.

Isaacson, Walter, *Leonardo da Vinci*. New York: Simon & Schuster, 2017.

Isbouts, Jean-Pierre and Brown, Christopher H., *Young Leonardo: The Evolution of a Revolutionary Artist, 1472-1499*. New York: Thomas Dunne Books, 2017.

Isbouts, Jean-Pierre and Brown, Christopher H., *The Da Vinci Legacy*. New York: Apollo Publishers, 2019.

Kemp, Martin, *Leonardo da Vinci: The Marvelous Works of Nature and Man*. Oxford: Oxford University Press, 2006.

Kemp, Martin, Kemp, *La Bella Principessa: The Story of the New Masterpiece by Leonardo da Vinci*. London: Hodder & Stoughton, 2010.

Marani, Pietri C., *Leonardo da Vinci: The Complete Paintings*. New York: Harry N. Abrams, 2000.

Nicholl, Charles, *Leonardo da Vinci: Flights of the Mind*. New York: Penguin, 2004.

Pedretti, Carlo. *Leonardo, a Study in Chronology and Style*. Los Angeles: University of California Press, 1982.

Syson, Luke et al., *Leonardo da Vinci: Painter at the Court of Milan*. Exhibition catalog. London: National Gallery Company, 2011.

Vezzosi, Alessandro. *Discoveries: Leonardo da Vinci*. New York, NY: Harry N. Abrams, 1997.

LEONARDO'S NOTEBOOKS, DRAWINGS AND TREATISES

Farago, Claire J. (Ed), *Leonardo's Writings and Theory of Art*. New York: Garland Publishing, 1999.

Kemp, Martin (Ed.), *Leonardo on Painting*. New Haven: Yale University Press, 1989.

MacCurdy, Edward, *The Notebooks of Leonardo da Vinci*. New York: George Braziller, 1954.

O'Malley, Charles D., *Leonardo on the Human Body*. New York: Dover, 1983.

Richer, Paul (Ed.), *The Notebooks of Leonardo da Vinci* (Vols. I and II). New York: Dover, 1970.

Suh, Anna (Ed.), *Leonardo's Notebooks*. New York, NY: Black Dog & Leventhal Publishers, 2005.

Taglialagamba, Sara and Pedretti, Carlo, *Leonardo & Anatomy*. Poggio a Caiano: CB Publishers, 2010.

Zöllner, Frank, and Johannes Nathan. *Leonardo da Vinci: Sketches and Drawings*. Taschen, 2006.

Nicholl, Charles, *Leonardo da Vinci: Flights of the Mind*. New York: Penguin, 2004.

Pedretti, Carlo. *Leonardo, a Study in Chronology and Style*. Los Angeles: University of California Press, 1982.

Syson, Luke et al., *Leonardo da Vinci: Painter at*

the Court of Milan. Exhibition catalog. London: National Gallery Company, 2011.

Vezzosi, Alessandro. *Discoveries: Leonardo da Vinci.* New York, NY: Harry N. Abrams, 1997.

LEONARDO'S NOTEBOOKS, DRAWINGS AND TREATISES

Farago, Claire J. (Ed) *Leonardo's Writings and Theory of Art.* New York: Garland Publishing, 1999.

Kemp, Martin (Ed.), *Leonardo on Painting.* New Haven: Yale University Press, 1989.

MacCurdy, Edward, *The Notebooks of Leonardo da Vinci.* New York: George Braziller, 1954.

O'Malley, Charles D., *Leonardo on the Human Body.* New York: Dover, 1983.

Richer, Paul (Ed.), *The Notebooks of Leonardo da Vinci* (Vols. I and II). New York: Dover, 1970.

Suh, Anna (Ed.), *Leonardo's Notebooks.* New York, NY: Black Dog & Leventhal Publishers, 2005.

Taglialagamba, Sara and Pedretti, Carlo, *Leonardo & Anatomy.* Poggio a Caiano: CB Publishers, 2010.

Zöllner, Frank, and Johannes Nathan. *Leonardo da Vinci: Sketches and Drawings.* Taschen, 2006.

THE MONA LISA

Bülent Atalay, *Math and the Mona Lisa: The Art and Science of Leonardo da Vinci.* New York: Harper/ Smithsonian Books, 2006.

Carminati, Marco, *Leonardo/Mona Lisa.* Milano: 24 ORE Cultura, 2012.

Chastel, André, *L'illustre incomprise: Mona Lisa.* Paris: Éditions Gallimard, 1988.

Eyre, John R., *The Two Mona Lisa: which was Giocondo's picture?* London: J.M. Ouseley & Son, 1922.

Isbouts, Jean-Pierre and Brown, Christopher H., *The Mona Lisa Myth.* Los Angeles: Pantheon, 2013.

Kemp, Martin and Pallanti, Giuseppe, *Mona Lisa: The People and the Painting.* Oxford: Oxford University Press, 2017.

Mona Lisa Foundation, The, *Leonardo da Vinci's Earlier Mona Lisa.* 5th Edition, Zurich, 2018.

Mariotti, Josephine R., *Monna Lisa: La 'Gioconda' del Magnifico Giuliano.* Firenze: Ediziono Polistampa, 2009.

McMullen, Roy, *Mona Lisa: The Picture and the Myth.* Boston: Houghton Mifflin Co., 1976.

Mohen, Jean-Pierre et al., *Mona Lisa: Inside the Painting.* New York: Harry N. Abrams, 2006.

Pallanti, Giuseppe, *Mona Lisa Revealed: The True Identity of Leonardo's Model.* New York: Rizzoli, 2006.

Probst, Veit, *Zur Entstehungsgeschichte der Mona Lisa.* Heidelberg: Verlag Regionalkultur, 2008.

Sassoon, Donald, *Becoming Mona Lisa: The Making of a Global Icon.* New York: Harcourt, 2001.

About the Editor

Jean-Pierre Isbouts (Santa Monica, CA) is an art historian, National Geographic author and filmmaker, specializing in the art of the Renaissance and Near East archaeology. A doctoral professor at Fielding Graduate University in Santa Barbara, CA, he gained worldwide renown with his 2006 book *The Biblical World*, which became an international bestseller and is now in its fourth print. This success led to a series of National Geographic books, including the bestsellers *In the Footsteps of Jesus* (2011) and *The Story of Christianity* (2014).

In July of 2017, St Martin's Press published his book *Young Leonardo*, written with Christopher H. Brown, which shows that a large copy of Leonardo's *Last Supper*, now in a remote convent in Belgium, was actually painted by Leonardo and his workshop for the French King Louis XII. His new publications include *The Da Vinci Legacy* (2019), in which he shows how Leonardo da Vinci evolved from a reclusive 16th century figure to a global celebrity today. The book has inspired a film, *The Search for the Mona Lisa*, narrated by Morgan Freeman and broadcast on PBS stations nationwide in May of 2019. In 2020, National Geographic plans to publish his new book *The Visual History of the World*.

Dr. Isbouts has written and directed a number of television specials on art and history, featuring Leonard Nimoy, Dick van Dyke and Sir David Frost. As a musicologist, he has produced a number of recordings by the Los Angeles Chamber Orchestra, the Amsterdam Baroque Orchestra and other ensembles and soloists.

In 2013, Dr. Isbouts established Fielding University Press as the publishing arm of Fielding Graduate University. Since then, he has edited 18 books on a range of disciplines, including the dissertation research of more than 70 Fielding doctoral graduates as well as over 25 contributing scholars from around the world. Fielding University Press's website is www.fielding.edu/universitypress. Dr. Isbouts' website is www.jpisbouts.org.

About Fielding Graduate University

Fielding Graduate University, headquartered in Santa Barbara, CA, is an accredited, nonprofit leader in blended graduate education. Founded 45 years ago in 1974, the university offers master's and doctoral degrees for professionals and academics around the world. Fielding's faculty members represent a wide spectrum of scholarship and practice in the fields of educational leadership, human and organizational development, and clinical and media psychology. Fielding's faculty serve as mentors and guides for self-directed students who use their skills and professional experience to chart a highly individualized learning path through their programs, and become powerful, socially-responsible leaders in their communities and workplaces. For more information, please visit Fielding at www.fielding.edu.

ILLUSTRATION CREDITS

COVER: Leonardo da Vinci, Earlier *Mona Lisa*/The Mona Lisa Foundation.

CHAPTER 1. Fig. 1. Leonardo da Vinci, *Mona Lisa*/RMN/DCoetzee. Fig 2. The Heidelberg marginalia/ ub.uni-heidelberg.de. Fig 3. Giorgio Vasari, *Le vite de' piu eccellenti pittori*/Magnus Manske. Fig. 4. Leonardo da Vinci and assistant, *Madonna of the Yarnwinder*, Buccleuch version/Web gallery of Art. Fig. 5. Leonardo da Vinci and assistant, *Madonna of the Yarnwinder*, Lansdowne version/Bogdan. Fig. 6. Leonardo da Vinci, *Study for a Nativity*/Pantheon Studios. Fig. 7. Leonardo da Vinci, *Study for Leda and the Swan*/Pantheon Studios. Fig. 8. Giampietrino, *Leda and the Swan*/Web gallery of Art. Fig. 9. Leonardo da Vinci, *Head of a Young Woman*/Pantheon Studios. Fig. 10. Leonardo's residence in Amboise, the *Manoir de Cloux*/Pantheon Studios.

CHAPTER 2. Fig. 1. Unknown artist (Salai or Melzi?), The Prado *Mona Lisa*/Escarlati. Fig. 2. Unknown Artist, *Mona Lisa with Columns*/The Mona Lisa Foundation. Fig. 3. Leonardo da Vinci, The Louvre *Mona Lisa*/RMN/DCoetzee. Fig. 4. Unknown artist (Salai or Melzi?), The Prado *Mona Lisa*/Lcsrns. Fig. 5. Comparison between the Prado *Mona Lisa* and the Louvre *Mona Lisa*/Lcrns and RMN/DCoetzee. Fig. 6. The Reynolds *Mona Lisa*/ The Mona Lisa Foundation. Fig. 7. The Isleworth *Mona Lisa*/ The Mona Lisa Foundation. Fig. 8. Raphael, *Head and shoulders of a woman*/ The Mona Lisa Foundation. Fig. 9. The Oslo *Mona Lisa*/ The Mona Lisa Foundation. Fig. 10. Comparison of the columns/ The Mona Lisa Foundation. Fig. 11. Comparison of the left column in the Isleworth, Oslo Louvre, and Prado *Mona Lisa*/ The Mona Lisa Foundation. Fig. 12. Comparison of the right column in the Isleworth, Oslo, Louvre, and Prado *Mona Lisa*/ The Mona Lisa Foundation. Fig. 13. Comparison of the embroidery on the Isleworth, Louvre, Oslo and Prado *Mona Lisa*/ The Mona Lisa Foundation. Fig. 14. Leonardo da Vinci, *Lady with an Ermine*/ Pantheon Studios.

CHAPTER 3. Fig. 1. Leonardo da Vinci, Earlier *Mona Lisa*/The Mona Lisa Foundation. Fig 2. Domenico Ghirlandaio, *Adoration of the Magi*/Pantheon Studios. Fig. 3. Masaccio, *Portrait of a Young Man*/Pantheon Studios. Fig 4. Leonardo da Vinci, *Portrait of Ginevra de' Benci*/Pantheon Studios. Fig. 5. Leonardo da Vinci, *The Lady with an Ermine*/Pantheon Studios. Fig. 6. Ambrogio de Predis, *Portrait of Bianca Maria Sforza*/Pantheon Studios. Fig. 7. Leonardo da Vinci, *Last Supper*/Quibik. Fig. 8. Leonardo da Vinci, *Portrait of Isabella d'Este*/ RMN / Michèle Bellot. Fig. 9. Leonardo da Vinci, *Burlington Cartoon*/Pantheon Studios. Fig. 10. Leonardo da Vinci, *Map of the Town of Imola*/ Web gallery of Art. Fig. 11. Leonardo da Vinci, *Study of Tuscany with the Arno River*/ Pantheon Studios. Fig. 12. The Via della Stufa/Pantheon Studios. Fig. 13. Leonardo da Vinci, The Earlier *Mona Lisa*/The Mona Lisa Foundation. Fig. 14. Raphael, *Portrait of a Young Woman*/ The Mona Lisa Foundation. Fig. 15. Leonardo da Vinci, *La belle ferronnière*/Pantheon Studios. Fig. 16. Young vs. Old: detail of the Earlier *Mona Lisa* (left) and the Louvre *Mona Lisa*/ The Mona Lisa Foundation and RMN/DCoetzee. Fig. 17. Raphael, *Portrait of Maddalena Doni*/www.aiwaz.net. Fig. 18. Leonardo da Vinci, *Study for the Battle of Anghiari*/Pantheon Studios. Fig. 19. Leonardo da Vinci, *Study for the Battle of Anghiari*/Pantheon Studios.

Fig. 20. Michelangelo Buonarotti, *David*/ Jörg Bittner Unna. Fig. 21. Verrocchio, *David*/Rufus46. Fig. 22. Leonardo da Vinci, *Battle of Anghiari*/Pantheon Studios. Fig. 23. Leonardo da Vinci, *Battle of Anghiari* (Tavola Doria)/Web Gallery of Art. Fig. 24. Giovanni Francesco Rustici, *Battle Scene*/Paolo Villa. Fig. 25. Paolo Giovanni Lomazzo, *Self-Portrait*/Alamy.com. Fig. 26. Leonardo da Vinci, *John the Baptist*/ Pantheon Studios.

CHAPTER 4. Fig. 1. Leonardo da Vinci, the Earlier *Mona Lisa* (detail)/ The Mona Lisa Foundation. Fig. 2. Rembrandt van Rijn, *Self-portrait in a Velvet Beret*/RKDImages. Fig. 3. Comparison of geometrical features/John Asmus. Fig.4. Histograms of digitized images/John Asmus. Fig. 5. Five *Mona Lisas*/The Mona Lisa Foundation. Fig. 6. Histograms of digitized images/John Asmus. Fig. 7. Histograms of digitized images/John Asmus. Fig. 8. Result of matching of histograms/John Asmus. Fig. 9. 3D-plot of the statistical variances/The Mona Lisa Foundation. Fig. 10. Overlay of images of the Louvre *Mona Lisa* and Earlier *Mona Lisa*/John Asmus and Vadim Parfenov. Fig. 11. Overlay of images of the Louvre *Mona Lisa* with the Oslo *Mona Lisa*/ John Asmus and Vadim Parfenov. Fig. 12. Overlay of images of the Louvre *Mona Lisa* with the Reynolds copy/John Asmus and Vadim Parfenov.

CHAPTER 5. Fig. 1. Leonardo da Vinci, Louvre *Mona Lisa* (detail), RMN/DCoetzee. Fig. 2. Raphael, *Portrait of a Young Woman*/ The Mona Lisa Foundation. Fig. 3. The Flemish *Mona Lisa;* the Oslo *Mona Lisa;* and the Isleworth *Mona Lisa*/ The Mona Lisa Foundation.

CHAPTER 6. Fig. 1. Leonardo da Vinci, *Constant and Parabolic Curvatures*/Pantheon Studios. Fig. 2. The Earlier *Mona Lisa* and the Louvre *Mona Lisa*/ The Mona Lisa Foundation. Fig. 3. The Earlier *Mona Lisa* and the Louvre *Mona Lisa*/Albert Sauteur. Fig. 4. A comparison of the two *Mona Lisa* portraits/Albert Sauteur. Fig. 5. Traditional Perspective vs. Reinvented Perspective/Albert Sauteur. Fig 6. Louvre *Mona Lisa* and the Earlier *Mona Lisa* superimposed/Albert Sauteur. Fig. 8. Location of the plane/Albert Sauteur. Fig. 9. Angle of binocular creep/Albert Sauteur. Fig. 10. Vanishing points/ Albert Sauteur. Fig. 11. A modern reconstruction of the refectory/Pantheon Studios.

CHAPTER 7. Fig 1. Leonardo da Vinci, the Earlier *Mona Lisa* and the Louvre *Mona Lisa*/The Mona Lisa Foundation and RMN/DCoetzee. Fig. 2. Salaì (?), the Prado *Mona Lisa*/Escarlati. Fig. 3. Salaì (?), the Prado *Mona Lisa*/Lcsrns. Fig. 4. Leonardo da Vinci, The Earlier *Mona Lisa* (detail)/The Mona Lisa Foundation. Fig. 5. The Goldblatt Thesis/The Mona Lisa Foundation. Fig 6. Leonardo da Vinci, *Allegory of Pleasure and Pain*/Alamy.com. Fig 7. Leonardo da Vinci, *Adoration of the Magi*/Pantheon Studios. Fig 8. Leonardo da Vinci, *Lady with an Ermine*/Pantheon Studios. Fig 9. Leonardo da Vinci, *La belle Ferronnière*/ Pantheon Studios. Fig 10. Leonardo da Vinci, *Burlington Cartoon*/Pantheon Studios. Fig. 11. Francesco Melzi, *Vertumnus and Pomona*/Anagoria. Fig. 12. Francesco Melzi, *Flora*/Alamy.com.

CHAPTER 8. Fig. 1. Alessandro Botticelli, *Virgin and Child with Pomegranate*/Alamy.com. Fig. 2. Hugh Oswald Blaker, *Self-portrait*/Alamy.com. Fig. 3. Michiel van Musscher. *Self Portrait*/ theleidencollection.com. Fig. 4. Leonardo da Vinci, The Isleworth *Mona Lisa* and the Louvre *Mona Lisa*/The Mona Lisa Foundation.

Fig 5. Leonardo da Vinci, *Portrait of Isabella d'Este*/ RMN / Michèle Bellot. Fig. 6. Quinten Massys, *A Grotesque Old Woman*/ Alamy.com. Fig. 7. Peter Paul Rubens, *Portrait of Isabella Brant*/ Paul Hermans. Fig 8. After Hans Holbein the Younger. *Portrait of Sir Brian Tuke*/Pantheon Studios. Fig. 9. Attributed to Diego Velázquez (1599-1660). *Saint John the Baptist in the Wilderness*/ Alamy.com. Fig. 10. Georges de La Tour, *St Joseph the Carpenter*/ Pantheon Studios.

CHAPTER 9. Fig. 1. Leonardo da Vinci, Louvre *Mona Lisa*/ RMN/DCoetzee. Fig. 2. Use of the "Golden Rule"/The Mona Lisa Foundation. Fig. 3. Anonymous Artist, *Portrait of Giuliano de' Medici*/Pantheon Studios. Fig. 4. Comparison of the far background in the *St Anne* and the *Mona Lisa*/Pantheon Studios. Fig. 5. Leonardo da Vinci, *Anatomical study of a woman*/ Pantheon Studios. Fig. 6. Leonardo da Vinci, *St. Anne, Virgin and Child*/Pantheon Studios. Fig. 7. Leonardo da Vinci, Louvre *Mona Lisa* (detail)/ RMN/DCoetzee. Fig. 8. Leonardo da Vinci, *Study for Leda and the Swan*/Pantheon Studios. Fig. 9. Giampietrino, *Leda and the Swan*/ Web gallery of Art. Fig. 10. Leonardo da Vinci, *Anatomical Study of an embryo*/Pantheon Studios. Fig. 11. Leonardo da Vinci, *Study for Leda and the Swan*/Pantheon Studios.

CHAPTER 10. Fig. 1. Earlier *Mona Lisa* and the Louvre *Mona Lisa*/The Mona Lisa Foundation and RMN/DCoetzee. Fig. 2. Details of the eyes in the Earlier *Mona Lisa* and the Louvre *Mona Lisa*/The Mona Lisa Foundation and RMN/DCoetzee. Fig. 3. Leonardo da Vinci, *Drawing of an Old Man in Profile*/Pantheon Studios. Fig. 4. Leonardo da Vinci, *Profiles of an Old Man and a Youth*/Pantheon Studios. Fig. 5. Leonardo da Vinci, *Self-portrait*/ Pantheon Studios.

CHAPTER 11. Fig. 1. Composite of the face in the Earlier *Mona Lisa* and the Louvre *Mona Lisa*/ The Mona Lisa Foundation and RMN/DCoetzee. Fig. 2. The Louvre *Mona Lisa,* the Earlier *Mona Lisa* and a composite/Joe Mullins. Fig. 3. The Louvre *Mona Lisa* regressed/Joe Mullins. Fig. 4. The 12-year regressed image of the Louvre *Mona Lisa* and the Earlier *Mona Lisa*/Joe Mullins.

APPENDIX. Fig. 1. Results of the CD14 test dating the Earlier *Mona Lisa*/The Mona Lisa Foundation. Fig. 2. Key to the probe samples taken from the Earlier *Mona Lisa*/The Mona Lisa Foundation. Fig. 3. Leonardo da Vinci, Earlier *Mona Lisa* (detail)/The Mona Lisa Foundation.

www.ingramcontent.com/pod-product-compliance
Lightning Source LLC
Chambersburg PA
CBHW050713180526
45159CB00003B/1012